Keynes's impact on monetary economics

To
Elizabeth

Keynes's impact on monetary economics

J. C. Gilbert
Emeritus Professor of Economics
The University of Sheffield

Butterworth Scientific
London - Boston - Sydney - Wellington - Durban - Toronto

© Butterworth & Co (Publishers) Ltd. 1982

British Library Cataloguing in Publication Data

Gilbert, J. C.
  Keynes's impact on monetary economics
  1. Keynes, John Maynard – General theory of
    employment, interest and money
  I. Title
  330.15′6   HB99.7

  ISBN 0-408-10718-9

Typeset by Butterworths Litho Preparation Department
Printed in England by Mackays of Chatham, Chatham, Kent

Contents

HB
99.7
.64x
c.1

Preface

This book is an academic monograph which should be useful to advanced students and of interest to professional economists. I was a student at The London School of Economics in the 1920s, experienced the influence of Professor Hayek at The School during the session 1930/31, was greatly influenced by Keynes's *The General Theory* of 1936 and shared in the great interest of the debate and the varying interpretations which followed the publication of this great work. The general reader should find the early chapters fairly straightforward but some of the later chapters are demanding and he could omit the more technical passages.

I have pleasure in acknowledging the financial help I have received from The Leverhulme Trust Fund, having been awarded an Emeritus Fellowship by the Research Awards Advisory Committee, and from the Bank of England's Houblon-Norman Fund.

I wish to thank Professor G. Clayton, Professor J. L. Ford and my other colleagues in economics at The University of Sheffield for their help. I also wish to thank Professor M. T. Sumner and Mr D. Gowland for all the trouble they have taken over the book.

Sheffield   J. C. Gilbert
December, 1980

Chronology

Marries Lydia Lopokova	1925
Visits Russia	1925 and 1928
Fellow of the British Academy (F.B.A.)	1929
Member Macmillan Committee on Finance and Industry	1929–1931
Member Economic Advisory Council	1930–1939
A Treatise on Money (two volumes)	1930
Opening of the Arts Theatre, Cambridge	1936
The General Theory of Employment, Interest and Money	1936
First cardiac infarction	1937
Adviser to the Chancellor of the Exchequer, (Kingsley Wood, Anderson, Dalton)	1940–1946
Director of the Bank of England	1941–1946
Trustee of the National Gallery	1941–1946
Chairman of the Council for the Encouragement of Music and the Arts, later the Arts Council	1942–1946
Becomes Lord Keynes (Baron Keynes of Tilton)	1942
High Steward of the Borough of Cambridge	1943–1946
Bretton Woods Conference	1944
Washington Negotiations on Stage II of Lend-Lease Assistance	1944
Washington Negotiations for U.S. loan to Britain	1945
Honorary Doctor of Science, University of Cambridge (Hon.Sc.D.)	1946
Savannah Conference with inauguration of the International Monetary Fund and International Bank	1946
Elected Fellow of the Royal Society (F.R.S.)	1946
Asked and accepts appointment to (but died before receiving) the Order of Merit (O.M.)	1946
Dies at Tilton in Sussex, aged sixty-two	21 April 1946

This chronology is based on Chronology and Bibliography in Milo Keynes, ed., *Essays on John Maynard Keynes*, London 1975, pp. XV–XVI: Cambridge University Press.

Part I

Introduction

Chapter 1

Keynes the man

To write of Keynes the man is difficult but necessary for two reasons. First, as indicated in the preface, a path can be followed through this book by the non-professional economist who would certainly want to know something of the personality of the greatest economist of the twentieth century. Second, Keynes's personality had an important influence on the way in which he presented his ideas on economic theory and policy. The controversies which arose over *The General Theory of Employment, Interest and Money*[1] while he was still living and those which arose after his death in 1946, the period of post-Keynesian economics, were shaped not only by his contributions to the development of economic theory but also by the manner in which he, Keynes, being the person he was, made them. His personality affected the influence he had on economic thinking, regarded by many economists as the Keynesian Revolution, the misunderstandings and unnecessary controversies of professional economists, and the heart-searching as to how fair or unfair he had been to his predecessors and contemporaries. Much progress had been made by 1946 in assessing Keynes's contribution but reassessments and reinterpretations continue to the present day. This second reason for considering Keynes's personality is important for professional and non-professional economists.

However, before undertaking this difficult and delicate task, a brief account of Keynes's life seems appropriate. John Maynard Keynes was born in 1883 and died in 1946. His influence on economic theory and policy in the United Kingdom and elsewhere was immense. It would be fair to say that no other economist in this century has had the same international reputation as Keynes, although other economists may have been more accomplished in technical economic analysis. In a lecture that I gave in Hamburg in March 1956 while on a lecture tour in Germany for the Foreign Office I said, 'In England, if the man in the street were asked for the name of an economist, he would give that of Keynes. The increasing respect for economics shown by people in my country, who are not economists, is to a very considerable extent due to Keynes.' This is still true today although there has been much controversy between the Keynesians and the monetarists, for example Professor Milton Friedman and the Chicago School, and among the various brands of Keynesians.

Friedman himself on occasion has praised Keynes. Economics is no longer on the rising tide of the quarter of a century after World War II but is in the doldrums with the onset of the serious world depression of the 1970s. The controversies will be discussed later but Keynes's influence remains very important.

Keynes believed that economic problems could be solved by rational thought and action. Keynes has sometimes been criticized for being over-optimistic. Rationalism must certainly be tempered with a recognition of the emotional and political complications. Keynes developed his theory of employment during a period of mass unemployment and falling or relatively stable prices. He was also an ardent advocate of policies for reducing unemployment, publishing such pamphlets as *Can Lloyd George Do It?* (1929) and *The Means To Prosperity*(1933)[2]. Keynes concerned himself with the inflationary pressure during World War II, when our productive resources were fully stretched, in *How To Pay For The War* (1940)[3]. Today in this country we have a relatively high level of unemployment, although, as a percentage of the labour force, not comparable to the mass unemployment with which Keynes was concerned, and a high rate of inflation. Nevertheless the apparatus of thought developed by Keynes is helpful in dealing with our present problem. In present circumstances, economists who would not agree with all the tenets of the monetarists would accept the importance of an appropriate control of the total money supply which has been emphasized by them. Keynes himself would also no doubt have agreed to this. How long it will take for the United Kingdom to solve this problem of high unemployment and high inflation remains to be seen. It is a general problem of the non-communist industrial countries although these countries are faced with varying degrees of unemployment and rates of inflation.

The persistence of the influence of Keynes is a mark of his greatness as an economist. He was one of the great economists of all time and may be ranked with Adam Smith and David Ricardo. This reputation rests on his book *The General Theory of Employment, Interest and Money* which he published in 1936[4]. Without this book, he would be regarded as an important economist who had made very significant contributions to the discussion of the economic problems of the day, a powerful advocate of economic policies which were generally right and an economic statesman to whom the nation owed a great debt. Some economists have recently maintained that his *magnum opus, A Treatise on Money* (1930)[5], is a greater work than *The General Theory*. It is certainly a seminal work which has been unduly neglected but for various reasons it failed to make the great impact of *The General Theory*.

The General Theory is the culmination of Keynes's intellectual development as an economist. Keynes won scholarships to Eton and King's College, Cambridge. For his King's scholarship he combined classics with mathematics but his intellectual interests were even wider. Keynes read mathematics, not economics, as a student at Cambridge. He was a very competent mathematician and he was bracketed twelfth Wrangler in the first class of the mathematical tripos examination list. As Sir Roy Harrod puts it 'Some congratulated; some condoled. The result was respectable, but not triumphant. Mathematics were not his love – although he was to remain deeply interested in mathematical philosophy.'[6] Professor E. A. G. Robinson wrote that Keynes 'had come to Cambridge with a very considerable Eton reputation as a mathematician. But it fairly quickly became apparent that by the exacting standards of Cambridge he was not in that narrow superlative class which alone can hope to achieve fame in the field of pure mathematics.'[7] Keynes's aptitude and interest in logic and mathematics led him to take probability as the subject of his dissertation for a Fellowship at King's. His work was greatly influenced by G. E. Moore's *Principia Ethica* (1903) and Bertrand Russell's *Principia Mathematica* (1903) in which A. N. Whitehead had been much involved[8]. He obtained his Fellowship in 1909 having been unsuccessful when he first submitted his dissertation in 1908. Keynes's work in this area was finally published in 1921 as *A Treatise on Probability*[9]. It is not surprising that Keynes, having written as he did on probability and having a wide knowledge of the real world with all its uncertainties, placed so much importance on uncertainty in *The General Theory*. What is somewhat surprising is that he did not spend more time on defining and elaborating the concept of which he made so much use.

Keynes first studied economics as a university subject when working at Cambridge in 1905/06 for the Civil Service Examination. In letters written to Lytton Strachey in November 1905 he says 'I find Economics increasingly satisfactory, and I think I am rather good at it' and 'Marshall is continually pestering me to turn professional economist and writes flattering remarks on my papers to help on the good cause.'[10] Keynes passed the Civil Service Examination but with relatively low marks in economics. He expressed his indignation by saying 'I evidently knew more about economics than my examiners.'[11] After a short period in the Civil Service, at the India Office, he returned to Cambridge in 1908 as a lecturer in economics. Keynes's first book was *Indian Currency and Finance* (1913)[12] and he was a member of the Royal Commission on Indian Finance and Currency from 1913 to 1914. It is interesting to note that Keynes's father, John Neville Keynes, took a somewhat similar path to economics. His first degree was in mathematics, his first book was *Formal Logic* (1884) and his second book was *The Scope and Method of Political Economy* (1891).

Without wishing to minimize in any way the great contributions made to economics by non-mathematicians such as Adam Smith, David Ricardo and Carl Menger, the founder of the Austrian School, it is important to acknowledge the debt economics owes to the mathematicians who took up economics. One thinks of Cournot, Walras, Jevons, Marshall and Keynes. In Keynes's greatest work, *The General Theory*, the mathematics are not obvious. Like Marshall, whose pupil Keynes was and who dominated Cambridge economics when Keynes was turning from mathematics to economics and long afterwards, Keynes kept the mathematics behind the scenes. Marshall did this in his great book, *Principles of Economics* (1890)[13] because he wanted his economics to be widely understood by businessmen and others. No doubt Keynes's similar method of presentation of his ideas was because of his urgent desire to affect public policy and to contribute to the welfare of the nation by eliminating mass unemployment. In the Preface he writes 'This book is chiefly addressed to my fellow economists. I hope that it will be intelligible to others . . . it is my fellow economists, not the general public, whom I must first convince. At this stage of the argument the general public, though welcome at the debate, are only eavesdroppers. . . .'[14] It must be remembered, however, that in 1936 a much smaller proportion of professional economists had mathematical competence than today. It was thus important to keep the mathematics in the background if he was to influence as many economists as possible to make a change, which he regarded as of vital importance, in their economic thinking. It seems clear from the ease with which later economists formulated Keynes's employment theory in mathematical terms that Keynes had a mathematical analysis in mind.

It is not appropriate to trace here the development of Keynes's economic thought from the pre-World War I period up to *The General Theory*. This has been done in the biographies of Keynes by Harrod[15] and Professor D. E. Moggridge[16], in Professor Don Patinkin's *Keynes's Monetary Thought*[17], in part in D. E. Moggridge's article 'From the *Treatise* to *The General Theory*: An Exercise in Chronology'[18] and elsewhere. Two general points may, however, be made here. First, Keynes always started with contemporary economic problems and made his contribution to the development of economic theory by developing economic theory when he found the existing tools of analysis insufficient for his purpose. Secondly, of the inter-war trilogy, *A Tract on Monetary Reform* (1923)[19], *A Treatise on Money* (1930)[20] and *The General Theory* (1936)[21], *A Tract* utilizes existing economic theory with great success while *A Treatise* and *The General Theory* make important original contributions to the development of economic theory[22]. To these last two books must be added Keynes's article, 'The General Theory of Employment'[23]. This article is described by Professor Shackle as 'that "third edition", that ultimate distillation of the *Treatise* and the *Theory*, which Keynes wrote for the QJE in answer to his critics, . . .'[24].

There are many aspects of Keynes that I do not discuss but only mention here. He was not merely a mathematician and academic economist. He was an economic adviser to governments, an economic statesman, whose work at the Treasury in World War I and World War II was outstanding. By speculation in foreign currencies, stocks and shares, and commodities he made a fortune for himself and enriched King's College as its Bursar. He was a great editor of *The Economic Journal*. In the City, Keynes became chairman of the National Mutual Life Assurance Society in 1921 and had other financial interests. Keynes was also a man of wide culture. He was for years associated with the Bloomsbury group of writers and painters, Lytton Strachey, Duncan Grant and Virginia Woolf among them. Some of these friends questioned his aesthetic appreciation but he was an artist himself, a master of English prose, a biographer. He loved the ballet and in 1925 married the Russian ballerina Lydia Lopokova. This was a happy marriage and according to Mrs Alfred Marshall, 'the best thing that Maynard every did'[25]. He was a collector of books and a buyer of modern paintings. Keynes by his generosity with his money and time (he was a very good administrator) encouraged the Arts which meant so much to him, the visual arts, ballet, music and the theatre. He gave the Arts Theatre to Cambridge. Keynes was Chairman of the Council for the Encouragement of Music and the Arts, later the Arts Council[26].

In 1937 Keynes had a heart attack. Despite his serious heart condition, he made an immense contribution at the Treasury throughout World War II and until his death in April 1946 (as a result of a sharp heart attack). He was involved in long and arduous negotiations in the United States as described by Harrod[27]. His courage and devotion to duty are beyond praise. As E. A. G. Robinson puts it, 'For some years before 1946 both Keynes himself and his friends had known the possibility, even the likelihood, that if he continued to work as he was working the end would come one day just as it did. Despite this knowledge he carried on. This was his contribution to the war and to the future of his country.'[28] Keynes was honoured by his sovereign, becoming a CB in 1917, Lord Keynes (Baron Keynes of Tilton) in 1942 and was offered the Order of Merit but died before the award could be made.

Michael Holroyd, referring to Keynes as an undergraduate at Cambridge, writes: 'Already, by the time he was elected to the Apostles[29], Keynes's cleverness was prodigious, and his intellect, in the opinion of Bertrand Russell, "was the sharpest and clearest I have ever known".'[30] Keynes was not, however, only clever: he was a genius. His strength lay not only in his great logical powers but in his intuition, the quality to which Keynes attributed Isaac Newton's pre-eminence[31]. The genius, Newton, is described by Keynes as Cambridge's greatest son[32]. Professor Schumpeter is referring to this quality of intuition of Keynes, I think, when he points to his social vision and his vision of an economic process[33]. Schumpeter also wrote referring to Keynes's *General Theory* that 'The first condition for simplicity of a model is, of course, simplicity of the vision which it is to implement. And simplicity of vision is in part a matter of genius . . . .' He continues that if we 'choose to accept his vision of the economic process of our age as the gift of genius whose glance pierced through the welter of surface phenomena to the simple essentials that lie below, then there can be little objection to his aggregative analysis that produced his results'[34]. Schumpeter makes a similar point in his *History of Economic Analysis* where he points out that 'Keynes's work presents an excellent example for our thesis that, in principle, vision of facts and meanings precedes analytical work, which, setting in to implement the vision, then goes on hand in hand with it in an unending relation of give and take.'[35] Here Keynes's vision is traced through his various work. In 1919 he was Principal Representative of the Treasury at the Paris Peace Conference. Following his resignation in June of that year Keynes wrote his brilliant and highly critical book *The Economic Consequences of the Peace* (1919)[36]. His vision was of great importance in other works, in particular *The General Theory* (1936).

As was indicated at the beginning of this chapter, an understanding of Keynes's personality is important when considering Keynesian and post-Keynesian economic theory and policy. Economists owe a great debt to Sir Roy Harrod for writing his biography of Keynes[37] so soon after his death. However, at an appropriate time, another biography must be written with the emphasis placed on Keynes's personality. The author will need great psychological insight to deal with his complex character[38]. At present all we have are varying accounts of him by friends and acquaintances, valuable though they are. I only met Keynes once, at a tea party in Lord

Robbins's room at The London School of Economics in about 1930. On this occasion the argument was mainly between Keynes and Evan Durbin, at that time a young economist[39]. Keynes was very benign. There are advantages and disadvantages in my not having known Keynes personally. There is the advantage of objectivity in making an assessment of his personality although I would not claim complete objectivity. One's emotions are easily stirred by Keynes. Harrod in *The Life* is not conscious of any suppression in regard to Keynes's faults and writes, 'Criticisms have been made by the malicious or ill-informed which have no foundation in fact.'[40] One would dearly like to have an elaboration of this statement, giving the nature of these criticisms and the reasons for their having been made.

There is a difference of opinion among economists as to whether Keynes was fair or unfair to the classical economists and to his contemporaries such as Marshall and Pigou. Keynes was criticized by Harrod when writing to him about a draft of *The General Theory* for being unduly polemical in his discussion of the classical economists. Keynes replied, 'I *want* so to speak to raise a dust; because it is only out of the controversy that will arise that what I am saying will get understood.'[41] Professor Sir Dennis Robertson also attempted to get Keynes to alter his attitude to Marshall and Pigou but the only result was Keynes's Appendix on Professor Pigou's *Theory of Unemployment* in *The General Theory* and Robertson was left unsatisfied[42]. In the Preface to *The General Theory* Keynes states that he can only achieve his purpose (a reconstruction of economic theory) by much controversy, a view shared by Friedman, but writes, 'I must ask forgiveness if, in the pursuit of sharp distinctions, my controversy is itself too keen.'[43] Keynes's polemics were a result of his character and his view of the best way of influencing his fellow economists. Keynes's attitude to the classical and neoclassical economists raised a new economics 'industry' which has greatly developed since his death.

Professor Paul A. Samuelson writing of *The General Theory* in 1946 states, 'It is arrogant, bed-tempered, polemical, and not overly generous in its acknowledgements.'[44] However, he goes on to say that it is a work of genius. In 1941, when reviewing Professor Pigou's *Employment and Equilibrium*, Samuelson raises the question whether Keynes was deliberately Machiavellian in his treatment of the 'classical' economists but says that only he can tell[45]. As a result of the rift between Keynes and Robertson which he dates as being from *A Treatise on Money* (1930), 'a new note enters into Robertson's writing which was to remain until the end – a querulous note of protest over the pretensions and correctness of so-called new ideas . . .'[46]. Samuelson does not regard this Robertsonian querulousness as sterile. He points out that 'Many of Robertson's points, had they come from within the Keynesian camp, would have been recognized as valuable contributions.'[47] The rift between the two men thus hindered the development of economic thought.

Patinkin refers to Pigou's sharply critical review of Keynes's *General Theory* in *Economica* and points out that 'This sharpness stemmed primarily from Pigou's justified feeling that in order to "win attention" for his *General Theory*, Keynes had presented the ideas of this book "in a matrix of sarcastic comment upon other people" . . . In particular, Pigou deeply resented what he considered to be Keynes's misrepresentation of Pigou's own views, and even more those of Keynes's "old master", Marshall.'[48] On later occasions Pigou paid high tribute to Keynes's constructive work. Keynes in a letter to Robertson of 20 September 1936 rightly expresses grief that his contribution was not understood and appreciated by Pigou, but surely shows a lack of sensitivity when he writes, 'I was distressed by the Prof's review and even more so that you should think it worthy of him . . . I had often wondered how he would take my book but I never hit on the right answer (though perhaps I ought to have!) that his predominant emotion would be that of a sixth-form boy who had been cheeked.'[49] Later in the letter Keynes writes, 'It's awfully difficult to keep off Economics but I don't, dear Dennis, feel differently, and we must try to come to closer touch again.'[50] Keynes as well as being astringent had an affectionate nature and this is a touching attempt to remove the personal rift between them. Robertson spent a great deal of time on the early drafts of *The General Theory* and in a letter to Keynes of 10 February 1935 he expresses sorrow that he will feel 'the general tenor of my comments (which seem almost to have reached the dimensions of a book [are] rather hostile'.[51] He ends the letter with a pleasant touch, 'Yours ever – in spite of these bites at the hand that fed me –'.[52] The whole correspondence seems amiable and yet the rift between them remained. In the Preface to *The General Theory* he acknowledges a number of economists from whom he has received help, but not Robertson.

Professor Sir Austin Robinson in his article 'Pigou, Arthur Cecil (1877–1959)' in the *International Encyclopedia of the Social Sciences* (1968) writes of the relationships of Keynes with Pigou and Robertson as follows:

'Whether Keynes could have achieved a radical rethinking of economics without wounding, as he did, Pigou and Robertson, among others, is a question that will be eternally debated. I have always believed that this was the sad but necessary cost of the revolution of thought. With Robertson, the wounds went so deep that they never could be healed. With Pigou, time brought a healing. And indeed the wounds were never as severe . . . . It was an oddly tolerant and mutually admiring relationship which never came near to reaching the misery of the cleft between Robertson and Keynes.'[53]

Robinson in A Personal View, in *Essays on John Maynard Keynes* (1975)[54] takes a rather less serious view. He again refers to the misery of the break between Keynes and Robertson, his close friends, but thinks the break has been greatly exaggerated. In support of this he mentions their long correspondence now published in *The Collected Writings*, Volumes XIII and XIV[55]. Robinson has, I think, in mind the tone of their correspondence. In 1944 Pigou retired from the chair of Political Economy at Cambridge which had been held by Marshall before him. The electors offered the chair to Keynes, but Robinson points out that when Keynes declined the offer he pressed the claims of Robertson. Robinson writes, 'While Keynes was alive there was, I am convinced, no break between them that could not have been mended. The antipathy of Robertson was not to Keynes himself living, but after his death to some of his younger friends and colleagues and their more radical interpretations of Keynesian policies which differed increasingly widely from his own more and more right-wing liberal views.'[56] Robinson refers to the break that could have been mended but whether it was is certainly unproven. Professor Harry G. Johnson is more critical of the way Keynes presented his new theory and refers to him having sacrificed 'the subtle and sensitive, intellectually more menacing but emotionally more vulnerable, personality of his former student Robertson to his coterie of young lions in the bitter in-fighting that followed the revolution'[57].

Lord Robbins refers to the deterioration of personal relations at Cambridge long before the death of Keynes. He refers to Robertson taking the chair of Money and Banking at The London School of Economics in 1938 as a result of the distress this caused him. Robbins refers to Robertson as warmly responsive to friendship and writes, 'His differences with Keynes; with whom he had worked so fruitfully, were a source of much unhappiness.'[58] Robbins states that on Robertson's side, the differences began as intellectual ones. He was candid about his disagreements with certain developments in *A Treatise on Money* and more so in *The General Theory* but Keynes, under the stress of illness and excited by his new theories, found Robertson's criticisms a source of irritation and resentment. Robbins continues, 'So the intimacy of earlier years was disrupted and there can be no doubt that, till the end of his life, this was a recurrent sorrow for Dennis.'[59] Robbins like Robinson warns against exaggerating the extent of the rupture and also refers to the pain Robertson felt from the intellectual and personal divisions among Cambridge economists during the years after his return to Cambridge at the end of World War II. Robbins refers to faults on both sides, a lack of imagination and charity of his Keynesian critics and Robertson's over-sensitivity.

Professor Sir John Hicks dates the turning-point of the relationship between Keynes and Robertson not from *A Treatise on Money* (1930) but from 1931 when they were working on very different lines[60]. Hicks refers to Robertson taking the chair at The London School of Economics in 1938 after an agonizing decision that the Cambridge of the 'Keynesian Revolution' was no place for him. In 1944 Robertson returned to Cambridge as the prefessorial successor of Pigou, but Hicks thinks that 'he must often have wondered, in after years, whether he had chosen right . . . . It was only too clear (back in Cambridge) that the division was very deep.'[61]

The suggestion by Robinson, Robbins and others that the rift between Keynes and Robertson must not be exaggerated is partly based on their being able to work together in the Treasury during World War II on international monetary problems[62]. Sir Roy Harrod quotes a letter from Keynes to Sir Richard Hopkins of the Treasury of 22 July 1944 in which he praises Robertson's work at Bretton Woods very highly. He also gives the famous quotation from Keynes's letter to his mother of 25 July 1944, 'Dennis Robertson is perhaps the most useful of all – absolutely first-class brains do help!'[63] However, Hicks points out that, although superficially there was a reconciliation, it must be remembered that they were working in the international monetary field in which they had had no great differences. Hicks thinks that the temporary reconciliation was not easy and that Keynes was condescending. Hicks writes, 'I am afraid that is how I read the well-known passage in which Keynes reported (to his mother) on

Bretton Woods: "absolutely first-class brains do help" . . ."[64]. Hicks states that Robertson was easily hurt and that the rift remained until Keynes's death.

Robertson visited Sheffield on a number of occasions and I always found him very pleasant, cultured, scholarly and modest, although aware of his academic achievement. He stayed at my home twice[65] and I was very conscious of his hurt feelings and how isolated he felt himself to be at Cambridge. It may be asked why I have spent so much time on the personal relations between Keynes and Robertson. The reason is that, whatever the nature of the rift between them was, it was lamentable and counter-productive, in my view, to the development of economic theory. It not only affected developments during Keynes's lifetime but also post-Keynesian economics. One cannot but regret that their fruitful co-operation referred to in the introductory chapter of Robertson's *Banking Policy And The Price Level*[66] of 1926 could not have been continued throughout their lives. One is reminded of the break between Freud and Jung in psychology.

Sir Roy Harrod describes Keynes as a dear friend and writes,

> 'He was very sensitive, indeed I think I can say gentle, in his relations with human beings; but as soon as you got into controversy he was no longer sensitive and gentle; he was rebarbative in the extreme, he had no mercy for those who advanced fallacious arguments, he crushed them brutally. . . . He crushed you with great rudeness: his fierce manners on these occasions injured his relationships with some people for life.'[67]

Keynes's controversy with Professor F. A. von Hayek provides a well-known example of such behaviour[68]. Hayek had written a long critical review of Keynes's *A Treatise on Money* in *Economica*. In replying, Keynes referred to Hayek's *Prices and Production*[69] in the following terms,

> 'The book, as it stands, seems to me to be one of the most frightful muddles I have ever read . . . and yet it remains a book of some interest, which is likely to leave its mark on the mind of the reader. It is an extraordinary example of how starting with a mistake, a remorseless logician can end up in Bedlam.'

Keynes had felt that Hayek had not read his book with that measure of 'goodwill' which he could have expected[70]. Sir Roy Harrod says that 'Hayek replied with a powerful and dignified protest against this kind of behaviour.'[71] He is able to add, however, that Keynes and Hayek later achieved a happy, friendly relationship.

Hayek's *Prices and Production* contained a very incomplete theory and in places there are very serious logical errors. The policies he advocated during the Great Depression were quite wrong and diametrically opposed to the appropriate Keynesian policies. I think, however, that Hayek's work has been unduly neglected and I tried at the British Association in 1953 to explain the nature of Hayek's contribution and show that he had analysed a theoretically important limiting case[72]. How important such a case has been in the real world can only be shown by further detailed empirical research. Robertson, writing to Keynes on 3 February 1935 regarding a draft of *The General Theory*, says 'I don't think these pages are at all a fair account of Hayek's own exposition.'[73]

Keynes's friends and acquaintances have referred to his patience and impatience. *A Treatise on Money*, although in many ways a great book, failed to provide an adequate theoretical explanation of the factors determining the level of employment and thus an adequate support for his policy proposals. It also contained errors in the analysis which were quickly criticized by his contemporaries. Keynes with his usual energy and courage started all over again and produced *The General Theory*. This time he took the precaution of circulating drafts of the work among a number of economists. It is surprising that the masterpiece appeared with so many blemishes in view of the voluminous correspondence[74]. With the benefit of hindsight, it is clear that if Keynes could have patiently explained what he was doing and why he was doing it in the way he adopted, much confusion, misunderstanding and bitterness would have been avoided. However, perhaps one cannot expect this from a genius fully stretched in creative work.

Very different accounts have been given of Keynes's character and personal relations. Harrod, Robinson, Robbins and others refer to him in very affectionate terms[75]. He has been referred to as idealistic, affectionate, kind and tolerant to the young if not to the eminent when he regarded them as obstinate in holding views dangerous to human welfare. However, there was another side to him. Milo Keynes, his nephew, quotes from Kingsley Martin's obituary notice, 'Keynes was the most formidable of antagonists, ruthless and sometimes unscrupulous in argument, and always unsparing of all that seemed to him silly and insincere . . . . His wit was shattering and his capacity for rudeness unequalled.' He also quotes Harold Nicholson as saying that 'Keynes was impatient, iconoclastic, rude. Yet although with incisive cruelty he would snub the eminent, he never snubbed the humble or the young.' As Milo Keynes says, Maynard was not always an easy companion[76]. There are many other references to Keynes's rudeness, for example, by Harrod[77] and in *The Times* obituary where his good personal qualities are also emphasized[78].

Robbins has shown that if an offence was pointed out to Keynes, 'there was noone who could better make the *amende honorable*'[79]. Robbins himself had certainly been treated disgracefully by Keynes when he was a member of a small secret committee of the Economic Advisory Council in the early 1930s. Robbins found himself in opposition to Keynes who was furious and treated him very roughly. This was painful to Robbins who, however, recognizing Keynes's quality and character, considered the personal behaviour as unimportant[80]. Within a few weeks they were on easy terms and eventually developed a real friendship[81]. P. D. Proctor writing of Keynes at the Treasury, 1940–1946, refers to the magnificent contribution he made and also to the good and bad sides of his personal relations. Having recounted his faults, Proctor recognizes Keynes's greatness and ends with the question 'what did it matter?'[82]

Things did not always turn out as happily as this. Lord Balogh describes his acquaintance with Keynes over 16 years during which his relations with Keynes had their violent ups and downs and finished at their lowest[83]. In 1944 Keynes and Balogh held very different views on international economic policy and in a letter to *The Times* Keynes had a wounding sentence about Balogh being a disciple of the German central banker, Dr Schacht. In subsequent letters to *The Times* Keynes conjectured that Balogh knew no English and no Latin[84]. At the Savannah first meeting of the International Monetary Fund and the International Bank in 1946, Keynes and Mr Vinson, the Secretary of the United States Treasury were unable to establish a good relationship[85]. However, Keynes proved to be a great negotiator in the United States on behalf of his country throughout World War II and until his death[86].

Keynes was a great conversationalist and could take hard knocks himself. His rudeness and his wounding words occurred when he was arguing about problems the importance of which he felt deeply. To many, Keynes was not only a great man but a great friend. Schumpeter refers to him as the pleasantest fellow you can think of. He adds, 'contrary to a widely spread opinion, he could be *polite*, polite with an old-world *punctilio* that costs time'[87]. Keynes had great self-confidence and has sometimes been charged with arrogance, but too much need not be made of this. He would, in general, have been even more effective in controversy if he had been able to use calm persuasion to a greater degree.

Keynes was kind and generous to his friends; for example, after conscription was introduced in 1916 he appeared before military tribunals to support Duncan Grant, James Strachey and David Garnett as conscientious objectors[88]. Keynes was greatly concerned with the social distress resulting from unemployment. His main concern for many years was to develop economic theory and policy so that mass unemployment could be eliminated. He advocated government intervention in certain fields, while preserving democracy, in his famous essay, *The End of* Laissez-Faire (1926)[89]. He developed his employment policies throughout his life in such a way that they were consistent with a free economy which provides scope for individual initiative. Harrod points out that Keynes had no egalitarian sentiment but that he wanted to improve the lot of the poor, not for the sake of equality but to make their lives happier and better. However, the 'good life' could only be enjoyed by the few for the time being and this must not be destroyed[90]. He supported Beveridge's Report on Social Insurance and Allied Services of 1942, the famous 'cradle to the grave' report for the post-war welfare state[91]. Keynes was a 'do-gooder' in the best sense of the term. Given his background, it is not surprising that he was somewhat paternalistic and thought of the United Kingdom as being governed by an intellectual élite who would guide and persuade the general public.

Elizabeth Johnson pays tribute to Keynes for his great leap forward with regard to the government's responsibility for a high level of employment, but thinks that two problems did not trouble him because of his comfortable upbringing in Cambridge[92]. We still have not solved them – the problem of equal opportunity and the problem of the boring nature of many jobs. Keynes had a valuable view of the good society but, unlike Marshall, he had not attempted to study and understand working-class life. In Keynes's case there was only his interest in agricultural workers on college estates and on his farm. Moggridge points out that whether this mattered is open to discussion but Elizabeth Johnson holds the view that it did[93].

The influences which affected Keynes's character, interests and work are clear. He loved his parents – his father, John Neville Keynes, a don and administrator at Cambridge and his mother, Florence Ada Keynes, a daughter of a Congregationalist divine, John Brown, author of a life of Bunyan. His mother was an early student of Newnham College and a pioneer of social services for the needy, the unemployed and for those suffering from chronic tuberculosis by being concerned with the establishment of Papworth Village Settlement. He had a Congregationalist upbringing[94]. Robinson refers to Keynes in the 1920s as an atheist with a devotion to King's College Chapel[95]. A second influence on Keynes was the long tradition of Cambridge economics established by Sidgwick, Neville Keynes, Marshall and Pigou that economics should be studied to improve the lot of man, raise the standard of living to make possible a better life and reduce social suffering[96]. Pigou wrote of Keynes and Marshall that they were alike 'in their desire that the study of economics should serve, not as a mere intellectual gymnastic, but directly, or at least indirectly, for the forwarding of human welfare'.[97]

The final significant influences on Keynes were his membership of 'The Society' (The Apostles), a Cambridge University society which at that time was dominated by the ideas of G. E. Moore's *Principia Ethica* (1903), and later his being one of the Bloomsbury Group. Keynes describes in 'My Early Beliefs' (1938) what he and his friends got from Moore, 'Nothing mattered except states of mind, our own and other people's of course, but chiefly our own. These states of mind were not associated with action or achievement or with consequences. They consisted in timeless, passionate states of contemplation and communion, largely unattached to "before" or "after".'[98] The prime objects in life were love (coming a long way first), the creation and enjoyment of aesthetic experience and the pursuit of knowledge. The relationship of pleasure and pain to states of mind was complicated[99]. There was another important element in Moore's work, the question of the rightness of actions and the justification of general rules of conduct. This, Keynes tells us, was mainly ignored in the early years, but in practice, at least as far as he was concerned, the outside world was not forgotten. Keynes, writing in 1938, realized that he and his friends were seriously mistaken in the rationality they attributed to human nature and ignored powerful and valuable springs of feeling[100]. The whole Memoir is well worth reading for an understanding of Keynes. He depended on his Bloomsbury friends to a great extent for the artistic side of the good life. Keynes used the wealth he had acquired by his own efforts to give himself independence, a good but not lavish standard of living and to show generosity. He liked good food and wine, particularly champagne. (I am not a Keynesian with respect to champagne!) During World War I, Mrs Asquith (Lady Oxford) said of Keynes, 'He is such a good man.'[101] Some two years after Keynes's death, his cowherd told Harrod that Keynes 'was a *good* man'[102].

Keynes was overoptimistic, as many post-Keynesian economists have been, with respect to solving the problem of mass unemployment. At present the non-communist world is faced with a serious recession associated with high unemployment and inflation. Keynes also showed undue optimism in 'Economic Possibilities for our Grandchildren' (1930) although he was assuming no important wars and no important increase in population. He wrote, 'the *economic problem* may be solved, or be at least within sight of solution, within a hundred years. This means that the economic problem is not – if we look into the future – *the permanent problem of the human race.*'[103] At the end of the essay he warned against overestimating the importance of the economic problem and urged the encouragement of the arts of life. Keynes rightly defined the role of economics when he gave 'the toast of the Royal Economic Society, of economics and economists, who are the trustees, not of civilization, but of the possibility of civilization'[104]. At the present time, considering both the developed and the underdeveloped countries, the economic problem is very serious. We are a long way from eliminating poverty. The economic problem is not only serious *per se* but can give rise to grave political problems, strife and war. In these circumstances economic growth is of great importance. Keynes did not deal with the theory of economic growth but it is important in post-Keynesian economics. Keynes, however, was right to stress the arts of life, civilization, with which economics does not deal. I made a similar point in my Inaugural Lecture in 1958 when I said that the real problem 'which faces humanity is that of the goals for the development of the individual and of societies, goals which must be related to the propensities of man. What is man to make of the splendour and terror to be found within each individual and throughout nature?'[105]

Notes*

1. J. M. Keynes, *The General Theory of Employment, Interest and Money* (1936). (In *C.W.*, Vol. VII (1936, 1973).)
2. *Essays in Persuasion*, Keynes, *C.W.*, Vol. IX (1972). *Can Lloyd George Do It?* was written jointly with Sir Hubert Henderson.
3. Keynes (1972a).
4. Keynes, *C.W.*, Vol. VII (1936, 1973).
5. Keynes, *C.W.*, Vols. V and VI (1971).
6. R. F. Harrod, *The Life of John Maynard Keynes* (1951), p. 103.
7. E. A. G. Robinson, 'John Maynard Keynes 1883–1946', *Economic Journal*, 1947 (reprinted in R. Lekachman, *Keynes' General Theory Reports of Three Decades* (1964), p. 22.
8. *See* Harrod, *The Life of John Maynard Keynes* (1951), p. 654, n.1.
9. Keynes, *C.W.*, Vol. VIII (1973). For an assessment of this work, *see* Professor R. B. Braithwaite's editorial foreword and his contribution, 'Keynes as a Philosopher', in Milo Keynes, *Essays on John Maynard Keynes* (1975). *See also* Harrod (1951), pp. 122 *et seq.* and Appendix.
10. Harrod (1951), p. 111.
11. *Ibid.*, p. 121.
12. Keynes, *C.W.*, Vol. I (1971).
13. 1st edn.
14. Keynes, *The General Theory of Employment, Interest and Money*. In *C.W.*, Vol. VII (1973), p. xxi.
15. Harrod (1951).
16. D. E. Moggridge, *Keynes* (1976).
17. D. Patinkin, *Keynes' Monetary Thought* (1976a).
18. 1973.
19. Keynes, *C.W.*, Vol. IV (1971).

* Throughout, *C.W.* refers to *The Collected Writings of John Maynard Keynes*. London: Macmillan.

20. Keynes, *C.W.*, Vols. V and VI (1971).
21. Keynes, *C.W.*, Vol. VII (1936, 1973).
22. D. Patinkin, 'John Maynard Keynes: from the *Tract* to the *General Theory*', *Economic Journal* (June 1975).
23. J. M. Keynes, 'The General Theory of Employment' (1937). In *C.W.*, Vol. XIV (1973).
24. G. L. S. Shackle, *Keynesian Kaleidics* (1974), p. 37.
25. Harrod (1951), p. 365.
26. *See* Harrod (1951); Milo Keynes (1975); D. E. Moggridge, *Keynes: Aspects of the Man and His Work* (1974); Council of King's College Cambridge, *John Maynard Keynes 1883–1946. A Memoir* (1949); M. Holroyd, *Lytton Strachey and the Bloomsbury Group: His Work and Their Influence* (1971a); M. Holroyd, *Lytton Strachey: a Biography* (1971b); Q. Bell, *Bloomsbury* (1974).
27. Harrod (1951), Chapters XII–XV.
28. E. A. G. Robinson, 'John Maynard Keynes, 1883–1946', in Lekachman (1964), p. 84.
29. A club known as 'The Society' which was founded in the 1820s. Its membership of undergraduates and senior members was an intellectual elite. Keynes was elected a member in 1903.
30. M. Holroyd (1971b), p. 241.
31. J. M. Keynes, *Essays in Biography* (1933). In *C.W.*, Vol. X (1972b), p. 365.
32. Keynes, *C.W.*, Vol. X (1972b), p. 363.
33. J. A. Schumpeter, 'Keynes the Economist'. In S. E. Harris, *The New Economics* (1948), p. 91.
34. *Ibid.*, p. 92.
35. J. A. Schumpeter, *History of Economic Analysis* (1954), p. 1171.
36. Keynes, *C.W.*, Vol. II (1971).
37. Harrod (1951).
38. Whether Keynes's bisexuality is of much relevance is at present an open question.
39. Durbin was a man of courage and he died courageously. In September 1948 'he saved two children from a rough sea on the Cornish shore; and, having lifted the second child on to a rock, himself fell back beneath the waves' (E. H. Phelps Brown, 'Evan Durbin, 1906–1948', *Economica*, 18 February 1951, p. 91).
40. Harrod (1951), p. vi.
41. Patinkin (1976a), p. 115, and references to Keynes, *C.W.*, Vol. XIII, *The General Theory and After: Part I, Participation* (1973a), pp. 530–531, 535–537, 546 and 548.
42. Keynes, *C.W.*, Vol. XIII (1973a), pp. 520–524.
43. Keynes, *C.W.*, Vol. VII (1936, 1973), p. xxi. *See also* Patinkin (1976a), p. 115, n.12.
44. Preface to Paul A. Samuelson, *The General Theory* (1946), in Lekachman (1964), p. 318.
45. J. E. Stiglitz, *The Collected Scientific Papers of Paul A. Samuelson*, Vol. II (1966), p. 1183.
46. Stiglitz (1966), p. 1596.
47. *Ibid.*
48. Patinkin (1976a), p. 138. The quotations are from Pigou's review in *Economica*, May 1936, p. 115.
49. *The General Theory and After: Part II, Defence and Development*, Keynes, *C.W.*, Vol. XIV (1973b), p. 88.
50. *Ibid.*
51. Keynes, *C.W.*, Vol. XIII (1973a), p. 506.
52. Keynes, *C.W.*, Vol. XIII (1973a), p. 507. Robertson had been a student of Keynes.
53. Austin Robinson in *International Encyclopedia of the Social Sciences* (1968), p. 96.
54. Robinson in Milo Keynes (1975).
55. Keynes, *C.W.*, Vols. XIII and XIV (1973a, b), pp. 12–13.
56. *Ibid.*
57. Harry G. Johnson, 'Keynes and British Economics', in Milo Keynes (1975), p. 116.
58. Lord Robbins, *Autobiography of an Economist* (1971), pp. 221–222.
59. *Ibid.*
60. D. H. Robertson, *Essays in Money and Interest* (1966) (selected with a memoir by Sir John Hicks), pp. 15–17.
61. Hicks in Robertson (1966), p. 19.
62. Robinson in Milo Keynes (1975), p. 14; Robbins (1971), p. 222.
63. Harrod (1951), pp. 578–579.

64. Hicks in Robertson (1966), p. 19, n.10.
65. In July 1961, when he received an honorary degree from the University of Sheffield, and on 16 February 1962, the night of the great gale. On that night none of us slept: we went downstairs at 5 a.m. for cups of tea, and Robertson, in his early seventies, recited A. E. Housman's 'On Wenlock Edge'.
66. D. H. Robertson, *Banking Policy and the Price Level* (1926), p. 5.
67. Moggridge (1974), p. 2.
68. *Economica*, August and November 1931 and February 1932.
69. 1st edn, 1931.
70. *See* Moggridge (1974), p. 64. *See also* Keynes, *C.W.*, Vol. XIII (1973a), pp. 243ff.
71. Harrod (1951), pp. 435–436.
72. J. C. Gilbert, 'Professor Hayek's Contribution to Trade Cycle Theory', in J. K. Eastham, *Dundee Economic Essays* (1955), pp. 51–62.
73. Keynes, *C.W.*, Vol. XIII (1973a), p. 504. This was a reference to a passage which appeared in *The General Theory*, pp. 192–193.
74. Keynes, *C.W.*, Vol. XIII (1973a).
75. In the works cited above.
76. Milo Keynes (1975). p. 4. For Keynes's personal relations as an undergraduate at Cambridge, *see* Holroyd (1971b), pp. 214, 241–244.
77. Harrod (1951), p. 559.
78. *The Times*, 22 April 1946.
79. Robbins (1971) p. 193. Harrod (1951), p. 559, makes the same point.
80. Robbins (1971), pp. 150–152.
81. *Ibid.*, p. 135.
82. King's College, *Keynes: a Memoir* (1949), p. 28.
83. Lord Balogh, in A. P. Thirlwall, *Keynes and International Monetary Relations* (1976), p. 68.
84. Thirlwall (1976), pp. 79–80.
85. Harrod (1951), pp. 625–637.
86. *Ibid.*, Chapters XII–XV.
87. Schumpeter in Harris (1948), p. 83.
88. R. Jenkins, *Nine Men of Power* (1974), p. 9. David Garnett's position seems to have been different in 1914.
89. Keynes, *C.W.*, Vol. IX (1972a), pp. 272–294.
90. Harrod (1951), p. 333.
91. *Ibid.*, p. 535. For the 'good life' *see* p. 14.
92. Elizabeth Johnson, 'John Maynard Keynes: Scientist or Politician?', in Joan Robinson, *After Keynes* (1973), pp. 24–25. Elizabeth Johnson is one of the editors of *The Collected Writings of John Maynard Keynes*.
93. Moggridge (1974), p. 68 and n.66.
94. For details of these early influences, *see* Harrod (1951), Chapter I.
95. Robinson in Milo Keynes (1975), p. 11.
96. D. E. Moggridge, *Keynes* (1976), pp. 25–29. *See also* p. 13.
97. King's College (1949), p. 21.
98. *Essays in Biography*, Keynes, *C.W.*, Vol. X (1972b), p. 436.
99. *Ibid.*, pp. 441–442.
100. *Ibid.*, p. 449.
101. King's College (1949), p. 12.
102. Harrod (1951), p. 650.
103. Keynes, *C.W.*, Vol. IX (1972a), p. 326.
104. Harrod (1951), pp. 193–194.
105. J. C. Gilbert, 'Economic Theory and Policy', *Yorkshire Bulletin* (1959).

Chapter 2

A survey of the literature*

Lord Keynes has had an enormous influence on monetary economics, both on monetary theory and monetary and fiscal policies. In assessing Keynes's influence on monetary economics it is helpful to know something about his personality and the part he played in public affairs. The importance of the latter is shown by the fact that 13 of the 30 volumes of *The Collected Writings of John Maynard Keynes* will relate to his *Activities*. My Chapter 1, 'Keynes the man', depicts some personal traits that are relevant. Sir Roy Harrod's *The Life of John Maynard Keynes* was published in 1951 not long after Keynes's death in 1946. He was well aware that it was too early for a definitive biography. In fact, it was a very good and comprehensive biography. Keynes, the greatest economist of the twentieth century, rightly appears in the Fontana series of Modern Masters for which Professor D. E. Moggridge wrote *Keynes*, published in 1976. He was well placed to do this, being an editor of the Royal Economic Society's *The Collected Writings*. Moggridge's short biography deals well with Keynes as economist, economist statesman and patron of the arts.

Essays on John Maynard Keynes, published in 1975, was edited by one of his nephews, Milo Keynes. The book is designed for the general reader and for economists. It is a biography in the form of papers on the many aspects of Keynes's life and work written by specialists in the various fields to which he had contributed so much. In view of the fact that *The General Theory* is Keynes's greatest work, the volume of the Proceedings of a conference held in 1975, *Keynes, Cambridge and The General Theory*, published in 1977 and edited by Professors Don Patinkin and J. Clark Leith, is of great interest. The conference considered the influences of criticism and discussion which aided Keynes in creating a masterpiece. Although primarily a book for economists, it contains material of interest to the general reader. Elizabeth S. Johnson and Professor Harry G. Johnson, both being Canadians, give an outside view in *The Shadow of Keynes* published in 1978. Some of the material in this book will be of interest to the general reader.

* The literature surveyed here is referred to in the text in such a way that further details are easily obtainable from the list of References.

Keynes's *A Tract on Monetary Reform* (1923) was based on the traditional Cambridge quantity theory of money equation. His seminal work is to be found in his trilogy, *A Treatise on Money* (1930), *The General Theory of Employment, Interest and Money* (1936) and 'The General Theory of Employment', an article in *The Quarterly Journal of Economics* (1937). *A Treatise on Money*, which consists of two volumes, *The Pure Theory of Money* and *The Applied Theory of Money*, was an elaborate work which Keynes expected to be his main contribution to monetary economics. His method was that of dynamic theory in which disequilibrium analysis was undertaken and was influenced by D. H. Robertson's period analysis in his *Banking Policy and the Price Level* (1926). In *A Treatise* Keynes set out to provide a more elaborate theory of the factors determining changes in the value of money, in other words the general level of prices, than in the accepted monetary theory of the time. In doing so he also provided an early form of a macrodynamic theory of changes in the levels of employment and output. *A Treatise on Money* was subjected to much criticism and it must have been a grave disappointment to Keynes when he had to recognize that his great endeavour had failed. After years of great intellectual effort and help from associates he produced his masterpiece, *The General Theory*. After careful consideration he changed his method to that of comparative statics. The thrust of the book was directed to an analysis of the factors determining the levels of employment and output, the problem of the general level of prices taking a secondary place. This does not mean that Keynes was not very concerned about inflation if it were likely to occur. Although *The General Theory* had its critics the book was an outstanding success and economists began to refer to the Keynesian Revolution.

The third of Keynes's trilogy is his 1937 article 'The General Theory of Employment'. This article was partly a reply to some of his critics but mainly a lucid restatement of his main ideas. His further explanation of what he meant by the uncertainty of our knowledge of the future and the important economic effects of this is valuable. In recent years *A Treatise on Money* has had a renaissance, economists realizing that on some issues it is necessary to consider his analysis in that work as well as in *The General Theory*. Keynes's influence on monetary economics has been so great because *The General Theory* is a seminal work. His basic macroeconomic model has been important in the development of econometric models for the management of an advanced economy despite Keynes's critical attitude towards econometrics as shown in his 1939 *Economic Journal* review of Professor J. Tinbergen's *Statistical Testing of Business Cycle Theories*. The richness of *The General Theory* (apart from the way in which it was written) has led to a number of different interpretations, placing the emphasis on different strands of thought, which have provided important developments in monetary economics.

There is a difference of opinion among economists as to whether Keynes was fair to Professor A. C. Pigou in his criticism of classical and neoclassical economics. Keynes's polemics, which he thought necessary to bring about the Revolution in economic thought, caused a great deal of controversy which might otherwise have been avoided. In the case of Pigou, I think Keynes was unfair as he did not consider the whole relevant range of Pigou's work. It should also be noted that they were in general agreement on the appropriate monetary and fiscal policies to deal with unemployment. Pigou's 1936 review article in *Economica*, 'Mr J. M. Keynes' *General Theory of Employment, Interest and Money*', was highly critical. In 1941 (2nd edn 1949) Pigou published his important book *Employment And Equilibrium* which has been unduly neglected by professional economists to whom it was mainly addressed. He dealt with macroeconomic issues raised by Keynes but in a more rigorous manner. The book is mainly devoted to problems of short-period flow equilibrium although it also contains analysis of economic systems in disequilibrium. Pigou put forward the concept which later became known as the Pigou effect in his 1943 *Economic Journal* article 'The Classical Stationary State'. This concept is of great theoretical importance as it goes far towards completing the classical and neoclassical theories of equilibrium which Keynes had attacked but it is generally recognized that it is of no practical importance in relation to employment policy. In 1950 Pigou published *Keynes's General Theory*, an appraisement of the achievements and limitations of Keynesian theory which was intended for readers with some knowledge of economics. Here he acknowledges that in his 1936 review article he failed to grasp the significance of Keynes's fundamental conception.

Professor Sir Dennis Robertson and Keynes were closely associated in the development of their ideas in monetary economics during the 1920s. Robertson had published his textbook *Money* in 1922 which went through a number of editions. His main work during this decade was *Banking Policy and the Price Level* (1926) in which he used dynamic period analysis to explain the causes of changes in the general level of prices and of output. The relations between forms of saving and of investment were analysed in detail. Keynes's *A Treatise on Money* (1930) was a more detailed treatment of these problems along somewhat similar lines. About 1931 their ways parted and Robertson, while continuing to extend his own dynamic theory of a monetary economy, became a critic of Keynes. His main contributions are to be found in *Essays in Money and Interest* selected with a Memoir by Sir John Hicks (1966) and in Part III of his *Lectures on Economic Principles* (1963). These were Robertson's Cambridge lectures and those in Part III were last delivered in 1957.

Professor Harry G. Johnson was greatly impressed in the 1950s and early 1960s with the importance of Keynes's *General Theory* for the development of economics despite what he regarded as certain weaknesses in the theory. This is shown by two lectures included in his *Money, Trade and Economic Growth* (1962). In later years Johnson was influenced by Milton Friedman and other monetarists and while recognizing Keynes's importance became a severe critic of Keynesian theory. This is exemplified in his Richard T. Ely Lecture of 1970 reprinted in his *Further Essays in Monetary Economics* (1972) and his paper in *Essays on John Maynard Keynes* (1975) edited by Milo Keynes. Professor Friedrich A. von Hayek has been a critic of Keynes since 1931. Hayek was an economist of the Austrian School in Vienna when he published his basic work on monetary economics *Prices and Production* (1st edn 1931). This book remains important although it was rightly subjected to much criticism. Much of Hayek's criticism is to be found in *A Tiger by the Tail – A 40-Years' Running Commentary on Keynesianism* by Hayek (2nd edn 1978), compiled and introduced by Sudha R. Shenoy. Hayek has published a number of Institute of Economic Affairs' occasional papers such as *Full Employment at Any Price?* (1975). Hayek's studies of the causes and economic consequences of the post-World War II inflation are valuable, but I would not accept his attribution to Keynes of responsibility for the inflation problem.

Professor Milton Friedman's *The Optimum Quantity of Money and Other Essays* (1969) contains reprints of his main articles and papers over many years. His 1956 paper 'The Quantity Theory of Money: a restatement' may be regarded as the origin of his development of monetarism. Friedman regarded the velocity of circulation of money as a relatively stable magnitude or at least changes in it as predictable, being dependent on a few variables. Thus an increase in the quantity of money would cause a predictable increase in total money income although subject to a variable time lag. Much work remains to be done on the division of the increase in money income between increases in the price level and in real output. Friedman undertook and stimulated much empirical work in monetary economics. *A Monetary History of the United States 1867–1960* (1963) by Milton Friedman and Anna Jacobson Schwartz is a monumental work. Friedman's paper *The Counter-Revolution in Monetary Theory* (1970) sets out his claim that monetarism is the counter-revolution to the Keynesian Revolution. There had been criticism that Friedman's empirical work lacked an adequate theory. This led him to write two articles 'A Theoretical Framework for Monetary Analysis' (1970) and A Monetary Theory of Nominal Income' (1971). These were reprinted in *Milton Friedman's Monetary Framework: A Debate with His Critics*, edited by Robert J. Gordon (1974). The debate left many problems unresolved. In his writings Friedman has stressed what he regards as an appropriate monetary policy and attacked Keynesian demand management.

In the Prefaces of *A Treatise on Money* and *The General Theory* Keynes expressed his great indebtedness to R. F. Kahn, a young economist at King's College, Cambridge. In *The General Theory* the multiplier in its static form plays a very important role. It was Professor Lord Kahn who had developed this concept in its dynamic form in his path-breaking 1931 *Economic Journal* article 'The Relation of Home Investment to Unemployment'. Kahn's important contributions to monetary economics in the period following Keynes's death, along with the multiplier article, are contained in his *Selected Essays on Employment and Growth* (1972). Sir Roy Harrod played an important part in dynamizing Keynesian theory. In 1936 he published *The Trade Cycle* which combined the multiplier with the accelerator. His 1939 *Economic Journal* article 'An Essay in Dynamic Theory' is an important preliminary attempt to develop a dynamic theory of an economy. Harrod's main contribution to the subject was made in *Towards a Dynamic Economics* (1948) which was followed by *Economic Dynamics* (1973). Professor Joan Robinson was another close associate of Keynes. She expounded and developed Keynesian theory. Her important developments in dynamic economics were influenced by Keynes's work. She published in 1956 the first edition of her important book *The Accumulation of Capital* in which she developed a theory of an expanding economy in the long run. There followed her *Essays in the Theory of Economic Growth* (1962) which is closely related to the former book. Joan Robinson's five volumes of *Collected Economic Papers* show her wide range as an economist and include many papers on monetary economics of great interest.

The neoclassical synthesis stems from Professor Sir John Hicks's famous 1937 *Econometrica* article 'Mr Keynes and the "Classics"'. Professor Don Patinkin developed this neo-Walrasian system in great detail in the first edition of his scholarly book *Money, Interest And Prices* (1956). Professor James Tobin is taken as a representative of the neoclassical synthesis and his work considered in detail. He emphasized the importance of the rate of interest and regarded the market value of equities relative to the replacement costs of physical assets as the major determinant of new investment. Tobin has written many important papers such as 'Liquidity Preference as Behaviour towards Risk' (1958); 'Money, Capital and Other Stores of Value' (1961); 'An Essay on the Principles of Debt Management' (1968); and (with William C. Brainard) 'Pitfalls in Financial Model-building' (1968), all of which are included in his *Essays in Economics Volume 1: Macroeconomics* (1971). Professor G. L. S. Shackle is the chief fundamentalist Keynesian. He regards uncertainty as the essence of Keynesian theory and recognizes its great importance in relation to the rate of investment. Shackle stresses that crucial unique decisions are taken under uncertainty, in the sense of the future being unknowable and probability theory not being applicable. This has been his main theme since his first book of 1938. In 1949 Shackle published the first edition of his very important book *Expectation in Economics*. Other important books followed such as *Uncertainty in Economics* (1955), *A Scheme of Economic Theory* (1965), *The Years of High Theory* (1967) and *Epistemics and Economics* (1972). Professor Paul Davidson, another fundamentalist Keynesian, published the first edition of his *Money And The Real World* in 1972.

Professor Robert Clower published his path-breaking paper 'The Keynesian Counter-revolution: a theoretical appraisal' in 1965. This was an attack on the neoclassical synthesis which he referred to as the Keynesian counter-revolution. His own contribution is the dual-decision hypothesis. Clower points out that in the case of Keynesian involuntary unemployment the effective demand which determines the output of producers is less than desired consumption as given by the full-employment equilibrium of orthodox analysis. The relevant market signals are not given; there is inadequate information. Clower developed his theory further in his 1967 article 'A Reconsideration of the Microfoundations of Monetary Theory'. Professor Axel Leijonhufvud's important book *On Keynesian Economics and the Economics of Keynes* (1968) follows Clower's interpretation of Keynes. He attacks the income–expenditure theory, the neoclassical synthesis, as an incorrect interpretation of Keynes's *General Theory*. Leijonhufvud does not accept that Keynes's model is basically that of comparative statics and interprets Keynesian Theory as being disequilibrium analysis. He stresses the problem of the co-ordination of economic activities and the failure of communication because of information costs, for example the search costs of an unemployed worker. Leijonhufvud's book is open to criticism but it has had a stimulating influence on monetary economists.

Keynes was concerned in *The General Theory* with the possibility of economic stagnation, serious longterm unemployment. The stagnation thesis has been much debated. Professor Alvin H. Hansen developed and strongly supported this thesis in the United States in *Full Recovery or Stagnation?* (1938), *Fiscal Policy and Business Cycles* (1941) and *Economic Policy and Full Employment* (1947). Robertson gives a well-balanced discussion of the stagnation thesis in his *Lectures on Economic Principles* (1963).

Keynes had an important influence not only on the development of economic theory but also on the problem of monetary and fiscal policies appropriate for the management of an advanced free-enterprise or mixed economy. In addition to what is to be found in *A Treatise on Money* and *The General Theory*, Keynes wrote extensively on monetary and fiscal policies. Volume IX *The Collected Writings, Essays in Persuasion*, contains reprints of a number of important pamphlets. There are a number of important studies of this problem: Professor T. W. Hutchison's *Economics and Economic Policy in Britain 1946–1966* (1968) and his *Keynes v The 'Keynesians' . . .?* (1977); Professor Donald Winch's *Economics and Policy* (1972); D. E. Moggridge and Susan Howson, 'Keynes on monetary policy, 1910–1946' (1974).

Chapter 3

The Keynesian Revolution

Six months after coming down from Trinity College, Cambridge, in 1906, Lytton Strachey wrote to Keynes envisaging how happy the situation would be if they and some of their friends could live together and you 'would revolutionize political economy'[1]. This remarkable statement was made some years before the publication of Keynes's first book, *Indian Currency And Finance* (1913)[2]. It was not until after the appearance of *The General Theory* in 1936 that we begin to hear of the Keynesian Revolution. Keynes himself certainly thought of *The General Theory* in terms of a revolution. He wrote to George Bernard Shaw on January 1935,

> 'To understand *my* state of mind, however, you have to know that I believe myself to be writing a book on economic theory which will largely revolutionize – not, I suppose, at once but in the course of the next ten years – the way the world thinks about economic problems. . . . I can't expect you, or anyone else, to believe this at the present stage. But for myself I don't merely hope what I say, in my own mind I'm quite sure.'[3]

In recent years there has been much discussion among academic economists as to whether there was a real revolution and if so, would a Keynesian evolution have been more appropriate. An extreme view has also been put forward that the whole crisis in economic thought was in one sense unnecessary. However, it is clear that in Keynes's view there was the Keynesian Revolution.

Professor Gottfried Haberler in his two essays on Keynes, '*The General Theory* after Ten Years' (1946) and 'Sixteen Years Later' (1962)[4] recognizes Keynes's genius and greatness as an economist in lucid expositions of the place of *The General Theory* in the development of economic thought. He warns us against the exaggerated claims of some Keynesians, but states that *The General Theory* marks a conspicuous milestone in the development of economic theory. He does not regard it as a revolution or a new beginning or even a break in economic thought[5]. While Keynes understressed the continuity of the development of economic theory, Haberler overstressed it. In fact, Haberler ruled out the consideration of the possibility of a Keynesian Revolution on general grounds in his 1962 essay.

He writes,

> 'As I see it, what is true of other sciences, among them the queen of sciences, mathematics, is also true of economics, pure and applied: the accumulated mass of knowledge is so enormous that it has become impossible for any single man, however great a genius he may be, to bring about a real revolution. It does, of course, require men of genius to increase the stock of knowledge but the contribution of any single one is small compared with the existing stock.'[6]

Haberler asks us to admire great genius while avoiding untenable exaggerations.

My own view is that it is useful to characterize a breakthrough, a peak of achievement, in the development of a science as a revolution. As I have already stated (*see* Blake, p. 32), I think it is useful to speak of revolutions in economics such as the Keynesian Revolution. In this case, it follows that post-Keynesian monetary economics is discussed in terms of counter-revolutions and developments of Keynesian theory. Admittedly, it may be helpful at times to think in Lakatosian terms (*see* Latsis, 1976) of a Keynesian methodology of scientific research programme, but there are problems of its beginning and eventual ending.

Certainly *The General Theory* is one of the great classic works in economics because of the new vision of the economic process and the basic analytical model which it contains. Samuelson writing in 1946, suggests that possibly the future historians of economic thought will place *The General Theory* 'in the first rank of theoretical classics, along with the work of Smith, Cournot, and Walras. Certainly, these four books together encompass most of what is vital in the field of economic theory.'[7] Walter Eltis has stated, 'It would be universally agreed today that Keynes's *General Theory of Employment, Interest and Money* is, together with Smith's *Wealth of Nations* and Marx's *Das Kapital* one of the three truly great books that political economists have written.'[8] Harrod, having quoted the letter to Shaw, emphasizes that Keynes claimed to be promoting a revolution of thought. He regards the essence of Keynes's contribution as a reclassification of economic phenomena, states that the advantages of his new system can only be judged by its actual use and that in this way 'Keynes has been, and will, I am confident, continue to be triumphantly vindicated.'[9] Harrod puts Keynes in a class with Adam Smith and Ricardo but doubts whether his star, as an economist, was quite of their magnitude. However, he admits that this may not be the final judgement. Harrod does state definitely that Keynes did not produce a book (including *The General Theory*) that will survive as well as the *Wealth of Nations*[10].

Unfortunately, Keynes's masterpiece, *The General Theory* despite some fine passages, is badly organized, although Keynes was a brilliant writer of English prose. Quite apart from the treatment of his predecessors, the book contains many confusions, obscurities and inconsistencies of method, and lacks a clear design. This seems surprising in view of the detailed criticisms of the Cambridge economists and also of Harrod and Sir Ralph Hawtrey to whom he submitted early drafts. He received much effective criticism from his younger colleagues, Kahn, Joan Robinson and Harrod, who had adopted his basic approach, but, after lengthy correspondence with Robertson and Hawtrey, Keynes never reached a real understanding with them[11]. It should be noted that his pre-publication critics were a small group and he did not obtain the advantage which can be derived from publishing preliminary articles in the academic journals. However, partly because of Keynes's lengthy correspondence with a few economists during the various stages of the development of the book, *The General Theory* was not undermined by criticism after its publication, as happened to a considerable extent in the case of *A Treatise on Money*. Patinkin writes that 'the basic structure of the book not only remained intact, but also defined the framework of both theoretical and empirical research in macroeconomics for decades to come – truly a scientific achievement of the first order'[12]. While recognizing the greatness of Keynes, Milton Friedman and the other monetarists would certainly wish to qualify this statement.

Paul Samuelson, the distinguished American Keynesian economist and a Nobel Prize-winner in economics, regards *The General Theory* as a work of genius. However, he emphasizes its obscurity and goes so far as to say that it 'seems the random notes over a period of years of a gifted man . . .'[13]; this is, of course, an exaggeration. He compares *The General Theory* to Joyce's *Finnegan's Wake*, both of which are much in need of companion volumes providing 'skeleton keys' and guides to their contents. Samuelson points out that 'Certainly in its present state, the book does not get itself read from one year to another even by the sympathetic teacher and scholar.'[14] I always advised my students to read *The General Theory* and not merely the textbook models which are provided in such abundance. Incidentally these models have come under severe criticism in recent years from a number of economists, notably Axel Leijonhufvud, who have been re-interpreting Keynes[15]. I used to say to my students that by reading *The General Theory* they would share the experience of creative work in economics which only a masterpiece, a great classic, could provide. I was interested to find that Patinkin took the same view. He writes 'In so far as *The General Theory* is concerned – this is the book that made the revolution which has continued to mould our basic ways of thinking about macroeconomic problems. And so the reading of it – at least in part – is an intellectual experience that no aspiring economist even today can afford to forgo.'[16]

By the middle of the 1940s the Keynesian Revolution had become widely recognized. Lawrence R. Klein's *The Keynesian Revolution*[17], first published in 1946, was a doctoral thesis written in 1944 with all the enthusiasm of a revolutionary disciple. Professor Klein is now one of the most distinguished American economists who can be described as a Keynesian. There are contributions in *The New Economics*[18], published in 1947, which give Keynes recognition similar to that of the book's title. In 1946 Professor E. A. G. Robinson had paid tribute to the greatness of Keynes as an economist and in 1963 he wrote, 'I am persuaded that we could not have had a Keynesian revolution without Keynes . . . .'[19] Claims for a Keynesian Revolution have been made by recent writers. For example Professor H. P. Minsky states, 'If Keynes, along with Marx, Darwin, Freud and Einstein belong in the pantheon of seminal thinkers who triggered modern intellectual revolutions, it is because of the contribution to economics, both as a science and as a relevant guide to public policy, that is contained in his *General Theory of Employment, Interest and Money*.[20] Robert Lekachman refers to Keynes, 'As fundamental a revolutionary as Freud or Marx, Keynes re-wrote the language of economics for the Western world.'[21] He further states, 'It has been said that we are all Keynesians now. In the main this is a justified if slightly hyperbolic claim.'[22]

The claim that we are all Keynesians now is certainly not justified. One only has to think of the monetarists, of Milton Friedman's *The Counter-Revolution in Monetary Theory*[23]. It is true, of course, that Keynes's influence in monetary economics is very pervasive and Milton Friedman has acknowledged this influence on himself. Two other counter-revolutions will also be discussed. They are, however, basically Keynesian economics. There is the neoclassical synthesis or neo-Walrasian equilibrium analysis which, despite its name, has been referred to as a counter-revolution. There is also the development of disequilibrium economics which some economists regard as a reinterpretation of Keynes but I regard Keynes's *General Theory* as basically equilibrium economics. I shall also consider the dynamizing of Keynes's basically static system.

Hicks's point that 'There was not one Keynesian Revolution, there were several'[24], is a reference to the very pervasive influence of Keynes on the development of economics. It is thus possible to speak of the Keynesian Revolution and then consider post-Keynesian developments. Hicks refers to the classical economists of the eighteenth and nineteenth centuries and the neoclassical economists of 1870 to 1920 as having been interested in dynamic problems of the causes of economic growth. However, they often used the static method, which considers the economy at a point in time, and not a dynamic method, which traces the path of economic change over time. Keynes's method was basically static, the method of comparative statics: his main objective was to analyse the determinants of the levels of employment and income. By assuming different magnitudes of economic variables, such as the rate of investment (expenditure on capital goods), he was able to obtain different levels of employment and income. He was not, in general, analysing the processes of change from one level of employment to another. We can say that this method involves snapshot photographs of the economy at different points of time or different hypothetical levels of employment in the economy at a point of time, because of different magnitudes assumed in the analysis of the determinants of the level of employment. Hicks stresses the limitations of the static method, although it must be remembered that Keynes achieved a great deal by its use. Three 'post-Keynesian' dynamic methods are distinguished by Hicks and their importance emphasized. He is, however, eclectic and states that we need all four methods and should 'be aware of their weaknesses and strengths'[25]. Hicks points out that there are dynamic elements in *A Treatise on Money* and *The General Theory*. Some economists point to *A Treatise* as being more dynamic than *The General Theory* and take the view that it was unfortunate that Keynes moved in the direction he did. Professor Shackle put forward this view strongly in conversation with me. However, as I have pointed out (*see above*), the static model served Keynes's main objective well.

Much of the work in macroeconomics since Keynes has taken the form of attempts to 'dynamize' the Keynesian model. There have been three lines of development. First, there has been the development of a theory of the trade cycle, the periodic upward and downward swings in economic activity, without an upward trend, economic progress. Keynes did not develop a theory of the trade cycle, but he gave important leads to the development of such a theory using the framework of *The General Theory*. Chapter 22, entitled 'Notes on the Trade Cycle' is devoted to this subject. Second, there has been the development of a theory of trade cyclical fluctuations about an upward trend. Third, economic growth theory has concentrated on the conditions for steady economic growth. The classical and neoclassical economists, as already mentioned, had been interested in dynamic problems. Their interests included both the problems of the trade cycle and of secular economic growth. The development of dynamic economics in the terms of period analysis, the tracing of the path of economic change over time, owes much to Robertson's *Banking Policy and The Price Level* of 1926. Also, before Keynes, the Swedish School had developed period analysis in the late 1920s and early 1930s following Knut Wicksell's great work, *Geldzins und Güterpreise* of 1898[26]. Wicksell had used period or sequence analysis, for example, in his famous 'cumulative' process. Professor Bertil Ohlin surveyed the development of Swedish sequence or process analysis which took place before *A Treatise on Money* of 1930 and in the early 1930s[27]. However, it remains true that Keynes set the stage for the development of dynamic economics in the United Kingdom and the United States although he retained the older method of comparative statics.

Before considering the attitudes of economists towards the Keynesian Revolution it may be helpful to state Keynes's main contribution in *The General Theory* in simple terms. It was a path-breaking work on the factors which determine the levels of employment and income of a free-enterprise economy. As has been stated, the analysis was static. Keynes analyses an equilibrium position with given data, including expectation. The introduction of expectations along with uncertainty makes the analysis more applicable to the real world, but expectations are taken to be given at a point in time. Unlike much of classical and neoclassical economics, Keynes's analysis is short-term and 'full' employment equilibrium is only the limiting case. In a modern advanced economy there is a whole range of underemployment equilibrium positions. Keynes emphasized the importance of the rate of investment (expenditure on capital goods, machinery, factory buildings, etc.) for the level of employment. Given certain assumptions the levels of income and employment depend upon aggregate money demand which consists of expenditure on consumption goods and investment. The multiplier, the figure by which an increment of additional investment must be multiplied to give the corresponding additional increment of income, depends upon the marginal propensity to consume. This refers to the proportion of an additional increment of income which is consumed. Without going into detail here, it is clear that if there is a net increase in investment (expenditure on capital goods), employment and incomes will be higher in the capital goods industries. Thus more money will be spent on consumption goods and, assuming general unemployment of productive resources, the production of capital goods and consumption goods are *complementary*; therefore an increase in the output of capital goods is associated with an increase in the output of consumption goods. In classical and neoclassical economics, full employment of productive resources was assumed as the general case although unemployment because of trade cyclical depression and other causes was, of course, recognized. On the assumption of full employment, the outputs of capital goods and consumption goods are *competitive*; therefore an increase in the output of capital goods involves a decrease in the output of consumption goods.

Keynes's great contribution was made in the 1930s at the time of the Great Depression and the prolonged heavy unemployment. He started with the assumption of general unemployment of productive resources and analysed the forces that would raise the economy to full employment level. It was a great achievement of Keynes to emphasize the simple point that, on the assumption of general unemployment, the production of capital goods and of consumption goods are complementary. Government intervention by means of appropriate monetary and fiscal policies can raise aggregate money demand by influencing its constituents, investment and consumption. Investment and saving are equal by definition in *The General Theory*. This obscures somewhat the fundamental point that an increase in investment could be matched by an increased amount of saving out of the resulting higher level of income. Thus, starting with general unemployment, there is no need to worry about the source of the savings to finance the additional investment. Here Keynes was combatting the so-called Treasury view of the 1920s that an increase in public investment would be offset by a decrease in private investment. In recent years the related concept of crowding-out has been much discussed. If there is widespread high unemployment crowding-out in terms of productive resources is not serious although there may be bottleneck problems regarding particular supplies of commodities and there may be a balance of payments problem. Crowding-out is also used to refer to a financial constraint. This constraint depends on the monetary policy adopted.

Unemployment because of a deficiency of aggregate money demand may be a long-period problem of economic stagnation or a problem of trade cyclical depression. Private investment is shown to depend on the expected rate of return on capital goods and the rate of interest and is considered to be unstable. If there is a deficiency of demand, money rates of interest may be lowered by increasing the quantity of money in order to stimulate private investment. Government tax revenue may be decreased and/or public expenditure increased to create a budgetary deficit which is associated with an increase in the quantity of money and/or its velocity of circulation.

Keynes regarded the full-employment equilibrium of the classical and neoclassical theories as a special case of his more general theory and one which required special assumptions. In a free-enterprise economy with conditions mainly of *laissez-faire*, the objective of his analysis was to show that the forces present will not necessarily bring about a full-employment equilibrium. Thus, state intervention in the form of monetary and fiscal policies is required. Keynes put forward his theory in the context of a severe criticism of the classical and neoclassical economists and of Say's Law in particular.

This simple statement of the Keynesian theory of the determination of the levels of income and employment avoids many difficulties in the analysis which will be considered later. It should also be noted here that Keynes assumed a closed economy, an economy without international trade and financial transactions, although in places he allows for such international relationships. Post-Keynesian economics has been much concerned with converting his model of a closed economy into that of an open economy.

Keynes's *General Theory* has sometimes been referred to as depression or slump economics. Samuelson refers to 'the fallacious belief that Keynesian economics is good "depression economics" and only that. Actually, the Keynesian system is indispensable to an understanding of conditions of over-effective demand and secular exhilaration.'[28] Malcolm R. Fisher pays tribute to three of Hicks's contributions to the exposition and elaboration of Keynes's *General Theory*, but it is surprising to find him conclude his review article, written in 1976, of John Hicks's, *The Crisis in Keynesian Economics* (Oxford, 1974) with the sentence, 'The economics of the *General Theory* is the economics of depression. In 1976, even after reconstruction we are less sure than formerly that it is more.'[29] Fisher's statement is very misleading. Keynes would have been the first to admit that he had not solved all the problems of full employment, over-full employment, mass unemployment because of deficiency of demand, and other kinds of unemployment. His claim in the Preface of *The General Theory*, to which I have already referred, that he had produced 'a more general theory, which includes the classical theory with which we are familiar, as a special case'[30] is perfectly justified. Keynes's model provides an analysis of the determinants of the levels of income and employment. The theory is general in the sense (but not only in this sense) that the determinates, income and employment, can be at any levels. The slump or depression economics depends on certain empirical assumptions. It is true that this case is emphasized in *The General Theory* because Keynes was writing his book during The Great Depression of the early 1930s which followed the years of high level unemployment in the United Kingdom of the 1920s. His primary concern was with the problem of mass unemployment because of trade-cyclical depression, weak cyclical booms and secular stagnation.

As early as 1937[31] Hicks had extracted a set of three simultaneous equations which give the equilibrium rate of interest and the equilibrium level of income at which savings are equal to investment out of Keynes's general theory of income and employment[30]. The volume of employment is related in a simple way to the value of income. The model is presented as the famous IS–LM diagram which has been widely used in the textbooks. The model clearly shows that the level of income depends on the empirical assumptions made. Keynes's depression economics or slump economics is therefore a special case. In 'Recollections And Documents', Hicks quotes a letter dated 31 March 1937 from Keynes to him in which Keynes says of the 1937 *Econometrica* article, 'I found it very interesting and really have next to nothing to say by way of criticism.'[33] Keynes went on to make a few interesting comments but did not point out that the equality of saving and investment in Hicks's model was not an identity as in *The General Theory*.

Hicks concludes that Keynes accepted the IS–LM diagram as a fair statement of the nucleus of his position[34]. The important point here is that Keynes is accepting a general equilibrium presentation of his theory and implicitly agreeing that his slump or depression economics depended on specific empirical assumptions.

In January 1937 Keynes was using the apparatus of his general theory in three articles in *The Times* on 'How To Avoid A Slump'[35]. In November 1939 Keynes wrote two long articles for *The Times* which formed the basis of his booklet, *How to Pay for the War*, which was published in February 1940[36]. Again he was using the same theoretical apparatus but to deal with the entirely different problem of controlling aggregate demand in a full employment war economy so as to avoid or minimize inflation. Thus Keynes himself showed that the basic macroeconomic model of *The General Theory* could be used in an analysis of a full-employment economy as in a depressed economy with mass unemployment. Samuelson suggests that we 'paste into our copies of the *General Theory* . . . the famous chapter in *How to Pay for the War* which first outlined the modern theory of the inflationary process'.[37] Incidentally, it may be noted that although it was largely because of the influence of Keynes that World War II was a 3 per cent longterm rate of interest war in contrast to the 5 per cent World War I, his proposals in *How to Pay for the War* were only partially adopted. The ingenious proposal of deferred pay or compulsory saving as a method of offsetting inflationary pressures, which it was envisaged had the added advantage of the release of such saving to combat post-war depression, was only adopted in the scheme of post-war credits to a relatively small extent. The annual average amount raised would have had to have been much greater if deferred pay was to have played the key role in war finance as proposed by Keynes[38]. It should be noted that there was no post-war slump in the case of World War II as there was following the post-war boom after World War I. The United Kingdom economy showed great flexibility in adapting to the changed pattern of demand. Nevertheless it is regrettable that the post-war credit scheme was adopted only in such a moderate form.

A much more important contribution to financial control of a full employment war economy was made by Keynes in his development of national income and expenditure accounting. The model of *The General Theory* provided the theoretical basis for this development and the statistics used in *How to Pay for the War* were the starting point. Under the stimulus of Keynes, Mr Richard Stone and Mr James Meade (as they were at that time) produced *An Analysis of the Sources of War Finance and an Estimate of the National Income and Expenditure for 1938 and 1940* (1941, Cmd 6261) which was published at the time of the 1941 Budget. This was the Chancellor of the Exchequer, Sir Kingsley Wood's first budget and it and the accompanying budget speech was thoroughly Keynesian. As Professor Winch points out, the use of national income and expenditure estimates in relation to the formation of the budget 'was a major event in the history of the application of economics to policy formation'[39]. Subsequent wartime budgets and those of the post-war period have been produced in association with such national income and expenditure White Papers. The narrow Treasury view of the nature of the budget had been transformed into an instrument of overall financial control of the economy on the basis of Keynesian macroeconomic theory. Such national income and expenditure accounting has been adopted by many other countries as well as the United Kingdom as a tool for formulating fiscal policies in relation to the objectives of a high level of employment, the control of inflation and dealing with international balance of payments disequilibrium.

The degree of success of the management of aggregate demand by means of fiscal policy during the post-war years in the United Kingdom and the extent to which it has reflected 'true Keynesian' or 'pseudo-Keynesian' doctrines have been much debated. Further, there has been the attack of Milton Friedman and other monetarists on such methods of control and their strong advocacy of the control of the money supply as the only appropriate instrument of control in the present state of knowledge. What I have been emphasizing here is that Keynes's *General Theory* does provide a general model for determining the level of employment and is not merely depression economics. Sir Austin Robinson, a pupil and colleague of Keynes, points out that 'Keynes's own Cambridge pupils regarded Keynesian economics as being a way of thinking about the factors determining the level of activity, equally applicable to depression and boom.'[40] This sums up the view which I have put forward and strongly hold and is, of course, not confined to Keynes's pupils. Whether actual 'Keynesian' policies have been appropriate in particular situations is another matter.

Mr Colin Clark stated in 1970,

> 'Even now we are still standing too close to make a real assessment of Keynes's contributions to economics, how far they represented permanent additions to our methods of analysis, to what extent they were *ad hoc* proposals to put right the tragic and unnecessary unemployment and depression of the 1930s, which would have been valuable if applied at the time *but which may have become irrelevant or positively misleading later.*'[41]

In the light of this statement one can understand that at the present time some economists are maintaining that Keynes did not make a fundamental contribution to the development of economic theory while others differ as to the essential nature of the contribution while accepting it as a revolution or important advance. Anyone versed in the history of economic thought will recognize the importance of Colin Clark's caution, but I think that it is possible at the present time to make a rational assessment of Keynes's contribution and to recognize it as a revolution. It remains true, of course, that *The General Theory*, Keynes's masterpiece, a seminal work, will be subject to close scrutiny and interpretation as well as acting as a stimulus to further economic thought for many years to come.

Notes

1. M. Holroyd, *Lytton Strachey and the Bloomsbury Group: His Work and Their Influence* (1971a), p. 18.
2. Keynes, *C.W.*, Vol. I (1971).

3. Keynes, *C.W.*, Vol. XIII (1973a), pp. 492–493.
4. G. Haberler (1946, 1962). 'The General Theory after Ten Years' and 'Sixteen Years Later' in R. Lekachman, *Keynes' General Theory Reports of Three Decades* (1964).
5. Haberler (1946) in Lekachman (1964), p. 284.
6. Haberler (1962) in Lekachman (1964), p. 296.
7. Paul A. Samuelson, *The General Theory* in Lekachman (1964), p. 319.
8. W. Eltis, 'The Failure of the Keynesian Conventional Wisdom', *Lloyds Bank Review* (1976), p. 1.
9. R. F. Harrod, *The Life of John Maynard Keynes* (1951), p. 463.
10. *Ibid.*, pp. 466–467.
11. D. Patinkin, *Keynes' Monetary Thought* (1976a), pp. 61–62.
12. Patinkin (1976a), p. 139.
13. Samuelson (1946) in Lekachman (1964), p. 319.
14. *Ibid.*
15. *See* A. Leijonhufvud, *On Keynesian Economics and the Economics of Keynes* (1968).
16. Patinkin, 'The Collected Writings of John Maynard Keynes: from the *Tract* to the *General Theory* (1975), p. 269.
17. 2nd edn, 1968.
18. S. E. Harris, *The New Economics* (1948 (US copyright 1947)).
19. E. A. G. Robinson (1963), 'Could there have been a 'General Theory' without Keynes?, in Lekachman (1964), p. 95.
20. H. P. Minsky, *John Maynard Keynes* (1976), p. 1 (first published in the USA 1975).
21. R. Lekachman, *The Age of Keynes* (1967 (first published in the USA 1966)). The statement is on the jacket.
22. Lekachman (1967), p. 5.
23. 1970.
24. J. Hicks, *Capital and Growth* (1965, 1st edn), p. 29.
25. *Ibid.*
26. The English translation is K. Wicksell, *Interest and Prices* (1936).
27. B. Ohlin, 'Some Notes on the Stockholm Theory of Savings and Investment', *Economic Journal* (1937).
28. Samuelson (1946) in Lekachman (1964), p. 320.
29. M. R. Fisher, 'Professor Hicks and the Keynesians', *Economica* (1976), p. 314.
30. *The General Theory*, p. XXIII.
31. J. R. Hicks, 'Mr Keynes and the "Classics"', *Econometrica* (1937); reprinted in J. R. Hicks, *Critical Essays in Monetary Theory* (1967). Coddington discusses Hicks's life-work in relation to that of Keynes. *See also* Hicks's reply. (Alan Coddington, 'Hicks's contribution to Keynesian economics'. *Journal of Economic Literature* (December 1976), and John Hicks, 'On Coddington's interpretation: a reply'. *Journal of Economic Literature* (September 1979)).
32. 'Mr Keynes and the "Classics"', in Hicks, *Critical Essays* (1967), p. 134.
33. Reprinted in J. R. Hicks, *Economic Perspectives* (1977), p. 144.
34. Hicks, *Perspectives* (1977), p. 146.
35. Reprinted as Appendix A in T. W. Hutchison, *Keynes versus the 'Keynesians' . . .?* (1977).
36. Reprinted in Keynes, *C.W.*, Vol. IX (1972a).
37. Samuelson (1946) in Lekachman (1964), p. 319.
38. Harrod (1951), p. 494.
39. D. Winch, *Economics and Policy* (1972, 2nd edn), p. 273.
40. Hutchison (1977), p. 58.
41. C. Clark, *Taxmanship* (1970, 2nd edn), p. 53, as quoted by Hutchison (1977), who added italics, p. 45.

Part II

The critics

Chapter 4

A. C. Pigou, his criticism and final recognition of Keynes

Professor Pigou was a distinguished economist[1] whose work was severely criticized by Keynes in his attack on classical and neoclassical economic theory in *The General Theory*. His work was based on that of his revered teacher, Marshall, but he systematized and elaborated Marshallian economics while making original contributions. His development of welfare economics reached its final stage in *The Economics of Welfare*[2]. In the first edition entitled *Wealth And Welfare* (1912), his Part IV dealt with the variability of the national dividend (national income) which was later to become a separate book, *Industrial Fluctuations*[3]. It was his *Theory of Unemployment*[4] which was the major object of Keynes's attack. Subsequent to Keynes's *General Theory*, Pigou wrote *Employment And Equilibrium*[5] which was a systematic and subtle analysis of short-period equilibrium and the level of employment on 'classical' lines. Pigou generally has not been accorded his proper place as a great economist. However, Kaldor in a critical but eulogistic review–article of *Employment And Equilibrium* writes, 'The fact that it is the sixth major treatise on economic theory the author has produced bears witness to a record of achievement which must surely be unique among economists.'[6]

Pigou's review–article[7] of *The General Theory*, published in 1936, was highly critical. Keynes was unfair in his criticism of Marshall, Pigou and others. Pigou castigated Keynes for presenting his ideas in a 'matrix of sarcastic comment upon other people'[8]. Pigou himself was at the centre of Keynes's attack on 'classical' economics as according to Keynes his *Theory of Unemployment* is 'the only detailed account of the classical theory of employment which exists'[9]. In these circumstances it was natural for Pigou to react strongly against Keynes's criticisms of the 'classicists'. He defended himself on a number of issues and raised a number of important objections to Keynes's analysis. Sir Austin Robinson writes, 'Thus Pigou was on the defensive – principally, I think, because of Marshall; while he had a great sense of authority as professor he was not a vain man, and as subsequent events showed, he was not unprepared to admit that he had been wrong. His defence took the form of a severe review of the *General Theory* in *Economica*. He condemned Keynes's "patronage extended to his old master Marshall", and his iconoclastic treatment of classical economists as a group.'[10] Robinson also states that Keynes 'was very conscious that in attacking Pigou, he was attacking ideas which he himself had held only a few years earlier'[11].

Keynes's attack on the 'classical' system was basically a denial that a competitive private-enterprise economy possessed forces which made it an automatic, self-regulating economy with a tendency to full-employment equilibrium. This economic harmony depended on the rate of interest being at a level at which investment would be equal to saving out of a full-employment level of real income. Keynes showed that the rate of interest could not fall below a minimum somewhat above zero while the rate of investment might be insensitive to a fall in the rate of interest. Thus, with given investment opportunities, a reduction of the rate of interest to its minimum might not give a rate of investment equal to the rate of saving at a full-employment level of income. In this case, we have Keynes's under-employment equilibrium, employment and income being low enough to give a rate of saving sufficiently low to equal the rate of investment at the minimum rate of interest[12]. It was soon pointed out by Haberler and many other economists that this under-employment equilibrium depended on Keynes's assumption of fixed money-wage rates. If money wages were flexible downwards, unemployment would cause wages to fall in a competitive labour market and this was inconsistent with Keynes's under-employment equilibrium. On the other hand, as Haberler points out, 'There is no difficulty in "classical theory" with any amount of involuntary unemployment, if wages are rigid and the rigid floor is pushed high enough.'[13]

Earlier, in 1946, Haberler states, 'Keynes assumes that (money) wages are rigid downward. If this assumption, which is certainly not entirely unrealistic, is rigidly adhered to, ... Under-employment equilibrium is then possible.'[14] With flexible wages under-employment equilibrium is impossible as wages and prices will fall continuously which 'cannot well be described as an equilibrium position'[15]. Haberler then refers to Keynes's analysis, on the assumption of flexible wages, in chapter 19 of *The General Theory* in which it is shown that a reduction in money wages can cause a fall in the rate of interest. However, the rate of investment at the minimum rate of interest may not be sufficient for full employment. This fall in the rate of interest is called the 'Keynes effect' but it may be exhausted before full employment is reached. Therefore, money wages and prices continue to fall. Haberler was the first economist to show that, theoretically, full-employment equilibrium could be established by the rise in the real value of the money stock resulting from the fall of prices. This increase in wealth held by the general public will lead to an increase in consumption and full employment. Thus consumption is not only a function of the level of income but also of the amount of wealth held. Consumption of a given level of income increases with the increase in the amount of wealth held. This is the famous 'Pigou effect', but it was first formulated by Haberler in the first edition of his *Prosperity And Depression* (1937)[16].

Haberler recognized the theoretical importance of the 'Keynes effect' and he regarded the 'Pigou effect' as constituting 'a permanent enrichment to our analytical apparatus: this we largely owe to the stimulus provided by the *General Theory*. Keynes forced the classical writers to rethink, restate and to refine their theories.'[17] The theory of the 'classical' economists and the basic model of *The General Theory* were comparative statics. The Pigou effect was formulated on a high level of abstraction which provided flexible wage rates, perfect homogeneity and perfect mobility of labour. On this basis, the Keynesian under-employment equilibrium and the associated secular stagnation thesis are not tenable. The Pigou effect was not developed as an instrument of employment policy, but in order to complete the classical static system which had overlooked an important theoretical relationship. At the same time, it made clear the dependence of Keynes's concept of under-employment equilibrium on fixed money wages. Haberler writes, 'in the static, Keynesian world with competitive, flexible wages, full employment will be effectively maintained even without the operation of the Pigou effect, except in the extreme cases where either the liquidity preference is infinitely elastic at a positive rate of interest or the marginal efficiency of capital is entirely inelastic with respect to the interest rate'[18]. The rate of investment at the minimum rate of interest may be too low to give full employment. Haberler continues, 'The Pigou effect need be called upon to bring about full employment only in the extreme cases just mentioned whose actual occurrence in a static world is highly questionable.'[19]

As we shall see, Pigou rightly analyses in detail in comparative static terms the case of a positive rate of saving at a minimum rate of interest where investment is zero. It is here that the Pigou effect is required. In a barter economy it is not required, as saving can only take the form of an accumulation of physical goods which is investment. However, in such a highly abstract equilibrium system as the Walrasian system it is possible to have money acting as a medium of exchange[20] and in a money economy the Pigou effect may be required. There is perfect certainty[21] regarding the system of relative prices and quantities that constitutes the static equilibrium, but not perfect knowledge which excludes the possibility of money. To simplify, assume a closed economy with the money stock consisting of a fixed nominal amount of gold coins. It is conceivable in this case that the establishment of full-employment equilibrium requires an appropriately low level of money wages, other factor prices and prices of consumption goods and services, to provide a sufficiently high real value of the money stock (its value in terms of the constituents of final income). The real money in addition to other forms of wealth held gives the community total wealth which is so high that the whole of current income is consumed, net saving and investment are equal to zero at the minimum rate of interest.

Perfect knowledge excludes the possibility of money because there is 'no need for records of any kind'[22]. As I have stated, 'If an unqualified certainty is assumed, each individual's wealth (capital) is known for all points of time in the future, and no evidence in the form of titles to wealth and money balances is required. Unforeseen dishonesty cannot occur. Such an economic model need not be timeless. Exchange can take time, but there is no money because there are no money transactions, a form of record.'[23]

Haberler emphasizes that the Pigou effect has been developed in terms of highly abstract static theory[24]. Money-wage rates and prices are perfectly flexible downwards and the static analysis avoids the possibility of unfavourable price expectations affecting employment which must be taken into account in dynamic analyses. Labour is perfectly mobile, there are no bottlenecks and no disturbance from fixed money contracts such as debenture debt of companies. The latter point is discussed in more detail below but it is obvious that there could be bankruptcies if firms no longer remained profitable because, for example, it is assumed that product money prices have fallen while the same amount of debt interest in money terms has to be paid to the debenture holders.

Pigou introduced the relationship which became known as the Pigou effect in his important but somewhat neglected, difficult book, *Employment and Equilibrium*, first published in 1941[25]. As I have already emphasized Keynes's basic model in *The General Theory* was in terms of comparative statics although at times he considered dynamic aspects of a problem. In *Employment and Equilibrium*, Pigou formalized and generalized Keynes's comparative static system but started from a classical background. He gives a detailed analysis of the conditions of short-period flow equilibrium and the special case of long-period flow equilibrium. Pigou analysed the behaviour of the economic system as a whole and the relation between equilibrium and 'full employment'. He makes use of simplified models, abstracting from important aspects of reality, in order to concentrate on the essential characteristics of an economy[26]. The book owes much to the stimulus of *The General Theory*. Pigou writes in the Preface, 'Whatever may be thought of the value of his [Keynes's] criticisms upon other people, or of the solutions which he himself offered, the author of that book rendered a very great service to economics by asking important questions.'[27] He acknowledged that in this field Keynes was a true pioneer. Pigou's contribution here was a defence and elaboration of classical and neoclassical economics. He showed that Keynes's underemployment equilibrium depended on the assumption of fixed money wages and that with wage flexibility the Pigou effect ensured full employment. Pigou, like Haberler, recognized the great advance in economics made by Keynes but did not think of it as a revolution. Both economists emphasized the continuity of economic thought. In 1946 Haberler wrote, 'A classical treatise like Pigou's monumental work, *Equilibrium and Employment* (which is so much more general than the *General Theory* that the latter by comparison appears as a special case), would never have been written without the Keynesian challenge, although it is not in contradiction to, but rather constitutes a clarification of, Pigou's own pre-Keynesian, "classical" position.'[28] Pigou not only clarified classical and neo-classical economics, but also added a missing link. At an admittedly highly abstract level, the free-price system was shown to establish a full-employment equilibrium and Adam Smith's invisible hand could be retained. The Pigou effect shows that with a given quantity of money, money wages and prices will be reduced to increase the real value of money and therefore people's real wealth so that in the extreme case of a zero rate of investment at the minimum rate of interest, the rate of saving is zero. The whole of income is consumed at a full-employment level of income. Samuelson writes, 'While Pigou, rightly in my opinion, did not consider this mechanism a useful one for policy, it did serve to save face and honour for the believers in the harmony of equilibrium. This was a worthy achievement, purchased at little cost. And now the air was cleared to tackle matters of substance and not of ideology.'[29] However, I accept Haberler's view that the Pigou effect is an enrichment of economic theory. It is important to 'complete' the classical and neoclassical theory by inserting the missing link and to understand the implications of Keynes's concept of an under-employment equilibrium. Professor Abba P. Lerner referred to the Pigou effect as logically unassailable, but emphasized that it was not a practical alternative to Keynesian employment policies, a point which is generally admitted. Lerner adds that 'the argument does serve to show a certain abstract consistency and correctness in some interpretations of the pre-Keynesian or "classical" theory of employment'.[30]

Lloyd A. Metzler describes Pigou as the principal architect of the rconstruction of classical theory to meet Keynesian criticisms[31]. The innovation was to show that saving out of a given income depended not only on the interest rate but also on the real value of privately held wealth. Metzler uses the expression 'saving–wealth relation' for the functional relationship between current saving and private wealth. The saving–wealth relation takes the form that 'Other things remaining the same . . . real saving tends to be smaller and real expenditure for consumption tends to be larger, the larger the real value of private wealth.'[32]

Pesek and Saving argue that the wealth effect is to be found in *The General Theory* and is included in Keynes's analysis of the determinants of consumption, but it was subsequently neglected perhaps because in his mathematical treatment he made consumption a function of a single variable income[33]. The wealth effect was not included in his basic model. They write, 'Had Keynes incorporated wealth into his final analysis, he would not have reached the conclusion, so provocative to the classicists, that a less-than-full-employment equilibrium in a perfectly competitive model is possible; the bitter controversy surrounding this claim could have been avoided.'[34]

It is important to distinguish two kinds of non-human wealth[35]. Firstly, the community owns wealth in the form of capital goods used in the process of production. The individual may own the physical goods or titles to them in the form of ordinary shares (equities). Keynes makes it perfectly clear that changes in such wealth because of a change in the rate of interest which is used to capitalize a given expected income from capital goods and a change in its expected rate of return (its expected yield) will affect the propensity to consume and therefore expenditure on consumption.

In discussing the principal objective factors that influence the propensity to consume, Keynes emphasizes the importance of *'windfall changes in capital-values not allowed for in calculating net income'*[36]. They are stated to be important because they 'bear no stable or regular relationship to the amount of income'[37]. Keynes continues, 'The consumption of the wealth-owning classes may be extremely susceptible to unforeseen changes in the money-value of its wealth. This should be classified amongst the major factors capable of causing short-period changes in the propensity to consume.'[38] He considers that changes in the rate of interest have an important influence on consumption expenditure out of a given income because these changes cause an appreciation or depreciation in the prices of securities[39] and other assets. Keynes writes, 'For if a man is enjoying a windfall increment in the value of his capital, it is natural that his motives towards current spending should be strengthened, even though in terms of income his capital is worth no more than before; and weakened if he is suffering capital losses.'[40]

In chapter 22 'Notes on the Trade Cycle', Keynes emphasizes the importance of changes in the marginal efficiency of capital, the expected rate of return on capital, during the upward and downward swings in business activity. This instability of the marginal efficiency of capital is regarded as an essential characteristic of the trade cycle, because it is the cause of the fluctuations in investment which cause fluctuations in income which are magnified by the multiplier. Associated with the changes in income are the changes in employment (unemployment) with which Keynes was so much concerned. However, the fluctuations in the marginal efficiency of capital also affect the propensity to consume[41]. Keynes writes,

'Unfortunately a serious fall in the marginal efficiency of capital also tends to affect adversely the propensity to consume. For it involves a severe decline in the market value of stock exchange equities. Now, on the class who take an active interest in their stock exchange investments, especially if they are employing borrowed funds, this naturally exerts a very depressing influence. These people are, perhaps, even more influenced in their readiness to spend by rises and falls in the value of their investments than by the state of their incomes.'[42]

Pesek and Saving point out that Keynes justified the inclusion of wealth as an independent determinant of consumption in the same way as modern economic theorists. This is 'because changes in income are not a good index of changes in wealth'[43].

It is very important to realize that this first kind of wealth effect, clearly recognized and emphasized by Keynes, has nothing to do with the second kind of wealth effect, the Pigou effect. The first kind of wealth effect is excluded by the conditions assumed for the economy which require the Pigou effect to establish full-employment equilibrium. These conditions are firstly that the rate of interest has reached it minimum and will remain at this level. Secondly, that the rate of investment is zero and will remain at this level so that fluctuations in the marginal efficiency of capital are excluded. As we have seen, Pigou's wealth effect operates by money wages and prices falling, assuming competition, to bring about a rise in the real value of money, the purchasing power of a given stock of money in terms of consumption goods. The value of the community's total wealth in terms of consumption goods is increased to the amount at which saving equals investment[44] equals zero, the whole of current income being spent on consumption goods and services. As a simplification, I assumed that we were dealing with a closed economy with a given stock of money in the form of gold coins. Later, I consider what other forms of money should be included in Pigou's analysis and also what other assets. Until then, I shall quote freely without always referring to this basic problem. However, it should be noted that Pigou and others undertaking this analysis have emphasized the role of the asset, money, but not always defining money for this purpose in the same way. The Pigou effect is thus sometimes referred to as the real-balance wealth effect[45], the real balance being the value of the money stock, appropriately defined, in terms of consumption goods and services. Real-balance wealth thus increases as money wages and prices are reduced. In the first kind of wealth effect, the importance of fluctuations in the money value of capital goods, factories, machines, etc. was stressed[46]. However, it may be noted here that such capital goods will not be included in the assets taken into account for the Pigou effect. As money wages and prices of consumption goods and services fall so do the prices of capital goods such as machines. The value of, for example, machines in terms of consumption goods is constant.

Pesek and Saving maintain that Keynes's *General Theory* contains the second kind of wealth effect, the Pigou effect, although this has not been generally recognized. They state that Keynes 'has a rudimentary but still adequate statement of the price-induced wealth effect'[47]. Hicks refers to Pigou's criticism of the Keynesian theory and states, 'I cannot myself attach much practical importance to it [the Pigou effect], but I have no doubt that it is valid theoretically, and in principle it ought to be allowed for.'[48] As has already been mentioned Pigou himself did not regard the 'Pigou effect' of any importance as an instrument of employment policy. Pesek and Saving refer to Hicks's statement and continue, 'Ever since, the moderate disciples of Keynes admit that Keynes overlooked the wealth effect, but excuse him on the grounds of justifiable neglect. His less moderate disciples even claim that Keynes must have considered the effect only to discard it after reaching a conclusion that in view of the existing price and wage rigidities it has no empirical significance.'[49] However, Pesek and Saving undertake a careful piece of exegesis of *The General Theory* and appear to show that Keynes did state the second kind of wealth effect, the price-induced wealth effect (the Pigou effect), but I think in a very obscure way[50]. This is interesting, but of little significance because Keynes never analysed the relationship of this concept to classical theory or to his own theory. Pesek and Saving argue that Keynes believed that the effects of these two changes in capital-values on consumption were of great importance[51]. I cannot think that Keynes believed the price-induced wealth effect (the Pigou effect) was of empirical importance and had significance for economic policy. He emphasized the importance of money-wage rigidity and the disturbing effects on the economy of falling money wages. If Keynes had analysed the price-induced wealth effect, he would undoubtedly have come to the same general conclusions as Pigou and almost all other economists who have discussed it[52].

In 1941 Pigou first formulated the price-induced wealth effect in his *Employment and Equilibrium*. In chapter IX of Part II, 'The Special Case of Long-Period Flow Equilibrium', Pigou shows that on classical assumptions the stationary state must be a full-employment equilibrium[53]. It is not necessary here to discuss the determinants of the proportion of income saved[54]. I merely state that the incentives to save out of a given income are the income derived from the saving, which is related to the rate of interest, and the amenity value (utility) of possessing some saving (capital). Pigou points out that 'people desire additions to accumulated wealth, not merely for the income they will presently yield, but also for the amenity, in sense of power, sense of security and so on, which the *possession* of them carries'[55]. It is conceivable that capital will have been accumulated to the point where investment opportunities[56] have been exhausted at the minimum rate of interest which Pigou considers not to be appreciably higher than zero[57]. The rate of investment at this rate is zero. People may, however, wish to hold a larger amount of capital because of its amenity value. In a money economy they can hold money at negligible cost. Pigou considers the case where the rate of interest has fallen to nil, the rate of investment is zero but people still desire to save. Pigou's representative man[58] 'will try to satisfy this desire by making purchases of already existing durable things. Those persons who possess such things, since the quantity of them cannot be increased, will continually ask, and those who do not possess them will continually offer, higher and higher prices in terms of consumable goods. Thus the value of land and similar property and, above all, the value of money, which is an especially convenient store of value, will continually rise.'[59] On the next page, Pigou adds Old Masters as an example of the sort of property which is very suitable for the embodiment of saving.

Pigou explains the process by which the stationary state which is a full employment equilibrium is established. He assumes full employment at the stage when the rate of investment falls to zero. It is now assumed that the community wishes to continue to make net savings and that people do not spend the whole of their money incomes on consumption but hoard money[60]. This causes a continuous fall in money income (aggregate money demand) but on classical assumptions full employment is maintained by reductions in money-wage rates and prices of consumption goods[61]. As money income, money-wage rates and prices fall, the fixed amount of money and certain kinds of property such as land and Old Masters become more valuable in terms of consumption goods. Since investment in capital goods is zero, the community's real income is constant but its holding of wealth in terms of consumption goods is increasing. A stage will be reached when people feel so well off that they spend the whole of their money income on consumption goods at a constant price level. This is the full-employment stationary state[62].

In a footnote, Pigou points out that the fact that an equilibrium position exists does not necessarily mean that it will be attained. There could be oscillations round it. However, he thinks that it is probable that people 'will learn by experience, . . . the oscillations must eventually fade away, . . .'[63]. However, this problem does not arise if an appropriate assumption of certainty is made. In view of Pigou's statement that there is no uncertainty about the future rate of interest referred to above (*see* p. 54, n.58), it is surprising that he does not do this. Indeed, Pigou's explanation of the *process* by which the stationary state is reached involves a departure from his basic model of comparative statics, a generalization of Keynes's model. It involves dynamics which raises far more serious problems.

In a number of other writings Pigou put forward much the same case for the price-induced wealth effect. His 1943 article, 'The Classical Stationary State'[64], is a reply to Professor Hansen's criticism of the classical economists in which he had maintained that without technological progress etc. net investments would fall to zero and the price system would not provide full employment. Pigou quotes Hansen, 'thus total expenditures decline and the economy falls towards an equilibrial self-perpetuating income level far short of full employment'[65]. Pigou emphasizes that the classical economists had the concept of a full-employment stationary state on the assumption of flexible wages but that they did not deny that if wage-earners were not acting competitively and that the real rate of wages were 'too high' the stationary state would be one of less than full employment. The analysis of the price-induced wealth effect is the same as in 1941. At the stage when investment in producers' goods (machines etc.) falls to zero, there is not 'an endless state of disequilibrium with money-wage rates falling for ever'[66]. As money wages fall, employment and real income being constant, prices fall and 'the stock of money, as valued in terms of real income, correspondingly rises. But the extent to which the representative man desires to make savings otherwise than for the sake of future income yield depends in part on the size, in terms of real income, of his existing possessions. As this increases, the amount that he so desires to save out of any assigned real income diminishes and ultimately vanishes.'[67] In his *Lapses from Full Employment* (1945), Pigou refers to people saving for reasons of prestige, security and so on, apart from any income yield. With zero investment in producers' goods, money is drawn out of circulation and held 'in stockings or in savings deposits'[68]. Thus with falling money wages and prices, 'as valued in terms of income goods, such accumulated wealth as is embodied in the stock of money – and also in certain other non-reproducible types of durable goods that are specially attractive as stores of value – grows continuously larger'[69]. People's desire to save is reduced sufficiently to establish a new equilibrium[70].

In the 1947 article, 'Economic Progress in a Stable Environment', Pigou refers to the assets that rise in value in terms of consumption goods with the fall in prices as being 'the stock of money, and, along with this, that of other sorts of non-instrumental property, such as Old Masters'[71]. It is interesting to note that in this article Pigou accepts Kalecki's criticism[72] and states that not the whole of the stock of money held by the public is a net asset as the public's debts to the banks in the form of advances (loans) and discounts must be deducted. Pigou's last statement of the 'Pigou effect' is in his 1949 Cambridge lectures[73], but no addition is made to the analysis.

As I have already emphasized, Pigou's contribution of the price-induced wealth effect was to clarify and elaborate classical economic theory in relation to Keynesian theory and not to forge an instrument of economic policy to control the level of employment. This is made clear in the Preface to *Lapses From Full Employment* where he writes, 'Professor Dennis Robertson . . . has warned me that the form of the book may suggest that I am in favour of attacking the problem of unemployment by manipulating wages rather than by manipulating demand. I wish, therefore, to say clearly that this is not so.'[74] In his 1947 article, Pigou points out that no government would allow the Keynesian equilibrium with massive unemployment nor the degree of money-wage rate and price decline required for his full-employment stationary state. He writes, 'Thus the puzzles we have been considering . . . are academic exercises, of some slight use perhaps for clarifying thought, but with very little chance of ever being posed on the chequer board of actual life.'[75] In his last work, *Keynes's 'General Theory'*,

Pigou points out that Keynes thought that his equilibrium with mass unemployment might come about within a generation but not that it was inevitable. The former possible terminal position (Keynes's hell) was regarded by Keynes, he says, 'not at all as an academic plaything, but very seriously'[76]. Pigou does not do this. He wrote, 'Since, however, there is every reason to expect that scientific discoveries will continue to be made, and so that new openings for profitable investment will appear in the future, as they have in the past, it may well be that no stationary state of any kind, neither heaven nor hell, will ever be attained; but economic man for the remainder of his career will continue to live and move in purgatory.'[77]

Professor Don Patinkin discussed the Pigou effect in detail in his well-known 1948 article, 'Price Flexibility and Full Employment'[78]. He concludes that, subject to two reservations, 'Haberler and Pigou have demonstrated the automaticity of full employment within the framework of the classical static model.'[79] The mechanism is shown to be the price-induced wealth effect. Patinkin formulates the Pigou effect in terms of the theorem, '*There always exists a sufficiently low price level such that, if expected to continue indefinitely, it will generate full employment.*'[80] This real-balance wealth effect plays an important role in his *magnum opus, Money, Interest, and Prices*[81], the main aim of which is to integrate monetary and real value theory beyond the stage reached by Keynes.

In this article Patinkin discusses the implications of the Pigou effect for dynamic analysis and economic policy, while recognizing that Pigou did not recommend a policy of allowing money wages and prices to fall, the real value of money balances to rise and the elimination of unemployment by the consequent increase in consumption. Patinkin thinks that Pigou's disclaimer was because of the impractability of the necessary wage and price flexibility while his aim is to show that a deflationary policy will not work because of dynamic factors, given perfect flexibility of money wages and prices. The important factor in Patinkin's dynamic analysis relates to the role played by price expectations. He writes, 'It is quite possible that the original price decline will lead to the expectation of further declines. Then purchasing decisions will be postponed, aggregate demand will fall off, and the amount of unemployment increased still more.'[82] For example, adverse expectations will be formed which reduce the rate of investment. Further, firms which have debts fixed in money terms such as debenture interest may get into financial difficulties and even go bankrupt. The real value of the debt interest fixed in money terms rises with the fall in prices, the firm is paying out the same amount of money as interest while its receipts fall with the fall in prices of its product. The bankruptcies will cause dislocation and unemployment[83]. They will also strengthen the adverse expectations[84]. Anticipating his later works[85], Patinkin interprets Keynes in terms of dynamic disequilibrium economics. He writes, 'what Keynesian economics claims is that the economic system may be in a position of under-employment *dis*equilibrium (in the sense that wages, prices, and the amount of unemployment are continuously changing over time) for long, or even indefinite periods of time'[86]. The dynamic analysis is undertaken on the assumption of uncertainty which is appropriate in view of Keynes's emphasis on uncertainty and that Patinkin is considering employment policy in the real world. However, it would be useful also to develop the dynamic analysis at a more abstract level, on an appropriate certainty assumption[87].

Although we are dealing with Pigou's comparative static analysis, Patinkin's article raises in a useful way two important and difficult problems with which we have to deal. The first is the appropriate definition of money and any other assets through which the price-induced wealth effect is taken to operate. I avoided this problem in my earlier discussion by assuming money consisted only of gold coins and a closed economy. The second problem is the effect of a reduction of prices on debtors which is clear in Patinkin's dynamic analysis and which I shall eliminate in static analysis. These two complex problems are discussed in the following paragraphs.

Patinkin in the Static Analysis part of his article deals with the first problem. The appropriate definition of money is currency (coin and bank notes) held by the public plus demand deposits (current accounts) to the extent that they are not backed by bank loans to the private sector and discounted trade bills of exchange. Government interest-bearing debt (securities) is added to money because a price decline increases its real value. A deduction from demand deposits is made for bank loans and discounts as the gains of deposit holders are offset by the losses of bank debtors[88]. As government securities are included as a relevant asset, it follows implicitly that any bank demand deposits backed by government securities are included in money. Patinkin explicitly mentions that the deposits backed by cash reserves in the form of cash in the till and balances at the central bank are money for our purpose[89]. Pigou's money and other assets are 'the existing stock of money – as also the stock of land and of some other sorts of property, such as Old Masters, which are specially suitable as embodiments of, or receptacles for, saving'[90]. Pigou refers to the argument that a large part of the stock of money including bank money[91] is offset by Government debt so that the increase in net wealth because of a fall in the price level is much smaller than assumed. However, he accepts Robertson's point that 'what chiefly affects the attitude of the public towards saving is the real value of the capital wealth held by the public, not that of the capital wealth held by the public and the Government together'[92]. As we shall see, this matter is much more complicated than stated here.

The development of thought along these lines led to a widely adopted distinction between inside money and outside money as defined by John G. Gurley and Edward S. Shaw although their problems of analysis differed in some respects from our problem. Inside money is 'Money based on private domestic primary securities'[93]. Commercial bank deposits backed by bank loans to business and industry, for example, are inside money. A fall in the general price level does not increase net wealth because the rise in the real value of deposits is offset by the rise in the real value of the bank debts (the loans obtained by firms)[94]. Outside money is 'Money that is backed by foreign or government securities or gold; or fiat money issued by the government.'[95] We can omit foreign securities as we are dealing at present with a closed economy. It was only outside money which was relevant for the Pigou effect as it was believed that a rise in its real value resulting from a fall in the price level was not offset by a rise in the real value of liabilities. Thus, for the Pigou effect, money was commodity money such as gold money, paper money which was convertible into gold, fiat money (inconvertible paper money issued by the government)[96], bank notes and bank deposits as far as they were backed by government securities and not firms' debts. It follows that to outside money must be added government securities held by the public.

Professor Harry G. Johnson denied that interest-bearing government debt was a net asset of the public and if this were the case money backed by government securities would also not be a net asset. Johnson wrote, 'The existence of government debt implies the levying of taxes to pay the interest on it, and in a world of reasonable certainty these taxes would be capitalized into liabilities equal in magnitude to the government debt; hence if distribution effects between individuals are ignored, a change in the real amount of government debt will have no wealth-effect.'[97]

Boris P. Pesek and Thomas R. Saving have shown that there is not a complete offset so that government debt in part is net wealth and a fall in the price level will increase it in real terms. They point out that human capital is not separable from its owner[98]. An example of human capital is investment in a person's education. Human capital is not marketable so that the owner cannot consume all or part of it if conditions are such that he wishes to do so. On the other hand, the owner of non-human capital can do this. He can, for example, sell government securities and spend the proceeds on consumption goods and services. From this point of view, human wealth is inferior to non-human wealth and the income from it will be capitalized at a higher discount rate. Thus, taxes on personal income to pay interest on government debt are capitalized at at a higher rate than the interest received by the owners of the government securities. The capitalized value of the taxes is less than the capitalized value of the interest, the market value of the government debt. Hence, there is net wealth. Thus, when there is a fall in the price level and the real level of the government debt and its interest increase, the capitalized value of the increased real taxes increases less than the capitalized value of the increased real interest. There is a price-induced increase in real net wealth; the Pigou effect works[99].

Pesek and Saving define money as the generally acceptable medium of exchange which is net wealth; a fall in the price level will increase this real net wealth. For this to be the case it must be non-interest-bearing. A monetary asset on which the market rate of interest is paid is not money. They show clearly that commodity money (for example, gold coins) and fiat money are part of net wealth[100]. Bank demand deposits (current accounts) are included in the stock of money but not necessarily to their full amounts[101]. Bank time deposits in the United States are excluded; they are similar to deposit accounts in the United Kingdom. They do not act as a medium of exchange and must be regarded wholly as a money-debt on which interest is paid by the bank and received by the holder[102]. In the case of demand deposits the question arises whether their full amount is to be included in the stock of money or only a fraction of the value. Demand deposits may not only be a medium of exchange but also in part a debt certificate. The holder obtains the convenience of money as a medium of exchange, avoiding the difficulties of barter, but he may also obtain interest. The rate of interest paid on the money-debt aspect of the demand deposit is 'the value of the non-medium of exchange flow of services per unit of money value'. As far as the United States is concerned, at the time of writing, Pesek and Saving conclude that demand deposits are almost wholly money. They write, 'demand deposits have a fraction of their value, probably a very small one, which is nonmonetary wealth (free accounting service)'[103]. Their view of demand deposits may be clarified by reference to their theoretical discussion of money-debt. They write 'only for that portion of the value of private money-debt [say demand deposits] that is due to its being a medium of exchange will price changes affect the net wealth of the community'[104]. Pesek and Saving consider the case of a private producer who sells (creates) a joint product, money and bonds. We may take this case to represent a commercial bank which sells (creates) demand deposits which may only provide the holders with the convenience of having a medium of exchange or may also pay interest. They state that 'the extent to which privately produced money-debt (demand deposits) represents a net addition to wealth . . . is a function of the difference between the rate of interest paid on private money and the market rate'[105]. If the commercial bank creates a deposit on which it pays the market rate of interest, it has created a pure 'bond' which is not a net addition to wealth.

Harry G. Johnson in his 1968 paper, 'Inside Money, Outside Money, Income, Wealth and Welfare in Monetary Theory'[106], accepted the correctness of Pesek and Saving's argument in their important new book[107] that the distinction between 'inside' money and 'outside' money whereby the former in contrast to the latter involved no net wealth for the community as a whole was incorrect. He criticizes their analysis, but accepts that 'provided that money is defined to be non-interest-bearing, both types of money will constitute net wealth for the community'[108].

Patinkin's paper 'Money and Wealth'[109], based on a paper of 1969, is an alternative criticism of the inside/outside money distinction. Pesek's and Saving's book provided the initial stimulus for his analysis but there are similarities and differences compared with their work[110]. The conclusion of Patinkin's elaborate analysis is that money provides a real-balance (net real monetary wealth) effect 'only to the extent that there is a difference between the value of the stock of money and the present value of the costs of maintaining that stock constant'[111]. Gold and government fiat money will be included in net monetary wealth because such costs are negligible. On the other hand, bank deposits provided by a competitive banking system will be excluded because these costs equal the value of the bank deposits, only the normal rate of return being earned on the capital invested in the banking industry[112].

For Pigou's defence of the classical and neoclassical economists in terms of his classical stationary state analysis we can take as net monetary wealth the simple case of gold coins in a closed community. We may also take gold coins and government notes convertible into gold or coins and fiat money (inconvertible paper money issued by the government). To this must be added a part of the government debt (securities) held by the public as explained above[113]. In view of the present state of the debate, I leave open the question of whether bank demand deposits should be included at all. The classical state under consideration is one with a minimum rate of interest determined by the cost of bringing borrowers and lenders together, according to Pigou not 'appreciably higher than nothing'.[114] In these circumstances, the rate payable on demand deposits would be zero while depositors would pay the bank costs of operating the deposit payments mechanism as bank charges. Bank borrowers would pay a small rate of interest, the cost of bringing borrowers and lenders together. To this monetary wealth must be added Pigou's land[115] and non-reproducible goods such as Old Masters. We have now considered all the items eligible for inclusion in net wealth through which the Pigou effect can operate.

The second complex problem is the effect of a reduction in the general level of prices on debtors, the real value of whose debt and interest are increased. We have seen that in dynamic analysis under conditions of uncertainty serious distribution effects between creditors and debtors occur and the problem arises of the financial difficulties and bankruptcies of firms. Pigou discusses this problem in these terms in *Industrial Fluctuations*[116]. In chapter XVI of Part I, The Modification of the Terms of Past Contracts, he states that 'price changes wrench the terms of contracts for loans and wages away from the terms that were intended when these contracts were made'[117]. At the time of writing, it was reasonable for Pigou to assume that people almost always underestimate future changes in the general price level. He points out that dealers and manufacturers are in general borrowers rather than lenders. Thus, when prices have fallen, they have to make larger real payments to debenture-holders and other lenders at fixed interest. In chapter III of Part II, A Tabular Standard for Long Contracts, Pigou suggests that 'contracts for loans and so far as they cover periods of any length for wages should be made in terms not of money, but of a tabular standard of value based upon a considerable number of items'[118]. This proposal was made by Marshall whom he quotes at length[119]. Loans could be made in terms of the standard unit of purchasing power which would have a constant real value, adjustments being made for changes in the prices of all important commodities. The adoption of this proposal would solve the bankruptcy problem[120]. It is, of course, the same as the proposal, to some extent adopted, of index-linking[121] at the present time.

This analysis has to be adapted to the comparative statics of the Pigou effect which Pigou failed to do. We can consider in terms of comparative statics a stationary state which is in full-employment equilibrium at the minimum rate of interest just above zero[122]. The whole of current income is consumed, saving is zero. This state can be compared with a stationary state having the same rate of interest but is only in full-employment equilibrium because the real value of money and other assets through which the Pigou effect operates is higher. The general level of prices of consumption goods and services is sufficiently low for the price-induced wealth effect to ensure that the total wealth of the community is such that the whole of current income is consumed, saving is zero. In Pigou's stationary state, fixed-interest securities may be present. Indeed, Pigou refers, as we have seen, to the existence of government securities and we can have fixed-interest industrial securities, debentures. Bank loans to business and industry which bear the minimum rate of interest, can be outstanding, associated with an equivalent amount of demand deposits. Now comparative statics deals with hypothetical static situations. Thus in the stationary state with lower money wages and prices and a higher real value of net monetary wealth, land and Old Masters etc., the nominal money value of fixed-interest industrial securities and the nominal amounts of money interest paid will be lower in proportion to the lower price level. Government securities may be adjusted in the same way. Similarly, firms will have smaller nominal amounts of bank loans which will be associated with a smaller amount of demand deposits. Firms require a smaller nominal amount of funds to finance the same real level of production, the money wage and price level being lower. The dynamic problem involving bankruptcies has been eliminated by a hypothetical application of Marshall's tabular standard or index-linking to comparative static situations.

If the tabular standard was hypothetically applied to all assets and liabilities it is obvious that the Pigou effect could not operate[123]. It is appropriate to assume that net monetary wealth, land and non-reproducible durable goods such as Old Masters are not indexed. The Pigou effect can then be used to establish the stationary state with the hypothetically lower money wages, prices and nominal fixed-interest debts[124]. The nominal amount of bank deposits is lower.

If demand deposits are not included in net monetary wealth, their smaller nominal amount leaves the stock of nominal money constant, the normal assumption for comparative static analysis[125]. If they are included, the nominal money stock is lower but this deviation from static assumptions is not serious. It remains true that the real value of this reduced total nominal stock of money has increased. The real value of demand deposits is constant, their nominal amount declining in proportion to the fall in prices[126].

A further difficulty arises in relation to the ratio of coin and fiat paper money to bank demand deposits. Before introducing the Pigou effect, this ratio depends on the techniques of payments. Some payments are made more conveniently than others by coin and paper money, others by transfers of demand deposits by cheque. Certain advantages of bank deposits such as security from theft must also be taken into account[127]. Once the Pigou effect is introduced, the real value of coin and paper money has increased and these monies are acting as a store of value in addition to the store of value, temporary abode of purchasing power, inherent in the use of money as a medium of exchange. To avoid the complications which would follow from the assumption that coin and paper money to this additional extent would not be held, the substitute, demand deposits, perfect security (no burglaries), is assumed[128].

We have seen that in terms of comparative statics it can be stated that there must always be a sufficiently low price level to ensure full employment, given the amount of net monetary wealth and certain other assets. It follows, alternatively, that there could always be a sufficiently large amount of monetary net wealth and certain other assets to ensure full employment, given the general level of prices. Thus, hypothetically, full employment is ensured by assuming a large enough amount of coin and fiat money (inconvertible paper money issued by the government) given the general level of prices. The whole of current income is consumed, saving is zero. This case was not considered by Pigou because he was defending and elaborating classical theory on the assumption of a given stock of money and flexible prices. In practice, departing from comparative statics, the policy of increasing people's money balances avoids the difficulties of adverse expectations and bankruptcies but there are administrative difficulties in increasing people's holding of money.

A number of methods have been suggested. David Hume in 1752, in spite of his atheism, supposes 'that, by miracle, every man in Great Britain should have five pounds slipped into his pocket in one night'[129]. Milton Friedman, over two centuries later, in 1969, asks us to 'suppose now that one day a helicopter flies over this community and drops an additional $1000 in bills [an amount of money] from the sky, which is, of course, hastily collected by members of the community'[130]. Pesek and Saving refer to a number of economists who assume an increase of fiat money by gift, for example, Metzler who 'gives money to the existing holders of money in proportion to their money assets'[131]. As far as employment policy is concerned, the direct increase of people's money balances can be ignored. The government's monetary and fiscal policies as now pursued are more suitable.

Pigou's most important contribution to an understanding and criticism of Keynes's *General Theory* was the Pigou effect. It has had a great influence on post-Keynesian theory. He provided other important insights and criticisms. Pigou's final statement of his position is to be found in his two 1949 Cambridge lectures published as *Keynes's 'General Theory' A Retrospective View*[132]. Here he attempts an appraisement which recognizes Keynes's great achievement but remains a critical commentary. Pigou recognizes 'Keynes's main and very important contribution to economic analysis'[133], finding it in Keynes's summary statement of his basic model which he developed to explain the determinants of national income and employment[134]. Pigou's final recognition is clearly stated in his second lecture. He finds the kernel of Keynes's contribution in the summary already quoted and writes 'Whatever imperfections there may be in his working out of the fundamental conception embodied there, the conception itself is an extremely fruitful germinal idea. In my original review –article on the *General Theory* [In *Economica*, 1936] I failed to grasp its significance and did not assign to Keynes the credit due for it. Nobody before him, so far as I know, had brought all the relevant factors, real and monetary at once, together in a single formal scheme, through which their interplay could be coherently investigated.'[135] Pigou does not regard Keynes's contribution as a revolution, giving his reasons for this, but he does recognize its great importance and originality. Professor Sir Austin Robinson refers to these lectures as even more moving to hear than to read and, having in mind Pigou's frank acknowledgement of his failure to appreciate the importance of *The General Theory*, writes, 'It was the noble act of a scrupulously honest man, who put truth before vanity and another's reputation beyond his own.'[136]

Notes

1. For a good general review of Pigou's life and work, *see* Pigou, Arthur Cecil by Sir Austin Robinson in *International Encyclopaedia of the Social Sciences* (1968). He was Marshall's successor as Professor of Political Economy at Cambridge, 1908–1943.
2. 4th edn, 1960.
3. 1st edn, 1927; 2nd edn, 1929.
4. 1933.
5. 1st edn, 1941; 2nd edn, 1949.
6. N. Kaldor, 'Pigou on Employment and Equilibrium', *Economic Journal* (1941); reprinted in his *Essays on Economic Stability and Growth* (1960), p. 100
7. A. C. Pigou, 'Mr J. M. Keynes' *General Theory of Employment, Interest and Money*', *Economica* (1936).
8. Pigou (1936), p. 115; referred to by S. E. Harris, *The New Economics* (1948), p. 29.
9. Keynes, *C.W.*, Vol. VII (1973), p. 7. Keynes's Appendix to Chapter 19 is a critical examination of Pigou's book.
10. E. A. G. Robinson in *International Encyclopaedia of the Social Sciences* (1968), p. 95.
11. *Ibid.*, p. 96.
12. In Keynes's basic model, S ≡ I, an identity, but it is convenient to state the position in the above terms.
13. Gottfried Haberler, 'Sixteen Years Later' (1962), in R. Lakachman, *Keynes's General Theory Reports of Three Decades* (1964), p. 293. If wages are above the marginal productivity of labour, there will be unemployment.
14. Gottfried Haberler, 'The General Theory after Ten Years' (1946), in Lekachman (1964), p. 275. *See also* Haberler, *Prosperity and Depression* (1958), p. 242.
15. Haberler (1946) in Lekachman (1964), p. 276. This statement is qualified in footnote 12 but the qualification involves a very high degree of abstraction.
16. Haberler (1946) in Lekachman (1964), p. 278, n.15. Haberler refers here to the question of whether the whole of the money stock is to be included in the analysis. The whole problem of what assets fixed in money terms are relevant to the Pigou effect is discussed below.
17. Haberler (1962) in Lekachman (1964), p. 292.
18. Haberler, 'The Pigou Effect Once More', *Journal of Political Economy* (June 1952). Reprinted in Haberler (1958), p. 496.
19. *Ibid.*, p. 496.
20. J. C. Gilbert, 'The Demand for Money: The Development of an Economic Concept', *Journal of Political Economy* (1953), pp. 149–152. *See also* Gilbert, 'The Compatibility of any Behaviour by the Price Level with Equilibrium', *Review of Economic Studies* (1956, 1957), pp. 177–178.
21. The professional economist will know that this is achieved by Walras's tâtonnement process or Edgeworth's recontracting. Alternatively, an appropriate definition of certainty which does not involve perfect knowledge may be made.
22. S. P. Chambers, 'Fluctuations in Capital and the Demand for Money', *Review of Economic Studies* (1934), p. 39.
23. Gilbert (1953), p. 151. In this world of perfect knowledge the person who is thinking of burgling a house knows that the house-owner knows this!
24. *See* Haberler (1958), Appendix II (1952), pp. 495 *et seq.* and 'Sixteen Years Later' in Lekachman (1964), p. 292.
25. A. C. Pigou, *Employment and Equilibrium* (1st edn, 1941; 2nd edn, 1949).
26. Pigou, *Employment and Equilibrium* (1949), pp. 3–5, 2nd edn. The book is devoted to static analysis although in the short Part IV Pigou turns his attention to the dynamic analysis of transitions between equilibrium positions and disequilibrium positions.
27. *Ibid.*, p. v.
28. Haberler (1946) in Lekachman (1964), p. 288. Haberler is not in any way belittling Keynes here and recognizes that *The General Theory* 'has exerted a tremendously stimulating influence on economic thinking'. Indeed, Keynes's 'special case' continues to influence economists far more than Pigou's 'so much more general' system.
29. Paul A. Samuelson, A brief survey of post-Keynesian developments (1963b), in Lekachman (1964), p. 333.
30. Abba P. Lerner, Keynesian Economics in the Sixties (1963), in Lekachman (1964), p. 226.

31. L. A. Metzler, 'Wealth, Saving, and the Rate of Interest', *Journal of Political Economy* (1951). Reprinted in his *Collected Papers* (1973), p. 311. He refers also to T. Scitovsky, 'Capital Accumulation, Employment and Price Rigidity', *Review of Economic Studies* (1940–1941), and Haberler (1958).
32. Metzler (1973), p. 312.
33. Boris P. Pesek and Thomas R. Saving, *Money, Wealth, and Economic Theory* (1967), p. 20.
34. *Ibid.*, p. 23.
35. Human wealth refers to the capital invested in human beings such as expenditure on education.
36. Keynes, *C.W.*, Vol. VII (1936, 1973), p. 92.
37. *Ibid.*, p. 92.
38. *Ibid.*, pp. 92–93.
39. Securities must include here fixed-interest government securities as well as ordinary shares, preference shares and debentures.
40. Keynes, *C.W.*, Vol. VII (1936, 1973), p. 94.
41. Changes in the marginal propensity to consume involve changes in the multiplier referred to above.
42. Keynes, *C.W.*, Vol. VII (1936, 1973), p. 319. It should also be noted that in a letter to D. H. Robertson, 13 December 1936, *C.W.*, Vol. XIV (1973c), p. 92, Keynes wrote, 'As wealth increases, undoubtedly the marginal propensity to consume diminishes.' Here Keynes is considering that investment over time increases the community's wealth.
43. Pesek and Saving (1967), p. 19.
44. Pigou defines aggregate real saving and real investment so that they are identically equal in the same way as Keynes in *The General Theory*. *See* Pigou, *Employment and Equilibrium* (1949), 2nd edn, p. 28.
45. This concept must be clearly distinguished from Keynes's real-balance interest effect already discussed.
46. The corresponding change in real private wealth involved the implicit assumption that the price level of consumption goods and services was constant or at least changed less than proportionally with the money value of the capital goods.
47. Pesek and Saving (1967), p. 16.
48. J. R. Hicks, *Value and Capital* (1946, 2nd edn), p. 335.
49. Pesek and Saving (1967), p. 15. They quote D. G. Champernowne as a moderate disciple: Champernowne, Expectations and the links between the economic future and the present (1963), in Lekachman (1964), p. 191; and Abba P. Lerner as a less moderate disciple: Lerner, 'The General Theory after Twenty-Five Years: Discussion'. *American Economic Review* (May 1961), p. 22.
50. Pesek and Saving (1967), pp. 17–19.
51. *Ibid.*, pp. 19–20.
52. There has been much detailed analysis of the price-induced wealth effect and a great deal of controversy since Haberler and Pigou formulated it.
53. Pigou, *Employment and Equilibrium* (1949, 2nd edn), pp. 123–134.
54. *See* Pigou, *ibid.* Chapter VIII of Part II.
55. *Ibid.*, p. 130.
56. We are considering the stationary state case in which there are no changes in technique (inventions), no changes in population and no discovery of new territories.
57. Pigou, *Employment and Equilibrium* (1949, 2nd edn), p. 129. On p. 128 Pigou quotes from Keynes's *General Theory*, 'The costs of bringing borrowers and lenders together and uncertainty as to the future of the rate of interest set a lower limit, which in present circumstances may perhaps be as high as 2 per cent or 2½ per cent on long term.' Pigou regards these figures as much too high for a stationary state which is very different from Keynes's 'present circumstances'. There is no uncertainty about the future rate of interest and it is the marginal cost of bringing borrowers and lenders together which is relevant. He points out that 'many people invest in their own businesses, where these costs are nil', (p. 129).
58. *Ibid.* Defined on p. 127, n.1.
59. *Ibid.*, p. 131. the same passage appeared in the 1st edn, 1941, p. 127.
60. As the nominal stock of money is fixed, people as a whole cannot increase their holdings of nominal money. The income-velocity of circulation falls (K in Chapter 5, p. 54, increases), prices of consumption goods fall and the real value of the money stock

increases. Pigou included bank deposits in his total stock of money. Pigou, *Employment and Equilibrium* (1949, 2nd edn), p. 133, n.10.

61. At this level of abstraction, units of labour are assumed to be homogeneous and perfectly mobile. When net investment ceases, some labour is transferred from the capital goods industries to the consumption goods industries.
62. Pigou, *Employment and Equilibrium* (1949, 2nd edn), p. 133.
63. *Ibid.*, p. 133, n.2.
64. *Economic Journal* (1943).
65. A. H. Hansen, *Fiscal Policy and Business Cycles* (1941), p. 306; quoted by Pigou (1943), p. 343.
66. *Ibid.*, p. 349.
67. *Ibid.*, pp. 349–350.
68. Pigou, *Lapses from Full Employment* (1945), p. 23.
69. *Ibid.* (1945), p. 24.
70. Professional economists should note that according to Pigou here, this is not a full-employment equilibrium but one much nearer to that than Keynes's low-level equilibrium. The reason Pigou gives is a time lag between the initial fall in money wages and prices. However, in introducing a time lag, he is departing from comparative statics. Further, I suspect that if the only dynamic factor is this time lag, a full-employment stationary state will be established.
71. Pigou, 'Economic Progress in a Stable Environment', *Economica* (1947). Reprinted in American Economic Association (1952), p. 249.
72. M. Kalecki, 'Professor Pigou on the Classical Stationary State – a Comment', *Economic Journal* (April 1944).
73. A. C. Pigou, *Keynes's 'General Theory': A Retrospective View* (1950).
74. Pigou (1945), p. v.
75. Pigou (1947), reprinted in AEA *Readings* (1952), p. 251. Pigou is over-modest in saying 'of some slight use perhaps for clarifying thought'. In *Employment and Equilibrium* (1949, 2nd edn), p. 135, admittedly, Pigou does refer to the possibility of Keynes's equilibrium with mass unemployment, Keynes's Day of Judgement, as he calls it, being avoided by the price-induced wealth effect. However, I do not think this reflects Pigou's general position.
76. Pigou (1950), p. 37. 'Very seriously', assuming that appropriate Keynesian employment policies were not adopted.
77. Pigou (1950), pp. 37–38.
78. *American Economic Review* (1948); reprinted, corrected and modified, in American Economic Association, *Readings in Monetary Theory* (1952) to which all references are made.
79. Patinkin, in AEA, *Readings* (1952), p. 269. The two reservations relate to the possibility that with regard to expenditure a price decline may discourage debtors more than it encourages creditors, and Pigou's implicit assumption as to the intensity of the effect. I deal with the former reservation in detail below.
80. *Ibid.*, p. 271. He points out that the qualifying phrase is the restriction to static analysis.
81. 1st edn, 1956; 2nd edn, 1965.
82. Patinkin, in AEA *Readings* (1952), p. 273.
83. The bankruptcy point is emphasized in Kalecki's 'Professor Pigou on the Classical Stationary State – a Comment' (1944).
84. Patinkin, AEA *Readings* (1952), p. 273.
85. For example, *Money, Interest, and Prices* (1956, 1965), and *Keynes' Monetary Thought* (Durham, North Carolina, 1976a).
86. AEA *Readings* (1952), p. 280. This interpretation is discussed further in Chapter 12.
87. Along the lines of my article, 'Compatibility of any Behaviour of the Price Level with Equilibrium' (Gilbert 1956–1957) which, however, deals with different problems.
88. Kalecki, *Economic Journal* (1944), Patinkin refers to a complication arising from the possibility of a differential reaction. Debtors may be discouraged by a decline in the price level more than creditors are encouraged. *See* AEA *Readings* (1952), p. 263.
89. For this discussion *see* AEA *Readings* (1952), p. 264. I have made a formal change.
90. Pigou, *Employment and Equilibrium* (1949, 2nd edn), p. 132.
91. Pigou does not distinguish between current and deposit accounts.
92. Pigou, *Employment and Equilibrium* (1949, 2nd edn), p. 133, n.1. Pigou does not refer to Kalecki's criticism regarding the omission of bank loans, bank debtors, in his analysis.

93. John G. Gurley and Edward S. Shaw, *Money in a Theory of Finance* (1960), p. 363.
94. Like Patinkin above, Gurley and Shaw refer to distribution effects. *Ibid.*; pp. 67–68, 87–88 and 138–139.
95. *Ibid.*, p. 364.
96. The Bank of England one pound note is fiat money in spite of the 'Promise to Pay Bearer on Demand the Sum of One Pound'. All one can do is to exchange one pound note for another at the Bank until one decides to give up being a nuisance!
97. Harry G. Johnson, 'Monetary Theory and Policy', *American Economic Review* (June 1962), reprinted in his *Essays in Monetary Economics* (2nd edn, 1969b), p. 24.
98. Pesek and Saving (1967), p. 265. Their discussion of the assumptions required to compensate for nonseparability need not be considered here. *See* pp. 265–269.
99. Johnson refers to the non-existent wealth effect for change in real balances after writing 'Finally, if this logic applies to interest-bearing government debt, why should it not apply to the limiting case of non-interest-bearing government debt [fiat money], which is equally a debt of the public to itself, and to commodity moneys, which are the same thing though based on custom rather than law?'. This argument is not valid and Johnson later abandoned it. Harry G. Johnson (1969b), pp. 24–25.
100. Pesek and Saving (1967), p. 48 *et seq.*, pp. 206–208, 72 *et seq.* and p. 208 *et seq.*
101. Pesek and Saving stress that the constituents of the total stock of money depend on the current institutional arrangements of the economy under consideration. *See* Pesek and Saving (1967), pp. 187–189, n.29, where examples are given including the reference to interest at times having been paid on currency as in the case of the Greenbacks in the United States.
102. Pesek and Saving show that this statement is correct in spite of the fact that 'Time deposits can frequently be shifted into a demand deposit on the basis of a phone call' (Pesek and Saving (1967), p. 185). They also point to the fact that time deposits have been transferable by cheque in the past. In this case they acted as a medium of exchange and were money. To the extent that interest was paid on them, their full value would not be included in the stock of money (*ibid.*, p. 186). The latter point is explained below in the discussion on demand deposits.
103. Pesek and Saving (1967), p. 197. The matter is complicated. There is the question of the costs incurred by the bank in operating the demand deposit transmission mechanism, clearing of cheques etc. and the extent to which they are met by bank charges paid by the depositor. If such costs are not covered completely by bank charges, an implicit rate of interest is being paid. It is interesting to note that the Price Commission Report on Bank Transmission Services of 18 April 1978 recommends as a possible line of commercial bank action the charging for the services of making payments etc. in connection with current accounts according to the costs involved and paying interest on current accounts. A recent practice in the United States is to pay interest on demand deposits.
104. *Ibid.*, p. 112.
105. *Ibid.*, p. 121. I do not discuss here the question of the degree of bank competition.
106. Harry G. Johnson (1969a). *J.M.C.B.* (February 1969) reprinted in his *Further Essays in Monetary Economics* (London, 1972).
107. Pesek and Saving (1967).
108. Johnson (1969a), p. 114. *See also* Harry G. Johnson, 'Recent Developments in Monetary Theory – a Commentary', in David R. Croome and Harry G. Johnson, *Money in Britain 1959–1969* (1970), reprinted in Johnson, *Further Essays* (1972), pp. 33–34.
109. Don Patinkin, *Studies in Monetary Economics* (1972), Chapter 9.
110. *See* Patinkin's review article of the Pesek–Saving book, 'Money and Wealth: A Review Article', *Journal of Economic Literature* (December 1969).
111. Patinkin, *Studies on Monetary Economics* (1972), p. 190.
112. *Ibid.* If the banks obtain monopoly profits, 'bank money should be included in net wealth for the purpose of the real-balance effect to an extent equal to the capitalized value of these profits. For this value represents the difference between the stock of bank money and the costs of maintaining it'. *See also* David Laidler, 'On Definition of Money: Theoretical and Empirical Problems', *Journal of Money, Credit and Banking* (August 1969).
113. Pigou's stationary state involves an appropriate certainty assumption. If we assume uncertainty and approach the conditions of the real world, the Pigou effect with respect to government securities will be much stronger. Referring to the fall in the price level and the rise in the real taxes to pay the increased real interest, Dr Goodhart writes, 'Even if the increase in the present value of the future financial imposts matches the rise

in the present value of the bond, the latter is here and sure while the former represents an uncertain future contingent liability. An asset in the hand is worth more than a contingent future liability in the bush. Thus an expectation of future higher tax charges (in real terms) to meet the interest payments is likely to offset some, but not all, of the expansion resulting from a higher present value of 'outside' public-sector bonds'. C. A. E. Goodhart, *Money, Information and Uncertainty* (1975), p. 204.

114. Pigou, *Employment and Equilibrium* (1949, 2nd edn), p. 129.
115. There are two aspects of land. It is a productive factor which in combination with labour and capital produces a final product, say corn. As money wages and prices fall, the price of corn falls which is associated with a fall in the price of land; to this extent its real value in terms of consumption goods and services does not increase. However, there is also the amenity value of land, a possession suitable as a receptacle for saving. It follows that the price of land falls less than proportionately to the fall in consumption goods and services; its real value increases. It is necessary to have a rate of interest slightly above zero, using the borrower's rate or in some other way, to avoid a zero rate of interest which raises the problem of an infinite price of land when a given money yield is capitalized.
116. A. C. Pigou, *Industrial Fluctuations* (1st edn, 1927; 2nd edn, 1929). The references are made to the 1st edition.
117. *Ibid.*, p. 157. Pigou explains that if borrowers and lenders have correct foresight, the change in the price level can be allowed for in the money rate of interest so that the appropriate real rate is paid and received (pp. 157–158). For a detailed discussion of Irving Fisher's real rate of interest doctrine, see my article, 'The Compatibility of Any Behaviour of the Price Level with Equilibrium' (Gilbert 1956–1957), p. 178 *et seq.*
118. Pigou (1927), p. 231.
119. A. C. Pigou, *Memorials of Alfred Marshall* (1925), pp. 197–199; reprint of an article in the *Contemporary Review* (March 1887).
120. Marshall's tabular standard and Pigou's discussion of it cannot be considered in detail here.
121. Index-linking refers to contracts which are, for example, in the United Kingdom adjusted for changes in the retail price index number.
122. The rate of interest may be markedly above zero, depending on time preference, the amenity value of capital and the opportunities for investments.
123. I do not analyse the consequences of this assumption.
124. In contrast, in the dynamic case with uncertainty there are the problems already referred to, possible adverse expectations and bankruptcies and also the problem of the positive real rate of return in which money balances yield during the process of falling prices.
125. It is assumed that the central bank reduces the banks's cash reserves in the form of cash in the till and balances held with it, which are retained in a constant ratio to deposits, in a way which minimizes disturbance. The main point is that the real economic position must be the same in the two static states which are compared.
126. It might be possible to assume an institutional arrangement under which the nominal amount of bank deposits is constant, a compensatory increase being provided in a way which minimizes disturbance and ensures that cash reserves remain the same. As in the previous footnote, the real economic position must be the same in the two static states compared.
127. Pesek and Saving (1967), pp. 97–98.
128. It has been shown above (*see* p. 39) that perfect knowledge cannot be assumed, but this assumption of perfect security can be added to the appropriate certainty assumption.
129. David Hume, *Essays Moral, Political and Literary* (1903), p. 307. This is in his essay, 'Of Interest'.
130. Milton Friedman, *The Optimum Quantity of Money and Other Essays* (1969), pp. 4–5. It is supposed that each individual picks up an amount of money equal to the amount he already holds.
131. Pesek and Saving (1967), pp. 210–211. They are referring to Metzler, 'Wealth, Saving, and the Rate of Interest' (1951), reprinted in Metzler (1973). The gift of fiat money can, of course, be treated in terms of comparative statics or dynamics.
132. Pigou (1950).
133. *Ibid.*, p. 20.
134. Pigou quotes the whole of Keynes's summary statement. The reference to *The General Theory* is pp. 246–247.
135. Pigou (1950), p. 65.
136. Austin Robinson, 'Pigou, Arthur Cecil', *International Encyclopaedia of the Social Sciences* (1968), p. 96.

Chapter 5

D. H. Robertson, a Cambridge critic of Keynes

Professor Sir Dennis Robertson was a distinguished economist and critic of Keynes. Robertson and Pigou were Cambridge economists much influenced by Marshall as indeed was Keynes. Pigou and Keynes had been Marshall's pupils; Robertson went up to Cambridge originally to read classics in 1908, the year of Marshall's retirement and that of Pigou's appointment as his successor in the Chair of Political Economy. In 1910 Robertson changed to economics and became a pupil of Keynes. At this time, and long after, the Marshallian tradition was dominant at Cambridge. As Hicks put it, Marshall's *Principles of Economics* was 'the Bible of Cambridge economics'[1]. Robertson held the view that it was important to realize the continuity of the development of economic theory. In this respect he was like Marshall, who stressed that his own contributions were part of the continuing development of economic theory. Robertson examined Keynes's contribution in these terms and considered what advances he had made but did not accept the Keynesian Revolution. On the contrary, he emphasized the closeness of the relationship of Keynes's theory to the work of his predecessors and contemporaries while differing on the importance of his actual contribution.

Robertson was in the main a critic of Keynes's *General Theory*. With the publication of volumes XIII and XIV of *The Collected Writings of John Maynard Keynes*[2], which relate to *The General Theory*, and the publication of a number of journal articles since Keynes's death, it is now possible to understand better Robertson's attitude to Keynes's work. In the 1920s they had both worked happily and creatively together. Reference has already been made to Robertson's acknowledgement of this in his introduction to *Banking Policy and the Price Level* (1956)[3]. Keynes wrote to Robertson on 13 December 1936, 'I certainly date all my emancipation from the discussions between us which preceded your *Banking Policy and the Price Level*.'[4] The personal break between Robertson and Keynes has already been discussed[5]. Their disagreements in economics first became apparent following the publication of Keynes's *A Treatise on Money* (1930). Hicks states that Robertson had found the *Treatise* 'less congenial than he had expected'[6], but points out that his article on the *Treatise* published in *The Economic Journal* (September, 1931) was not in the form of a severe and explicit attack. Hicks considers that the critical years during which their disagreements developed were those between the *Treatise* (1930) and *The General Theory* (1936). Patinkin suggests that their paths diverged before 1930[7]. Harry Johnson states that 'they broke over the *Treatise* basically, but it became worse as *The General Theory* began to emerge'[8]. He refers to the attacks on Robertson[9] and the harrying of Robertson through the 1930s both in print and personally [at Cambridge]; the latter was much more serious[10].

It is sometimes said that the break occurred at the time of the *Treatise* and not at that of *The General Theory*, surprise being expressed that this was the case in view of the fact that the methodological approach of the *Treatise* differed far less than that of *The General Theory* from Robertson's own approach. Further, the emphasis and empirical speculations of *The General Theory* differed from the position taken by Robertson. Another important point is that it was not in the *Treatise* but in *The General Theory* that Keynes made his polemical attack on the classical and neoclassical economists, on Marshall whom Robertson so admired, and on Pigou whose position was very similar to that of Robertson. Keynes showed a serious lack of scholarship in the history of economic thought and was unfair to his contemporaries including Pigou whom he singled out as the most convenient representative of classical or rather neoclassical economic theory. Keynes's treatment of his predecessors and contemporaries deeply offended Robertson. There does not, on the other hand, seem to be much in the *Treatise* to upset Robertson. The defects in the new version of the quantity theory of money in the form of the fundamental equations and other theoretical weaknesses were criticized by Robertson and other economists. Keynes accepted much of the criticism and realized that he still needed to provide a satisfactory theoretical basis for the economic policies he advocated.

In the preface to the Japanese edition of *A Treatise on Money*, dated 5 April 1932, Keynes, having referred to his year and a half of further reflection and the advantage obtained from much criticism and discussion of his work, writes, 'I propose to publish a short book of a purely theoretical character, extending and correcting the theoretical basis of my views . . .'[11] In a letter to R. G. Hawtrey of 1 June 1932, Keynes wrote, 'As I mentioned to you, I am working it out all over again.'[12] In the *Treatise*, the theory related to changes in prices although some attention was paid to changes in output while in *The General Theory* the position was reversed and the emphasis was placed on changes in output with changes in prices being a secondary consideration. This does not mean that Keynes's theory is inflationary as has sometimes been asserted. An examination of *The General Theory* and some of his subsequent writings shows that his model is well suited to the analysis of the problem of inflation. He had been concerned with the problem of an 'appropriate' degree of stability in the general level of prices since his book, *A Tract on Monetary Reform* (1923)[13]. The change of emphasis to that of the general level of economic activity (output and employment) occurred soon after the publication of the *Treatise*. The development of his new analysis was greatly aided by a group of young economists, Richard Kahn, James Meade, Piero Sraffa, Joan and Austin Robinson, who formed 'The Cambridge Circus' of

1930–1931. Professor Donald Moggridge writes that 'Dennis Robertson did not wish to be deeply involved and attended, if memories serve, on only one occasion.'[14] In the autumn of 1932 the title of Keynes's lecture course was changed from 'The Pure Theory of Money' to 'The Monetary Theory of Production'[15]. Exactly when the personal break between the two men came is not clear but no doubt Hicks is correct in believing that their main disagreements developed between 1930 and 1936, when Keynes was moving from the *Treatise* to *The General Theory*. Patinkin points out that the breach between Keynes and Robertson became 'official' when Keynes did not include Robertson's name in his acknowledgements in the Preface to *The General Theory*[16]. The cause of diagreement could certainly not have been Keynes's change of emphasis to that of output and employment. After all Robertson's first book, *A Study of Industrial Fluctuations* (1915)[17] was devoted to cyclical changes in output with the emphasis on real rather than monetary factors. From his book, *Money*, first published in 1922, he had devoted himself mainly to monetary theory, but concerned himself with changes in output and employment as well as the price level.

The reasons for Robertson's critical attitude towards Keynes's work are clearer today than before Keynes's death in 1946, apart from Keynes's misrepresentations of his contemporaries and predecessors to which reference has already been made. Robertson maintained his critical attitude until his death in 1963. As Professor of Political Economy at Cambridge he gave the lectures on Economic Principles from 1945–1946 to 1956–1957 and in the third term of his last economic year he said at the beginning of his lectures on money and the fluctuations of economic activity, 'If I may strike a personal note, this has always been to me to the most interesting part of economics – the only part to which I can hope to be remembered as having made any personal contribution.'[18] Robertson continued with some remarks about his attitude to Keynes's work which are so enlightening that they must be quoted at length. He said

'I regret too that some part of what I have to say is inevitably controversial, and critical of the work of my generous friend and brilliant teacher Maynard Keynes. There is no doubt that the modern concentration of interest on this range of subjects is due to him more than to any other single person. But if you have read any of my writing on these themes you will know already that I am definitely of the opinion that in his later work Keynes while he continued to contribute to, also marred by distortions and exaggerations of various kinds, a fruitful body of doctrine which had been moulded over several decades by many hands.'[19]

S. R. Dennison, a personal friend and great admirer of Robertson, refers to Robertson's criticisms of the Keynesian system as being regarded in some quarters as '*carping* at minutiae of a fundamental revolution in economic thinking'[20]. He goes on to show that there were important points at issue and that Robertson played by his constructive criticism an important role in the development of the Keynesian system. Samuelson refers to a new note entering into Robertson's writings after the break with Keynes, which remained until the end, 'a querulous note of protest over the pretensions and correctness of so-called new ideas and a somewhat repetitious defence of earlier wisdom . . .'. This Robertsonian querulousness was not, I conclude on reflection, sterile. Many of Robertson's points, had they come from within the Keynesian camp, would have been recognized as valuable contributions.'[21]

Hicks points out that one can now see that Robertson was right to perceive the weaknesses of Keynes's model, 'but he was too much occupied with its weaknesses to perceive its strengths'[22]. Keynes saw that the differences between himself and Robertson (and Pigou) were theoretical, not differences relating to economic policies. He wrote to R. F. Kahn, 20 October 1937 'Many thanks for sending me a copy of the Prof's new book, [A. C. Pigou, *Socialism versus Capitalism*]. As in the case of Dennis [Robertson], when it comes to practice, there is really extremely little between us. Why do they insist on maintaining theories from which their own practical conclusions cannot possibly follow? It is a sort of Society for the Preservation of Ancient Monuments.'[23] Here, on the other hand, we find Keynes not perceiving the strength of Robertson's and Pigou's theoretical structures which he regarded as neoclassical and misleading. Robertson and Pigou were not misled by their theoretical systems; they advocated monetary and fiscal policies very similar to those of Keynes and these policies were consistent with their theories. Keynes and Robertson seemed to be incapable of recognizing the relationship of their theories. This is very clear in their correspondence before and after the publication of *The General Theory*. It persisted until Keynes's death and as we shall see, after 1946, Robertson remained the critic and never succeeded in producing a synthesis which would have clarified their positions. I shall try to explain this.

Before *The General Theory*, Robertson wrote to Keynes, 3 February 1935, that he took the proposition that there was a chronic and epidemic deficiency of aggregate money demand in the modern world to be the real *differentia* of the book, marking it off from the *Treatise* and most of the other literature dealing with trade-cyclical fluctuations around a norm but not considering a chronic failure to reach a norm[24]. Robertson commented with sympathy on this point but by considering, as other economists have done, that this speculation of Keynes was the *real differentia*, showed that he was misled by the economics-of-depression tone of the book and prevented from recognizing the main contribution, the model providing a general theory of employment[25]. The essence of Keynes was not stagnation economics. Again, Robertson wrote to Keynes, 10 February 1935, saying that he feared that his comments on the book would be felt to be rather hostile and expressing sorrow for this as he was not unsympathetic to what he regarded as the most important practical thing Keynes was saying, 'that there were certain long-term depressive influences at work'. On the other hand, Robertson writes, 'a large part of your theoretical structure is still to us almost complete mumbo-jumbo'[26]. Thus Robertson was unable to grasp the great advantages of Keynes's simple theoretical model. After a prolonged and inconclusive correspondence, they agreed to break off the discussion[27]. After *The General Theory*, Keynes wrote to Robertson, 13 December 1936, saying that he felt that there was not a great deal that was fundamental which divided them and less perhaps than Robertson thought[28]. He returned to this point at the end of the letter and referred to their minds having 'been changing continuously and enormously, though on parallel lines that all but, yet don't quite, meet, over the last eleven years'[29]. Having said that the last thing he would accuse Robertson of was being classical or orthodox, Keynes complained 'But you won't slough your skins, like a good snake'[30]. Robertson replied on 29 December 1936 saying that he was pleased to feel that the chances of *practical* disagreement were less than he had feared, but defended himself regarding bad snakehood on a number of grounds. He writes that he is 'acutely conscious . . . of the *educational* disadvantages of the present tendency . . . to exaggerate differences and represent all knowledge as brand new'[31].

There are two main reasons why Robertson remained the critic, apart from Keynes's unscholarly and misleading treatment of the classical and neoclassical economists and perhaps the break in their personal relationship. The first is suggested by Professor T. Wilson in a survey article of Robertson's work when he writes 'Yet it was, I suspect, the very enlightenment of his own views which made it difficult for Professor Robertson to appreciate the revolution in thought which followed the publication of the *General Theory*.'[32] Robertson's enlightenment becomes clear in the later discussion of his criticism of Keynesian theory. The second reason is suggested by Hicks in *A Memoir*, that Robertson's equilibrium was equilibrium over time while Keynes's equilibrium was equilibrium of the short period. Hicks writes, 'Yet that new equilibrium of Keynes was a powerful weapon; because it cut out just those things which Robertson felt to be most essential, he was reluctant to admit how very powerful it was.'[33]

Keynes's model was basically comparative statics while Robertson's was dynamics. The methodology was fundamentally different, Keynes compared short-term equilibrium on different assumptions while Robertson used a period approach or step-by-step method of analysing economic processes over time. Robertson's period analysis was developed as early as 1926 in *Banking Policy and the Price Level* and he felt strongly that Keynes had taken a backward step by using comparative statics in *The General Theory* of 1936. Associated with their different methodologies there is a difference in the problems with which they are concerned, for example Keynes's concern with the raising of the level of employment from a low to a high level and Robertson's concern with the conditions required for a stable money economy the real income of which was growing steadily for various reasons which he distinguished. Of course, there was a good deal of common interest and Robertson was certainly concerned with the problem of raising the level of employment during the depression and Keynes did at times refer to economic growth, for example capital accumulation. They both contributed to the analysis of the trade cycle although Keynes's *General Theory* contains only the one highly suggestive chapter, Notes on the Trade Cycle. Thus, there was a very different emphasis in the work of the two economists which is related both to their methodologies and their objectives in economic analysis. Although I agree with Professor John Vaizey that differences between Keynes's approach and Robertson's were exaggerated in the controversy over the *General Theory*, I fail to understand how he can state that 'Harry Johnson's work has shown that formally the two can be reduced to very similar formulations.'[34]

There is a great deal, I am sure, in Wilson's point that Robertson failed to appreciate the Keynesian Revolution because his own work in the field of monetary macroeconomics had advanced so far. Wilson, writing in 1953, points out that Robertson's contributions on Keynesian economics consisted mainly in criticism and 'a vindication of earlier views on these matters'[35]. Samuelson in his obituary article of 1963, as we have seen, refers to Robertson's 'somewhat repetitious defence of earlier wisdom . . .'[36]. Robertson used to think 'it's all in Marshall'. On reading the whole of Robertson on Keynes one gets the impression that he is saying 'it's all in Robertson'. I cannot resist this quip although I am well aware of his scholarship, his acknowledgement of the work of earlier economists and his modesty. Indeed, as a young member of The London School of Economics staff, I attended his lectures on Money in 1930–1931, when a visiting lecturer, and noticed how sensitive he was when referring to his own work before a large audience. However, he must have felt deeply the lack of detailed acknowledgement of his work by Keynes. That Keynes did not relate his Revolution to Robertson's work must have made it more difficult for Robertson to accept the Revolution. The main point, however, is that Robertson did not see the importance of the Keynesian vision, the thrust of Keynes's simple basic model. In a letter to Keynes of 29 December 1936, Robertson wrote, 'Both over the *Treatise* and this book [*The General Theory*] I have gone through real intellectual torment trying to make up my mind whether, as you often seem to claim, there is some new piece on the board or rather a re-arrangement, which seems to you superior, of existing pieces. It has been an intellectual relief to me to find Hicks (e.g. review pp. 246–248) and Harrod (*Econometrica* paper) both taking the latter view, though agreeing far more with you than with me about the merits of the re-arrangement.'[37] In 1946 Austin Robinson stated that Keynes 'was only in a limited sense a tool-maker'[38] but he emphasized the importance of his analysis of 'the general pattern of forces at work'[39]. In 1963, Austin Robinson pointed out that it was not possible for any economist to build without any of the bricks of his predecessors. He wrote, 'The greatness of a Corbusier lies not in an impossible attempt to use none of the normal materials of building, but in his ability to put them together differently and to make out of them something essentially new and more appropriate to his own age. The break-away is not in every detail but in a new total conception. That is what, I think, Keynes was achieving.'[40] The essence of the Keynesian Revolution was the new total conception and it was this which Robertson failed to appreciate.

Robertson was given many honours but his contribution to economics was underestimated, in general, by professional economists. This was so in the case of most of his Cambridge colleagues and many economists elsewhere. It is exemplified in Samuelson's fears that he has done Robertson less than justice but he thinks that perhaps it could not have been otherwise as his own views differ so widely from those held by Robertson. They came from very different stables. Samuelson concludes his article with the words 'Let my tribute to him stand, then, as an underestimate.'[41] On the other hand, Robertson's work was fully appreciated by a number of economists. Hicks in his *A Memoir*[42] and in many favourable references to Robertson in his writings gives him recognition.

Professor William Fellner in his article 'The Robertsonian Evolution', refers to the heritage of the next generation being 'just as essentially Robertsonian and Swedish as Keynesian, regardless of what they will choose to call it'[43]. Dennison writes, 'The Keynesian system was considerably modified and developed under criticism, not least that of Robertson, and the accepted view on some matters became as much Robertsonian as Keynesian.'[44]

Before evaluating Robertson's criticisms of Keynes, it is necessary to consider in more detail their different methodologies, Keynes using comparative statics, and Robertson dynamics, period analysis. Keynes's basic method was to compare two static short-period equilibrium positions in which the given data differ. The short period could be a point of time or a short period of time. Keynes refers to a firm's behaviour in deciding its daily output as being determined by short-term expectations and writes in a footnote '*Daily* here stands for the shortest interval after which the firm is free to revise its decision as to how much employment to offer. It is, so to speak, the minimum effective unit of time.'[45] On given assumptions it can be shown how the levels of employment and output differ, when the rates of investment, expenditure on capital goods, per unit period of time differ. It is explained in Chapter 12 why Keynes did not use the dynamic method of period analysis, tracing the path of economic processes through a succession of unit-time periods. The difficulty is that there is no determinate time unit, its length differing according to the nature of the economic factors under consideration. Thus, one is presented with time units of different lengths which overlap one another. These difficulties are avoided by using comparative statics, comparing two hypothetical static situations. Schumpeter states that Keynes once said to a pupil 'Forget all about periods.'[46] It is also pointed out in Chapter 12 that Keynes at times departed from his basic static model. There are various passages in *The General Theory* which deal with the different effects of a change in one variable on another variable according to the time period allowed between the change and the effect, for example, the effect of an increase in the rate of investment on income. In many such cases the analysis can be formulated in comparative static terms.

At times, however, Keynes's analysis is explicitly dynamic. On pages 47 and 48 of *The General Theory* he considers the effects of changes in short-term and longterm expectations on the level of employment and states that the full effect of such a change on employment requires the lapse of a considerable period of time. He gives examples of how the degree of adjustment of the economic system to the new expectations depends on the period of time assumed. In doing this, Keynes indicates some of the kinds of processes occurring during the period of adjustment but there is no detailed analysis. Keynes continues, 'If we suppose a state of expectation to continue for a sufficient length of time for the effect on employment to have worked itself out so completely that there is, broadly speaking, no piece of employment going on which would not have taken place if the new state of expectation had always existed, the steady level of employment thus attained may be called the long-period employment corresponding to that state of expectation.'[47] In comparing such levels of employment on the assumption of different states of expectation comparative statics is all that is required. Later, Keynes undertakes much the same analysis in terms of his conception of the elasticity of employment[48]. On page 47 Keynes has a footnote in which he refers to a dynamic equilibrium. He writes, 'it is not necessary that the level of long-period employment should be *constant*, i.e. long-period conditions are not necessarily static. For example a steady increase in wealth or population may constitute a part of the unchanging conditions. The only condition is that the existing expectations should have been foreseen sufficiently far ahead.'[49] It is to this problem of dynamic equilibrium that Robertson devoted so much attention in his analyses of monetary equilibrium, from his book *Money*[50] and his article 'Theories of Banking Policy'[51], both published in 1928, to his last publication *A Memorandum Submitted to the Canadian Royal Commission on Banking and Finance*[52], written in 1962 and published in 1963, the year of his death.

In his New Introduction, dated January 1948, to *A Study of Industrial Fluctuation*, first published in 1915, Robertson wrote, 'To one so drenched with the vision of eternal ebb and flow, relapse and recovery, Keynes's final attempt in his *General Theory* to deal with the savings-investment complex in terms of a theory of static and stable equilibrium was bound to seem a step backwards.'[53] Further, in the Preface to the 1949 edition of *Banking Policy and the Price Level*, dated September 1949, Robertson elaborated this important point. He wrote, 'While Keynes must at the time have understood and acquiesced in my step-by-step method, it is evident that it never, so to speak, got under his skin; for in his two successive treatments of the savings-investment theme in his two big books [*A Treatise on Money* and *The General Theory*] he discarded it completely. This was naturally a great personal disappointment to me, and it is, I think, being increasingly recognized that it was also a misfortune for the smooth progress of theory.'[54] As Dennison points out, to Robertson, the Keynesian 'revolution', taking the form of an analysis of short-term equilibrium, was retrogression rather than an advance, in contrast to his own analysis of equilibrium over time[55]. Robertson, by using his step-by-step method, traces a path of economic processes from one unit period of time to subsequent unit periods. His objective is to provide the conditions for a dynamic equilibrium, the economy's real income growing as a result of increases in population, capital and productivity because of inventions. At the same time he shows how the path may be a disequilibrium one.

Robertson first used his unit of time, a 'day' in 1926 in *Banking Policy and the Price Level*[56]. In 1933, in his article 'Saving and Hoarding', he assumed 'the existence of a period of time, to be called a "day", which is finite but nevertheless so short that the income which a man receives on a given day cannot be allocated during its course to any particular use'[57]. Robertson recognized the objections made on the ground of the vagueness of the length of the minimum period of time, a 'day', but rightly stressed the importance of his use of the 'day', to give him the unit of time he required for his period analysis[58]. The 'day' is, of course, an abstraction from reality but a useful one for formal analysis. One 'day's' disposable income, which is spent or saved, is the income received on the previous 'day'. Investment, expenditure on capital goods, during the current 'day' will be greater than saving if it is financed not only out of the saving of the previous 'day's' income, but also by an increase in the supply of money and/or dishoarding, the investment of idle money balances. The 'day's' money income rises as compared with that of the previous 'day'. Investment will be less than saving if the supply of money is decreased and/or hoarding, the accumulation of idle money balances, occurs. In this case, the 'day's' money income falls as compared with that of the previous 'day's'. If saving equals investment during the 'day', money income remains unchanged. Thus, Robertson shows that money income may increase, decrease or remain the same from one 'day' to the next. By his period analysis, Robertson made an important contribution to dynamic economics. Saving equals investment, according to Robertson's terminology, is consistent with, but not a sufficient condition for, equilibrium.

According to Professor A. H. Hansen, Robertson's definitions only establish identities. He writes, 'They are merely truistic statements about today's and yesterday's income. They can have no value in *analysing* income changes. They are only descriptions of what has happened after the event.'[59]

Robertson was stating a truism which, like the quantity theory of money, provided useful heads under which the causes of changes in certain economic phenomena could be considered. Hansen regards Robertson as having partly redeemed himself by adding in 1936 the hypothesis that today's consumption is a function of yesterday's income[60]. However, this functional relationship was presumably implicit in his 1933 analysis[61]. Despite his criticism Hansen concludes that Robertson's definitions are useful and indeed necessary for period analysis[62]. Samuelson recognizes the justice of the claim that Robertson was an originator of period analysis, which became such a useful tool for economists developing dynamic economic analysis[63]. He complains that Robertson 'never conceded to Hawtrey and Keynes that he was merely uttering a tautology in asserting that income will rise (or fall) when observed investment exceeds (or runs short of) Robertsonian saving'[64]. My view is that Robertson's tautology is useful. Robertson himself made good use of it, while later writers elaborated his period analysis. Samuelson makes much of the fact that the tautology does not imply refutable causation and that Robertson did not realize the importance of analysing a dynamic causal sequence involving a hypothetical consumption function which could be tested[65]. Robertson, however, had stated that when he said there was an excess of saving over investment, he was trying to formulate in a convenient phrase the *cause* of a fall in income[66]. One can, I think, accept that Robertson used his tautology to do this, although he did not have a formal dynamic sequence model, which was developed later. Fellner in his 1952 appreciative article on Robertson, 'The Robertsonian Evolution', points out that his theory is dynamic in that it depicts a process of economic development and that this process may or may not satisfy the conditions of a moving equilibrium. Fellner contrasts Robertson's approach to the basic comparative static equilibrium approach of Keynes's *General Theory*[67].

Robertson's theory of the trade cycle involved instability because of the uneven rate of economic growth. His theory of dynamic equilibrium was an analysis of the conditions required for equilibrium over time when real income is increasing for various reasons. He was a forerunner of modern economic growth theory although a critic of much of the work done in this fashionable post-Keynesian field. In his Marshall Lectures given in the autumn of 1960, Robertson reviews the contributions of the neoclassical economists to growth theory which he shows to be important[68]. He refers to the modern growth models of Harrod, Domar, Joan Robinson, Kaldor Mark I, Kaldor Mark II, Kaldor Mark III, Hahn, Matthews, Goodwin, Champernowne, Hicks, Little, Duesenberry, Tobin, Fellner, Solow and Swan and devotes considerable attention to some of them[69]. Keynes did not deal with growth in his basic comparative static model although there are some references to growth in *The General Theory*, particularly regarding the possibility of the accumulation of capital over time exhausting the opportunities for investment and causing economic stagnation if appropriate action was not taken.

Robertson and Keynes, however, took a somewhat similar view regarding mathematical models and the application of econometric methods associated with them. Keynes was very conscious of the dangers in such econometric work and he did not hold very high hopes of the results likely to be achieved. Robertson in his 1956–1957 *Lectures* said that he did not think much had yet been added to the analysis of the trade cycle by the various mathematical models of recent years. He refers to the models of Kalecki, Kaldor, Samuelson and 'what should now perhaps be regarded as the fine flower of the "model" garden, Hicks's book *The Trade Cycle*.'[70] Robertson also refers to the notable attempts made by Tinbergen and other econometricians to incorporate statistical data into a closed mathematical system of the trade cycle. Robertson's view was that 'all these models do point the way to possible advances of theory beyond the comparative study of positions of short-period equilibrium outlined by Keynes and formalized by Pigou in his *Employment and Equilibrium*. At the same time I think they carry great dangers unless kept in control by a strong historical sense.'[71] Earlier in his 1948 new Introduction to the reprint of his *A Study of Industrial Fluctuation* (1915), he wrote,

'As to stylized models of the cycle, of the kind now so fashionable, they doubtless have their uses, provided their limitations are clearly understood. We must wait with respectful patience while the econometricians decide their elaborate methods are really capable of covering such models with flesh and blood. But I confess that to me at least the forces at work seem so complex, the question whether even the few selected parameters can be relied on to stay put through the cycle or between cycles so doubtful, that I wonder whether more truth will not in the end be wrung from interpretative studies of the crude data of the general type contained in this volume, but more intensive, more scrupulously-worded and more expert.'[72]

It is of great interest that Hicks tells us in 1977 that he takes the same view as Robertson and quotes the above passage in full[73]. Dr Colin Clark points out that Robertson was critical of Keynes's static method because he liked to analyse the intricate path of events on succeeding 'days'. Clark writes, 'This method of reasoning Keynes described, characteristically, as "barbarous".' Clark states somewhat unjustifiably that the method did not get Sir Dennis very far. It was certainly a good beginning. Clark quotes

Robertson's reply, 'I cannot get used to a world where everything happens all at once.' Clark concludes, 'We now know that Robertson was right, and that time-lags are of very great importance in short-period analysis, both of consumption and of investment, even though he was not able to formulate them.'[74]

I should like to add to this that not only was Keynes's comparative statics well suited to his purpose in the 1930s[75], but that we still need this model as well as the Robertsonian and post-Keynesian dynamic models. Its relative simplicity still gives it an advantage for the analysis of certain economic problems. It should also be pointed out that the Keynesian theory lent itself readily to dynamization and much of post-Keynesian dynamic theory relating to the trade cycle and economic growth stems directly from his work. Time-lags play a vital role in much of this analysis and some economists have failed to give due recognition to Robertson's early use of them. Some post-Keynesian economic growth theory has been developed from Keynes's *General Theory* without the use of time-lags, notably Sir Roy Harrod's growth model[76].

Keynes's attack on the assumption of full employment or a theoretical system, based on a competitive private capitalist economy, which provided for an automatic self-adjusting mechanism to give full employment equilibrium, took the form of an attack on the classical and neoclassical economists. Keynes's criticism was very misleading. Robertson in view of his own work complained in his 1948 Introduction to *A Study of Industrial Fluctuation* (1915) of 'a prevalent tendency to suppose that the behaviour of "output as a whole" first attracted the attention of economists in the 1930s'[77]. No doubt, he had Keynes's influence in mind. He points out that in his 1915 book the emphasis is on a study of fluctuations in real national income or output rather than of prices, profits or even employment. Further, he does not claim originality for this object of study as Part IV of A. C. Pigou's *Wealth and Welfare* (1912) dealt with fluctuations in the national dividend. Robertson laid stress on changes in investment causing changes in the level of general economic activity and on inventions as a very important cause of such changes in investment. In his 1949 Preface to *Banking Policy and the Price Level*, he points out that the ultimate concern of the book was with changes in output in a money economy and that Pigou in his *Industrial Fluctuations*[78] has analysed the monetary causes of changes in output. Again Robertson complains, 'it is bound to remain to me a source of some bewilderment that at some time in the period following 1930 the idea that monetary analysis . . . is concerned with the behaviour of output as well as of prices should apparently have struck Keynes, or at any rate the able little group who were then advising him, with the force of a new discovery'[79]. *Banking Policy and the Price Level* was a path-breaking work which did not have the influence it deserved, partly as a result of its title and apparent emphasis on changes in the price level rather than output, if not read with due care, and partly as a result of the somewhat weird but fascinating Robertsonian terminology with which I remember struggling in the 1920s as a student. However, it must be realized that one of Keynes's greatest contributions was to bring the study of variations in the level of output on to the front of the economics stage.

One of the characteristic features of Keynes's *General Theory* was the development of an analysis of the determinants of the general level of output and employment in a monetary economy, in which money played an essential role. This was important as economics had often in the past been treated in two separate compartments: the theory of value which dealt with relative prices and the allocation of productive resources, and the theory of money which dealt with the determination of the general level of prices. However, long before Keynes, attempts at such a synthesis had been made, Professor Ludwig von Mises, a member of the famous Viennese School, had published his *Die Theorie Des Geldes Und Der Umlaufsmittel* in 1912[80] in which the Austrian monetary over-investment theory was developed. This was an attempt to integrate monetary and real economic factors by showing how monetary influences could affect the allocation of productive resources and cause disequilibrium. As we shall see, when discussing Hayek's elaboration of this theory, it was a special case which had very unfortunate consequences for the development of economic theory and policy[81]. Robertson, having undertaken what was mainly a study of the real economic factors causing trade cycle fluctuations in 1915[82], tried to integrate the theory of money into that of the trade cycle in his book *Money*[83], first published in 1922. This integration is to be found in later editions of this book, in *Banking Policy and the Price Level* (1926), his essays on the trade cycle[84], and in the chapters on the trade cycle in his *Lectures* given in 1956–1957[85]. Further, in these books, in his 'Theories of Banking Policy'[86] of 1928, in his Marshall Lectures[87] for 1960 and *A Memorandum Submitted to the Canadian Royal Commission on Banking and Finance*, signed in 1962[88], Robertson developed his theory of steady economic growth of output or dynamic equilibrium in the terms of monetary equilibrium. It is thus not surprising to find him critical of Keynes's exaggerated claims to originality with respect to the integration of monetary and real economic theory.

Keynes seemed to believe that he was making a fundamental break with traditional economics by holding that a competitive private capitalist system was not self-adjusting so as to maintain a full-employment equilibrium. Thus government intervention in the form of monetary and fiscal policies was required. Robertson was certainly not subject to such criticism. He pointed out that he had not been brought up with any exaggerated respect for Say's Law and that he had subjected it to some rough handling in *A Study of Industrial Fluctuation* (1915)[89]. The progress of an economy, according to Robertson, involved instability. He studied the booms associated with the great innovations, railways, basic steel, electricity and oil and the depressions which followed. Robertson believed that the collapse of investment might be caused by a shortage of saving to provide funds for the high level of investment or, more often, by a temporary saturation of the economy with capital goods[90]. Depressions were regarded as the penalty to be paid for progress but he considered the possibilities of alleviating their consequences by appropriate policies. In *Banking Policy and the Price Level* (1926), Robertson gives the same two possible causes and adds a third, the strain on the banking system, i.e. rising interest rates[91]. A rise in the general level of prices during the upward swing of the trade cycle is regarded as acceptable as it facilitates the innovational investment, an essential element of economic progress. It imposes forced saving on the community in addition to the voluntary saving provided. Robertson, Pigou and the Austrian economists who developed the monetary over-investment theory of the trade cycle, all use this concept which has a long history going back to Jeremy Bentham's statement of it in 1804[92]. Despite the advantages of the concept it must be admitted that it is difficult to define precisely and Keynes gives reasons in *The General Theory* for not using the concept himself[93].

Robertson in his *Lectures* of 1956–1957[94] maintains that there is a great variety of reasons for the course of the trade cycle turning from boom to depression and refers specifically to the three causes given in his earlier work which I have already mentioned. He adds that the temporary saturation with important groups of capital instruments 'is frequently the most important underlying feature of the situation, and *would have* become operative before long even if the others hadn't'[95]. By 1956–1957 Robertson's view that trade-cyclical booms and depressions were a necessary concomitant of economic progress made possible by technical innovation had somewhat changed. This view was similar to that put forward by J. A. Schumpeter in his *Die Theorie Der Wirtschaftlicken Entwicklung*[96] of 1911 which Robertson had not seen when he was developing his own view. Robertson's view had not completely changed. The preservation of a stable economy associated with monetary equilibrium was still not the overriding objective of policy in all circumstances. He writes, 'Looking back on the history of capitalism, I should myself find it difficult to say dogmatically that such episodes as the English railways mania of the 1840s, or the American railway boom of 1869–1871, or the German electrical boom of the 1890s, each of which drenched the country in question with valuable capital equipment at the expense of inflicting inflationary levies and adding to the instability of employment, were on balance "a bad thing".'[97] Robertson also considers that at the present time a community which is making modest but steady progress, may find itself under an urgent need for fixed capital equipment for defence or for making technical improvements and that in such cases a monetary policy involving monetary disequilibrium may be desirable[98]. However, Robertson was now more conscious of the penalties of economic progress involving trade-cyclical booms, the immediate cost in human welfare and the risk (he would not say certainty) that such policies if pressed too far may lead to depression. He ends this lecture with the words, 'And for western countries at least, unless perhaps under the imminent threat of catastrophic war, I would now hold the pursuit of monetary equilibrium to be a sufficiently ambitious, and the wiser, path'[99].

Keynes's essential point that a deficiency of aggregate money demand could be responsible for unemployment and a low level of output is closely associated with the concept of hoarding which Robertson emphasized throughout his life. Hoarding was defined by Robertson as an increase in the demand to hold money, a decrease in money expenditure during a given period of time, which may also be expressed as a decrease in the rate at which a given nominal quantity of money circulates against the constituents of final real annual output (a decrease in the income-velocity of circulation). The self-adjusting forces of the economic system prove inadequate and a fall of prices associated with a fall in output and employment occur. The hoarding which is a form of saving is not reflected in a corresponding amount of investment, additional capital goods. In 1948 Robertson tells us that the common-sense remarks about hoarding by farmers in his *A Study of Industrial Fluctuations* (1915), with the help of the midwives Cassel and Pigou, became in *Banking Policy and the Price Level* (1926), 'transformed into the formal doctrine that under certain conditions the process of individual saving, so far from finding vent in the accumulation of useful stocks, may become completely abortive . . .'[100]. In his *Lectures* of 1956–1957, Robertson states clearly that an increase in hoarding creates a tendency to disequilibrium, a discouragement to output and employment[101]. Unfortunately, in *Banking Policy and the Price Level*, his analysis of the effects of an increase in hoarding is based on the assumption of constant production and sales. Thus an increase in hoarding by some individuals, unless steps are taken to ensure a corresponding increase in the output of capital goods, will merely lead to falling prices and an increase in the consumption of other individuals. The saving in the form of hoarding has been abortive[102]. Robertson's complaint in the Preface to the 1949 Edition that 'nobody who read the book as a whole with attention can have doubted that the ultimate concern of this section, as of the rest of the book . . . was with changes in *output*'[103], is hardly justified. In his book *Money* in which the public is assumed to increase its hoarding, prices fall, the real value of the money stock (consisting only of bank deposits as a simplification) increases so that increased saving in the form of money held is achieved, but consumption is not reduced, prices having fallen so that sales of goods and services are maintained. Once again, the saving is abortive unless the banks increase their loans to convert the saving into capital goods. However, here Robertson adds the vital footnote, 'Disregarding for the present any secondary effects of the falling price-level in checking the creation of wealth (Chapter 1, para. 7)'[104].

The relationship between Robertson's increased hoarding and Keynes's decreased aggregate money demand is somewhat complicated. Keynes writes in *The General Theory*, 'Moreover, it is impossible for the actual amount of hoarding to change as a result of decisions on the part of the public, so long as we mean by "hoarding" the actual holding of cash. For the amount of hoarding must be equal to the quantity of money . . . and the quantity of money is not determined by the public.'[105] Professor Abba P. Lerner follows Keynes on this point[106]. Wilson refers to Professor Villard's suggestion that the difficulty arose because 'the instantaneous approach of the *General Theory* avoids as far as possible specific reference to time periods, while "hoarding" in its usual meaning must have a time dimension'[107]. Wilson also quotes Robertson 'There are inevitable difficulties in expressing in statically-framed terms the situation existing *at a moment of time during a period of change* . . .'[108]. Wilson thinks this may be part of the explanation, but lays stress on the relationship of hoarding and dishoarding of a given quantity of money to the rate of interest in Keynesian theory[109]. Keynes himself wrote, 'All that the propensity of the public towards hoarding can achieve is to determine the rate of interest at which the aggregate desire to hoard becomes equal to the available cash [money].'[110]

The confusion over hoarding in *The General Theory* is not to be explained by the time dimension point. Robertson's increase in hoarding, a decrease in the income-velocity of circulation of money, is an increase in the demand for money to hold, the public wishing to hold a greater command over goods and services in the form of money balances. There is no difficulty in comparative statics in assuming different demands for money to hold and comparing, other things being equal, the two static situations. Keynes is misleading because he does not make explicit the necessary assumption for his statement that hoarding cannot increase unless the quantity of nominal money is increased. This assumption is that the price level of the constituents of real income is constant. If prices are flexible, then an increase in hoarding causes a fall of prices and a rise in the real value (purchasing power) of the given nominal stock of money as Robertson explains. This can easily be put in comparative static terms. If the price level is constant as Keynes must be assuming, an increase in hoarding causes the rate of interest to rise to equate the given supply of nominal money (and money in real terms) with the demand for it. Again, this can easily be stated in comparative static terms. One can analyse the effects of an increase in hoarding on prices and output in Robertsonian or Keynesian terms. It should be noted that Keynes does not assume throughout *The General Theory* that money wages are fixed, nor that the general price level is constant in this case.

The multiplier was a basic relationship in Keynes's model of the determination of the levels of income, or output, and employment in *The General Theory*. Robertson was never able to accept its importance. Keynes formulates the multiplier in terms of the relationship between an increment of investment and the corresponding increment of income which is a multiple of the former. He simplifies by considering a closed economy so that changes in imports and exports are excluded. He also excludes government taxation although the increase in investment could be an increase in government expenditure. Thus the multiplier depends on the marginal propensity to consume, the proportion of an additional increment of income which is consumed. Alternatively, it can be said to depend on the marginal propensity to save which is 1 minus the marginal propensity to consume as an increment of income will consist of an increment of consumption and an increment of saving which is identically equal to investment in Keynes's terminology. The marginal propensity to save relates to the increment of income which is not spent and so does not increase output. The greater the marginal propensity to consume, the lower the marginal propensity to save, the greater will be the multiplier. Saving is regarded as a leakage of money from circulation and if we were considering an open economy and government taxation, imports, which do not involve a direct demand for national output, and tax revenue would be leakages, or withdrawals as they are sometimes called, and would affect the multiplier. An increase of exports would be an injection in the same way as an increase of investment. However, we are not concerned with these complications here.

Retaining Keynes's simplifications we can show how the multiplier gives us the increment of income which will be associated with an increment of investment, expenditure on capital goods. The unit of measurement may be a money unit as assumed here, or a real unit such as Keynes's wage unit which is not considered here. Having taken a money unit, allowance must be made for any change in the general level of prices before the change in real output is obtained. Let ΔY, ΔC and ΔI stand for additional increments of income, consumption and investment.

We then have:

$$\Delta Y \quad = \quad \Delta C \quad + \quad \Delta I$$
$$(100 \text{ units}) = (80 \text{ units}) + (20 \text{ units})$$

If k = the multiplier, we have:

$$\Delta Y \quad = \quad k\Delta I$$
$$(100 \text{ units}) = (5 \times 20 \text{ units})$$

The marginal propensity to consume, c, is

$$\frac{\Delta C}{\Delta Y}\left(\frac{80}{100} = \frac{4}{5}\right)$$

and the marginal propensity to save, s, is

$$1 - \frac{\Delta C}{\Delta Y}\left(1 - \frac{4}{5} = \frac{1}{5}\right)$$

The multiplier k =

$$\frac{1}{1-c}\left(\frac{1}{1-4/5}\right) = \frac{1}{s} = \left(\frac{1}{1/5}\right) = 5.$$

Thus in this case, the multiplier is 5 and a net increase of investment of 20 units, say by additional private investment or government investment in the form of public works, gives an increase of income of 100 units. This is the investment multiplier. In the same way there is an employment multiplier which shows the relationship between an increase in employment resulting directly from the increase in investment and the associated total increase in employment.

Clearly, these multiplier relationships are very important although, as we shall see, they must be treated with care as they are not stable, particularly in the short run. In general, however, the concept that an increase in public or private investment will lead to an increase in income which is a multiple of the increased investment is very important for economic policy during depression. The government can increase its own public expenditure, for example on public works, such as roads, while maintaining the same level of taxation, thus involving a budgetary deficit, and/or stimulate private investment. Aggregate money demand and national income will be increased by an amount which will be greater, the greater the multiplier. Associated with the increased output of capital goods is an increase in the output of consumers' goods. Starting with general unemployment, the increase in primary employment in the capital goods industries will be associated with an increase in secondary employment in the consumption goods industries. The total increase in employment will be a multiple of the increase in primary employment and will be greater the greater the employment multiplier. On the assumption of general unemployment, the increased output of capital goods is associated with a complementary increase in the output of consumption goods. The government can also raise the level of income and employment by reducing taxation while maintaining public expenditure, involving a budgetary deficit. If the government increases the degree of equality of the distribution of income, it will raise the average propensity to consume, as it will transfer income from individuals who spend a smaller proportion of their incomes on consumption goods to individuals who spend a larger proportion. The average propensity to consume will be increased and the corresponding multiplier so that a given level of investment will be associated with a higher level of income.

Keynes made very important use of the multiplier both in *The General Theory* and in the various forms of publication preceding that book in which he advocated policies to deal with mass unemployment in the form of government fiscal policies. He did not, however, originate the multiplier principle which had been used in an informal way much earlier[111]. It was finally formulated precisely in Lord Kahn's classic article, 'The Relation of Home Investment to Unemployment', published in *The Economic Journal* (June, 1931). This formulation was of great help to Keynes although his multiplier was static while Kahn's was dynamic. As Keynes's model was basically one of comparative statics, he compared two static positions of the economy with a given multiplier but different rates of investment and therefore different levels of income and employment.

Robertson was very critical of Keynes's multiplier and the multiplier principle in general. He ends the section on the multiplier in his review article of *The General Theory* with the statement, 'it seems to be doubtful whether, for the analysis of a fluctuating world, the "multiplier" constitutes much advance over more crudely "monetary" weapons of thought'[112]. Robertson is critical of Keynes's analysis because the multiplier is static; this criticism merely follows from their different methodological approaches which have been discussed earlier in this chapter. Keynes, however, does at times depart from his basic comparative static method as has already been pointed out. He does so in the case of the multiplier when he considers a gradual expansion in the capital-goods industries over a period of time and subject to time-lags. This analysis includes a temporary departure of the marginal propensity to consume from its normal value, that is, a temporary change in the value of his multiplier during a process of economic change[113]. It is important to recognize when Keynes is departing from his basic comparative static model and the implications of such a departure.

Robertson's second criticism of Keynes's multiplier analysis is that it excludes the acceleration principle or accelerator. He points out that the increased expenditure on consumption goods will stimulate a further increase in investment as well as the initial increase in investment, causing an increase in consumption by the multiplier. As Robertson puts it, 'Dogs wag tails, as well as tails dogs.'[114] The acceleration principle states that a given percentage increase in the demand for and output of consumption goods will cause a larger percentage increase in the output of capital goods. This relationship, the capital-output ratio or accelerator, is related to the durability of capital goods but is subject to many qualifications such as no excess capacity[115]. The principle had for long played an important role in trade cycle theory and explained in part the greater instability in the output of capital goods compared with that of consumption goods. Haberler gives a long list of economists who have developed and made use of the acceleration principle, starting with Albert Aftalion, *Les Crises Périodiques De Surproduction* (Paris, 1913)[116]. It should be noted that some theorists substitute income or total output for consumption goods in the statement of the principle.

Robertson is perfectly correct in pointing to the limitations of Keynes's theory resulting from the exclusion of the acceleration principle. He was misleading, however, in not explaining that this omission followed logically from Keynes's adoption of the method of comparative statics. The acceleration principle is a dynamic principle and cannot be included in a static system. Thus, Robertson is again criticizing Keynes's static method and I have already shown that it suited Keynes's purpose and indeed that we still need this method in addition to other methods.

In one of the additional chapters included in the 1948 edition of *Money*, Robertson refers to the marginal propensity to save, which gives us the multiplier, as a 'potentially useful little brick, but not yet a very firm foundation for that imposing edifice of combined prosperity and stability which we should all like to build if only we knew how'[117]. He had earlier referred lightly to the little piece of algebra giving the multiplier, which was used as a magic carpet to waft us from one level of employment to a higher level. However, he rightly questioned the stability of the marginal propensity to save, the stability of the multiplier[118]. Much theoretical and empirical work has been done on the multiplier since the death of Keynes and this has completely justified Robertson's questioning. It has been shown that the multiplier depends on a considerable number of factors and that it is of great importance to make allowance for its instability. Further, it became clear that a number of different multipliers had to be distinguished. There is no doubt that Keynes oversimplified the multiplier. Wilson asks, 'But would Professor Robertson, for his part, be prepared to concede that the size of the marginal propensity to consume [the marginal propensity to save equals 1 minus the marginal propensity to consume], whether steady or not, is a critical factor – not merely "a potentially useful little brick" – and one which his own earlier models neglected?'[119]

For Robertson's answer to this question, one naturally turns to his treatment of the multiplier in his *Lectures* of 1956–1957. He gives an exposition of the dynamic multiplier and then writes that it seems 'to be quite a self-consistent little piece of apparatus, worth setting out, so to speak, under a glass case in order to get clear about its implications'. He then considers some of the complications which must be taken into account before applying the multiplier to the real world. Firstly, while the multiplier is working itself out over time, other things may change which will upset its operation. However, Robertson admits that this is a general difficulty in economic analysis. Secondly, 'the very processes depicted are almost certain to set in motion forces modifying their own operation'[120]. These difficulties are, of course, the result of Robertson's formulation of the multiplier in dynamic terms and do not arise in the case of Keynes's static multiplier. They are however, important difficulties and show the limitations of Keynes's static model and the care with which it must be used. Robertson distinguishes three cases of his second general complication[121].

(1) The increase in consumption is likely to stimulate a further increase in investment. This is the acceleration principle to which we have already referred. Many economists who have dynamized the Keynesian static system to develop theories of the trade cycle and of economic growth have combined the multiplier and the accelerator.
(2) The marginal propensity to consume (save), the multiplier, may change during the process of economic expansion caused by the initial increase in the rate of investment. Robertson gives examples of how this may occur as a result of a redistribution of income between entrepreneurs, the recipients of profits, and wage-earners.
(3) The increase in saving may itself lead to an increase in investment, expenditure on capital goods. Thus not all the additional saving is available to finance the initial increase in investment. This is a partial return to classical economics and a reversal of Keynes's causal sequence, a higher rate of investment on certain assumptions is associated with a higher rate of saving out of a higher level of income and is equal to the higher rate of investment. Robertson quotes the distinguished Polish economist, Mr Michal Kalecki, in his support[122].

The third complication which Robertson considers arises when the supply of consumption goods is not perfectly elastic which he regards as the normal case. Here the real multiplier is less than the money multiplier.

In pointing to these complications, Robertson is criticizing the '*simpliste* exposition of the theory of the multiplier, which, like so much of the rest of analysis of which it forms part, becomes a somewhat treacherous guide to policy once we leave conditions of extreme depression'[123]. This, by implication is a criticism of Keynes's *The General Theory*. Keynes's consumption function relates consumption to the level of current income and, in general, he assumes that the marginal propensity to consume (save), and so the multiplier, are stable. He does, however, recognize in Chapter 22, Notes on the Trade Cycle, that a serious fall in the marginal efficiency of capital, the expected rate of return on investment, reduces the propensity to consume and the multiplier. This is because the much less favourable outlook for profits causes a severe decline in the market values of stock exchange ordinary shares (equities) and an individual's consumption depends not only on his income but also on the amount of wealth he holds[124]. Keynes also recognized that the multiplier was affected by the way in which an increase in income is distributed among persons[125]. Robertson refers to the work undertaken by many economists of high ability to improve the multiplier as a tool of prediction after its serious failure in the United States in 1946. He points out that account is now taken of the effects on an individual's consumption out of a given level of income of his capital resources, especially his holdings of money and other fairly liquid assets. He refers to Professor Duesenberry's[126] emphasis on the importance of whether the individual's current income is his peak income or has fallen from a higher level and the importance of the behaviour of his income relatively to those of other people rather than being seen as absolute income. We may add Professor Milton Friedman's permanent income hypothesis, that consumption is related not to actual current income but to what is regarded as permanent or normal income[127]. A number of other variables has also been put forward[128]. Robertson concludes his discussion with the statement, 'But unless and until these various modifications can be effectively sorted and tested out, that concept [the multiplier] must remain, it seems to me, an extremely unreliable instrument for short-run or cyclical prediction.'[129] He was thus reluctant to accept the multiplier and did not incorporate it in his theoretical work. This seems inconsistent with the fact that he made use of the acceleration principle and the accelerator is by no means constant. Samuelson wrote in his obituary article of 1963 that he feared that Robertson 'was wrong in suggesting that the world could be the same after Richard Kahn's 1931 multiplier article, and that no useful empirical analysis could be made of $\delta C/\delta Y$ and the shifts in schedules of C as a function of Y'[130]. This is perhaps a little harsh but shows the impression Robertson had made on Samuelson.

Colin Clark has stated, 'Having been present at the birth of the multiplier, I should also like to be present at its funeral.'[131] He points out that Robertson was right in emphasizing the very great importance of time-lags in short-period analysis of consumption and investment although he did not formulate them. Clark hates to think of students still being taught the crude 1931 form of the multiplier which would have been very useful if applied during the deep depression of that time, 'but merely darkens counsel now'[132]. Clark states that its central defect, as Robertson suggested, is that it did not allow for time-lags and that they are so complex that no simple multiplier is permissible.

This extreme position of Clark's is not acceptable. No competent university teacher would put forward the simple multiplier without explaining it was a first approximation and giving a warning of its limitations. The complications of the multiplier do not arise only from time-lags but also from the number of possible variables to be taken into account. It has already been shown that much theoretical and empirical work has been done in this field since 1946. Different multipliers have been distinguished and a multiplier must be chosen according to the problem in hand. Econometric work has shown how unstable the multiplier can be in the short period. Like many other tools of economic theory, the multiplier must be used with care, but there is no case for its demise. It remains a very important relationship in post-Keynesian monetary macroeconomics.

Following the publication of Keynes's *General Theory*, there was unfortunately a protracted and confused controversy in the learned journals over the appropriate definitions of saving and investment and their implications. In his basic model, Keynes defined the equality of saving and investment as an identity, both equal to income minus consumption, $S \equiv I$. However, at times he referred to the equality of saving and investment, $S = I$, as an equilibrium condition. He argued that an increase in the rate of investment increased the level of income until saving, which was a function of income, was increased to match the higher rate of investment. An explicit example of this is to be found in Keynes's article, 'Alternative Theories of the Rate of Interest', in the June 1937 issue of *The Economic Journal*. He stated, 'The novelty in my treatment of saving and investment consists , not in my maintaining their necessary aggregate equality, but in the proposition that it is not the rate of interest, but the level of incomes which (in conjunction with certain other factors) ensures this equality.'[133] The controversy eventually led to a clarification of the issues, although there is still some confusion. In 1948, Robertson was quite right in criticizing some expositors of Keynesian theory, and presumably Keynes, for asserting that two quantities are by definition equal and then asserting that the establishment of equality between them is a condition of equilibrium[134]. He makes the same point in his *Lectures* of 1956–1957 when discussing the meaning of monetary equilibrium[135]. Samuelson in 1946 pointed out that Keynes's thinking remained fuzzy on this important analytical distinction throughout his life[136]. In 1963, Samuelson referred to Robertson having rightly pointed out this mistake[137].

Despite the justification of Robertson's criticism, Wilson in 1953 rightly asks whether he would 'not think it desirable to pay more attention than he formerly did to the effect on the volume of savings of variations in real national income – an effect which receives no more than a passing mention even in his remarkable essay of 1934?'[138] Wilson clearly thinks the answer should be in the affirmative and that Keynes deserved a slightly more sympathetic treatment than Robertson had given him. Indeed, it was a great achievement of Keynes, starting with the assumption of general unemployment of productive resources, to analyse the forces which would raise the economy to full employment level. The equality of saving and investment by definition in *The General Theory* obscured somewhat the fundamental point that an increase in investment could be matched by an increased amount of saving out of a higher level of income. This is a very important point for government economic policy during a period of mass unemployment. Investment can be increased, for example, by public works and the levels of employment and real national income raised. There is no need to worry about the source of the savings to finance the increased rate of investment.

The quantity theory of money in its primitive form stated that the general level of prices rose and fell in the same proportion as the quantity of money was increased or decreased. Keynes refers to this as the strict interpretation of the quantity theory[139]. While understandable in its context, the statement in general is very misleading. Fellner points out that the French political philosopher Jean Bodin (1530–1596), referring to the influx of South American gold and silver into Western Europe via Spain in the sixteenth century, stated that the increase in the quantity of monetary metal not only raised prices, the great inflation, but also led to increased consumption and production although monopolies were tending to restrict output[140]. Keynes referred to the quantity theory of money relating the total quantity of money to money income (final output during a given period of time multiplied by the general level of prices), taking into account the income-velocity of circulation (the rate at which money circulates against the constituents of final income during a given period of time) as a truism. It was said to hold in all circumstances although without significance[141]. Truisms and tautologies are very useful in economics and it is unfortunate that Keynes was so critical of the quantity theory which, in my view, he so greatly enriched in his Chapter 21, The Theory of Prices. It would have been a great advantage if he could have integrated such a quantity theory into his general theory.

Keynesian economists have perhaps been more critical than Keynes himself. Robertson, before discussing the quantity theory in terms of the so-called 'Cambridge monetary equation' in his *Lectures*, reminds his students of the passionate scorn of some modern writers aroused by the simple equation. He refers in particular to Mrs (now Professor) Joan Robinson's article of 1933[142], written after Keynes's *A Treatise on Money* (1930) and during the period when Keynes was developing his thought which led to *The General Theory*. Later, Robertson refers to Joan Robinson's witty comment 'We have been telling the equation what is happening, it has not been telling us.' In Robertson's view 'One of the attractive features of the Cambridge equation is precisely that which rouses Mrs Robinson's ire, namely its complete generality, so that we can use it to order our thoughts about a great number of different sequences of events, some of them starting at one point in the causal chain and some at another.'[143] Lord Kahn, another distinguished Keynesian economist, spoke disparagingly of the quantity theory in 1956. He referred to those who wished to avoid the awkward implications of credit restriction and dear money, high interest rates, as having 'recourse to some manifestation of what is called the quantity theory of money, the idea that inflation is the direct cause of expansion of credit rather than physically too much investment and consumption, no matter how brought about'[144]. There is no need for a quantity theorist to mislead himself or others when dealing with a restrictive monetary policy. Kahn said that the quantity theory mentality had become far less common, but that Keynes had been involved in continual controversies over the theory. He referred to the advice Keynes offered the editor of the *Financial News* in a letter published in 1940. 'If you are not too old, as to which I have no information, I strongly recommend an operation. By modern methods an inflamed Quantity Theory can be removed with much less danger than formerly.'[145] Harry Johnson stated that 'The Keynesian Revolution left the quantity theory thoroughly discredited on the grounds either that it was a mere tautology (the quantity equation), or that it "assumed full employment" and that the velocity factor it emphasized was in fact highly unstable.'[146] However, he points out that 'Keynes, unlike many of his followers, was prepared to concede that traditional quantity theory becomes relevant under full employment conditions.'[147]

Robertson gave an exposition of the quantity theory in his *Money*[148] and continued to use it throughout his life, giving a detailed discussion of it in his *Lectures*[149] of 1956–1957. The *quaesita* are values of money or general levels of prices, a fall in the value of money being the same thing as a rise in the general level of prices. There is no *the* value of money or *the* price level, the value of money depending on the goods and services which are considered as being purchased by a unit of money. Robertson distinguishes four main values of money, the transaction-value (its value in terms of all the things which are exchanged with its aid), the consumption-value (its value in terms of consumption goods and services), the income-value (its value in terms of the constituents of real income or output, consumption goods and services plus new capital goods) and the labour-value (its value in terms of the amount of labour of a given quality)[150].

Robertson explains the two approaches to the theory of the value of money, the velocity-of-circulation approach and the demand-to-hold approach, both of which can be formulated in terms of a given value of money, general level of prices, in relation to real income or output. The velocity-of-circulation approach, then considers the flow of money coming on to the market during a given period of time (the quantity of money multiplied by its average income-velocity of circulation) and the real income or output which it purchases during a given period. If M is the quantity of money, V is its income-velocity of circulation, R is the real national income for a given period of time, and P the income price-level, the quantity equation is

$$MV = PR$$

$$\therefore P \quad = \frac{MV}{R}$$

Thus the price level rises with an increase in M and/or V and falls with an increase in R. MV = PR is a truism in that it looks at the same thing, total money expenditure on real output, from two points of view. It is, however, a useful truism as it provides convenient heads under which to consider possible causes of changes in P, the general level of prices.

The definition of the quantity of money is a question of convenience and will partly depend on the existing institutional arrangements relating to the functions of 'money' as a generally acceptable medium of exchange and store of value. We are not here concerned with the other important function of money as a unit of account or *numéraire* in which the relative values of all goods and services and factors of production are expressed in terms of relative money prices. Money also acts as a unit of account over time, a standard for deferred payments, for example loans in terms of money and life assurance policies. In my article 'The Demand for Money', I discuss the problem of defining money and show that the definition must be somewhat arbitrary because of the difficulty of drawing a line between money and money substitutes[151]. The correctness of the analysis is not affected by the exclusion of a particular money substitute from the quantity of money as it will then be taken into account as affecting the velocity of circulation of money or the demand for money in the demand-to-hold approach. I finally define the quantity of money as the quantity of common money (coin and bank notes) and commercial bank deposits (current accounts and deposit accounts). Coin and bank notes held by the banks are excluded. This is the definition which both Keynes and Robertson find convenient. Overdraft facilities are not included in the quantity of money and are regarded as increasing its velocity of circulation or reducing the demand for it[152]. A difficult question is the extent to which the quantity of money is to be regarded as exogenous, controlled by the central monetary authority, and endogenous, determined by the economy's level of economic activity. This problem is discussed later[153].

In my day, as a student in the 1920s, V was not considered a constant but a useful heading under which a number of changes were considered. The distinction was made between changes in V which were independent of changes in M and P and those which were dependent on them. In the first category were included the frequency and regularity of wage payments, the distribution of personal income, the general economic outlook and the habits and customs of the public which gave one general cover! An improvement in the general economic outlook, an upswing in the trade cycle, would be associated with an increase in V. In the second category, V increased if the quantity of money and the price level rose and inflation was expected to continue. People were less inclined to hold money, an asset depreciating in real terms. Conversely, V decreased if the quantity of money and the price level fell and deflation was expected to continue.

R, real income or output, was also not assumed constant although the quantity theory has been criticized as involving this assumption. It was recognized that R increased owing to an increase in the amount of productive resources employed and/or an increase in their productivity because of technical progress.

The analysis of changes in the general level of prices in terms of the quantity theory has to allow for the interdependence of the variables. It is perfectly true that the simple equation is only an aid to the study of causal sequences.

The alternative approach, the demand-to-hold approach, is a stock approach or point-of-time approach; the velocity approach is a flow or period-of-time approach. There are advantages and disadvantages in the two approaches and both are needed[154]. They lead to approximately the same P and R. According to the demand-to-hold approach, the general level of prices, the value of money, depends on the supply of and demand for money at a point of time. The theory of the value of money is a special case of the general theory of value. For the simple equation, often referred to as the 'Cambridge monetary equation', one further symbol, K, is required. K is the proportion of R, real national income or output over a period of time, over which people wish to hold command in the form of money. The quantity equation is now

$$M = PKR$$

$$\therefore P = \frac{M}{KR}$$

The general price level depends on the supply of money and the demand for money which is shown to depend on K and R. V is approximately equal to 1/K; an increase in V corresponds to a decrease in K. Thus, all the factors we considered under the heading V are now considered under the heading K.

These two approaches to the theory of the value of money have a long history, the velocity-of-circulation approach being the more important until early in this century. The distinguished American economist, Irving Fisher, published *The Purchasing Power of Money* in 1911[155] in which he formulated the theory in terms of his famous equation $MV = PT$[156] which has had a wide international influence. I traced the demand-to-hold approach, in my article 'The Demand for Money', back to the work of Marshall in 1888, who later pointed out that the approach goes back to Sir William Petty in the seventeenth century[157].

Keynes argued that for the purposes of the real world 'it is a great fault in the quantity theory that it does not distinguish between changes in prices which are a function of changes in output, and those which are a function of changes in the wage-unit [the money-wage of a labour-unit]'[158]. He thought this omission was perhaps due to the assumptions that there is no propensity to hoard and that there is always full employment. As we have seen, quantity theorists like Robertson were concerned with changes in the velocity of circulation owing to changes in hoarding and did not assume full-employment output. The assumptions to which Keynes referred were only made by classical and neoclassical economists when developing abstract equilibrium theory. It should also be noted that Robertson and many other economists analysed monetary expansions and contractions in terms of the extent to which there were associated changes in output and changes in prices. This remains an important theoretical problem at the present time.

However, it is in these two related areas, the causes of changes in prices because of changes in output and because of changes in money-wages, and the extent to which changes in monetary expenditure are associated with changes in output and with changes in prices, that Keynes enriched the quantity theory. Keynes gives a fairly detailed analysis of the effect of an increase in the quantity of money on the general level of prices of total output[159]. The increase in effective demand associated with an increase in the quantity of money will depend on the behaviour of the income-velocity of circulation of money. Keynes considers that the income-velocity of money[160] is merely a name which explains nothing and that it cannot be assumed constant since it depends on many variable factors. He writes, 'The use of this term obscures, I think, the real character of the causation, and has led to nothing but confusion.'[161] It is clear that neither Robertson nor I would accept this point of view from what has been already discussed.

Keynes then makes the important point that supply price will increase as output from a given capital equipment and unchanged technique is increased because of diminishing returns. Thus both output and prices will rise even if there is no change in money-wages. This concept of the elasticity of the supply of output in general is followed by taking into account different elasticities for different commodities, so that 'bottle-necks' will be reached when outputs of commodities can no longer increase and only prices rise. A second reason for rising prices is the tendency for the wage-unit (money-wage) to rise before full employment[162] is reached because of trade union pressures. To allow for the fact that the money remunerations of the different factors of production entering into the marginal prime costs of production do not change in the same proportion, Keynes substitutes the cost-unit for the wage-unit[163].

Once full employment is reached and no further increases in output are possible, increases in effective demand cause proportionate increases in the cost-unit and the general level of prices. In some notes sent to Keynes by Harrod, 19 August 1935, Harrod confesses that he can make nothing of a state in which output is absolutely inelastic. Keynes's marginal comment on this is interesting, 'Quantity theory of money in full control.'[164] In Chapter 20, The Employment Function, which precedes Chapter 21, The Theory of Prices, Keynes also refers to the quantity theory. He states that when full employment has been reached the conditions of strict equilibrium require that 'Wages and prices, and consequently profits also, shall all rise in the same proportion as expenditure, the "real" position, including the volume of output and employment, being left unchanged in all respects.'[165] Keynes regards this situation as one in which 'the crude quantity theory of money'[166] is fully satisfied. However, he qualifies this conclusion by referring to entrepreneurs' errors and the redistribution of personal incomes[167]. Keynes's analysis was mainly in terms of the short period, but he added some historical generalizations for the long period[168].

It is clear from my discussion of the quantity theory that I agree with Robertson that 'the "ancient ceremony" of the Cambridge equation should be retained'[169]. Fellner is also right in suggesting that the problem of the price level is likely to stimulate interest in a proper synthesis of the saving-investment analysis with the quantity theory, a synthesis already present in the early work of Robertson[170].

Notes

1. Robertson, *Essays in Money and Interest*. Selected with a Memoir by Sir John Hicks (1966), p. 11.
2. Both published in 1973.
3. *See* p. 11.
4. *CW*, Vol. XIV (1973), p. 94.
5. *See* pp. 8–11.
6. Robertson (1966), p. 15.
7. Patinkin (1976a), *Keynes' Monetary Thought*, pp. 30–31 and note 6.
8. Johnson (1975), *On Economics and Society*, p. 114.
9. *Ibid*.
10. *Ibid*., p. 116.
11. *C.W.*, Vol. V (1930, 1971), p. XXVII.
12. *C.W.*, Vol. XIII (1973), p. 172.
13. *C.W.*, Vol. IV (1923, 1971).
14. *C.W.*, Vol. XIII (1923), p. 338.
15. Moggridge, *ibid*., p. 343.
16. Patinkin (1976a), p. 61.
17. London school of Economics: London, 1948.
18. Robertson, *Lectures on Economic Principles* (1963a), p. 325.
19. *Ibid*., p. 326.
20. S. R. Dennison, *International Encylopaedia of the Social Sciences* (1968), p. 531.
21. Joseph E. Stiglitz, ed., *The Collected Scientific Papers of Paul A. Samuelson*, Vol. ii (1966), p. 1596.
22. John Hicks, 'Recollections and Documents', *Eca* (February 1973), reprinted in John Hicks, *Economic Perspectives* (1977), p. 143, p. 11.
23. *C.W.*, Vol. XIV (1973), p. 259.
24. *C.W.*, Vol. XIII (1973), p. 500.
25. *See* p. 30.
26. *C.W.*, Vol. XIII (1973), p. 506.
27. *Ibid*., letters on pp. 520, 522 and 523.
28. *C.W.*, Vol. XIV (1973), p. 89.
29. *Ibid*., p. 94.
30. *Ibid*., pp. 94–95.
31. *Ibid*., pp. 95–96.
32. T. Wilson, 'Professor Robertson on Effective Demand and the Trade Cycle', *E J.* (September 1953), p. 570.
33. Robertson (1966), p. 17.

34. Skidelsky, ed. (1977), *The End of the Keynesian Era, Essays on the Disintegration of the Keynesian Political Economy*, Chapter 2, 'Keynes and Cambridge', by John Vaizey, p. 14.
35. Wilson (1953), p. 553.
36. Samuelson (1963a) in Stiglitz (1966), p. 1596.
37. *CW*, Vol. XIV (1973), p. 95. I deal with Hicks's and Harrod's attitudes to the Keynesian Revolution on pp. 30, 159. The reference to Hicks's review article is to that in *Economic Journal* (June 1936). Harrod's paper was published in *Econometrica* (January 1937).
38. E. A. G. Robinson (1946) in Lekachman (1964).
39. *Ibid.*, p. 59.
40. *Ibid.*, p. 87.
41. Samuelson (1963a) in Stiglitz (1966), p. 1612.
42. Robertson (1966), pp. 9–22.
43. William Fellner, 'The Robertsonian Evolution', *American Economic Review* (1952), pp. 267–268.
44. Dennison (1968), p. 531.
45. *C.W.*, Vol. VII (1936, 1973), p. 47, n.1.
46. Joseph A. Schumpeter, *History of Economic Analysis* (1954), p. 1184, n.28.
47. *C.W.*, Vol. VII, p. 48.
48. *Ibid.*, pp. 287–288.
49. *Ibid.*, p. 48, n.1.
50. 1st edn, 1922. The 4th edn, 1948, to which all references are made is the 1928 edition with minor changes and two additional chapters.
51. *Economica* (June 1928), reprinted in Robertson (1966).
52. *Essays in International Finance*, No. 42, May 1963 (Princeton).
53. Robertson (1915/48), p. xvi.
54. Page XI.
55. Dennison (1968), p. 531.
56. Page 59.
57. *Economic Journal* (September 1933), reprinted in Robertson (1966), p. 47.
58. 'Industrial Fluctuation and the Natural Rate of Interest', *Economic Journal* (December 1934), reprinted in Robertson (1966), p. 64.
59. Hansen, *A Guide to Keynes* (1953), pp. 61, 62). Hansen points out correctly that Keynes stated Robertson's definition in an awkward manner on p. 78 of *The General Theory* but he makes Keynes appear more critical of Robertson than I think he was in this passage.
60. *Ibid.*, p. 62. Robertson's article in which he did this appeared in the *Quarterly Journal of Economics* (November 1936) as 'Some Notes on Mr Keynes' General theory of Employment'.
61. Robertson (1933).
62. Hansen (1953), p. 64.
63. Samuelson (1963a) in Staglitz (1966), p. 1594.
64. *Ibid.*, p. 1601.
65. *Ibid.*
66. Robertson (1966), p. 141. This reference is to the reprint of part of his *Quarterly Journal of Economics* (November 1936) article.
67. Fellner (1952), p. 269.
68. Robertson, *Growth, Wages, Money*, The Marshall Lectures for 1960 (1961), pp. 5–11.
69. *Ibid.*, pp. 11–31.
70. Robertson (1963a), p. 418. The book referred to is J. R. Hicks, *A Contribution to the Theory of Trade Cycle* (1950).
71. *Ibid.*
72. Pages XVI–XVII.
73. J. R. Hicks, *Economic Perspectives* (1977), pp. 180–181.
74. Clark, *Taxmanship* (1970), p. 54.
75. *See* p. 27.
76. R. F. Harrod, *Towards a Dynamic Economics* (1948).
77. Page IX.
78. A reference to A. C. Pigou, *Industrial Fluctuations* (1st edn, 1927; 2nd edn, 1929).
79. Robertson (1949), p. XIII.
80. *See* Ludwig von Mises, *The Theory of Money and Credit*, English translation (London, 1934).
81. *See* pp. 90–91.

82. *A Study of Industrial Fluctuation.*
83. *See also ibid.*, p. XV.
84. Robertson (1966).
85. Robertson (1963a).
86. Robertson (1966).
87. Robertson (1961).
88. Robertson (1963b).
89. 1948 New Introduction, p. XII.
90. *Ibid.*, p. XIII.
91. Pages 90–91.
92. *See* F. A. Hayek's *Q.J.E.* article, 'A Note on the Development of the Doctrine of "Forced Saving"' (November 1932), reprinted in Friedrich A. Hayek, *Profits, Interest and Investment* (1939).
93. *CW*, Vol. VII (1936, 1973), pp. 79–81.
94. Robertson (1963a), pp. 412–415.
95. *Ibid.*, p. 414.
96. The English translation is *The Theory of Economic Development* (Cambridge, Mass., 1934).
97. Robertson (1963a), p. 360.
98. *Ibid.*
99. *Ibid.*, p. 361.
100. Robertson (1948), p. XV.
101. Robertson (1963a), p. 366.
102. Robertson (1949), p. 46.
103. *Ibid.*, pp. XII–XIII.
104. Robertson, *Money* (1948), p. 95.
105. *CW*, Vol. VII (1936, 1973), p. 174.
106. Lerner (1963) in Lekachman (1964), p. 212.
107. Wilson (1953), p. 557. The reference is to editor Howard S. Ellis, *A Survey of Contemporary Economics* (1948), Chapter 9, 'Monetary Theory' by Henry H. Villard.
108. Wilson (1953). The reference is to Robertson, *Essays in Monetary Theory* (London, 1940), p. 17).
109. *Ibid.*, p. 558.
110. *C.W.*, Vol. VII (1936, 1973), p. 174.
111. *See* A. L. Wright, 'The Genesis of the Multiplier Theory', *Oxford Economic Papers* (June 1956).
112. Robertson (1936), a section reprinted in Robertson (1966), p. 145.
113. *C.W.*, Vol. VII (1936, 1973), pp. 122–125.
114. Robertson (1966), p. 144.
115. One of the best accounts of the acceleration principle is in Gottfried von Haberler, *Prosperity and Depression* (1958; *see* in particular, pp. 85–105, 308–309, 486–491).
116. *Ibid.*, p. 87.
117. Page 212.
118. *Ibid.*, p. 211.
119. Wilson (1953), p. 576.
120. Robertson (1963a), p. 420.
121. *Ibid.*, pp. 420–422.
122. *Ibid.*, pp. 421–422. Robertson quotes from M. Kalecki, 'A New Approach to the Problem of Business Cycles', *Review of Economic Studies* (1949–1950).
123. *Ibid.*, p. 423.
124. *C.W.*, Vol. VII (1936, 1923), p. 319.
125. *Ibid.*, p. 299.
126. J. S. Duesenberry, *Income, Saving and the Theory of Consumer Behaviour* (1949).
127. M. Friedman, *A Theory of the Consumption Function* (New York, 1957).
128. For very useful surveys of the theoretical and econometric work done in this field, *see* R. A. Gordon, *Business Fluctuations* (1961) and Thomas F. Dernburg and Duncan M. McDougall, *Macroeconomics* (1972), pp. 111–119).
129. Robertson (1963a), p. 425.
130. Samuelson (1963a) in Stiglitz (1966), p. 1600.
131. Clark (1970), p. 54.
132. *Ibid.*
133. *CW*, Vol. XIV (1973), p. 211.

134. Robertson *Money* (1948), p. 209.
135. Robertson (1963a), p. 353.
136. Samuelson (1946) in Lekachman (1964), p. 327. Dennison (1968) makes the same point, p. 531.
137. Samuelson (1963a) in Stiglitz (1966), p. 1600.
138. Wilson (1953), p. 56–58. The reference to the 1934 essay is to his *Economic Journal* (December 1934) article, 'Industrial Fluctuation and the Natural Rate of Interest', reprinted in Robertson (1948a).
139. *C.W.*, Vol. XIV (1973), p. 106. The point is made in his contribution, The Theory of the Rate of Interest, to *The Lessons of Monetary Experience: Essays in Honour of Irving Fisher* (1937).
140. William Fellner, *Modern Economic Analysis* (1960), pp. 38–39.
141. *C.W.*, Vol. VII (1936, 1973), p. 209 and footnote 1. It should be noted that Keynes divided the total quantity of money (M) into M_1 (held for the transactions . . . and precautionary motives) and M_2 (held for the speculative motive, discussed in his Chapter 13). He relates M_1 to the level of income, taking the appropriate V. Robertson (1963a), p. 334, gives reasons why he takes M and what is the equivalent of the appropriate V.
142. Robertson (1963a), p. 327. Mrs Joan Robinson's article appeared in *Review of Economic Studies* (1933–1934) entitled 'The Theory of Money and Analysis of Output', reprinted in Joan Robinson, *Collected Economic Papers*, Vol. 1 (Oxford, 1951).
143. Robertson (1963a), p. 345.
144. Richard Kahn, *Selected Essays on Employment and Growth* (1972), p. 109. The quotation is from Lord Keynes and Contemporary Economic Problems, two radio talks on the B.B.C., 3 and 10 May 1956.
145. *Ibid.*, p. 110.
146. David R. Croome and Harry G. Johnson, eds, *Money in Britain 1959–1969* (1970), p. 85.
147. Harry G. Johnson, 'The General Theory after Twenty-five Years', *American Economic Review* (May 1961), reprinted in Johnson, *Money, Trade and Economic Growth* (2nd edn, 1964), p. 143.
148. Robertson (1948), pp. 27–40 and 180.
149. Robertson (1963a), pp. 325–346.
150. Robertson (1948), p. 18. *See also* Book II of J. M. Keynes, *A Treatise on Money* (1930), *C.W.*, Vol. V (1930, 1971).
151. J. C. Gilbert, 'The Demand for Money: The Development of an Economic Concept', *Journal of Political Economy* (April 1953), p. 148.
152. *See* Keynes, *C.W.*, Vol. VII (1936, 1973), p. 196 and Robertson (1963a), p. 329.
153. *See* pp. 124–127.
154. *See* Gilbert (1953), pp. 144–145 and Robertson (1963a), p. 335.
155. New York, 1st edn.
156. V is the average velocity of circulation of money against real transactions during a given period of time; P, the transactions price level; and T, the real volume of transactions during the given period.
157. Gilbert (1953), p. 145.
158. *C.W.*, Vol. VII (1936, 1973), p. 209. The wage-unit is defined on p. 41.
159. *Ibid.*, pp. 295–306.
160. *Ibid.*, p. 299. There is a complication arising from the distinction between expected and realised income.
161. *Ibid.*
162. A precise definition of full employment raises difficulties.
163. *C.W.*, Vol. VII (1936, 1973), p. 302. For the concept of marginal prime cost, *see* pp. 66–69.
164. *C.W.*, Vol. XIII (1973), p. 543.
165. *C.W.*, Vol. VII (1936, 1973), p. 289.
166. *Ibid.*
167. *Ibid.*, pp. 290–291.
168. *Ibid.*, pp. 306–309.
169. Robertson (1963a), p. 346.
170. Fellner (1952), p. 282. The reader's attention is drawn to the renewed interest in Robertson's work as shown by the work of Thomas Wilson (1980), Danes (1979) and Presley (1979).

Chapter 6

Some Keynesian critics: H. G. Johnson, F. A. von Hayek, W. H. Hutt

Professor Harry G. Johnson has argued in effect that there was no need for the Keynesian Revolution. In 1958[1] he was quite happy to talk about the Keynesian Revolution. He writes, 'The essence of the Keynesian revolution was to shift the subject-matter of monetary theory, placing the emphasis on the level of employment as the central subject of monetary theory and posing the determination of the rate of interest as a specifically monetary problem.'[2] Johnson concludes the article with a general evaluation of the Keynesian Revolution which as a theory of employment and inflation, he regards as 'a great and pervasive advance, the essence of which is to look at the relations between aggregate demand for and availability of resources, rather than the quantity of money'[3]. In monetary theory, the main contribution is considered to be the treatment of money as an asset, alternative to other assets, and the breaking of the quantity-theory assumption of a direct connection between money quantity and aggregate demand. At this time, Johnson thus accepted the Keynesian Revolution and was not a monetarist although he does refer to Keynes tending 'to play down the influence of monetary conditions, which may at times be very important'[4]. In 1961[5] Johnson was still happily referring to the Keynesian Revolution, although now recognizing the importance of Milton Friedman's work on the quantity theory of money.

Johnson in his Richard T. Ely Lecture in 1970, 'The Keynesian Revolution and the Monetarist Counter-Revolution'[6], refers to the Smithian revolution, the Ricardian revolution and the marginalist revolution of the 1970s which constituted the neoclassical economics. He regards contemporary economics as being based on this development and on at least four 'revolutions' which occurred in the late 1920s and in the 1930s, the imperfect/monopolistic competition revolution, the empirical or econometric revolution, the general equilibrium revolution resulting from the introduction here by Hicks and Allen of the Walrasian–Paretoan system (the Lausanne School) to replace, or, we may say, to provide a complementary approach to, the Marshallian partial-equilibrium system. Referring to the fourth of these revolutions, Johnson writes, 'Finally, and most sweeping in its effects, there was the Keynesian revolution in monetary theory.'[7] Johnson's criteria for identifying revolutions and counter-revolutions and distinguishing them from the gradual evolution of economic thought are the relative speed of change and the degree to which the speed is justifiable. On one or both of these grounds he regards most of the revolutions already mentioned as not being really revolutionary and he is left with three real intellectual revolutions, the Ricardian, the Keynesian and the monetarist counter-revolution.

Johnson distinguishes two elements which were responsible for the rapid acceptance of *The General Theory* by professional economists – the objective social situation at the time and the scientific characteristics of the new theory. The first of these was described as the prevailing orthodoxy not being able to explain or cope with the mass unemployment in Britain of the 1920s and 1930s. It is at this point that we may note the change in Johnson's thought to the idea that the Keynesian Revolution was unnecessary. As far as the 1920s are concerned, Johnson emphasizes that the mass unemployment was associated with industrial senescence and an over-valued foreign exchange rate. As far as the 1930s are concerned, he attributes Britain's and the industrial world's unemployment problems to monetary mismanagement. In Johnson's view, it was the economists who were at fault as there already existed monetary analysis of which they did not make proper use. This is, of course, a monetarist view which would not be accepted in its entirety by many economists. The scientific characteristics of the new theory to which Johnson attributes its quick success are also discussed[1], but are not relevant here. The rejection of the Keynesian Revolution, Johnson thinks, is due in an important way to the conviction of most Keynesians that the mass unemployment of the 1930s is the normal state of capitalist society and Keynesian management is required to deal with this most urgent social problem, while Keynes's critics do not accept this. The essence of the Keynesian Revolution does not depend on the concept of economic stagnation, although the problem of mass unemployment is of the greatest importance. Johnson ends his article on a note less critical of Keynes, recognizes the weaknesses of the monetarist counter-revolution and approves of the attempts of some monetarists to bring about a synthesis[9].

In a talk given in February 1973, 'Cambridge in the 1950s'[10], Johnson criticizes Joan Robinson's effort and that of many of her disciples to prove that private capitalism cannot work. He refers to the fact that 'by and large, the world has enjoyed full employment and fairly successful capitalism for about a quarter of the post-war century and that, that being so, the fact that Britain had mass unemployment for twenty years and the rest of the world for about eight years in the inter-War period is not really a very great violation of the long run of historical experience'[11]. Without accepting much of Professor Joan Robinson's 'economic philosophy', it should be pointed out here that once again Johnson is tending to underrate the importance of mass unemployment as a serious defect of private capitalism. Keynes developed his theory and policies so that private capitalism could survive. Admittedly, Johnson would have argued that private capitalism will work at a high level of employment if the growth of the money supply is controlled as required by the monetarists.

In 1975 in Keynes and British Economics[12], Johnson takes a definite and highly critical view of the Keynesian Revolution. He states 'no "Keynesian

Revolution" was really necessary (what was necessary, however, was for economists to apply the economics they had)'. He goes on to explain 'why a Keynesian Revolution nevertheless occurred (and may indeed have been necessary after all, given the inability or refusal of economists to apply the tools of their trade to their society's most pressing social and economic problem)'[13]. Johnson points out that the mass unemployment in Great Britain in the 1920s, far more than the mass unemployment of The Great Depression which hit many countries after 1929, was the origin of Keynes's concern with unemployment theory and policy. The unemployment in the 1920s in Great Britain was due firstly to her gradual loss of her nineteenth century industrial supremacy, which began possibly in the 1870s, and secondly to the return to the gold standard in 1925 at an overvalued foreign exchange rate which reduced British exports and necessitated a restrictive monetary policy. Johnson writes 'Had the exchange value of the pound been fixed realistically in the 1920s – a prescription fully in accord with orthodox economic theory – there would have been no need for mass unemployment, hence no need for a revolutionary new theory to explain it.'[14] With regard to the universal mass unemployment in the capitalist world after 1929, Johnson's view is that this was due to inappropriate national and international management. He takes the monetarist view that the deepest and most prolonged depression of all time was due to the failure of the United States monetary authorities. Johnson argues that 'Keynes's *The General Theory* distracted attention from all this background – which fits without trouble into the orthodox tradition of economic theory, unless one rejects a great deal of work on the trade cycle as not belonging to that theory . . .'.

According to Johnson *The General Theory* was not needed. His view is that the Great Depression could have been nipped in the bud if the policy-makers of the 1930s had understood the required policies and applied them or the economists had understood the position, by developing existing monetary theory, and explained it effectively to the policy-makers. It should be noted that 'Keynesian' policies had been advocated by Keynes and many other economists since the late 1920s, well before *The General Theory* of 1936. While most economists would agree that the overvalued foreign exchange rate of 1925 and the inappropriate industrial structure were important causes of unemployment in the United Kingdom in the 1920s and that the Great Depression was allowed to develop without governments adopting appropriate policies, Keynesian and many economists who would not describe themselves as strictly Keynesian would not agree with Johnson. His view reflects, of course, the influence of Milton Friedman and the monetarist school. As will be shown later in this chapter, *The General Theory*, the Keynesian Revolution, was required to provide a model of the economy in which the main determinant of the levels of employment and income was effective demand, the aggregate money demand for goods and services. Many of Keynes's policy prescriptions were not new, but he improved their rational foundation and he brought about a change in the attitude of governments to their responsibilities in the field of employment policy. Despite this critical approach to the Keynesian Revolution, Johnson recognizes that *The General Theory* is one of the few classics in the history of economic thought. In his view, Keynes's main contribution to theoretical economics was the application of capital theory to the theory of the demand for money, money held being one of the capital assets held by the individual, and the emphasis on quantity adjustments, such as changes in the amounts of output and labour employed, as well as price changes, to changes in aggregate money demand[15]. On the other hand, Johnson thinks it is difficult to avoid the conclusion 'that Britain has paid a heavy long-run price for the transient glory of the Keynesian Revolution . . .'[16]. He believes that it has led to the corruption of standards of scientific work in economics[17] and an overemphasis of the advantages of a very high level of employment without due regard to the effects of this on inflation, balance-of-payments problems, economic efficiency and economic growth.

In Johnson's last article on this subject written at the time of the 200th anniversary of The American Revolution or The War of Independence[18], he stresses that *The General Theory*, although interpreted as a revolution, was basically a struggle for independence of thought. Keynes himself had stated in the Preface to *The General Theory* that the book for him had been 'a long struggle of escape, . . . The difficulty lies, not in the new ideas, but in escaping from the old ones . . .'[19]. However, Keynes's idea of a struggle of escape from traditional ideas is consistent with the concept of a Keynesian Revolution as I have conceived it and, as has been stated, Keynes viewed his work as revolutionizing economics.

I have been critical of Johnson's assessment of Keynes's *The General Theory* with regard to the concept of the Keynesian Revolution, an assessment which is influenced by his monetarist view. At the same time it must be acknowledged that Johnson's work has thrown a great deal of light on Keynesian economics and the monetary controversies of the post-World War II period. His untimely death in 1977 was a great loss to economics. As a creative thinker, lucid expositor and stimulator of young and not so young economists, he made a distinguished contribution to the progress of economic science.

Professor F. A. von Hayek has been a severe critic of Keynes's *The General Theory*, although when dealing with the post-World War II inflation his criticisms tend to be directed against Keynes's followers rather than Keynes, who, he says, would not have approved of certain policies. The Keynesian model itself is, however, regarded as having had a disastrous effect on the development of economic theory. Keynes, as we have seen, referred to his struggle to escape from traditional ideas, I had a struggle to escape from the Austrian monetary over-investment theory of the trade cycle as developed by von Mises and Hayek on the basis of the works of the Austrian economists, Menger and Böhm-Bawerk, and the Swedish economist Wicksell. I was under the influence of Hayek at The London School of Economics during the academic year of 1930/1931 and well remember friendly controversy with him over cups of tea although I went too far in the acceptance of his basic theory.

In simple terms, Hayek's explanation of trade-cyclical depression was in terms of a fundamental maladjustment in the economy resulting from over-investment during the boom. The rate of investment at the top of the boom was too high in relation to the rate of saving without a continuance of inflation. Sooner or later, and the later the greater the maladjustment, the rate of investment would have to fall and this would cause general unemployment, particularly in the industries producing capital goods[20]. Keynes's explanation of trade-cyclical depression was diametrically opposed to that of Hayek. His view was that the rate of investment fell because of an exhaustion of investment opportunities, the expected rate of return on capital goods falling relatively to the rate of interest. The fall in the rate of return caused unemployment in the capital goods industries, thus causing a fall in incomes and consumption which created further unemployment in the consumption goods industries. Whether a cyclical depression is due to over-investment in Hayek's sense or under-investment in Keynes's sense, or for some other reason, can only be determined by empirical research. It might well be shown that there have been depressions which could be explained on Hayekian lines, but it is probable that the most frequent explanation would be found to be on Keynesian lines, if we simplify the situation for the moment by considering only these two possibilities. As I point out, 'Even if it were shown that depressions were almost always due to under-investment, Hayek would still have analysed an important limiting case.'[21]

Hayek in *Prices and Production* began with the assumption of full employment of productive resources although in later work he did make the initial assumption of general unemployment. Keynes on the other hand, in his work leading up to *The General Theory* made the initial assumption of general unemployment. Hayek overemphasized the possibilities of malinvestment, while Keynes's neglect of these possibilities was much less serious. Hayek's diagnosis of the Great Depression of 1929–1932 in terms of his theory was wrong as were the policies he advocated on this basis. This would be recognized by most economists. His main cure was a cut in expenditure including public expenditure to reduce the adjustment to be made because of investment having run ahead of voluntary saving. Hutchison refers to a letter in *The Times*, 17 October 1932, when unemployment was over 20 per cent, signed by Keynes, Professors Pigou and Macgregor, Sir Walter Layton, Sir Arthur Salter and Sir Josiah Stamp, which attacked the 'orthodox' maxims of saving and economy, private and public in conditions of deep depression. Two days later, in *The Times*, 19 October 1932, a letter in reply appeared signed by Professors Gregory, von Hayek, Plant and Robbins, all at The London School of Economics. This letter in particular criticized the method of increased government borrowing and spending as a method of promoting economic revival[22].

Lord Robbins frankly acknowledges that he was wrong in opposing increased public expenditure as a policy for combating the depression both before and after we left the gold standard in September 1931 which had involved too high a foreign exchange rate. He points out that he was not a deflationist, that he had never believed in a deliberate contraction of public and private expenditure, but 'I was certainly an anti-expansionist where public expenditure was concerned, at a time when, as I now think, I should have been on the other side.[23] Robbins attributes his mistaken views at the time of the World Depression to his having been unduly influenced by the Austrian or Viennese School of Mises and Hayek. While still thinking there is much in this theory as an explanation of some booms and depressions, Robbins now considers it was misleading as applied to the 1930s. One admires his academic honesty when he writes, 'I shall always regard this aspect of my dispute with Keynes as the greatest mistake of my professional career, and the book, *The Great Depression*, which I subsequently wrote, partly in justification of this attitude, as something which I would willingly see forgotten.'[24]

Government policy was in line with Keynes's policies of monetary expansion by means of low interest rates and increasing expenditure as far as a cheap money policy was adopted, the first step being taken in 1932. The Keynesian policy of budgetary deficit financing, increasing government expenditure and/or reducing government taxation, was not adopted as a policy for economic recovery in the 1930s[25].

In the early 1930s Keynes and Hayek produced rival theories which led to much controversy. As the years passed, Keynesian theory came to dominate and Hayekian theory came into disrepute amongst academic economists, with a few exceptions. The dominance of Keynesian theory was partly due to certain logical errors being shown up in Hayek's theory and partly due to its misleading character at a time of deep and prolonged depression. As Hicks has stated, 'It is in its application to deflationary slumps that the Hayek theory is at its worst; and it is a terrible fact that it was in just such conditions – in 1931/1932 – that it was first propounded. In such conditions its diagnosis was wrong; and its prescriptions could not have been worse.'[26] The dominance of Keynesian theory is reflected in Susan Howson's book on domestic monetary management in Great Britain during the period 1919 to 1938. Her bibliography includes seven publications of Keynes and none of Hayek. Professor Erich Streissler, a Viennese economist, points out that Hayek's tragic mistake was that he thought his theory was applicable to the violent disequilibrium of the 1930s and was an indication of the appropriate policies for such a depression. He refers to Keynes having gained 'an intellectual victory among economists of a completeness rare in our discipline'[27], which is attributed to his very short-term analysis and focus on depression.

However, in recent years there has been a revival in the work of Hayek as a theoretical economist. Perhaps I may refer to the fact that in a paper read to the Economics Section of the British Association at Liverpool as long ago as 1953, I attempted to rehabilitate Hayek's trade cycle theory[28]. I recognized the incompleteness and, in places, the logical errors in Hayek's work, but I maintained that it had been unduly neglected. I wrote 'It seems clear that a synthesis of Austrian and Keynesian theory would be a step in the right direction. The neglect of Hayek's work is unfortunate as in some ways it was nearer to dynamic economics than that of Keynes. Further, Hayek's particular emphasis on the immobility of labour and the heterogeneity of capital goods is of vital importance in certain contexts. There is a danger in thinking too much in terms of aggregates.'[29]

The revival of interest in Hayek's work is shown in Hicks's The Hayek Story to which reference has already been made. Although published in 1967 in *Critical Essays in Monetary Theory*, Hicks states in the Preface that he decided a couple of years earlier to write the article. After correspondence with Hayek, he rewrote the article, which he says remains something of an indictment[30]. However, Hicks acknowledges Hayek's contribution as well as subjecting Hayek's theory to severe criticism. Having referred to the diagnosis and policies during the Great Depression of the 1930s, based on Hayek's theory, as being wrong[31], Hicks writes, 'But because it was wrong then, it does not follow that it must always be wrong. It is possible that there may be conditions to which it is appropriate; and in these days (in 1967) one may not have to look very far before one finds them.' Hicks is referring here to the possibility of the Hayek 'slump'[32]. Unemployment develops, once inflation is not allowed to continue, and the economy's dislocation resulting from an attempted expansion greater than was feasible involves a reallocation of productive resources. Hicks does not quite say this but it is how I interpret the situation. He points out that the Keynesian prescription is as irrelevant as Hayek's was in 1931 to such conditions[33]. The Keynesian prescription referred to here is, of course, the packet of expansionary policies in the case of mass unemployment. Keynes was well aware of causes of unemployment other than a deficiency of aggregate money demand and of the importance of an appropriate allocation of productive resources. Hutchison quotes from an article in *The Times* of 12 January 1937, How to Avoid a Slump, by Keynes. He wrote at that time, 'I believe that we are approaching, or have reached, the point where there is not much advantage in applying a further general stimulus at the centre . . . It follows that the later stages of recovery require a different technique . . . We are in more need today of a rightly distributed demand than of a greater aggregate demand . . .'[34]

Streissler writing in 1969 considers the view that Hayek's work in economic theory in the 1930s and early 1940s 'only led to a gigantic intellectual blind alley; and that in the struggle for the survival of the fittest in economic doctrines Keynesian macro-economic thought has totally eliminated and replaced the reptilian monsters springing from the pen of (Hayek) . . .'[35] to be both unjust and wrong. Streissler discusses the interpretation of Hayek's work on trade cycle and capital theory in terms of economic growth theory, relates it to the main current theories of growth and considers those ideas of Hayek which could usefully be applied to the development of present growth theory.

In recent years, Hayek has returned to the discussion of monetary and employment theory and policy. He has blamed himself for having given up the struggle against Keynesian theories. This was partly due to Keynes having told him that he had changed his mind and no longer believed what he said in *A Treatise on Money* (1930) after Hayek had spent much time and energy criticizing the theoretical framework. This criticism appeared in the form of a long review article in two parts[36] and it was only after the appearance of the second part that Keynes told him this. Thus Hayek came to feel that it was useless to return to the charge because of the likelihood that Keynes would change his views again[37]. This attitude is difficult to understand but Hayek says this is one of the reasons why he did not return to the attack on the publication of *The General Theory*. Hayek feared that before he had completed his critical analysis, Keynes would again have changed his mind[38]. When *The General Theory* became accepted by most professional economists and some of his colleagues whom he most respected supported what Hayek calls the wholly Keynesian Bretton Woods agreement, he largely withdrew from the debate. The reason Hayek gives was 'to proclaim my dissent from the near-unanimous views of the orthodox phalanx would merely have deprived me of a hearing on other matters about which I was more concerned at the time'[39]. It was during this period that Hayek made important contributions to social philosophy. It remains unfortunate, however, that he did not develop his monetary and employment theory, perhaps along the lines I indicated in my 1953 British Association paper. He could have made a valuable contribution by taking into account the work of Keynes and other contemporary economists in the development of his own theory.

There is a return to the struggle by Hayek in 1966 in an article, 'Personal Recollections of Keynes and the "Keynesian Revolution"'[40]. Hayek says that in 1936, although Keynes had called his theory a 'general' theory, he regarded it as just another tract for the times and the result of Keynes's thought on the immediate policies required. At the time Hayek felt dimly, but in retrospect he feels decisively, that his disagreement with The General Theory referred to the general approach, which is now called macroanalysis. Hayek writes, 'I feel now that in a long-run perspective the chief significance of The General Theory will appear that more than any other single work it decisively furthered the ascendancy of macro-economics and the temporary decline of microeconomic theory.'[41] He regards this development as fundamentally mistaken. Professor L. M. Lachmann, a supporter of Hayek, is highly critical of macroeconomics, as it has developed, because of its neglect of the micro-foundations. It is held to be seriously deficient theoretically and this has led to the advocacy of incorrect policies[42]. Hayek emphasizes the narrowness of Keynes's knowledge of economics which was mainly Marshallian. He points out that he developed his own theories without being a highly trained economist, knowing little of what had been achieved by Walras, Pareto, the Austrians and the Swedes. This limitation of Keynes led to his misrepresentation of the classical and neoclassical economists as we have seen in Chapter 5. However, one cannot but be greatly impressed by the brilliant work which Keynes achieved in economics both with the equipment at his disposal and by the forging of a few new tools of analysis.

Keynes is criticized by Hayek for thinking in terms of a few 'measurable' aggregates such as total demand, investment and output and believing that there exist relatively simple and constant functional relationships between them. Hayek stresses that we cannot assume that these functional relationships are constant and that microtheory had shown long before Keynes that they will change over time. These relationships depend on the microeconomic structure, especially on relative prices. Hayek argues that they may change rapidly because of changes in the microeconomic structure and the assumption of their constancy will give misleading conclusions[43]. Keynes was right to create a simple model with a few aggregates to achieve his purpose, and Keynesians such as Klein have rightly emphasized the importance of disaggregation, the degree of disaggregation depending on the problem in hand. Keynes himself did not entirely neglect microeconomic theory as is shown clearly in his articles in The Times in 1937, How to Avoid a Slump[44]. Admittedly, Keynes was mistaken in assuming the constancy of certain functional relationships and post-Keynesian economists made mistakes in economic forecasting on the assumption of a stable multiplier. However, the instability of the multiplier in the short run was soon realized and much research was undertaken into the behaviour of the multiplier in the short and long run.

Hayek points out that Keynes had alleged, with only partial justification, that the classical and neoclassical economists had assumed full employment but that he assumed full unemployment, and that there normally existed unused reserves of all factors and commodities. Hayek writes, 'But the latter assumption is not only at least as unlikely to be true in fact as the former; it is also much more misleading. An analysis on the assumption of full employment, even if the assumption is only partially valid, at least helps us to understand the functioning of the price mechanism, the significance of the relations between different prices and of the factors which lead to a change in these relations. But the assumption that all goods and factors are available in excess makes the whole price system redundant, undetermined and unintelligible.'[45]

This criticism of Keynes is, I think, unjustified. Hayek's initial assumption was full employment equilibrium in *Prices and Production* (1931 and 1935) and this led to a theory which provided an incorrect diagnosis of the Great Depression. The fact that he did not also undertake an analysis on the assumption of general unemployment contributed to this and certainly caused much misunderstanding. His later work, starting with the assumption of general unemployment was incomplete. Keynes's theory is general, it has been shown, in that it deals with the determinants of the levels of income and employment which may be any levels. Admittedly, the emphasis of *The General Theory* was on depression economics, but he analysed the full employment case in *How to Pay for the War* as has already been explained. Keynes had also considered full employment equilibrium as a special case in *The General Theory* and discussed some of its implications. *The General Theory* placed the emphasis on quantity rather than price adjustments, changes in the quantities of investment, income or output, and employment. However, changes in prices are considered before full employment or 'bottlenecks' are reached. In the analysis, prices of consumers' and capital goods change, the rate of interest changes, and although the general assumption is made that money wages are fixed, this assumption is relaxed and the case of flexible money wages considered. Hayek's reference to some of Keynes's most orthodox disciples having given up the traditional theory of price and income determination 'and in consequence, in my opinion, to have ceased to understand any economics'[46] is clearly unjustified however critical one may be of some of their work.

The problem of the post-World War II inflation is serious. Hayek in his 1966 article expresses the opinion that he has little doubt that much of it was due to an over-simplified Keynesianism of which Keynes would not have approved. It appears from a conversation between Hayek and Keynes a few weeks before his death that Keynes would have strongly opposed inflation. This we already know from Keynes's *How to Pay for the War*. Hayek blames Keynes for calling 'a tract for the times' '*The General Theory*'[47] but, as has already been explained, this is not justified.

In Chapter 1 I stressed that Keynes was a great man who was many-sided. This is acknowledged by Hayek, but his assessment of Keynes is curious. He thinks Keynes's 'economics to be both false and dangerous', and 'his influence on economics and the fact that he will be remembered chiefly as an economist is both miraculous and tragic.'[48]

Hayek concludes this article by considering the future of Keynesian theory to depend on the development of the appropriate method of the social sciences and that Keynes's theories would be shown to have been the most influential instance of a highly questionable philosophical approach in economics. Hayek writes, 'Though with its reliance on apparently measurable magnitudes it *appears* at first more scientific than the older microtheory, it seems to me that it has achieved this pseudo-exactness at the price of disregarding the relationships which really govern the economic system.'[49] He continues with a prediction 'that once this problem of method is settled, the "Keynesian Revolution" will appear as an episode during which erroneous conceptions of the appropriate scientific method led to the temporary obliteration of many important insights which we had already achieved and which we shall then have painfully to regain.'[50]

In his Alfred Nobel Memorial Prize Lecture, *The Pretence of Knowledge*[51], delivered on 11 December 1974, Hayek developed further his criticism of the 'scientistic' attitude, the attempt to use the methods of the physical sciences in the social sciences without due allowance being made for the very different subject matter. He regards the 'Keynesian' policy of aggregate demand management to maintain 'full' employment as an example of a grave scientistic error and responsible for the post-World War II inflation. Hayek maintains that the main cause of unemployment is that the structure of relative prices has been distorted by monopolistic and governmental price-fixing and increases in the supply of money. He points out that we know the general conditions required for a 'full' employment 'equilibrium', but 'we can never produce statistical information that would show how much the prevailing prices and wages *deviate* from those that would secure a continuous sale of the current supply of labour'[52]. This is explained in terms of the complexity of a market economy. Hayek acknowledges the great advantage obtained by the use of mathematics to provide a comprehensive picture of the mutual interdependencies in the market, but thinks it has led to the illusion that we can also determine and predict the numerical values of the relevant magnitudes[53]. The Spanish schoolmen of the sixteenth century emphasized, Hayek points out, that the mathematical price 'depended on so many particular circumstances that it could never be known to man but was known only to God'[54].

The post-World War II inflation is regarded by Hayek as due to scientistic error, the policy of increasing aggregate demand associated with increasing the quantity of money which, when injected at points of the economic system, affects relative prices and the expectation of a continuing rise of prices. This causes an inappropriate allocation of resources at a level of employment which can only be maintained by a rate of inflation which would eventually lead to a disorganization of economic activity. The inevitable reversal of monetary policy will inevitably cause large-scale unemployment[55]. In 1969 Hayek said 'We now have a tiger by the tail: how long can this inflation continue? If the tiger (of inflation) is freed he will eat us up; yet if he runs faster and faster while we desperately hold on, we are *still* finished.'[56]

Here it must be pointed out that Hayek's general attack on Keynes's *General Theory* and the associated macroeconomic policy is not justified although one can admit mistakes have been made. It has already been pointed out that at appropriate times Keynes took due cognisance of microeconomic factors. Further, the limitations as well as the achievements of econometrics must be recognized. Hayek's rigid distinction between microeconomics and macroeconomics is unjustified as earlier reference to *The General Theory* has shown. Further, much work has been done in recent years in developing the micro-foundations of macroeconomic theory which Hayek does not mention[57]. Starting from the other end, the micro-end, the attempts made to develop a neo-Walrasian Equilibrium analysis which takes account of Keynes's model also receive no mention[58]. Hayek puts forward similar views in 'Inflation: the Path to Unemployment'[59]. In 1975 in *Full Employment at Any Price?*[60], he gives a detailed statement of his views. While again pointing out that Keynes would have opposed the post-World War II inflation, he regards the Keynes of the depressed 1930s as an inflationist or at least an avid anti-deflationist. These are two very different things, but one should regard him at that time as an expansionist by means of monetary and fiscal policy at a time of mass unemployment. It was at this time that Keynes became the intellectual leader and, according to Hayek, 'gained acceptance for the fatal idea: that unemployment is predominantly due to an insufficiency of aggregate demand . . .'[61]. Hayek argues that it is important not to aim at the maximum level of employment which is possible in the short run, by exerting monetary pressure, as the full employment target. The aim must be a high and stable level of employment and '*The primary aim must again become the stability of the value of money.*'[62] Writing in 1975, Hayek refers to the present economic crisis as marking 'the long overdue collapse of the Keynesian bubble of the fashionable doctrine that has dominated opinion for a generation. I am fully convinced that before we can hope to return to reasonable stability . . . we must exorcise the Keynesian incubus.'[63] He adds that this refers less to Keynes's teaching than to that of certain post-Keynesian economists. Economics has had its Malthusian nightmare of overpopulation for which it became known as the Dismal Science and is now presented with a Keynesian nightmare. This seems to me to be going too far despite the inflation of the post-War period culminating in the high rate of inflation and recession of the 1970s. The incubus, the evil spirit lying on a sleeping person, can hardly be applied to some of the post-Keynesian economists who may have advocated at times too much monetary pressure, but have been very much awake. However, Hayek's general attack on monetary inflation is salutary[64].

A further example of Hayek's extreme position is A Comment on Keynes, Beveridge, and Keynesian Economics[65], written in 1976, in which he compares Keynes with the great inflationist, John Law, of the early eighteenth century. Such a comparison is obviously quite unjustified. Once again, Hayek modifies his attack by writing 'it would be somewhat unfair to blame Lord Keynes too much for the developments after his death. I am certain he would have been – whatever he had said earlier – a leader in the fight against the present inflation.'[66] One can certainly agree that Keynes would have done all he could to have prevented the present inflationary problem, but Hayek's reference to 'whatever he had said earlier' is very misleading.

Hayek continues, 'But developments, at least in Britain, were also mainly determined by the version of Keynesianism published under the name of Lord Beveridge for which (since he himself understood no economics whatever) his scientific advisers must bear the responsibility.'[67] This again is very misleading. It is true that Beveridge did not have an expert knowledge of economic theory[68]. However, in 1909 he had published an enlightened book, *Unemployment, A Problem of Industry*, which led to the setting up of the Labour Exchanges. He was an authority on social insurance and produced for the Government his famous *Report on Social Insurance and Allied Services* in 1942. In 1936 Beveridge had given a paper, 'Employment Theory and the Facts of Unemployment' at The London School of Economics. This paper was unsympathetic to Keynes's *The General Theory* published in that year as is made clear in their correspondence during the summer[69]. By the time Beveridge wrote *Full Employment in a Free Society*, published in 1944, he had come to accept Keynes's general theory of employment, but was aware that he needed the advice of expert economists. Further, he had consultation with many people from different fields. Beveridge's book, or Report as he calls it, remains 'a document for which no one can be hanged except myself, but it is not one which I could have produced myself, without the cordial and helpful co-operation of many others'[70]. Beveridge, after considering the relevant conditions, takes 3 per cent as the aim to set for the average unemployment rate on the Government's adoption of a full-employment policy[71]. He also thinks that the full-employment policy should provide more vacant jobs than there are unemployed persons[72]. Beveridge was well aware of the dangers of inflation resulting from a full-employment policy. He discusses the problem of the increased bargaining strength of trade unions and the problem of the maintenance of a stable general level of prices[73]. Robbins was very critical, after the war, of the 'more vacant jobs than unemployed men' criterion of full employment and writes 'nothing that has happened in the intervening twenty or more years, in which so often there has prevailed this Beveridgean condition of the labour market, has led me to modify this opinion'[74].

This point of Robbins is important, but I do not think that this justifies Hayek's statement which I am criticizing regarding the Beveridge version of Keynesianism. Lord Kahn tells us that Keynes wrote to Beveridge in December 1944 warmly congratulating him on his book and that 'In a postscript he mentioned a point of criticism. "No harm in aiming at 3 per cent unemployment, but I shall be surprised if we succeed."'[75] Thus Beveridge's book had the general approval of Keynes. Beveridge himself had clearly stated that setting any particular rate of unemployment as the goal of a full-employment policy did not tie the policy to that figure[76]. It is only reasonable to assume that both Keynes and Beveridge would take into account all the circumstances of the time and be flexible with regard to the unemployment percentage and the vacancy–unemployment relationship. Some of Keynes's followers may have been overenthusiastic monetary expansionists in the post-World War II period and would have benefited from the degree of caution shown by such economists as Robbins and Professor Sir Dennis Robertson. It is stated in the *Council on Prices, Productivity and Incomes, First Report*, published in 1958, that 'the objective should be to stop, not merely to moderate, the inflation'[77]. This was the report of the Cohen Committee of the three wise men, one of whom was Robertson. This statement reflects his view. I think that Hayek's view of the post-war inflation and present recession as a straightforward economic problem is too simple, although he does deal with the political problem of the control of the money supply. I discuss the monetarists' position later[78]. I regard the inflation problem in terms of a complex pattern of economic, political and social factors. I emphasize, of course, the obvious fact that inflation can be controlled by an appropriate control of the money supply. We are all very conscious of the great social distress caused by unemployment. Hayek rightly stresses the inevitability of unemployment once inflation is stopped, or even slowed down, because of the adjustments required to the actual and expected relative prices. The degree of this unemployment and how far it can be alleviated in the short term are important problems. We are also very conscious of the great social distress and inequities that are caused by the effect of inflation on the distribution of real income and wealth. As early as 1923, Keynes in *A Tract on Monetary Reform* devoted a long section to the effects of changes in the value of money on distribution[79].

Mr Peter Lilley in Two Critics of Keynes: Friedman and Hayek, in *The End of the Keynesian Era*[80], discusses the three main criticisms of Keynes's *General Theory* made by Hayek who, he points out, rejects the whole Keynesian approach. The first criticism relates to Keynes's "conceptual realism" (the tendency to ascribe a real existence to arbitrary statistical aggregates such as consumption, the wage level, and capital)[81]. I believe there are undoubted advantages to be derived from Keynes's system being based on a few aggregates, while recognizing that important work has been undertaken by post-Keynesian economists in the direction of disaggregation. The aggregates were, of course, carefully chosen by Keynes and were not arbitrary ones. Much work is being done on the micro-foundations of the Keynesian system. The second criticism is said to derive from Hayek's 'total scepticism about the existence of quantitative functional relationships in economics'[82]. I have emphasized that such relationships as the consumption function relating consumption to income (and other variables) must be treated with caution. The short-term instability of the consumption function has been emphasized. However, Hayek's attitude is far too extreme and involves a hopelessness about much of the most important econometric work being undertaken. The third criticism relates to Keynes's capital theory or, as some economists would say, lack of it. Hayek criticizes Keynes for, in effect, treating capital as a homogeneous substance, ignoring 'its complex interlocking structure – remove one component (say a steelworks) and many other components (for instance, the iron and coal mines and steel fabricating plants) become useless'[83]. Hayek emphasizes the serious maladjustments which occur in the capitalistic structure of production. A vital distinction must be made between an initial assumption of full employment of productive resources and that of general unemployment. The peak of the trade cycle which is followed by depression may be characterized by over-saving in relation to the investment opportunities available, the normal Keynesian explanation, or possibly under-saving, Hayek's over-investment theory of the trade cycle, the rate of investment being too high in relation to the rate of saving undertaken without inflation. Both explanations are theoretically compatible and the explanation of a particular boom collapsing and depression developing involves detailed empirical research. I put the case in 1953 for a synthesis of Austrian and Keynesian theory and stressed that the heterogeneity of capital goods may be of vital importance, but I have not accepted Hayek's rejection of Keynes's great contribution[84]. Lilley also makes the point that Keynes's recommendation that interest rates be artificially depressed to stimulate employment will lead to 'boom and bust'[85]. Low interest rates may or may not lead to an inappropriate degree of capitalization of the structure of production (capital intensity). There is also the question of what is meant by 'artificially' depressed interest rates. These problems are discussed in the chapter on The Theory of Interest. No competent economist would deny that Keynesian theory requires modification and development. Keynes had already begun the process after 1936 and would no doubt have played an important part in it during the post-World War II period if he had not died in 1946. Lilley goes too far in referring to Keynes's critics as having now 'regained the intellectual upper hand'[86]. What is required is a greater emphasis on the relationship of different theories and an attempt at greater mutual understanding.

Hutchison quotes briefly from the work of Johnson and Hayek which I have considered in detail and then states, 'While fully conceding the force of Mr Eltis's question regarding the difficulties which 'Keynesian' policies had run into by the 1970s, we do not agree with the views of Professors Hayek and Johnson that Keynes's doctrines were fatally erroneous or irrelevant *from the start*.'[87] Hutchison gives five main grounds for rejecting 'their fundamental and comprehensive dismissal of Keynes's original doctrines' to which the reader is referred[88]. The post-World War II inflation, which reached its peak in the 1970s and became associated with depression (stagflation), is explained by Hutchison as being due basically to a serious political weakness, overoptimism regarding 'the possibility of enlightened management of the economy by popularly elected governments'[89]. Hutchison is also very critical of the alterations in Keynes's doctrines made by some of his followers whom he names the Pseudo-Keynesians.

Here, I merely wish to reiterate that my main criticism of Johnson and Hayek is that they do not accept the 'Keynesian Revolution' or Keynesian great advance in economic theory, in the sense that Keynes created a general model of the determinants of the levels of income and employment in which the concept of effective demand plays a dominant role, and do not accept that this model was necessary.

Professor W. H. Hutt in *A Rehabilitation of Say's Law*[90] states that in his book, *Economists and the Public* (London, 1936) which appeared shortly after *The General Theory*, he did not blame the prevailing orthodoxy of the 1930s but 'the ignoring of its basic teachings for the emergence and perpetuation of depression'[91]. He continues 'I believe also that *with all their shortcomings* the non-Keynesians of the inter-war period had deeper insight into the origins of chronic unemployment and depression than the overwhelming majority of today's professional economists.' Hutt believes that Britain is faced today with the same problem as that of the 1920s and

1930s and that the solution is to be found in the prevailing orthodoxy of the 1930s in which Say's Law was implicit but dominating.

Say's Law has been stated in many forms. Hutt maintains that if it is fairly interpreted Say's Law is the most fundamental 'economic law' in all economic theory, 'It enunciates the principle that "demands in general" *are* "supplies in general" – different aspects of one phenomenon.'[92] He adds that the suppliers may hold on to the money, that is, demand it instead of commodities. Hutt uses the Law to show that 'new "withhold-ings of inputs or outputs", mainly consequent upon the failure to price all such inputs and outputs for "market clearance" into consumption or stock accumulation, are the origin of depressed economies'; and that 'non-inflationary prosperity' is obtained by providing conditions under which the 'pricing of all inputs and outputs for "market clearance" '[93] occurs. Hutt says that he has written his book to show that this is the case in a money economy as well as in a barter economy. He adds that in a money economy 'deflation may magnify the consequences of defects in the pricing process and unanticipated inflation minimize those consequences'[94]. On the basis of Say's Law as he interprets it, Hutt argues that the Keynesian thesis that depression arises because of an 'excess' aggregate supply, a 'deficient' aggregate demand, or an aggregate demand somehow not being 'effective', is fallacious. In particular, Hutt stresses that the use of money does not frustrate the market-clearing process[95].

Hutt goes so far as to say, 'I am inclined to think that, had there been no Keynesian disturbance, even more progress in our understanding of monetary phenomena could well have been achieved.'[96] Hutt, unlike many neoclassical economists such as Pigou and Robertson in the 1930s, advocates money wage cuts at times of cyclical and chronic unemployment as part of the pricing process for market clearance and opposes incomes policies in that they are certain to be ineffective[97]. In general, I think that Hutt's book is interesting as an analysis of the conditions required for the 'equilibrium' of neoclassical economics and he allows for human error[98]. Thus we do not have a Walrasian equilibrium which in effect involves perfect certainty resulting from his tâtonnement process. I fail to see, however, why Hutt's analysis leads him to the rejection since 1936 of the Keynesian Revolution (or the fundamental advance) as I have described it in my discussion of the work of Johnson and Hayek.

Notes

1. H. G. Johnson, 'Monetary Theory and Keynesian Economics'. *Pakistan Economic Journal* (June 1958), reprinted in his *Money, Trade and Economic Growth* (2nd edn, 1964) to which page references refer.
2. *Ibid.*, p. 108.
3. *Ibid.*, p. 125.
4. *Ibid.*
5. Johnson, 'The General Theory After Twenty-Five Years', *American Economic Review* (May 1961), reprinted in Johnson (1964).
6. Published in the *American Economic Review* (May 1971).

7. *Ibid.*, p. 51.
8. *Ibid.*, pp. 54–56.
9. *Ibid.*, pp. 67–68.
10. Published in *Encounter* (January 1974) and reprinted in Johnson, *On Economics and Society* (1975) to which the page reference refers.
11. *Ibid.*, p. 122.
12. Milo Keynes, ed., *Essays on John Maynard Keynes* (1975) contains this contribution by Harry G. Johnson.
13. *Ibid.*, p. 109.
14. *Ibid.*, p. 110.
15. *Ibid.*, pp. 113–114 and p. 116.
16. *Ibid.*, p. 122.
17. *Ibid.*, pp. 117–119. This is attributed to the Keynesians and not to Keynes himself.
18. Harry G. Johnson, 'Keynes's *General Theory*: Revolution or War of Independence?', *The Canadian Journal of Economics* (November 1976).
19. *C.W.*, Vol. VII (1936, 1973), p. xxiii.
20. For a detailed discussion and critical analysis of Hayek's work, *see* my 'Professor Hayek's Contribution to Trade Cycle Theory', in Eastham, ed., *Dundee Economic Essays* (1955). The main works of Hayek referred to here are: *Prices and Production* (1st edn, 1931; 2nd edn, 1935); *Monetary Theory and the Trade Cycle* (1929); *Profits, Interest and Investment* (1939); *The Pure Theory of Capital* (1941); 'The Ricardo Effect', *Economica* (1942).
21. Gilbert (1955) in Eastham (1955), p. 52.
22. *See* T. W. Hutchison, *Economics and Economic Policy in Britain 1946–1966* (1968), pp. 20–21.
23. Lord Robbins, *Autobiography of an Economist* (1971), p. 153).
24. *Ibid.*, p. 153.
25. Susan Howson, *Domestic Monetary Management in Britain 1919–38* (1975), pp. 86–93.
26. John Hicks The Hayek Story, in Hicks, *Critical Essays in Monetary Theory* (1967), p. 214.
27. Erich Streissler, Hayek on Growth: A Reconsideration of his Early Theoretical Work, in Streissler, *Roads to Freedom, Essays in Honour of Frederick A. von Hayek* (1969), p. 248.
28. Published as Professor Hayek's Contribution to Trade Cycle Theory, in Eastham (1955).
29. *Ibid.*, p. 52.
30. Hicks (1967), p. IX.
31. *See* p. 91.
32. Hicks (1967), p. 214.
33. *Ibid.*, p. 215.
34. T. W. Hutchison, *Keynes versus the 'Keynesians' . . .?* (1977), p. 11. I have omitted Hutchison's italics. This article was one of three published by Keynes in *The Times* under this general heading on 12, 13, 14 January 1937, which Hutchison reprints as Appendix A.
35. Streissler (1969), p. 245.
36. 'Reflections on the Pure Theory of Money of Mr J. M. Keynes', *Economica* (1931 and 1932).
37. F. A. Hayek, *Choice in Currency* (1976), pp. 10–11.
38. F. A. Hayek, *A Tiger by the Tail* (1972), p. 100.
39. Hayek (1976), p. 11.
40. In *The Oriental Economist* (January 1966), reprinted in Hayek (1972).
41. Hayek (1972), p. 100.
42. L. M. Lachmann, *Macroeconomic Thinking and the Market Economy* (1973), editorial preface, pp. 4–5. *See also* p. 52.
43. Hayek (1972), p. 102.
44. *See* p. 240.
45. Hayek (1972), p. 103.
46. *Ibid.*
47. *Ibid.*
48. *Ibid.*, p. 104.
49. *Ibid.*, p. 105.
50. *Ibid.*, p. 106.

51. Reprinted in F. A. Hayek, *Full Employment at Any Price?* (1975).
52. *Ibid.*, p. 33.
53. *Ibid.*, pp. 34–35.
54. *Ibid.*, p. 36.
55. *Ibid.*, p. 37.
56. Caracas Conference Remarks, reprinted in Hayek (1972), p. 112.
57. *See* pp. 205–207.
58. *See* p. 178.
59. *Daily Telegraph*, 15 and 16 October 1974, reprinted as Addendum 2 to Lord Robbins *et al.*, *Inflation: Causes, Consequences, Cures* (1974).
60. F. A. Hayek, *Full Employment at Any Price?* (1975).
61. *Ibid.*, p. 19.
62. *Ibid.*, p. 27.
63. *Ibid.*, p. 43.
64. *Ibid.*, pp. 44 *et seq.*
65. In Hayek (1976), pp. 23–24.
66. *Ibid.*, p. 23.
67. *Ibid.*, pp. 23–24.
68. Lord Robbins, *Autobiography of an Economist* (1971), pp. 136 and 158. However, Beveridge must have had some regard for economics as on my appointment as an assistant (lecturer) at The London School of Economics in 1929, he told me to spend the summer vacation reading A. C. Pigou's *The Economics of Welfare*.
69. *C.W.*, Vol. XIV (1973), editorial note and letters, pp. 55–59.
70. Beveridge (1944), p. 14.
71. *Ibid.*, p. 128.
72. *Ibid.*, p. 132.
73. Pages 198–203.
74. Robbins (1971), p. 230.
75. Richard Kahn, Unemployment as seen by the Keynesians, p. 30. In G. D. N. Worswick, ed., *The Concept and Measurement of Involuntary Unemployment* (1976).
76. Beveridge (1944), p. 131.
77. Page 52.
78. *See* Chapters 7 and 8.
79. *C.W.*, Vol. IV (1971), pp. 4–30.
80. Robert Skidelsky, ed., *The End of the Keynesian Era, Essays on the disintegration of the Keynesian political economy* (1977).
81. *Ibid.*, p. 30.
82. *Ibid.*, p. 30.
83. *Ibid.*
84. *See* my contribution to Eastham (1955), pp. 51–52. *See also* p. 91 above.
85. Lilley in Skidelsky (1977), p. 32.
86. *Ibid.*
87. Hutchison, *Keynes versus the 'Keynesians' . . .?*, p. 5. He refers to Mr Eltis, having quoted on p. 4, from his 'The Failure of the Keynesian Conventional Wisdom', *Lloyds Bank Review* (October 1976), p. 1.
88. Hutchison (1977), pp. 5–8.
89. *Ibid.*, p. 9 and footnote 1.
90. Athens, U.S.A., 1974.
91. W. H. Hutt (1974), p. 2.
92. *Ibid.*, p. 3.
93. *Ibid.*, p. 5.
94. *Ibid.*, p. 8.
95. *Ibid.*, pp. 8–10.
96. *Ibid.*, p. 143.
97. *Ibid.*, pp. 145–147.
98. *Ibid.*, p. 5.

Chapter 7

Milton Friedman and monetarism
I. The quantity theory of money

The quantity theory of money has a long history but it was in the 1950s that Professor Milton Friedman brought about its revival and began its modern development. This revival was necessary because the importance of the quantity of money was not sufficiently emphasized or even denied in certain quarters as in the Radcliffe Report of 1959. This is true although Keynes and many Keynesian economists are not open to this criticism and recognized the importance of the quantity of money in certain circumstances. Milton Friedman developed monetary theory in a way which led to the great amount of empirical work undertaken in monetary economics since the mid-1950s to which he himself contributed so much. The development of economic statistics and econometrics in the post-World War II period facilitated the empirical testing of propositions in monetary as in other areas of economics and monetary economists stimulated such development. Although Friedman has done important work in other fields it is his work in monetary economics which has given him an international reputation. His recommendations for the conduct of monetary policy, which have to some extent been adopted in the United States and in this country, are based on his monetary theory and empirical analysis. In 1976 his great contributions were recognized by the award of the Nobel Prize in Economic Sciences.

Friedman was born in 1912 and has been based in the University of Chicago since 1946 where he has taught, supervised numerous postgraduate students, and undertaken his research. He became the leading monetarist economist in the world and his influence both in Chicago, where he is regarded as the leader of the so-called Chicago School of economics, and throughout the world has been immense. Discussing Friedman's work in monetary economics, Professor David Meiselman who had been one of his postgraduate students stated that 'his work has played a major role if not the major role in revolutionizing the entire field'[1]. Meiselman considers the combination of factors which led to the great and rapid success of Friedman's monetary analysis and policies since the early 1960s in addition to the prevalence of inflation. He refers to several real-world experiments and Friedman's and his laboratory (empirical) experiments[2] and states 'In both sets of experiments the Keynesians lost and the quantity theorists won.'[3] This is, of course, very much a monetarist's point of view. Keynesians would interpret events differently and there was much criticism of Friedman's and Meiselman's paper. However, it is true that Friedman's success is partly due to these 'experiments'. Reference is also made to the outstanding contributions of economists associated with Friedman's Money and Banking Workshop in Chicago. Meiselman also refers to Friedman's personal qualities of 'spirit, generosity, energy, and piercing intellect', and the importance of this method of positive economics by which questions are framed to be, at least in principle, answerable by evidence[4].

Clark Warburton has been recognized belatedly as the pioneer monetarist. His theories based on his empirical work were essentially completed during the period from the early 1940s to 1953 although after a break he continued to publish up to 1975. By 1953 Warburton had developed a monetarist position very akin to that of Friedman[5]. However, the roots of Friedman's work are to be found in the Chicago School. This term has been used in different ways. Friedman is often referred to as the leader of the Chicago School by which is meant the monetarist school as developed by him and his associates at Chicago. Professor Selden points out that although there is a Chicago School in economics it cannot be regarded as monolithic since Knight and Simons[6]. Friedman has referred to the Chicago School in the sense of those Chicago economists whose writings and teachings greatly influenced his work on money[7]. Professor Don Patinkin criticizes Friedman severely for maintaining that his work on monetary theory and policy is based on the writings and oral tradition of the Chicago School[8]. Friedman recognized that he had been much influenced by the Keynesian liquidity analysis[9] which recognition was ignored by Patinkin[10]. Professor Harry G. Johnson follows Patinkin's criticisms[11]. Friedman defended himself against Patinkin's and Johnson's criticisms in Comments on the Critics[12].

The revival of the quantity theory and the rise of monetarism are mainly due to Milton Friedman[13]. This began with his The Quantity Theory of Money: A Restatement of 1956[14] and developed into what Friedman regarded as the Counter-Revolution to Keynesian theory, the income-expenditure approach in which the emphasis was on the constituents of aggregate demand (investment and consumption) as determinants of the level of income. This development in economics became known as monetarism because it stressed once again the fundamental importance of the role played by the quantity of money in the economy. Friedman presented equations which showed the variables on which the income velocity of circulation of money and the corresponding element in the demand for money depend. They are to be found in the 1956 Restatement, his *International Encyclopaedia of the Social Sciences* article of 1968, 'Money: quantity theory'[15] and in his *A Theoretical Framework for Monetary Analysis*[16]. There are a few differences in the various presentations and some obscurities. I give here a synthetic statement which I hope would be acceptable to Friedman. Without denigrating Friedman's work it should be noted that all the variables used in his formulation of the quantity theory had been known to earlier writers. However, Friedman restated the quantity theory when it needed restating and he did so in an explicit form which enabled him and other economists to undertake the empirical research into the statistical relationships which had been lacking. Here his stimulus was very important although it has proved difficult to obtain definitive results in this area[17]. The demand for money is expressed in real terms – the demand to hold purchasing power over goods and services in the form of nominal money balances. M is the nominal money stock defined by Friedman as consisting of currency in circulation, demand deposits (current accounts) and time deposits (deposit accounts)[18] and P is the general price level. Thus M/P is the real value of the money stock which is equal to KR in the Cambridge equation[19]. Friedman writes the demand function for money as

$$\frac{M}{P} = f(y_p, w, r_m, r_b, r_e, r_g, u) \tag{1}$$

The symbols are for the variables on which the demand for money is considered to depend and must now be explained.

Friedman states that 'The quantity theory is in the first instance a theory of the *demand* for money. It is not a theory of output, or of money income, or of the price level.'[20] Admittedly, as Friedman points out, any statement about these variables requires specifications about other variables in addition to the demand function. However, Friedman is defining the quantity theory here more narrowly than has been usual in the literature in which the quantity equation has been taken as providing convenient heads under which the causes of changes in the general level of prices can be analysed.

Wealth is held in various forms of assets of which money is one kind. Thus the demand for money is analysed in terms of the theory of capital, an important aspect of Friedman's approach. The demand for money (or any other asset) by the ultimate wealth-owning units in the economy is also considered in an identical way to the demand for a consumption service in the theory of consumer choice. Thus the demand for money 'depends on three major sets of factors: (a) the total wealth to be held in various forms . . .; (b) the price of and return on this form of wealth and alternative forms; and (c) the tastes and preferences of the wealth-owning units'[21]. The factor (b) refers to the opportunity costs of holding money rather than interest-earning assets. Friedman starts his analysis by considering the demand for nominal money balances while I have started with the demand for real balances, purchasing power (M/P). However, Friedman shows that we may easily move from one formulation to the other by taking into account the general price level (P)[22]. This assumes the absence of money illusion.

The first variable is y_p, permanent real income which is used as a surrogate for wealth. Friedman adopted this method of representing wealth after he had developed his permanent income hypothesis in his important book *A Theory of the Consumption Function*[23]. He drew the distinction between current measured income and a longer-term concept which he called permanent income. Over the long period measured and permanent income tend to converge but in the short period measured income may be more or less than permanent income by the amount of positive or negative transitory income. Friedman maintained that consumption was a function of permanent income. He incorporated this concept in his monetary economics in his discussion of the behaviour of the velocity of circulation in the long and short run and as a surrogate for wealth which may be regarded as the source of permanent income. Permanent income was defined as a weighted average of current and past levels of measured income, the latter being given steadily declining weights (relative importance in the average) as we recede into the past, and the average being adjusted for secular growth at a percentage rate per annum[24]. Summarizing empirical work done by Anna J. Schwartz and himself, Friedman states that taking secular changes in the real stock of money per capita and secular changes in real income per capita[25] for the period from 1870 to 1954 in the United States. 'A 1 per cent increase in real income per capita has therefore, on the average, been associated with a 1.8 per cent increase in real cash balances per capita and hence with a 0.8 per cent *decrease* in income velocity.'[26] Thus the income elasticity of demand for money is greater than 1; money is regarded as a 'luxury' commodity[27]. Later Friedman modified his view and in his 'A Theoretical Framework for Monetary Analysis' of 1970 envisaged the possibility of a unit real income elasticity. Friedman's total wealth consists of all sources of income including the productive capacity of human beings. Capitalizing income by 'the' rate of interest, total wealth is

$$W = \frac{Y}{r} \tag{2}$$

where Y is money income and r 'the' rate of interest. For monetary analysis he excludes the services in the form of convenience etc. provided by money to the holder, the imputed income, from income and so money held by ultimate wealth-owning units from wealth[28]. Wealth consists of non-human and human wealth and there are only restricted possibilities of making a transfer from the one form to the other, for example by investing in a person's education. The ratio of non-human to human wealth or income from non-human wealth to income from human wealth, w, is taken as given at a point of time[29].

Apart from human capital, wealth is regarded as being held in four different forms, money[30], bonds, equities and physical goods. The relative amounts held by the individual depend on the expected rates of return and the tastes and preferences of wealth-owning units – u in equation (1).

Money in the form of currency and demand deposits (current accounts) may be taken as not yielding interest but interest is paid on time deposits (deposit accounts). Demand deposits may yield implicit interest in the form of reduced charges for financial services. Money acting as a medium of exchange and store of value yields a return in kind in the form of convenience and security at a given price level; it is held for Keynes's transactions and precautionary motives and gives the holder command over goods and services. This return in kind may be expressed as imputed income. The variable r_m in equation (1) is the expected yield from holding a unit of money. It does not appear in the 1956 version but does in the *International Encyclopaedia* article of 1968 and in his *A Theoretical Framework for Monetary Analysis* of 1970 where it is defined as 'the expected nominal rate of return on money'[31]. The equation here is the demand for money in real terms (M/P). The symbol r_b is 'the expected nominal rate of return on fixed-value securities, including expected changes in their prices'[32]. The prices of fixed-interest securities change inversely to changes in the market rate of interest. Friedman takes a 'standard' bond which is a 'claim to a perpetual income stream of constant nominal amount'[33].

Friedman should have stated explicitly here and elsewhere when putting forward this equation that the expected rate of increase in the price level affects the expected yield. An expected rise in the price level means an expected fall in the real value of nominal money balances, a negative rate of return and vice versa. He refers to Phillip Cagan's results in his The Monetary Dynamics of Hyperinflation, one of the 1956 *Studies in the Quantity Theory of Money*. The expected effect was obtained – the higher the (expected) rate of change of prices, the lower the demand for money or the higher the velocity of circulation[34].

The expected rate of change of prices also affects the money, or market rate of interest. This applies to the rate of interest on money in the form of time deposits (deposit accounts) and to the rate of interest on bonds (r_b). Indeed in A Monetary Theory of Nominal Income[35] Friedman incorporates in his theory Irving Fisher's distinction between the nominal and the real rate of interest[36]. In allowing for changes in the price level, we may distinguish between the *ex ante* and *ex post* concepts of the expected and realized real interest rates. In the demand for money equation we are concerned with the expected real rate in an uncertain world. One of the conditions in my article, The Compatibility of any Behaviour of the Price Level with Equilibrium, is that 'the maintenance of equilibrium requires an allowance in the money rate of interest for the known change in the price level during the unit period'[37]. As an example I state that 'If the price level is known with certainty to be rising at the rate of 10 per cent per unit period . . . the money rate of interest required to compensate for the depreciation would be 15½ per cent, if the marginal productivity of capital were 5 per cent.'[38] In the real world we have uncertainty and various market imperfections. For example, during a period of inflation the market rate of interest on 2½ per cent Consols may not allow fully for the expected and realized rates of inflation. The actual real rate of interest may be positive but less than the appropriate rate or indeed may be negative as occurred during the 1970s. The reasons for this are complicated.

At the 1970 Sheffield Money Seminar, Sir Roy Harrod stated in his Discussion Paper on Friedman's A Monetary Theory of Nominal Income, 'I do not accept the Irving Fisher view that we should expect the money rate of interest to exceed what that rate would be if there were a prospect of stable prices by an amount equal to the expected rate of inflation . . . . Keynes gave an outright denial of this doctrine and I am sure that Keynes was right.'[39] This is a reference to Keynes's analysis of the effect of an expected rise in the price level on investment and output and his criticism of Irving Fisher in *The General Theory*[40]. Keynes wrote that 'The mistake lies in supposing that it is the rate of interest on which prospective changes in the value of money will directly react, instead of the marginal efficiency of a given stock of capital.'[41] However, Keynes correctly recognized that 'the stimulus to output depends on the marginal efficiency of a given stock of capital rising *relatively* to the rate of interest'[42]. It is clear that this asymmetry is required. As Robertson said to me, 'This whole passage is one of the most muddled in *The General Theory*'. Harrod's argument was that 'Bonds and cash are two forms of asset denominated in money. Neither has a hedge against inflation . . . . The rate of interest represents the rate at which bonds can be exchanged for cash. Since neither contains a hedge against inflation the new-found expectation that inflation will occur cannot change their relative values or therefore the rate of interest.'[43] Harrod further argued that the growth of uncertainty about the prospective rate of inflation could increase the rate of interest and he attributed the recent rise to this factor[44]. It is the former point which is relevant to Friedman's appeal to Fisher although he is not assuming certainty. I attempted to refute Harrod's thesis in that part of the Introduction which I wrote. I pointed out that 'the opportunity cost of holding common money and current accounts is higher, owing to the negative rate of interest because of rising prices. The equilibrium, therefore, also involves less money in real terms being held, giving a higher marginal utility of "convenience".'[45] Thus Friedman's analysis can be accepted and my analysis in the 1956–1957 article is valid[46]. It is, of course, an empirical fact recognized by Harrod and all economists, that high money rates of interest prevail during inflation.

Friedman treats equities (ordinary shares) similarly to bonds in that he takes the 'standard' unit of equity 'to be a claim to a perpetual income stream of constant "real" amount; that is, to be a standard bond with a purchasing-power escalator clause, so that it promises a perpetual income stream equal in nominal units to a constant number times a price index'[47]. The nominal return to the holder of the equity is regarded as consisting of 'the constant nominal amount he would receive per year in the absence of any change in P [the price level]; the increment or decrement to this nominal amount to adjust for changes in P; and any change in the nominal price of the equity over time which may of course arise from changes either in interest rates or price levels'[48]. The symbol r_e is the market rate of interest on equities. Allowance is made for changes in the interest rate and the price level[49]. I take r_e to be 'the expected nominal rate of return on equities, including [all] expected changes in their prices'[50].

There is also a return to the ultimate wealth-owning unit on the physical goods he holds. In 'A Theoretical Framework' this is $(1/P \, dP/dt)$, that is, 'the expected rate of change of prices of goods and hence the expected nominal rate of return on real assets'[51]. I think it would be better to take the services expected to be derived from the holding of durable consumers' goods as expected imputed income to which the expected change of this price level is added. In the 1956 article Friedman explains his procedure of taking $I/P \, dP/dt$ by reference to 'the rapid depreciation of many of the physical goods held by final wealth-owning units'[52]. However, many durable consumers' goods are long-lasting in addition to the obvious case of housing. Further, one can regard depreciation as being met out of imputed income and replacement being made. I have therefore substituted r_g the expected rate of return on physical goods, for $I/P \, dP/dt$ in equation (1).

The treatment of the variables r_m, r_b, r_e, r_g involves an important simplification. Friedman points out that 'Each of the four rates of return stands, of course, for a set of rates of return, and for some purposes it may be important to classify assets still more finely – for example, to distinguish currency from deposits, longterm from short-term fixed-value securities, risky from relatively safe equities, and one kind of physical assets from another.'[53]

Finally, the equation contains u which is 'a portmanteau symbol standing for whatever variables other than income may affect the utility attached to the services of money'[54]. Under this head the degree of economic stability which is expected is regarded as important. Friedman stresses that wealth-holders will attach greater value to liquidity, the holding of money, 'when they expect economic conditions to be unstable than when they expect them to be highly stable'[55]. He points out that it is difficult to measure this variable empirically although the direction of change may be known from general information. Friedman instances the outbreak of war which may produce expectations of instability which cause a decline in the velocity of circulation, i.e. an increase in the demand for real balances, or more precisely an increase in the element in this demand which corresponds to velocity. Another possible variable is the volume of capital transactions relative to income because the higher the turnover of capital assets the higher the proportion of total assets people will hold as money[56].

Up to this point Friedman has considered the individual ultimate wealth-holder's demand for money. Equation (1) refers to the economy as a whole and involves certain problems of aggregation[57]. Further, the equation includes the demand for money by business enterprises. The same variables, with somewhat different interpretations, are relevant with the exception of w which is excluded. Again there are problems of aggregation[58].

Following Friedman's procedure in his 1956 paper[59] I rewrite equation (1), the demand for money to hold equation, as equation (3), the velocity of circulation of money equation:

$$Y = v(y_p, w, r_m, r_b, r_e, r_g, u)M \tag{3}$$

Y is the national money income per unit period of time and v is the velocity of circulation of money per unit period of time. Thus, this equation corresponds to Robertson's $MV = PR$[60]. Friedman has taken the traditional demand-to-hold and velocity-of-circulation approaches to the quantity theory of money and set out explicitly the variables on which the demand for money or an element of it and the velocity of circulation depend. He thus set the stage for his own and other economists' empirical work on these variables.

Friedman stresses the limitations of equation (3) (his equation 13). Changes in the nominal quantity of money will be associated with proportionate changes in money income only if the variables in v are taken as fixed or if 'the demand for money is quite inelastic with respect to the variables in v'[61]. In this case the velocity of circulation is constant, not changing with changes in the expected rates of return on the various assets or expected permanent income.

As early as 1956 Friedman stressed that the analysis relating to the equation gives us no information about how much of any change in money income is a change in real output and how much a change in the price level. If real output is at its practical maximum an increase in money can only affect the price level, for example[62]. Another monetarist, Professor David E. W. Laidler, in The Influence of Money on Economic Activity – A Survey of some Current Problems writes 'Exactly how fluctuations in aggregate demand spread their effects over time between prices and output remains mysterious, though it is coming to look increasingly as if the key to these problems will be found in the analysis of price expectations.'[63] Friedman in A Theoretical Framework for Monetary Analysis points out that one of the defects common to the three theories he has sketched in simplified terms, the quantity theory, the income-expenditure theory and his monetary theory of nominal income, is the lack of a theoretical explanation of 'the short-run division of a change in nominal income between prices and output'[64]. He regards this division between prices and output as depending on two major factors, anticipations about the be- haviour of prices and the current level of output or employment compared with the full-employment level of output or employment[65]. Friedman sketches a theory of the factors which determine this division of a change in nominal income[66]. However, he regards the question whether a change in nominal income impinges mostly on prices or on quantities of output as basically an empirical one. The interpretation of the economic data is shown to be difficult[67].

Sometimes it is incorrectly said or implied that Keynes made a simple contrast between quantity – and price – adjustments occurring in the case of an increase in the quantity of money associated with an increase in effective demand, depending on whether there was general unemployment or 'full' employment. In The General Theory he makes a contribution to this problem of the division between increases in output and increases in the price level in the case of monetary expansion in terms of his discussion of the elasticity of supply or of production[68]. Keynes points out that because of the law of diminishing returns, increasing output from a given capital equipment will be associated with rising prices, apart from any increase in money-wage rates. He also refers to the concept of 'bottle- necks' where the supplies of particular commodities become inelastic. Keynes stated, 'It is probable that the general level of prices will not rise very much as output increases, so long as there are available efficient unemployed resources of every type. But as soon as output has increased sufficiently to begin to reach the "bottle-necks" there is likely to be a sharp rise in the prices of certain commodities.'[69] Further, Keynes recognizes that money-wage rates will tend to rise before 'full employment' has been reached. Once 'full employment' has been reached, output can no longer be increased and the whole effect of an increase in the quantity of money associated with an increase in effective demand will be to increase costs, including money-wage rates, and the general level of prices.

Up to this point Friedman has developed the quantity theory of money particularly in terms of the demand-to-hold approach, an analysis of the factors which determine the demand for money as one of the assets in which wealth is held. Keynes concentrated on the demands for money and bonds. This is a very simple form of portfolio analysis. Friedman de- veloped his analysis of the demand for money in terms of a much wider portfolio as has been explained[70]. All economists presumably accept as very useful his detailed explicit elaboration of the factors determining the demand for money. The controversies, as will be seen, relate to his uses of this formal quantity theory. In developing his position Friedman refers to himself and those of his school of thought as quantity theorists. Monetarist is substituted for quantity theorist as the latter is much wider.

In his 1956 article Friedman sets out three basic issues about which there are differences of opinion: '(i) the stability and importance of the demand function for money; (ii) the independence of the factors affecting demand and supply; and (iii) the form of the demand function or related functions.'[71] His life work has been mainly devoted to econometric work and the elaboration of his ideas relating to these issues. It is convenient to take (i) and (iii) together as (i) because of their close relationship and then consider (ii).

Notes

1. Richard T. Selden, ed., *Capitalism and Freedom*, Proceedings of a Conference in honor of Milton Friedman (Charlottesville, 1975), p. 294.
2. Milton Friedman and David I. Meiselman, 'The Relative Stability of Monetary Velocity and the Investment Multiplier in the United States, 1897–1958', in the Commission on Money and Credit, *Stabilization Policies* (1963).
3. Selden (1975), p. 296.
4. *Ibid.*, p. 297.
5. *See* 'Clark Warburton: Pioneer Monetarist' by Michael D. Bordo, Carleton University and Anna J. Schwartz, National Bureau of Economic Research, New York, *Carleton Economic Papers* 78–101.
6. Selden (1975), p. 2.
7. Friedman has referred to this influence in a number of places. *See* Milton Friedman, ed., *Studies in the Quantity Theory of Money* (1956), 'The Quantity Theory of Money: A Restatement (1956b), reprinted in Friedman, *The Optimum Quantity of Money* (1969), pp. 51–52); Friedman, 'The Monetary Theory and Policy of Henry Simons', *The Journal of Law and Economics*, Vol. 10 (October 1967), reprinted in Friedman (1969), p. 81. For Simons' views on monetary theory as published during the years 1933 to 1945, *see* Henry C. Simons, *Economic Policy for A Free Society* (1948). For further references of Milton Friedman to Simons, *see* 'The Monetary Theory . . .', in Friedman (1969), pp. 82, 84.
8. Don Patinkin, 'The Chicago Tradition, the Quantity Theory, and Friedman', *J.M.C.B.*, Vol. 1 (February 1969), pp. 46–70, reprinted in Patinkin, *Studies in Monetary Economics* (1972a); Patinkin, 'On the Short-Run Non-Neutrality of Money in the Quantity Theory', *Banca Nazionale Lavoro Quarterly Review* (March, 1972b); Patinkin, Friedman on the Quantity Theory and Keynesian Economics, in Robert J. Gordon, ed., *Milton Friedman's Monetary Framework* (1974).
9. Milton Friedman, 'Post-War Trends in Monetary Theory and Policy', *National Bank Review*, Vol. 2 (September 1964), reprinted in Friedman (1969), p. 73.
10. Patinkin (1969a) in Patinkin (1972a), p. 93.
11. Harry G. Johnson, *Further Essays in Monetary Economics* (1972), pp. 23, 64–65.
12. Gordon (1974), pp. 133, 158–172.
13. *See Harry G. Johnson (1972), pp. 22–28.*
14. *All page references are to the reprint in Friedman (1969). See also* Friedman, 'Price, Income and Monetary Changes in Three Wartime Periods', *American Economic Review, Proceedings* (May, 1952), reprinted in Friedman (1969).
15. Reprinted in A. A. Walters, ed., *Money and Banking. Selected Readings* (1973).
16. New York: National Bureau of Economic Research, 1971, reprinted in Gordon (1974). This derived from two articles in the *Journal of Political Economy*. 'A Theoretical Framework for Monetary Analysis' (March/April 1970b) and 'A Monetary Theory of Nominal Income' (March/April 1971). The latter article was originally given as a paper to the 1970 Sheffield Money Seminar and was published in Clayton, Gilbert, Sedgwick, eds, *Monetary Theory and Monetary Policy in the 1970s* (1971).

17. For a review of the empirical evidence on the demand for money *see* David E. W. Laidler, *The Demand for Money: Theories and Evidence* (2nd edn, 1977).
18. For a discussion of his explicit definition of money, *see* 'Money and Business Cycles', Friedman (1969), pp. 207–209.
19. *See* p. 81.
20. Friedman (1956b) in Friedman (1969), p. 52.
21. *Ibid.*
22. *Ibid.*, p. 58.
23. Princeton, 1957.
24. 'The Demand for Money: Some Theoretical and Empirical Results', *Journal of Political Economy* (1959), reprinted in Friedman (1969), p. 124. Actually, this is an estimate of permanent income which Friedman calls expected income. *See also* 'The Demand for Money', *Proceedings of the American Philosophical Society* (June 1961), reprinted in Friedman, *Dollars and Deficits* (1968), p. 201.
25. As pointed out above, over the long period measured and permanent income converge.
26. Friedman (1969), p. 113.
27. For a more detailed discussion of the income elasticity of demand *see* Goodhart, *Money, Information and Uncertainty* (1975), pp. 22–30, 49–50 and 62–65.
28. Friedman (1969), p. 57.
29. *Ibid.*, p. 56.
30. Money is included despite the statement in Friedman (1969), p. 57 referred to previously.
31. Gordon (1974), p. 13.
32. *Ibid.*
33. Friedman (1969), p. 54.
34. *Ibid.*, p. 66.
35. Clayton, Gilbert, Sedgwick (1971), pp. 44–45. I had invited Professor Milton Friedman to give a paper to the 1970 Sheffield Money Seminar. The late Professor Harry Johnson was very helpful in supporting my invitation. In attending the Seminar, Friedman made important contributions to it and in a very pleasant way.
36. Irving Fisher, *The Theory of Interest* (1930), pp. 36–38 and 411–412). It is pointed out in Friedrich A. Hayek, *Prices and Production* (2nd edn, 1935), p. 23, n.2 that Fisher's real rate of interest doctrine was known to Marshall, Ricardo and Thornton.
37. Gilbert, *Review of Economic Studies* (1956/1957), p. 178.
38. *Ibid.*
39. Clayton, Gilbert, Sedgwick (1971), p. 61.
40. *C.W.*, Vol. VII (1936, 1973), pp. 141–143.
41. *Ibid.*, p. 142.
42. *Ibid.*, p. 143.
43. Clayton, Gilbert, Sedgwick (1971), pp. 61–62.
44. *Ibid.*, p. 62.
45. *Ibid.*, p. 4.
46. I said to Harrod in conversation at the Sheffield Money Seminar that if he was right my 1956/1957 *Review of Economic Studies* article would be washed out. He replied, in effect, *tant pis* for the article.
47. Friedman (1969), p. 54. Note 1 points out that this is a simplification.
48. *Ibid.*
49. Friedman (1969), p. 55. This allowance does not appear in the equations on p. 58.
50. Gordon (1974), p. 13.
51. *Ibid.*
52. Friedman (1969), p. 55, n.2.
53. Gordon (1974), p. 13. The distinction between current accounts and deposit accounts (time deposits) may be important.
54. *Ibid.*
55. *Ibid.*, p. 12.
56. *Ibid.*, p. 13. *See also* Friedman (1969), p. 56.
57. *Ibid.*, p. 13.
58. *Ibid.*, pp. 14–15. *See also* Friedman (1969), pp. 58–61.
59. Friedman (1969), p. 58, equations (11) and (13).
60. *See* p. 80, Y = PR, the constituents of real income multiplied by the income price level.
61. Friedman (1969), p. 62.
62. *Ibid.*

63. Clayton, Gilbert, Sedgwick (1971), pp. 119–120. Laidler gives a brief sketch of how the analysis of this problem could be pursued (pp. 120–122).
64. Gordon (1974), p. 48.
65. *Ibid.*, p. 49. Full employment does not mean, of course, 100 per cent employment of productive resources.
66. *Ibid.*, pp. 49 *et seq.*
67. *Ibid.*, pp. 61–62.
68. *C.W.*, Vol. VII (1936, 1973), pp. 298–304. I give here a simplified account of Keynes's analysis.
69. *Ibid.*, p. 300. Keynes also points out that the elasticity of supply depends partly on the time interval assumed for the adjustment.
70. For earlier treatments along these lines *see* J. R. Hicks, 'A Suggestion for Simplifying the Theory of Money', *Economica* (February 1935), reprinted in John Hicks, *Critical Essays in Monetary Theory*, Oxford (1967) and J. R. Hicks, 'Gleichgewicht und Konjunktur (*Zeitschrift Für Nationalökonomie*, Vol. 4, pp. 441–455).
71. Friedman (1969), p. 62.

Chapter 8

Milton Friedman and monetarism
II. Controversies

A general point must first be made regarding Friedman's econometric work on the variables he considers to be important in monetary economics. He uses a single equation, a reduced-form equation as equation (3) above in which money income (Y), the dependent variable, on the left-hand side of the equation is determined by the velocity of circulation (v) and the quantity of money (M), the independent variables, on the right-hand side. The symbols in brackets represent the factors on which velocity depends such as permanent income and rates of return on various assets which are taken as independent variables. The quantity of money is an independent variable as it is assumed to be exogenous, determined by, for example, the monetary authority.

Friedman does not have a large structural model consisting of a set of behavioural equations on which his reduced-form equation is based. The quantity of money may be endogenous, depending on the level of money income, in which case the causation would be the reverse of that shown in the equation. Friedman's critics argue that a large structural model[1] is required in which account is taken of the many interdependent variables. The econometric model is based on what is regarded as the appropriate economic theory. Whether money is exogenous or endogenous is shown in terms of the model. However, the specification of structural models also involves the difficult question of distinguishing between exogenous and endogenous variables.

At the 1970 Sheffield Money Seminar Friedman defended his use of reduced-form equations. He argued that 'on the basis of his experience and his study of monetary history he did not think that it was possible to resolve the exogeneity/endogeneity issue using large-scale models. He rejected large-scale models on the grounds of their complexity and because of the difficulty of obtaining all the information required to construct them correctly.'[2] Further, he argued that reduced-form equations could provide the answer 'if they were used in conjunction with the information and understanding gained from detailed studies of monetary history'[3]. Friedman relies on the 'Repetition of reduced-form studies taking different episodes in time and place.'[4]

The monetarist economists at the Federal Reserve Bank of St. Louis follow Friedman's reduced-form approach, using small simple models of a few equations. Some of this work is discussed by Professors G. R. Fisher and D. K. Sheppard particularly from the methodological point of view[5]. While recognizing the gain in simplicity and some of the useful contributions made by this empirical research, for example, by providing useful forecasts, they stress the loss of information from not having a large-scale structural model. Their view is that 'the use of the reduced-form approach essentially precludes the testing of theory and hence precludes empirical results from contributing significantly to the development of theory'[6].

In the United Kingdom an important contribution to the development of monetarism was made at the University of Manchester. Under Michael Parkin and David E. W. Laidler, Professors of Economics there (now at the University of Western Ontario), 'In July 1971 a group of some twenty economists, econometricians and accountants, financed by the Social Science Research Council, began work at the University of Manchester on a three-year research programme, on the problem of inflation.'[7] In all, six volumes were published from 1972 to 1978 containing the work of this group and other invited economists, including one volume of Laidler's work. A wide area was covered as indicated in note 7 and much detailed empirical work undertaken. No large-scale structural models were constructed, the reduced-form approach being used. This was shown at the 1974 Conference of the Association of University Teachers held in Manchester at which Parkin gave a very interesting and useful paper, The Causes Of Inflation: Recent Contributions And Current Controversies, and G. Fisher (University of Southampton) a Discussion paper[8]. Fisher criticizes Parkin's use of reduced-form models for the analysis of the causes of inflation which he maintains require a large structural model for their understanding, while a relatively small model may be acceptable for forecasting. He writes, 'In general, the major cost of a reduced-form approach is a loss of information, and hence a loss of power in structural testing.'[9] The debate regarding the advantages and disadvantages of the reduced-form and structural approaches continues.

As stated in the previous chapter the first head under which Friedman's work is considered is the stability, importance and form of the demand function for money and of certain other functions which play a role in macroeconomics[10]. Friedman as a monetarist accepts 'the empirical hypothesis that the demand for money is highly stable – more stable than functions such as the consumption function that are offered as alternative key relations'[11]. He stresses that this does not mean that the velocity of circulation is numerically constant over time. It means that there is a stable functional relationship between this velocity and a number of variables. Thus if changes in the relevant variables are known the change in the velocity of circulation can be predicted. Friedman states that the monetarist regards such a stable functional relationship 'as playing a vital role in determining variables that he considers of great importance for the analysis of the economy as a whole, such as the level of money income or of prices'[12]. Thus Friedman states one of the central propositions of monetarism to be 'There is a constant though not precise relation between the rate of growth of the quantity of money and the rate of growth of nominal income.'[13]

Friedman refers to the work of Phillip Cagan which shows that the velocity of circulation increases greatly during hyperinflations[14]. The expected increase in the price level is one of the variables in the stable functional relationship. If people expect prices to rise they expect money balances to be depreciating assets in real terms and therefore spend them more quickly. Friedman also refers to the work of Richard T. Selden which shows that in the United States over a long period the secular rise in real income has been associated with a decline in the velocity of circulation. The income elasticity of the demand for real money balances is greater than unity; they are a 'luxury commodity'[15]. Friedman raises the problem of Selden finding that 'for cyclical periods velocity rises during expansions and falls during contractions, a result that at first glance seems to contradict the secular result just cited'[16]. Friedman solves this problem by stating that Selden's velocity is the ratio of measured or current income to the stock of money while the appropriate variable in the demand-for-money and velocity equations is permanent income, y_p in equation (3) in the previous chapter (p. 110). This way of saving his stable relationship is not satisfactory. For the short-period analysis of trade cycles it is important to analyse the causes of changes in the velocity of circulation of money against measured or current income. Those economists who maintain that real factors such as changes in investment opportunities as well as monetary factors are causes of the trade cycle would regard the increase in the velocity of circulation during the upswing as partly a result of an improvement in the economic outlook. The decrease in the velocity of circulation during the downswing would be regarded as partly a result of a deterioration in the economic outlook. Thus such changes in velocity are associated partly with changes in the demand for money for the precautionary motive. In the long period, measured income tends to converge with permanent income and the distinction is not important.

Milton Friedman and Anna J. Schwartz discussed the cyclical behaviour of the velocity of circulation in their 1963 article Money and Business Cycles[17]. The empirical work was based on United States data from 1869 to 1960. They point out that the income velocity of circulation has declined from 4.6 to 1.7 over the period despite the increase in the post-World War II period. The secular decline in velocity has led to a slower rate of decline in expansions than in contractions in some trade cycles. In other trade cycles velocity has risen during expansions and fallen during contractions. They refer to an earlier article in which the cyclical pattern was explained largely by the distinction between measured income and current prices and permanent income and permanent prices[18]. This interpretation was criticized by Henry A. Latané as not recognizing the importance of interest rates. Friedman writes that Latané has argued that 'the whole of the movement of velocity, both over longer periods and over the cycle, can be accounted for by changes in interest rates, higher interest rates leading to economy in the use of money and so to higher velocities, and conversely'[19]. Latané's work is based on United States data from 1909 to 1958. Friedman shows that the different results arise primarily from Latané's definition of money which excludes time deposits[20].

Friedman points out that a more important question is whether velocity can be regarded as 'passively reflecting independent changes'[21] in money income and the quantity of money. As has been stated above, velocity may increase and decrease during the trade cycle because of changes in the economic outlook. The quantity of money may also increase during the upswing and decrease during the downswing. In this case the real factors, investment opportunities and so on, are regarded as important causes of the trade cycle although monetary conditions must be favourable and indeed may also be independent causes. Friedman believes that the private sector of the economy is inherently stable and that the trade cycle is basically due to changes in the quantity of money. Professor Thomas Mayer states that the monetarist 'looks upon the private sector as stable . . . and attributes most, though certainly not all, the actually observed instability to fluctuations in the money supply induced by the monetary authorities'[22]. Friedman's view that the trade cycle is basically a monetary phenomenon is put forward in the article under discussion[23] and much reliance at this stage is placed on his and Meiselman's well-known study, 'The Relative Stability of Monetary Velocity and the Investment Multiplier in the United States, 1897-1958'[24].

It is now generally recognized that the interest elasticity of demand for money (real money balances) is negative and significant. A rise in the rate of interest is associated with a decrease in the demand for money, an increase in the velocity of circulation. Milton Friedman stated in his 1959 article, The Demand for Money, that he and Anna J. Schwartz had been unable to find a statistically significant influence of the rate of interest[25]. Laidler, however, has pointed out that this was due to erroneous procedure[26]. In his later 1966 article, Interest Rates and the Demand for Money, Friedman wrote 'I know of no empirical student of the demand for money who denies that interest rates affect the real quantity of money demanded.'[27] He also stated that 'Almost all estimates, even for long rates, show an inelastic response, i.e. elasticities less than unity.'[28] Friedman also maintained that only the finding of a near-infinite elasticity of demand would raise fundamental issues in monetary theory although he admitted that 'It is important to determine as accurately as possible the size of the elasticities in order to have a better empirical basis for understanding the course of economic events and for guiding policy.'[29] The liquidity trap, an infinite elasticity of demand for money at some positive rate of interest, refers to a situation in which the rate of interest cannot be reduced by an increase in the real quantity of money, more money merely being held at this rate. He rightly pointed out that changes in the nominal amount of money will not affect interest rates and the real economy 'if prices react rapidly enough so that there are no changes in the *real* money stock, which is the desired magnitude affected by interest rates'[30]. Friedman concludes that no fundamental issues in monetary theory or policy 'hinge on whether the estimated elasticity can for most purposes be approximated by zero or is better approximated by -0.1 or -0.5 or -2.0, provided it is seldom capable of being approximated by $-\infty$'[31]. Commenting on Patinkin's criticism of his 1970 attempt to restate and clarify his position, A Theoretical Framework for Monetary Analysis, Friedman states that with regard to his demand function for money 'the inclusion of the interest rate is a minor feature of my framework'[32].

Laidler gives a very good summary of the main econometric studies of the demand for money. He refers to Professor A. H. Meltzer's 1963 article[33], based on United States data for 1900–1958 and using the rate of interest on 20-year bonds, as showing 'a significant negative relationship between the demand for money, however defined, and the rate of interest, regardless of the other variables included in the function'[34]. He adds that the elasticity of demand for money showed some variation but was about −0.7[35]. Laidler refers to his own 1966 article[36], based on United States data for 1892–1960, in which it was shown that 'regardless of whether the definition of money used included time deposits or excluded them, interest elasticities of demand for money of about −0.7 for the long rate of interest and of about −0.15 for the short rate were found'[37]. Laidler also refers to certain studies based on data of the United Kingdom and of other countries and states that 'all confirm the importance of one interest rate variable or another to the demand-for-money function for these countries'[38]. After consideration of some further studies Laidler finally concludes that 'there is an overwhelming body of evidence in favour of the proposition that the demand for money is negatively related to the rate of interest'[39].

Laidler also surveys the somewhat complicated econometric studies undertaken regarding the liquidity-trap hypothesis[40] and finds that 'the evidence on the liquidity trap is not quite clearcut. On the whole, the evidence goes against the hypothesis'[41]. However, he points out that until further work has been undertaken 'the conclusion to which we subscribe, that the liquidity-trap hypothesis is of no empirical significance, must rest on an uncomfortably high degree of personal judgement'[42]. A liquidity trap is possible because the costs of borrowing set a minimum rate of interest instead of Keynes's speculative motive (see p. 179). Harry Johnson refers to Latané's article[43] in which he 'adduces evidence for the existence of a liquidity trap, though he prefers to explain it by the cost of bond transactions rather than by Keynes's speculative motive'[44]. Much further econometric work needs to be done on the liquidity trap but during a trade-cyclical slump the interest elasticity of the demand for money may well be high. Meade states with approval Keynes's view that government expenditure financed by borrowing (the sale of government bonds) in such circumstances will only be associated with a small increase in interest rates because this will cause people to buy securities with their idle liquid balances[45]. He also refers to Keynes's contention that at a time of great economic depression there is 'an excess of idle funds waiting for profitable outlets'[46].

Dr C. A. E. Goodhart gives a very useful discussion of the empirical work on the interest elasticity of demand for money referring to Laidler's book[47] and the Table A of the article by C. A. E. Goodhart and A. D. Crockett (1970)[48]. Table A provides a useful summary of empirical work based on United States and United Kingdom data, showing for each study the period, the definition of money, the interest rate used and the interest elasticity. Goodhart states that the general conclusion of these surveys is that 'the interest elasticity of demand for money is highly significant, taking values that correspond reasonably closely to those which would be predicted on the basis of the micro-behavioural theories, i.e. around −0.5'[49]. He adds that 'The results would seem to contradict the expectations of more extreme Keynesians, who may have supposed that the availability of alternative liquid assets would have removed "any limit to the velocity of circulation".[50] This is a quotation from the Radcliffe Report[51]. Further, the results 'undermine the extreme version of the quantity theory, namely that there is a fixed short-term link between the stock of money and money incomes'. This depends on the assumption of a constant velocity of circulation.

In discussing the influence of monetary policy in terms of changes in interest rates Goodhart emphasizes that the important consideration is the relative sizes of the interest elasticities of the demand for money and of the demand for goods (a wider concept than Keynes's investment demand-schedule or the schedule of the marginal efficiency of capital). He states that 'The higher the interest elasticity of demand for money *relative* to the interest elasticity of demand for goods'[52] the less the effect of changes in the supply of money on the demand for goods, the level of economic activity. However, Goodhart points out that the *absolute* degree of substitution in an economy is important. He states that 'almost all the evidence indicates that the interest elasticities of demand, for money and for goods, are quite low, well below unity, for example'[53]. Goodhart considers that 'common observation makes it difficult to accept without hesitation the conclusion that the economic system is characterized by such generally low interest elasticities, such little response to relative price changes. A system of this kind would tend to exhibit large, erratic fluctuations in prices, interest rates and asset values, since relative prices would have to change very sharply to restore equilibrium.'[54] He also refers to the sensitivity of popular concern to interest rate changes.

In considering the predictability (the stability of the function) and degree of constancy of the velocity of circulation of money or the corresponding element in the demand for money, changes under v in equation (3) (*see* p. 110) are important. Friedman has since his 1956 paper treated v, the velocity of circulation, as a general head for a number of relevant variables (*see* p. 110 above). The expected degree of economic stability is stressed under this head. Such variables are difficult to measure empirically although the direction of change may be known. There may also be unexpected changes in these variables. Thus it may be difficult to formulate satisfactory short-term and longterm demand functions for money. Changes in the trade-cyclical velocity of circulation of money against measured or current income have already been discussed.

Friedman in his 1961 article, The Demand for Money[55], refers to the increase in the velocity of circulation of money in the United States during the post-World War II period in contrast to the general tendency for it to decrease throughout the period 1869 to World War II, which he attributes to the rise in real income per head. He thinks that some minor part of the increase in velocity may be due to the reasons commonly given: the rise in interest rates, expectations of inflation and the growth of savings and loan shares and other substitutes for money. Friedman's main explanation is a change in 'the public's expectations about the likely degree of economic stability'[56]. Post-war recessions proved to be mild and there was a growth of confidence in the maintenance of 'a high and relatively stable level of economic activity'[57]. Less money was held for the precautionary motive.

However, some economists have stressed the importance of the growth of money substitutes relatively to the quantity of money as a cause of an increase in the velocity of circulation. These near-money assets are provided by non-bank financial intermediaries such as building societies and hire purchase finance houses[58]. Professor N. J. Gibson points out that the interest in the role of financial intermediaries, banks and non-bank intermediaries, in the modern economy 'originated in the United States and was stimulated by the work of the American economists, J. G. Gurley and E. S. Shaw'[59]. Their classic book is *Money in a Theory of Finance* (1960)[60], but they had written their earlier articles (1955[61], 1956[62]) before the Radcliffe Report of 1959. They maintained that the growth of non-bank financial intermediaries[63] could reduce the effectiveness of a restrictive monetary policy. A relative increase in money substitutes increases the velocity of circulation. In the United Kingdom the Radcliffe Report (1959)[64] devoted a great deal of attention to the non-bank financial intermediaries in its emphasis on the importance of the concept of 'general liquidity'. Gibson questions 'the extreme position taken up by the Radcliffe Committee towards non-bank financial intermediaries as a threat to traditional monetary policy'[65]. His conclusion is that 'the available substitutes are in general not perfect and therefore cannot completely offset monetary policy'[66].

The relative growth of money substitutes reduces the demand for money, increases its velocity of circulation. Its effect on the interest elasticity of demand for money and the velocity of circulation must now be considered. Harry Johnson points out that Professor Alvin L. Marty in his review[67] of *Money in a Theory of Finance* 'makes the interesting theoretical point that the introduction of a substitute does not necessarily increase the elasticity of a demand' but 'Gurley and Shaw infer increased elasticity only in the special case of an unfunding of government debt, and present a satisfactory reason for it.'[68] Professor Phillip Cagan and Dr Anna J. Schwartz state that they estimated the short-run interest elasticity of demand for money for the 1920s and 1953–1965 and found that the growth of money substitutes did not increase it[69]. They used a narrow definition of money.

Important changes in the velocity of circulation of money do occur. To the extent that there is a stable demand function for money as emphasized by Friedman, such changes are predictable. For example, if the interest elasticity is known, the effect of a change in the rate of interest on the velocity of circulation is known. Approximate negative values for the elasticity have been given above but it is disquietening that the empirical evidence shows so much variation in the values which cannot be explained by the definition of money and the rate of interest which have been used. The parameters of the other variables in equations (1) and (3), as given by the empirical evidence, cannot be entirely relied on and important changes may occur under u for which it is very difficult or impossible to provide parameters, so that prediction is difficult. The velocity of circulation may also change because of shifts in the demand function and changes in the parameters for the various variables, which again makes prediction difficult.

Friedman has received considerable support for his belief in a stable demand function for money, a stable relationship between the velocity of circulation and a number of variables. The evidence at least suggests that for quite long periods of time relatively stable demand functions with significant negative interest elasticity have existed. Laidler concludes that the evidence seems to show a stable relationship between the demand for money and the rate of interest[70]. Goodhart's conclusion on the evidence relating the demand for money to money incomes and yields on alternative financial assets is that 'The relationships seem more stable, the income elasticities somewhat higher, and the interest elasticities rather lower than many Keynesians might have imagined.'[71]

However, the stability of the demand function for money has been questioned. Dr Douglas Fisher provided a Discussion Paper to the 1970 Sheffield Money Seminar in which he submitted that the evidence of the stability of the demand for money is 'under a cloud'[72]. Professor Hahn is critical of Friedman's claim that there is a relatively stable demand function for money 'in the absence of a theoretical explanation'[73]. Professor Newlyn and Mr Bootle refer to this stability problem in the United Kingdom, taking the 'narrow' (M_1) and 'broad' (M_3) definitions of money, the latter including deposit accounts[74]. They write, 'Events since 1971 have, however, called into question the stability of the demand for money, as previously understood. Although future research may reveal the underlying stability of a redefined money demand function, it is important that the stability of the demand function for M_3, accepted by the Bank [of England] at the time, appeared to collapse completely.'[75] They explain why 'The fact that this happened less to the demand function for M_1' may not provide a solution for monetary control[76]. There are a number of possible explanations of the instability which developed in the 1970s which require detailed examination.

Milton Friedman writes, 'I know of no monetarist who regards velocity as an unchangeable constant apart from stochastic disturbances.'[77] The problem is the degree of constancy and the extent to which changes can be more or less precisely predicted. Friedman stresses that the quantity of money and velocity generally move in the same direction[78]. Keynesian economists would accept this while holding that a decrease in velocity may be an offsetting influence to an increase in the quantity of money during a deep depression[79]. Friedman regards velocity as relatively constant and predictable while G. D. N. Worswick, a Keynesian, regards it as neither constant nor fairly exactly predictable[80].

Keynes of *The General Theory* and post-Keynesian economists have emphasized the importance of fluctuations in investment and other forms of 'autonomous' expenditure working through the multiplier to determine the levels of real and money income. Friedman's Counter-Revolution, or neo-quantity theory of money, emphasized that changes in the quantity of money, the velocity of circulation being relatively constant, determined the level of money income in the short and long run and could affect real income in the short run. Friedman has made great claims that his theory is vindicated by empirical work, in particular, his classic study with David Meiselman, 'The Relative Stability of Monetary Velocity and the Investment Multiplier in the United States, 1897–1958'[81]. In this study they attempted to show that the velocity of circulation was relatively constant compared with the Keynesian multiplier. Friedman writes, 'Both the stock of money and the level of autonomous expenditures are positively related to consumption and to income over both short and long spans of years. However, it turns out that the correlation is generally much higher for money than for autonomous expenditures.'[82] In his 1968 *International Encyclopedia* article, referring to the 1963 study, Friedman writes, 'The results are striking: velocity is consistently more stable than the multiplier'[83], but he does refer to the results having been challenged by critics, 'showing that this question is still far from settled'.

Harry Johnson in his 1963 lecture, Recent Developments in Monetary Theory, refers to Friedman's and Meiselman's major study and states 'for the period from 1897 until recently they found that the quantity of money worked better than the multiplier for all periods but the 1930s'[84]. While referring to the criticism of the study he did not evaluate it. Johnson merely pointed out that the significance of the result depended on one's view of the appropriate period for such a test and that 'any Keynesian can well argue that the 1930s was the period for which the Keynesian theory was designed'[85]. However, a Keynesian economist could not let the matter rest there.

Harry Johnson gave strong support to the Friedman–Meiselman thesis in his October 1969 Hove Conference paper[86], despite the criticisms to which it had been subjected. He states that 'The tests in question rested on some fundamental – and debatable – methodological principles; and the failure of the critics to understand these principles, as well as to appreciate the depth of the intellectual effort put into the tests, made their criticisms and attempted refutations less powerful and persuasive than they might have been.'[87] Johnson supports the view that 'the test of good theory is its ability to predict something large from something small by means of a simple and stable theoretical relationship'[88]. This is his justification for single or reduced-form equations containing the velocity function and the multiplier relationship. He contrasts this approach with the more common view that 'the full structure of a general-equilibrium model in the detail necessary to produce an adequately good statistical "fit"'[89] is required. Further, 'behavioural relationships should be invariant to institutional and historical change; hence the Friedman–Meiselman emphasis on a long run of data'[90]. The third principle, its application giving rise admittedly to legitimate criticism, is the classification of 'autonomous' and 'induced' expenditures by statistical tests of independence and interdependence[91]. That velocity and not the multiplier is relatively more stable and should be regarded as the key relationship has not been settled by the Friedman–Meiselman tests.

Methodologically, the single equations or reduced-form equations used for their tests have been considered inadequate. The tests require to be made in the context of the general structure of the economy. Laidler states in his paper to the 1970 Sheffield Money Seminar that 'we have learned a good deal less from studying reduced forms than is often supposed because the actual statistical hypotheses have been ill-devised to discriminate between the economic hypotheses that were alleged to underlyr them'[92]. He refers to Ando and Modigliani[93] having touched upon the fundamental issue 'of the ability of the tests to discriminate between the hypotheses at stake'[94]. There are serious specification problems. Consumption was substituted for income to avoid pseudo-correlation but there are difficulties relating to the borderline between consumption (induced expenditure dependent on income) and autonomous expenditure such as investment. Some durable consumer goods might be included in investment[95]. There is the related problem of the specification of autonomous expenditure. The articles by Hester[96] (1964), Ando and Modigliani[97] (1965) and De Prano and Mayer[98] (1965) showed how changes in the definition of 'autonomous expenditure' could increase the stability of the multiplier[99]. Kaldor refers to the latter two articles as showing that Friedman and Meiselman used 'arbitrary and inappropriate definitions of "autonomous" expenditures in a Keynesian model'[100]. De Prano and Mayer suggested a roughly equal influence of autonomous expenditures and the quantity of money on consumption. The Friedman–Meiselman study was also criticized for the assumption that the causal relationship was from money to consumption. (See pp. 125–126.)

Anderson's and Jordan's[101] tests performed at the Federal Reserve Bank of St. Louis were put forward in support of the Friedman–Meiselman thesis. The article deals with monetary and fiscal policies rather than directly with the rival theories of income determination; with the relative effects on income of monetary and fiscal changes. United States quarterly data from 1952 to 1968 were used and lags were introduced. De Leeuw and Kalchbrenner[102] criticized the way in which both the monetary and fiscal tests were undertaken. After making certain adjustments they repeated the estimations and obtained very different results. Further criticism was made by Davis[103]. Artis and Nobay[104] were critical of the Anderson–Jordan econometric methods and as Laidler points out, while using a similar procedure, they were 'unable to produce the kind of stable empirical relationship between the quantity of money and the level of money income for post-war Britain that Anderson and Jordan found for the United States'[105].

Goodhart, referring to the paper by Poole and Komblith[106], states 'Considerable further empirical digging suggested that it was a moot point whether or not the one statistical relationship fitted better than the other.'[107] However, he adds 'even if the Keynesian multiplier fitted very well also, it was undeniable that in the United States – though not in the United Kingdom – there was a very good statistical fit between monetary changes and subsequent changes in money incomes'[108].

Velocity and the multiplier are two key relationships in a monetary model. Whether one is a monetarist or a Keynesian should not depend on the results of empirical research as to their relative stability. Even if velocity was shown to be relatively more constant, a Keynesian could still argue that the analysis of the constituents of effective demand and of the role of the multiplier was essential. Rather one should look for an acceptable synthesis of the Keynesian Revolution and Milton Friedman's Counter-Revolution.

The second head under which Friedman's work is considered is the independence of the factors affecting the demand for and supply of money (see p. 112). Friedman realized its importance in his classic 1956 article. He wrote that the monetarist (quantity theorist) 'holds that there are important factors affecting the supply of money that do not affect the demand for money'[109]. He referred to such circumstances as 'technical conditions affecting the supply of specie' and 'political or psychological conditions determining the policies of monetary authorities and the banking system'[110]. He pointed out that a stable money demand function is only useful for showing the effect of changes in the quantity of money on money income if changes in money supply are not merely the effect of changes in demand. Basically, Friedman regards the supply of money as exogenous and not endogenous. He rejects the opposing view that 'changes in the demand for money call forth corresponding changes in supply [or] . . . that the same forces affect both the demand for and the supply of money, and in the same way'[111].

In 1964 Friedman considered what 'is in some ways the central issue in dispute about the role of money in business cycles, namely, whether the cyclical behaviour of money is to be regarded as a major factor explaining business fluctuations or as simply a reflection of business fluctuations produced by other forces . . . the issue is whether the major direction of influence is from money to business or from business to money . . . . Undoubtedly there can be and are influences running both ways . . . there can be and almost certainly are factors other than money that contribute to the cycle . . . . The question at issue is, therefore, whether money exerts an important independent influence'[112]. Friedman's main position is that money is exogenous and is a major independent influence. It is based on five kinds of evidence[113].

(1) Qualitative historical circumstances which are regarded as the most directly relevant. He cites his great book *A Monetary History of the United States, 1867–1960*[114].
(2) The behaviour of the determinants of the money stock for which he cites Cagan's monograph[115].
(3) The timing relationship, leads and lags, where he states that 'the regular and sizable leads of the money series are themselves suggestive of an influence running from money to business but they are by no means decisive'[116]. Friedman maintains that the rate of change of the money stock regularly reaches a peak and a trough before the general trade-cyclical peaks and troughs, the lead being variable[117].
(4) Serial correlation of amplitudes of cycle phases[118].
(5) Evidence from foreign countries[119].

Harry Johnson referred in 1969 to the criticism of Friedman by those who held that the supply of money responded passively to the demand for it ('reverse causation')[120] being quelled by the publication of the monumental volume of Friedman and Schwartz[121] and the companion volume by Cagan[122]. This was not justified because of the later support given to the view that the supply of money changed as a result of a change in the level of money income. Money was endogenous.

Barrett and Walters criticized the Friedman–Meiselman study's assumption of causality from money to consumption[123]. They point out that bank borrowing for investment and public expenditure is anticipatory – the increase in money precedes the increase in expenditure but is endogenous, being caused by it. In general, an anticipatory increase in money could be required to accommodate an increase in economic activity. An increase in the public sector deficit or the public sector borrowing requirement (PSBR) may be financed by sales of government securities to the public without increasing the quantity of money but it may in part or in whole involve increased holdings of government securities by the banks, an increase in bank deposits and the total quantity of money. During a depression the 'built-in stabilizers' begin to operate, government tax receipts decline while government expenditure such as unemployment benefit payments increase. The PSBR increases and the quantity of money may increase, setting the stage for an upswing in the trade cycle when real factors such as investment opportunities become favourable. This lead of money is recognizably Keynesian.

In their study of United Kingdom data from 1958 to 1967 Artis and Nobay[124] point out that the money supply is endogenous if monetary policy is accommodating or the money supply targets are decided in view of the real economic situation.

Kaldor[125] argues that the level of income determines the supply of money. He writes that 'The money supply "accommodated itself" to the needs of trade'[126], being perhaps the result of maintaining interest rates. The money supply is endogenous. The time lag does not prove the causal relationship as the money supply precedes the increase in income because of the way output is increased and the operation of the 'built-in fiscal stabiliser'[127]. Kaldor does not accept Friedman's arguments for exogeneity in terms of the Federal Reserve Board in the United States controlling the monetary base (high-powered money), that is, currency held by the public and member bank reserves with the Federal Reserve Banks. He argues that the monetary base is responsive to changes in income[128]. Kaldor also argues that in post-World War II Britain's money has been endogenous, reflecting changes in money income[129]. He stresses the importance of changes in the PSBR[130]. The core of Friedman's reply[131] was his summary of the influence of money given in a previous article[132].

Nobay studied the United Kingdom monetary authorities' behaviour from 1959 to 1969 and concluded that the money supply 'may more appropriately be considered to be endogenously determined – a result, of course, that is not surprising for an open economy with a fixed exchange rate'[133].

Goodhart writes that 'the authorities, both in the United Kingdom and in most other industrialised countries, at least until recently, have mostly operated to control *interest rates*, and this does make the money stock endogenous'[134]. He accepts the possibility of reverse causation but thinks that 'a finding that monetary changes have a significant relationship with subsequent income changes, but not vice versa, must imply a strong presumption that money changes cause the subsequent income changes'[135]. Goodhart argues that the money lead can hardly be explained by an anticipatory increase in money balances because of the opportunity cost (interest) and the credible behaviour of households[136].

Since 1976 the Bank of England has announced target growth rates for the money supply. To the extent that these have been achieved, money has been exogenous[137]. The money supply certainly can be controlled by the monetary authorities[138].

It is unwise to assert in general that the supply of money is exogenous or endogenous[139]. The behaviour of the monetary system for particular time periods and countries must be carefully examined. Sometimes money is both exogenous and endogenous which raises the question of relative importance.

The problem of the direction of causation between money and income is closely related to the problem of the relative importance of monetary and real factors as causes of the trade cycle. Friedman accepts that real factors play a role but he regards monetary policies of expansion and contraction as the basic reason for major trade cycles. Real theories have a long history and many economists regard real factors such as the instability of technical progress to be of major importance while realizing that monetary conditions must be sufficiently flexible and that monetary policy may greatly accentuate booms and slumps.

Friedman and Schwartz provided a detailed study of the Great Depression in their classic Chapter 7, The Great Contraction, 1929–1933[140]. It originated in the United States and was perhaps the most severe in United States history: unemployment reached 25 per cent in 1933. The Depression became worldwide. Friedman and Schwartz argued that the failure of the Federal Reserve System to stem the depression was widely and wrongly interpreted as meaning 'that monetary factors were not critical; that "real" factors were the key to economic fluctuations'[141]. Friedman and Schwartz stated that the main cause of the depression was the inept policy of the Federal Reserve, the money stock falling by 33 per cent with which was associated a decline in velocity by nearly one-third from 1929 to 1933[142].

Real factors have been regarded as basic by many economists. Keynes considered that in the United States in 1929 the exhaustion of investment opportunities, a very low marginal efficiency of capital resulting from previous large-scale investment, played a vital role[143]. Other real factors referred to by Fearon as tentative explanations are the approaching saturation of the markets for consumer durables, automobiles etc., and for housing[144]. Fearon concludes 'A sensible compromise would be to accept that a combination of deflationary forces, both monetary and non-monetary, was present in the U.S. economy during 1929, and that all contributed to the downturn.'[145]

The relative importance of real and monetary factors during the depression is still a matter of debate[146]. The Wall Street crash of October 1929 was deflationary. It is clear that inept Federal Reserve policies and the bank failures[147] of 1930, 1931 and 1933 greatly increased the severity and duration of the depression.

The difference between the Keynesian and monetarist model is sometimes stated over-simply in terms of elasticities. In the Keynesian model the interest elasticity of the demand for money is high while the interest elasticity of investment is low. In the monetarist model the interest elasticity of the demand for money is low while the interest elasticity of demand for goods is high. Friedman considers a wide range of goods, investment goods, durable and semi-durable consumer goods etc.[148]. It follows that monetary policy is relatively ineffective and fiscal policy relatively effective according to the Keynesian model and vice versa for the monetarist model. Actually Friedman regards monetary policy as highly effective and allows no role for fiscal policy.

Friedman has been much criticized for an inadequate transmission mechanism. According to Johnson's interpretation Friedman has put forward the view that 'because of the difficulty of sorting out the relevant rates of return one cannot hope to obtain useful results by looking at relations between interest rates and categories of spending'[149]. Further, 'The Friedman view is that this whole process is so difficult to trace that one should proceed instead by the direct route from money to income'[150]. Although Friedman has made some attempts to trace particular paths[151] there are constant references to the importance of the direct effect of monetary change (not analysed in detail) rather than the effect through the interest rate. He emphasizes the direct effects of monetary change on spending compared with that on investment *via* the interest rate[152]. In 1972 Friedman stated 'I too tend to minimize changes in market interest rates as the primary channel through which changes in the quantity of money affect spending, output, and prices.'[153]

In discussion at the 1970 Sheffield Money Seminar, Friedman stated that the method of injection of money was not important, that 'Different methods of injection gave rise to different initial results, but he was only interested in the end result, and the end result was not affected by the method and point of injection.'[154] In the Introduction I noted that 'in 1752 David Hume envisaged that "by miracle, every man in Great Britain should have five pounds slipped into his pocket in one night" while in 1969 Milton Friedman supposes a helicopter miracle, the helicopter flying over a community and dropping dollars from the sky.'[155] However, the main methods of injection are by open-market operations and fiscal policy. In the former case the increase of money is associated with a fall in the rate of interest and the effect on income and employment depends on the elasticities of demand for money and for goods. In the latter, where a budget deficit involves an increase of money at, say, a constant interest rate, government expenditure on goods and labour increases directly and the impact on income and employment will be greater[156].

Friedman in his 1967 American Economic Association Presidential address[157] stated that monetary policy could in the short run decrease unemployment below the 'natural' rate[158] but only by accelerating inflation because of price expectations. In the long run it could not control real variables such as unemployment and real income which depended on the real forces determining production[159]. A Keynesian who attaches more importance to real disturbances and advocates monetary and fiscal management would argue that what happens in the short run affects the long-run real economy.

The liquidity trap, wherein the interest elasticity of demand for money is infinite at some positive rate, is discussed above in this chapter. Friedman distinguishes between the short-run and long-run liquidity traps and identifies Keynes's theory with the liquidity trap[160]. Patinkin does not agree with this identification[161]. He quotes[162] Keynes, 'whilst this limiting case might become practically important in future, I know of no example of it hitherto'[163]. Hahn writes that 'Keynes did not build his revolution on the liquidity trap.'[164] Friedman points out that he made the same quotation from Keynes as Patinkin adding that Keynes 'treated velocity as if in practice its behaviour frequently approximated that which would prevail in this limiting case'[165]. Further, Patinkin does not recognize that 'this is the only disclaimer in *The General Theory*: while there are repeated statements in the opposite direction'[166]. Keynes was not consistent in his treatment of the liquidity trap, admittedly referring to it at times as a fact as well as a speculative possibility. However, *The General Theory* should not be identified with it as it did provide a general theory.

Friedman has been criticized for his lack of theory of the transmission mechanism and in general. Hahn writes, 'Friedman neither has nor claims to have a monetary theory'[167], his views being based on his empirical studies. Friedman's 'A Theoretical Framework for Monetary Analysis'[168] did not satisfy his critics. In 'Comments on the Critics' he shows his appreciation of Keynes as a great economist and gives reasons for rejecting his theory[169]. Hahn quotes Friedman, 'I continue to believe that the fundamental differences between us are empirical not theoretical.'[170] Hahn believes this view to be quite false[171]. He also states that 'The overwhelmingly most important postulate of the Monetarists is that the invisible hand works and that it works pretty swiftly'[172]. Keynesians would not accept this inherent stability of the market economy. Despite criticisms, Friedman's Counter-Revolution remains important for the development of economics in which the emphasis should now be on synthesis.

Friedman's views on policy are based largely on empirical work. He stresses that monetary policy can prevent money 'being a major source of economic disturbance' and can 'provide a stable background for the economy'[173]. Friedman's prescription is a steady rate of growth of the money supply (currency plus demand and time commercial bank deposits) of, say, 3 to 5 per cent a year which would achieve a roughly stable final product price level[174]. This rate of growth is to match the growth of output and decline in velocity because of increasing wealth per head[175]. He argues against the monetary authority having discretionary powers and for a legislative rule instructing it to maintain such a steady rate of growth of money[176]. Such a policy involves flexible exchange rates[177]. Friedman is against fine tuning, the general use of monetary and fiscal[178] policies to manage the economy. He believes that 'long and variable lags in the effect of monetary or fiscal policy may well render attempted countercyclical actions destabilizing'[179]. He states that monetary authorities' attempts 'have done far more harm than good'[180]. Keynesian economists while recognizing the great difficulties of economic forecasting and the lags problem are more optimistic. Professor M. J. C. Surrey and P. A. Ormerod write that demand management 'should in conjunction with exchange rate and incomes policies continue to play the central role'[181].

Friedman rejects the view that wage-push by trade union pressure was an important influence in some inflations. He states 'The important factor was always increases in the supply of money, irrespective of the reasons for the increases.'[182] Friedman therefore rejects incomes policies and states that he is absolutely appalled by the widespread belief in Britain that 'you can use the paper club of price and wage control to beat down the rigid power of trade unions'[183]. Michael Parkin states, 'there is no evidence at all either from the studies of the determinants of inflation or from more direct studies that wage and price controls materially affect the rate of inflation. All the evidence goes in the opposite direction'[184]. Many Keynesian or non-monetarist economists would claim minor successes for incomes policies while admitting their general failure. However, they would not accept the monetarist policy for 'full' employment without inflation which involves heavy unemployment so long as the trade unions use their monopoly powers to raise money wages excessively. They would advocate appropriate monetary and fiscal policies, and renewed efforts to obtain a voluntary or statutory incomes and prices policy with a permanent Prices and Incomes Board. A related proposal for the reform of wage-fixing arrangements has been made by Meade[185].

Keynes and other economists before his death had been aware of the danger of inflation in the case of 'full employment' but Keynes in *The General Theory* had assumed for the most part fixed money-wages and had not provided a theory of money-wage rate determination. In a letter to Benjamin Graham of 31 December 1943 Keynes wrote, 'The task of keeping efficiency wages reasonably stable (I am sure they will creep up steadily in spite of our best efforts) is a political rather than an economic problem.'[186] The Phillips curve was hailed in many academic quarters, without due caution, as filling the gap. Professor A. W. Phillips had made an empirical study of the relationship between the annual percentage change in money-wage rates and unemployment as a percentage of the labour force in the United Kingdom for the years 1861–1913. He found that money-wage rates rose rapidly when the unemployment percentage was low, fell when it was high, and remained unchanged when unemployment was about 5½ per cent. Phillips also studied the periods 1913–1948 and 1948–1957. His final conclusions were that 5½ per cent unemployment was associated with stable money-wage rates and 2½ per cent unemployment was associated with a stable level of product prices if productivity was increasing by 2 per cent a year. Phillips emphasized that his conclusions were tentative and subject to qualification[187]. Subsequent work on the Phillips curve introduced further qualifications or was critical of it, while many new 'Phillips curves' were produced for various countries and time periods. In a paper, The nature of economics and problems of appraisal with special reference to developments since 1931, I warned of the dangers of assuming that a functional relationship between two economic variables is constant, and referred to G. D. N. Worswick's statement of 1971 that the Phillips curve was a 'statistical failure'[188].

Reference has been made to Friedman's introduction of expectations into the Phillips-curve analysis. Laidler devoted a section of his paper, Monetarism: an interpretation and an assessment, to what has become known as the expectations-augmented Phillips curve[189].

Notes

1. For a useful discussion of the nature and advantages of a large structural model of behavioural equations *see* G. R. Fisher and D. K. Sheppard, Interrelationships Between Real and Monetary Variables: Some Evidence from Recent US Empiral Studies in H. G. Johnson and A. R. Nobay, eds, *Issues in Monetary Economics* (1974) especially p. 237. For certain difficulties *see* pp. 222–223.
2. Clayton, Gilbert and Sedgwick, eds, *Monetary Theory and Monetary Policy in the 1970s* (1971), p. 149.
3. *Ibid.*
4. *Ibid.*, p. 5.

5. Johnson and Nobay (1974), pp. 222–223 and 235–249.
6. *Ibid.*, p. 249.
7. Michael Parkin and Michael T. Sumner, eds, *Incomes Policy and Inflation* (1st edn, 1972, reprinted with minor amendments, 1974), Foreword. Five further volumes were published: D. Laidler and D. Purdy, eds, *Inflation and Labour Markets* (1974); D. E. W. Laidler, *Essays on Money and Inflation* (1975); Michael Parkin and George Zis, eds, *Inflation in the World Economy* (1976a); Michael Parkin and George Zis, eds, *Inflation in Open Economies* (1976b); Michael Parkin and Michael T. Sumner, eds, *Inflation in the United Kingdom* (1978).
8. Michael Parkin and A. R. Nobay, eds, *Current Economic Problems*. The Proceedings of the Association of University Teachers of Economics Manchester 1974 (1975), pp. 243–291.
9. Fisher, *ibid.*, p. 277.
10. The area of Friedman's (iii) has been widened for convenience.
11. Friedman, *The Optimum Quantity of Money and Other Essays* (1969), p. 62.
12. *Ibid.*, p. 63. Friedman adds that this leads the monetarist 'to put greater emphasis on the demand for money than on, let us say, the demand for pins, even though the latter might be as stable as the former'.
13. Friedman, *The Counter-Revolution in Monetary Theory* (1970a), p. 22.
14. Friedman (1969), p. 62. The reference is to Phillip Cagan, The Monetary Dynamics of Hyperinflation (1956) in Friedman, *Studies in the Quantity Theory of Money* (1956a), pp. 25–117.
15. Friedman (1969), p. 65. The reference is to Richard T. Selden, Monetary Velocity in the United States in Friedman (1956a), pp. 179–257.
16. *Ibid.*
17. Friedman (1969), pp. 189–235, reprinted from *The Review of Economics and Statistics*, Vol. 45, supplement (February 1963).
18. Friedman (1969), pp. 206–207. The article referred to is Friedman, 'The Demand for Money: Some Theoretical and Empirical Results', *Journal of Political Economy*, Vol. 67 (August 1959), reprinted in Friedman (1969), pp. 111–139.
19. Friedman (1969), p. 207. Friedman refers to H. A. Latané, 'Cash Balances and the Interest Rate – A Pragmatic Approach', *Review of Economics and Statistics*, Vol. 36 (November 1954, pp. 456–460) and H. A. Latané 'Income Velocity and Interest Rates: A Pragmatic Approach', *The Review of Economics and Statistics*, Vol. 42 (November 1960, pp. 445–449).
20. Friedman (1969), pp. 207–208.
21. *Ibid.*, p. 209.
22. Thomas Mayer *et al.*, *The Structure of Monetarism* (1978), p. 14.
23. Friedman (1969), pp. 209 and 211–213.
24. Milton Friedman and David Meiselman, 'The Relative Stability of Monetary Velocity and the Investment Multiplier in the United States, 1897–1958'. In Commission on Money and Credit *Stabilization Policies* (Englewood Cliffs, N.J.: Prentice Hall) (1963).
25. Friedman (1959), reprinted in Friedman (1969), p. 113.
26. David E. W. Laidler, *The Demand for Money: Theories and Evidence* (2nd edn, 1977), pp. 127–128.
27. Friedman, Interest Rates and the Demand for Money, *The Journal of Law and Economics*, Vol. 9 (October 1966), reprinted in Friedman (1969), p. 142. In note 1, pp. 142–143, Friedman explains how he has been misinterpreted as having asserted this.
28. Friedman (1969), p. 143.
29. *Ibid.*, p. 144.
30. *Ibid.*, p. 149. When Keynes stated in *The General Theory* that the money rate of interest was determined by the supply of and demand for money (liquidity preference), the supply of money was measured in real terms. Keynes's theory gave rise to a voluminous literature but his theory and the loanable-funds theory are complementary. *See* D. H. Robertson, A Survey of Modern Monetary Controversy, *The Manchester School*, Vol. 6 (1938, No. 1), reprinted in Sir Dennis Robertson, *Essays in Money and Interest* (1966), p. 119 (selected with a Memoir by Sir John Hicks). Compare the two approaches to the theory of the value of money, the demand-to-hold approach, a point of time, a stock approach and the velocity-of-circulation approach, a period of time, a flow approach. A real theory of interest which analyses the supply of and demand for capital, abstracting from monetary factors, must always be borne in mind when using monetary theories of interest.

31. *Ibid.*, p. 155.
32. In Robert J. Gordon, *Milton Friedman's Monetary Framework* (1974), p. 159.
33. A. H. Meltzer, 'The Demand for Money: The Evidence from the Time Series' (June 1963), pp. 219–246.
34. Laidler (1977), p. 125.
35. *Ibid.*
36. D. Laidler, 'The Rate of Interest and the Demand for Money – Some Empirical Evidence' (December 1966), pp. 545–555.
37. Laidler (1977), p. 126.
38. *Ibid.*
39. *Ibid.*, p. 130.
40. *Ibid.*, pp. 130–132.
41. *Ibid.*, p. 132.
42. *Ibid.*, p. 133.
43. H. A. Latané, Income Velocity and Interest Rates: A Pragmatic Approach' (November 1960), pp. 445–449.
44. Harry G. Johnson, 'Monetary Theory and Policy', *American Economic Review*, Vol. 52 (June 1962), pp. 335–384, reprinted in Harry G. Johnson, *Essays in Monetary Economics* (2nd edn, 1969), p. 39.
45. James Meade, The Keynesian Revolution, in Milo Keynes, *Essays on John Maynard Keynes* (1975), p. 86.
46. *Ibid.*, p. 87.
47. Laidler, *The Demand for Money: Theories and Evidence* (1st edn, 1969).
48. C. A. E. Goodhart and A. D. Crockett, 'The Importance of Money' (June 1970), pp. 188–189.
49. C. A. E. Goodhart, *Money, Information and Uncertainty* (1975), p. 54.
50. *Ibid.*
51. Radcliffe Report, Committee on the Working of the Monetary System Report (August 1959), Cmnd 827, para. 391.
52. Goodhart (1975), p. 179.
53. *Ibid.*, p. 180.
54. *Ibid.*, p. 182.
55. Friedman, 'The Demand for Money', *Proceedings of the American Philosophical Society*, Vol. 105 (June 1961), reprinted in Friedman *Dollars and Deficits* (1968a).
56. *Ibid.*, p. 204.
57. *Ibid.*, p. 205.
58. G. Clayton, 'British Financial Intermediaries in Theory and Practice' (December 1962).
59. N. J. Gibson, *Financial Intermediaries and Monetary Policy* (2nd edn, 1970), p. 17.
60. John G. Gurley and Edward S. Shaw, *Money in a Theory of Finance* (1960).
61. J. G. Gurley and E. S. Shaw, 'Financial Aspects of Economic Development', *American Economic Review* (September 1955), pp. 515–538.
62. J. G. Gurley and E. S. Shaw, 'Financial Intermediaries and the Saving-Investment Process' (May 1956), pp. 257–276.
63. Gurley and Shaw list the various kinds of non-bank financial intermediaries in the United States in Gurley and Shaw (1960), p. 193.
64. Committee on the Working of the Monetary System (1959).
65. Gibson (1970), p. 18.
66. *Ibid.*, p. 62.
67. A. L. Marty, 'Gurley and Shaw on Money in a Theory of Finance' (February 1961), pp. 56–62.
68. Harry G. Johnson, 'Monetary Theory and Policy' (1962), pp. 335–384; reprinted in Harry G. Johnson (1969b), p. 36, n.2.
69. Phillip Cagan and Anna Jacobson Schwartz, How Feasible is a Flexible Monetary Policy?, in Richard T. Seldon, *Capitalism and Freedom* (1975), p. 268.
70. Laidler (1977), pp. 133–134.
71. Goodhart (1975), p. 55.
72. Clayton, Gilbert, Sedgwick (1971), p. 147.
73. F. H. Hahn, Professor Friedman's Views on Money' (February 1971), p. 69.
74. W. T. Newlyn and R. P. Bootle, *Theory of Money* (3rd edn, 1978), p. 33.
75. *Ibid.*, p. 175.
76. *Ibid.*

77. Gordon (1974), p. 138, n.1.
78. *Ibid.*, p. 139, n.2.
79. Friedman writes in *The Counter-Revolution* (1970a), p. 17: 'Empirically, however, it turns out that the movements of velocity tend to reinforce those of money instead of to offset them. When the quantity of money declined by a third from 1929 to 1933 in the United States, velocity declined also.' This is not relevant to the case of an *increase* in the quantity of money during a deep depression.
80. G. D. N. Worswick, 'The End of Demand Management?' (1977), p. 13, n.1. Worswick is Director of the National Institute of Economic and Social Research.
81. Milton Friedman and David Meiselman (1963), pp. 165–268.
82. Milton Friedman and Anna J. Schwartz, 'Money and Business Cycles', *The Review of Economics and Statistics*, Vol. 45 (February 1963b), reprinted in Friedman (1969), p. 211.
83. Milton Friedman, 'Money: Quantity Theory', *International Encyclopedia of the Social Sciences* (1968), pp. 432–447: Free Press, reprinted in A. A. Walters, ed., *Money and Banking: Selected Readings* (1973), p. 62.
84. Harry G. Johnson, Recent Developments in Monetary Theory, reprinted with revisions from the *Indian Economic Review*, Vol. 6 (February and August 1963), as Chapter II in Harry G. Johnson (1969b), p. 102.
85. Harry G. Johnson (1969b).
86. Harry G. Johnson, Recent Developments in Monetary Theory – A Commentary, David R. Croome and Harry G. Johnson, eds, *Money in Britain, 1959–1969* (1970), pp. 83–114: reprinted in Harry G. Johnson, *Further Essays in Monetary Economics* (1972).
87. Harry G. Johnson (1972), p. 24.
88. *Ibid.*
89. *Ibid.*
90. *Ibid.*
91. *Ibid.*
92. D. E. W. Laidler, The Influence of Money on Economic Activity – A Survey of some Current Problems, pp. 73–135, in Clayton, Gilbert and Sedgwick (1971), p. 78.
93. Ando and Modigliani, 'The Relative Stability of Monetary Velocity and the Investment Multiplier' (September 1965b), pp. 693–728.
94. Laidler in Clayton, Gilbert and Sedgwick (1971), p. 79, n.5.
95. *Ibid.*, p. 80, n.7.
96. D. D. Hester, 'Keynes and the Quantity Theory: A Comment on the Friedman –Meiselman CMC Paper', and M. Friedman and D. Meiselman, 'Reply to Donald Hester', *The Review of Economics and Statistics*, Vol. 46 (November 1964), pp. 364–368, 369–376.
97. Ando and Modigliani (1956).
98. M. de Prano and T. Mayer, 'Tests of the Relative Importance of Autonomous Expenditure and Money'; M. Friedman and David Meiselman, 'Reply to Ando and Modigliani and to De Prano and Mayer'; A. Ando and F. Modigliani, 'Rejoinder'; M. De Prano and T. Mayer, 'Rejoinder', *American Economic Review*, Vol. 55 (September 1965), pp. 729–752, 753–785, 786–790, 791–792.
99. Laidler in Clayton, Gilbert and Sedgwick (1971), p. 79, n.5.
100. Nicholas Kaldor, 'The New Monetarism', *Lloyds Bank Review* (July 1970), pp. 1–17, reprinted in A. A. Walters, *Money and Banking. Selected Readings* (1973), pp. 264–265.
101. L. C. Anderson and J. L. Jordan, 'Monetary and Fiscal Actions: A Test of their Relative Importance in Economic Stabilization' (November 1968), pp. 11–24.
102. F. De Leeuw and J. Kalchbrenner, 'Monetary and Fiscal Actions: A Test of their Relative Importance in Economic Stabilization: A Comment' (April 1969).
103. R. G. Davis, 'How Much Does Money Matter? A Look at some Recent Evidence' (June 1969), pp. 119–131.
104. M. J. Artis and A. R. Nobay, 'Two Aspects of the Monetary Debate: The Attempt to Reinstate Money (August 1969), pp. 33–42.
105. Laidler in Clayton, Gilbert and Sedgwick (1971), p. 79, n.5.
106. W. Poole and E. Komblith, 'The Friedman–Meiselman CMC Paper: New Evidence on an Old Controversy' (December 1973), pp. 908–917.
107. Goodhart (1975), p. 188.
108. *Ibid.*, p. 189.

109. M. Friedman, The Quantity Theory of Money: A Restatement, in *Studies in the Quantity Theory of Money*, reprinted in Friedman (1969), p. 63.
110. *Ibid.*
111. *Ibid.*
112. M. Friedman, The Monetary Studies of the National Bureau, *The National Bureau Enters its 45th Year*, 44th Annual Report, pp. 7–25 (1964: National Bureau of Economic Research), reprinted in Friedman (1969), pp. 265–266.
113. *Ibid.*, pp. 266–277.
114. Milton Friedman and Anna Jacobson Schwartz (1963).
115. Phillip C. Cagan, *Determinants and Effects of Changes in the Stock of Money, 1867–1960* (1965).
116. Friedman (1969). Friedman gives three reasons why this evidence could be misleading. *See also* M. Friedman, 'The Lag in Effect of Monetary Policy', *Journal of Political Economy*, Vol. 69 (October 1961), reprinted in Friedman (1969). Here he refers to this 'long and variable lag' (p. 258).
117. M. Friedman and Anna J. Schwartz (1963b), reprinted in Friedman (1969), p. 234.
118. M. Friedman, The Monetary Studies of the National Bureau (1964), in Friedman (1969), pp. 271–275.
119. *Ibid.*, pp. 275–277.
120. Harry G. Johnson, Recent Developments in Monetary Theory – A Commentary, in David R. Croome and Harry G. Johnson (1970), pp. 83–114, reprinted in Harry G. Johnson (1972), p. 25. Johnson refers to this as the Banking School position. There is a linkage between the reverse causation view and the view of the Banking School in the famous Currency–Banking Schools controversy in the first half of the nineteenth century but this does not mean that the error in that view was being repeated.
121. Friedman and Schwartz (1963a).
122. Cagan (1965).
123. C. R. Barrett and A. A. Walters, 'The Stability of Keynesian and Monetary Multipliers in the United Kingdom' (November 1966), pp. 395–405.
124. M. J. Artis and A. R. Nobay (August 1969), pp. 33–51.
125. Nicholas Kaldor (1970), pp. 1–17, reprinted in Walters (1973).
126. *Ibid.*, p. 268.
127. *Ibid.*, pp. 271–272.
128. *Ibid.*, p. 273.
129. *Ibid.*, p. 276.
130. *Ibid.*, p. 277.
131. Milton Friedman, 'The New Monetarism: Comment', *Lloyds Bank Review* (October 1970), pp. 52–53, reprinted in Walters (1973).
132. M. Friedman (1964a), in Friedman (1969).
133. A. R. Nobay, A Model of the United Kingdom Monetary Authorities' Behaviour 1959–1969 in H. G. Johnson and A. R. Nobay (1974), pp. 290–322. *See also* Goodhart (1975), p. 191, where he refers to the United Kingdom as an open economy which maintained fixed exchange rates until 1972 and writes that in such an economy 'the private sector is in a stronger position to adjust its money balances to the current level of domestic expenditures . . . by transferring funds over the exchanges'. The foreign exchange rate devaluations of 1949 and 1967 must, however, be borne in mind.
134. Goodhart (1975), p. 52. *See also* p. 190 and p. 135, n.1.
135. *Ibid.*, p. 191.
136. Anticipatory bank borrowing was referred to on p. 125. Goodhart refers to the argument for an anticipatory increase in money balances by P. Davidson and S. Weintraub, 'Money as Cause and Effect' (December 1973), pp. 1117–1132, especially pp. 1117–1119.
137. To the extent that the Chancellor of the Exchequer in collaboration with the Governor of the Bank of England has taken the economic situation into account, for example, the existing rate of money growth which they may wish to reduce gradually, there is an endogenous aspect.
138. There may be difficulties in the short run but by controlling the monetary base, high-powered money, the monetary authorities can control the total supply of money. For discussions of the mechanics of monetary control *see* W. T. Newlyn and R. P. Bootle (1978); David Gowland, *Monetary Policy and Credit Control* (1978);

M. D. K. W. Foot, C. A. E. Goodhart and A. C. Hotson, 'Monetary Base Control' (June 1979), pp. 149–159; *Monetary Control*, Green Paper (March 1980).

139. Hahn leaves the question open. *See* F. H. Hahn, 'Professor Friedman's Views on Money', *Economica* (February 1971), pp. 61–80, pp. 68, 69, 72, 77. T. C. Mills discusses recent empirical work including his own study of United Kingdom data from 1963 I to 1977 III which contribute to the clarification and solution of this problem. He finds certain causal relationships but emphasizes the caution required at this stage. *See* T. C. Mills, 'Money, Income and Causality in the U.K. – A Look at the Recent Evidence' (May 1980), pp. 18–28.

140. Friedman and Schwartz (1963a), pp. 299–419.

141. Friedman and Schwartz (1963b) in Friedman (1969), p. 190.

142. Friedman and Schwartz (1963a), pp. 301–302. Friedman and Schwartz consider carefully the data for sub-periods which are necessary for diagnosis. Indeed much of the debate has turned on the interpretation of the data of a number of sub-periods.

143. *C.W.*, Vol. VII (1936, 1973), p. 323. *See also* the references to other economists holding this view in Peter Fearon, *The Origins and Nature of the Great Slump 1929–1932* (1979), p. 32.

144. Fearon (1979), p. 32.

145. *Ibid.*, p. 33. The monetary factors to which he refers are the reduction in the rate of growth of the money supply from 1928 and rising interest rates.

146. For example, Professor Temin advocates the Spending against the Money Hypothesis, particularly for a critical sub-period, in Peter Temin, *Did Monetary Forces Cause the Great Depression?* (1976). *See* pp. 169–178, especially pp. 170 and 178. Arthur E. Gandolfi and James R. Lothian, 'Did Monetary Forces Cause the Great Depression? A Review Essay' (November 1977), pp. 679–691, is a very critical review of Temin's book.

147. A consequence of the bank failures was an important improvement in the United States banking system by the introduction of compulsory insurance of bank deposits with the Federal Deposit Insurance Corporation in 1934 under the Glass–Steagull Banking Act of 1933. *See* Friedman and Schwartz (1963a), pp. 434–442.

148. Friedman (1961b) in Friedman (1969), pp. 237–260, pp. 255–256; Friedman, *The Counter-Revolution in Monetary Theory* (1970a), p. 25; Friedman (1970b) in Gordon (1974), pp. 1–62, p. 28.

149. Harry G. Johnson (1963) in Johnson (1969b), pp. 73–103, p. 101.

150. *Ibid.*, p. 102.

151. *See* for example Gordon (1974, pp. 48 *et seq.*).

152. Milton Friedman (1959) in Friedman (1969), pp. 111–139, p. 139.

153. Milton Friedman, 'Comments on the Critics', *Journal of Political Economy*, Vol. 80 (September/October 1972), in Gordon (1974), pp. 132–177, p. 172.

154. Clayton, Gilbert and Sedgwick (1971), p. 71.

155. *Ibid.*, p. 6. The references are to David Hume, *Essays Moral, Political and Literary* (1903) and Milton Friedman (1969), pp. 4–5. I added 'Such is the continuity of economic thought'. I also pointed out that 'Keynes had a more complicated vision of the Treasury filling old bottles with bank notes, burying them in disused coal-mines, and determining the conditions under which they could be dug up again.' J. M. Keynes, *C.W.*, Vol. VII (1936, 1973), p. 129.

156. For some further complications *see* Victoria Chick, *The Theory of Monetary Policy* (1973), pp. 55–57, 134–137 and 150; and Goodhart (1975), p. 188.

157. Friedman, 'The Role of Monetary Policy', *American Economic Review*, Vol. 58 (March 1968d), pp. 1–17), reprinted in Friedman (1969).

158. Friedman (1969), pp. 102–103. The 'natural' rate of unemployment refers to the rate determined by the structure of the labour market, costs of mobility, search costs etc. Michael T. Sumner discusses the effect of the benefit/earnings ratio. *See* his Wage Determination (pp. 75–92) in Michael Parkin and Michael T. Sumner (1978), pp. 89–90.

159. Friedman (1969), pp. 105 and 110.

160. Friedman (1970b) in Gordon (1974), pp. 15 and 21–26.

161. Don Patinkin, 'Friedman on the Quantity Theory and Keynesian Economics', *Journal of Political Economy*, Vol. 80 (September/October 1972) in Gordon (1974), pp. 111–131, p. 121, n.14.

162. *Ibid.*, p. 130.

163. J. M. Keynes, *C.W.*, Vol. VII (1936, 1973), p. 207.

164. Hahn (1971), p. 79.
165. Friedman (1972) in Gordon (1974), p. 169.
166. *Ibid*. Friedman's Appendix 1, Quotations from *The General Theory* Related to Absolute Liquidity Preference (Gordon (1974), pp. 173–174), provide impressive evidence of Keynes's concern about the liquidity trap.
167. Hahn (1971), p. 61.
168. Gordon (1974).
169. Gordon (1974), p. 134. Patinkin stresses the relationship of Friedman's work to Keynes's liquidity-preference theory. *See* Friedman on the Quantity Theory . . . , Gordon (1974), p. 112.
170. F. H. Hahn, 'Monetarism and Economic Theory' (February 1980), pp. 1–17, p. 1. The quotation is from Milton Friedman, Comments on Tobin and Buiter, in J. L. Stein, ed., *Monetarism* (1976), pp. 104–125. Friedman made a similar statement, Friedman (1970b) in Gordon (1974), p. 61.
171. Hahn (1980), p. 15.
172. *Ibid*., p. 16.
173. Friedman (1968d) in Friedman (1969), p. 106.
174. *Ibid*., p. 109.
175. Friedman, 'Monetary Policy', *Newsweek* (3 June 1968), reprinted in Friedman (1968a), p. 171.
176. Milton Friedman, Should There be an Independent Monetary Authority?, Leland B. Yeager, *In Search of a Monetary Constitution* (Cambridge, Mass., 1962; reprinted in Friedman (1968a), pp. 174–194).
177. Friedman, *A Program for Monetary Stability* (1960), p. 101.
178. Friedman emphasizes the importance of analysing fiscal and monetary policies separately although 'they operate jointly most of the time' Friedman (1970a), p. 18. He believes that government deficits not involving an increase in the quantity of money have little expansionary effect. *See* the *Newsweek* quotation in Friedman (1970b) (Gordon (1974), p. 140). A detailed analysis would require the consideration of a number of assumptions.
179. Friedman (1961b), in Friedman (1969), p. 258. *See also* Phillip Cagan and Anna Jacobson Schwartz (1975) in Selden (1975), pp. 262–293.
180. Friedman (1970a), p. 27.
181. M. J. C. Surrey and P. A. Ormerod, Demand Management in Britain 1964–1981, in Michael Posner, *Demand Management* (1978), pp. 101–125, p. 125.
182. Clayton, Gilbert and Sedgwick (1971), p. 71.
183. Friedman, *Unemployment versus Inflation? An Evaluation of the Phillips Curve* (1975), p. 31. In this study and in his 1976 Alfred Nobel Memorial Lecture, Friedman, *Inflation and Unemployment: The New Dimension of Politics* (1977), Friedman discusses the Phillips curve which shows an empirical relationship between the rate of increase of wages and the rate of unemployment. Expectations play an important role in the analysis and his conclusions are very different from those of Phillips.
184. Michael Parkin, Alternative Explanations of United Kingdom Inflation: A Survey, in Parkin and Sumner (1978), pp. 11–51, p. 49. *See* Parkin and Sumner, United Kingdom Inflation: an Overview and Summary, in Parkin and Sumner (1978), pp. 1–10, p. 6, for a useful summary of wage and price controls, 1948 to July 1977. For the three 'pay-round' years 1975–1978 there was a pay agreement between the Government and the TUC which then broke down and was followed by the Winter of Discontent of 1978–1979.
185. James E. Meade, *Wages and Prices in a Mixed Economy* (1971); James E. Meade, 'Employment without Inflation (1980).
186. J. M. Keynes, *C.W.*, Vol. XXVI (1980), p. 38. the whole of pages 30 to 40 are of interest. *See also* Austin Robinson, *John Maynard Keynes – Economist, Author, Statesman* (1971), pp. 13–14; and D. E. Moggridge, *Keynes* (1976). p. 130.
187. A. W. Phillips, 'The Relation between Unemployment and the Rate of Change of Money-wage Rates in the United Kingdom, 1861–1957' (November 1958).
188. J. C. Gilbert, The Nature of Economics and Problems of Appraisal with Special Reference to Developments since 1931, in C. Blake and S. G. E. Lythe, *Dundee School of Economics: A Further Commemoration* (1981).
189. Laidler, 'Monetarism: an Interpretation and an Assessment' (March 1981). *See also* Brian Kantor, 'Rational Expectations and Economic Thought' (December 1979).

Part III

The disciples

Chapter 9

Close associates of Keynes

Here I consider the work of some distinguished economists who were greatly influenced by Keynes and were explicit in their recognition of their debt to him. Much of their work was based on Keynes's model in *The General Theory*. In general, they recognized 'The Keynesian Revolution', the great break in the development of economic thought, and seized upon it as a starting point for their own contributions to its further development. I think in particular of Lord Kahn, Sir Roy Harrod and Professor Joan Robinson all of whom not only were influenced by Keynes but also influenced him[1].

Keynes's *The General Theory* was an important stage in the integration of monetary theory with the general economic theory of the determination of the relative prices of goods and services. It led Patinkin to write his *magnum opus, Money, Interest, and Prices*[2] which has the sub-title, An Integration of Monetary and Value Theory. Some progress had been made before Keynes. Firstly, the application of marginal utility analysis to the demand for money to hold by the Austrians, Menger and von Mises, by Marshall and the Cambridge School, and by Cannan at The London School of Economics, had made the theory of the value of money a special case of the general theory of value[3]. This gives us the statement that in equilibrium there will be equimarginal returns. The marginal utilities of, say, £1 spent on consumers' goods, £1 held as a money balance and £1 invested in an interest-earning asset are all equal[4]. The demand-to-hold approach to the theory of the value of money (the general level of prices) is a form of the quantity theory of money. Keynes wrote in the Preface to the French Edition of *The General Theory*, 'The following analysis registers my final escape from the confusions of the Quantity Theory, which once entangled me.'[5] Many Keynesian economists have taken a similar antagonistic view of the quantity theory. However, if this theory is correctly used, as in the hands of Professor Sir Dennis Robertson, it is useful and what is required is a synthesis of the quantity theory and Keynes's model.

Secondly, the analysis of the relationship between changes in monetary variables and changes in real variables played an important role in Wicksell's work beginning with *Interest and Prices* (1898), Ludwig von Mises, *The Theory of Money and Credit* (1912), J. A. Schumpeter, *The*

Theory of Economic Development (1911), von Hayek's work of the late 1920s and early 1930s and the work of D. H. Robertson of the same period. The doctrine of forced saving, investment imposed on the community by monetary change, must be included here and this goes back at least to Jeremy Bentham's passage in his 'Manual of Political Economy written in 1804 but not published until 1843'[6]. We also find David Hume describing the effect of changes in the supply of money on real variables as early as in 1752. He wrote, 'we find, that, in every kingdom, into which money begins to flow in greater abundance than formerly, every thing takes a new face: labour and industry gain life; the merchant becomes more enterprising, the manufacturer more diligent and skilful, and even the farmer follows his plough with greater alacrity and attention'[7].

I would say that Keynes's great contribution was to develop a model in which the determination of the levels of income and employment by aggregate money demand, effective demand, played the central part. We can find, I think, all the elements of the system of *The General Theory* in the writings of earlier economists. With the development of trade cycle (business cycle) theories from the beginning of the twentieth century we find fluctuations in effective demand playing an important role since great emphasis was placed on fluctuations in investment. This is obvious in Schumpeter's *The Theory of Economic Development* (1911), D. H. Robertson's *A Study of Industrial Fluctuation* (1915), theories in which the acceleration principle played an important role, and many others[8]. However, as a broad generalization one can say that until Keynes we had the theory of value, one of the glories of economic thought, which dealt with the allocation of resources on the assumption of a full-employment equilibrium, and theories of the trade cycle which dealt with fluctuations in income and employment, many of which stressed fluctuations in effective demand. Keynes's great achievement was to create a model in which these two areas were integrated. Although his formal model is static, trade cycle theory can be developed from it in a logical way as he indicates in Chapter 22 and it can also be said that he set the stage for dynamic economics. Much of post-Keynesian theory has been dynamising Keynes. However, it must be remembered that other economists, notably Robertson, developed techniques of dynamic analysis at an earlier date.

To put Keynes's work in perspective as I have done is by no means to diminish his great intellectual achievement. Austin Robinson, a student and close friend of Keynes, gave the British Academy Inaugural Keynes Lecture in April 1971[9]. It is an eulogy of Keynes appropriate to the occasion and yet given with restraint, showing a balanced judgement as far as was possible at the time. He points out that Keynes did not seek 'to write an economic bible, to survive as the verbally inspired truth for all time'[10]. He himself expected to move on, but this was largely denied him by serious illness, his war work and death in 1946. Despite the present unsatisfactory state of economics it is true to say that great progress has been made by Keynesian and other economists since *The General Theory*. Robinson points to two developments with which we shall be concerned. There is growth theory, 'descending in some important respects from the Keynesian thinking but not integrated into it in 1936'[11]. The other is the problem of avoiding the inflation which may arise in a full-employment economy.

Keynes foresaw this problem as has been made clear by a number of economists whose work is discussed in this chapter. Robinson gives the example of Keynes writing in 1944 'to an author who had submitted an over-formalistic analysis of the problem: I do not doubt that a serious problem will arise as to how wages are to be restrained when we have a combination of collective bargaining and full employment. But I am not sure how much light the kind of analytical method you apply can throw on this essentially political problem.'[12] Since 1974, during the world recession, the United Kingdom has been faced with the problem of inflation and relatively high rates of unemployment, a problem not foreseen by Keynes or any other economists.

Robinson regards Keynes's important contribution to economics to be found in a number of very fundamental new questions which he asked. Keynes asked what determined the level of employment, whether the economy was inherently stable at full employment and how the rate of interest is determined. Robinson writes with regard to these questions central to economics, 'If his own answers were all proved to be wrong (and I do not think they have been or will be) I would still regard the *General Theory* as one of the great milestones of all times in our subject.'[13]

Robinson considers that there are now two images of Keynesian economics. The first image sees Keynesian economics 'as a set of panaceas for the economic diseases of the 1930s applied uncritically to the entirely different world of the 1960s and 1970s – a belief that government policies should in all cases be expansionist and never disinflationary'[14]. In that sense, Robinson states that he and many others who were his pupils and admirers are not Keynesians. Further, he writes, 'Nor do I believe that Keynes himself would have been a Keynesian. After an evening spent discussing the prospects of the post-war world with economists in Washington in the fall of 1944, he commented to Lydia and myself at breakfast the next morning: "I found myself the only non-Keynesian present."'[15] Robinson refers to Keynes's definition of the perfectly consistent man as 'the man who has his umbrella up whether it rains or not'[16]. However, Robinson reminds us that Keynes attached great importance to maintaining the highest practicable level of employment. He was well aware of the social evil of unemployment as it affected the individual and the family despite the payment of unemployment insurance benefit.

The second image of Keynesian economics is the one Robinson himself holds and indeed which is held by all economists who have a just appreciation of its significance. It is stated by Robinson as being 'a system of thought in which one tries to see what are the factors influencing the propensities to consume and to save, to invest, to expand government expenditure; to see what factors are influencing and likely to influence the rate of interest; to see what is the current or expected loading of the economy and how far the elasticity of supply of output as a whole will permit expansion without more inflation than is regarded as tolerable'[17].

While absorbed in war finance, Keynes, as Robinson points out, was the inspiration of the White Paper, *Employment Policy*[18]. In this Coalition Government Paper, issued in 1944, the Government accepted 'as one of their primary aims and responsibilities the maintenance of a high and stable level of employment after the war'[19]. This was a big step forward in the Government's recognition of its responsibilities in economic affairs and was to a very considerable extent due to the work of Keynes. The Government no longer maintained that unemployment was largely beyond its control, somewhat like bad weather which had to be accepted when it came. The White Paper, while Keynesian in spirit, was a compromise document and was by no means a complete blueprint for employment policy. Robinson maintains, speaking in 1971, that it 'has done much in the past twenty-five years to mitigate the horrors of the world of unemployment'[20].

For the years 1953–1969 the average percentage unemployment rate in the United Kingdom was 1.6 as compared with 14.9 for 1934–1939[21]. This was a remarkable transformation although some economists, including D. H. Robertson, were critical of policies leading to what they regarded as over-full employment. The minimum percentage unemployment rate for Great Britain was 1.0 in 1955 and 1956 and the maximum rate 2.3 in 1968 and 1969. For the same period, 1953–1969, the average of the annual percentage increases (taking the level of one year as compared with that of the previous year) in retail prices in the United Kingdom was 3.3 as compared with 2.1 for 1934–1939. Admittedly the rate of inflation was increasing towards the end of the period and the percentage increases in retail prices were 4.7 in 1968 and 5.4 in 1969. Economic growth in the United Kingdom as measured by annual percentage increases of gross domestic product per man was satisfactory in the post-war period as compared with the pre-war period. The percentages are 1.7 for 1950–1957, 2.4 for 1957–1965 and for 1965–1974 as compared with 1.1 for 1922–1938. The rates of growth were, however, unsatisfactory as compared with those of most other industrial countries.

The claim made by Robinson and many other economists that Keynesian employment policies, monetary and particularly fiscal, have been the cause of the high and relatively stable level of employment in the United Kingdom from the end of the Second World War until the beginning of the world recession in 1974 has been questioned. The post-war period has been one of inflationary, not deflationary, pressure and the Government has not had to face a threat of mass unemployment. How far the maintenance of a very high level of employment from 1945 to 1970 was due to favourable underlying economic conditions and how far to the adoption of Keynesian policies is debatable. Certainly, there was no danger of economic stagnation in view of the investment opportunities available, defence expenditure and expenditure on the welfare state. However, the fact that the Government had accepted Keynesian policies to maintain a high level of employment increased confidence which contributed to the achievement of the objective. Keynes himself and other Cambridge economists such as Pigou had emphasized the importance of the confidence factor. We have had only minor recessions until the 1974 recession which were to some extent due to the Government's stop–go policy because of its other objectives such as an appropriate balance of international payments.

Some economists have argued that Keynesian policies of managing aggregate money demand have in fact been destabilizing while others have held the contrary view. Mr Kennedy discusses this question and refers to the review of studies of this problem by Worswick and himself[22]. Whatever is the final outcome of the controversy over the Government's past performance, I think that it was right to try to pursue appropriate demand management policies even with the somewhat blunt instruments at the Government's disposal. Economic forecasting has serious limitations but it has had a measure of success and there is reason to believe that it will become somewhat more reliable. Other difficulties of demand management can be expected to be partially overcome. It is a case of 'learning by doing' although unfortunately the social costs of mistakes can be very high. This seems to me to be a balanced Keynesian view.

Writing in 1970, Sir Alexander Cairncross, who was the first Head of the United Kingdom Government Economic Service and is a distinguished academic economist, stated that 'we have clearly no choice between control and no control. We all live in a managed economy and it is inconceivable that management will be discontinued. No one wants to go back to a world in which governments disclaim interest in the level of employment and output and leave them to be determined by blind market forces.'[23] After referring to forms of control, he writes that 'Whatever the imperfections of demand management – and there are many limitations to the available instruments, information and government powers – it seems to work, judged by experience since the war. We may have been lucky but it certainly has not been luck alone that has maintained continuous prosperity for so long.'[24] Cairncross admits that we have been less successful in avoiding inflation and this was before our very serious inflation of the 1970s. Mr G. D. N. Worswick, Director of The National Institute of Economic and Social Research, an institu*ion which operates a short-term economic forecasting model on Keynesian lines, is also a supporter of Demand Management. He stated in January 1977, 'On balance, I would conclude that fiscal and monetary policies contributed positively towards the achievement of a consistently high level of employment in the 1950s and 1960s.'[25] Worswick is well aware of the inflationary problem associated with the pursuit of a full-employment policy and argues strongly that it must be buttressed by an incomes policy. He takes the view that some form of incomes policy is needed[26]. Worswick concludes his article by stating that 'The lesson of the past is not that demand management did not work. It did – but it was not enough. The point is not to discard it, but to buttress it with additional instruments of management.'[27]

Some criticisms of Keynes and the Keynesians will be considered later in this chapter, but considering the wide publicity recently given to the views of Keynes's detractors it is well to reread Austin Robinson's Inaugural Lecture of 1971. He concluded this lecture by claiming for Keynes a true altruism, referring to his two objectives, 'To create a world monetary and financial system that could achieve adjustment without disaster to one of the parties to the adjustment; to create a world economy in which all countries all the time might be better able to use to the full their man-power and their resources'[28]. Robinson also claims that Keynes was a truly great man.

So far I have only referred to the post-war period of high employment up to the time of the world recession. The United Kingdom had had a number of minor recessions during the stop–go cycles and the position was much the same in the United States. Indeed, some economists had begun to regard the trade cycle as obsolete but this has proved not to be the case. With the world recession which began with the rise in oil prices and other primary product prices in 1973, unemployment became serious. As a result of the recession and other factors, unemployment in Great Britain in November 1980 amounted to 1.9 million, 8.2 per cent. During the early years of the recession the United Kingdom rate of inflation as measured by the percentage increase in retail prices as compared with the annual level of the previous year increased[29] and reached a peak of 24.2 in 1975. It was not until January 1978 that a single figure of inflation of 9.9 per cent (on a year-to-year basis) was reached. In November 1980 retail prices had risen by 15.3 per cent as compared with November 1979. The present recession, in its early years referred to as stagflation and later as depression, has persisted and it may be noted that the United Kingdom Government's policies are severely constrained by the balance of international payments and inflation problems. The incomes policy, in its various forms, of the Labour Government of 1974 achieved some success but the policy finally broke down. The Conservative Government of 1979 adopted a monetarist policy and was opposed to an incomes policy. Inflation and unemployment remain very serious problems at the time of writing[30]. The present recession, depression, is to be regarded as in part trade-cyclical and has nothing to do with the economic stagnation concept discussed in Chapter 13.

The basic short-term equilibrium condition in *The General Theory* is that the aggregate supply price of the output from a given level of employment of labour is equal to the aggregate demand price for this output, entrepreneurs thus maximizing their profits. Keynes takes 'a given situation of technique, resources and factor cost per unit of employment'[31]. Thus the schedule showing the aggregate supply prices for different levels of output is regarded as known[32]. On the other hand, the schedule showing the aggregate money demand for different levels of output and employment depends upon entrepreneurs' expectations of expenditure on consumption goods and on capital goods. The short-term equilibrium involves the equality of aggregate supply price and expected aggregate demand price, taking a small unit of time with given expectations under uncertainty. This aggregate demand price is the effective demand. Aggregate money demand plays a crucial role in *The General Theory* because, given the conditions of supply, the levels of employment and output are determined by expected aggregate money demand. Keynes emphasized in his 1937 lectures at Cambridge that aggregate demand is 'the proceeds which entrepreneurs *expect* to receive from employing N men'[33]. He showed that the time relationship between effective demand and income could not be made precise but argued that this did not matter as 'Employment is determined *solely* by effective demand which is influenced by realized results . . . .'[34] He went on to show how he came 'to lay all stress on effective demand as operative factor'[35].

Professor James E. Meade[36], awarded a Nobel Prize in Economics, writing on The Keynesian Revolution, regards one rather simple relationship as the quintessence of Keynes's intellectual innovation. He states that 'Keynes's intellectual revolution was to shift economists from thinking normally in terms of a model of reality in which a dog called *savings* wagged his tail labelled *investment* to thinking in terms of a model in which a dog called *investment* wagged his tail labelled *savings*.'[37] Keynes emphasized investment and expenditure on capital goods, as the constituent of aggregate money demand, the fluctuations of which played a crucial role in fluctuations in the levels of employment and output. His other constituent of aggregate money demand was consumption expenditure, which was mainly a function of the level of income. Total income is a multiple of investment according to the investment multiplier, the propensity to consume (save). In this way we obtain Keynes's operative factor.

Meade points out that before the Keynesian Revolution investment was regarded as dependent on the amount of savings made available for investment and expenditure on capital goods. The 'Treasury view' of the 1920s and early 1930s, based on this principle, opposed public investment (public works) as a method of reducing the mass unemployment because there was only a given amount of savings available and therefore there would be an offsetting reduction in private investment. This is only true in the case of full employment. Meade explains that Keynes started at the other end. He assumed a given rate of investment which determined the level of income according to the multiplier. If there is general unemployment, an increase in the rate of investment will be associated with a higher level of income and a higher rate of saving to match the increase in investment. Meade makes clear the fundamental role of aggregate demand when he writes, 'The greater the level of investment and the lower the proportion of their income which people decide to save [the higher the proportion they spend on consumption], the higher would be the level of the resulting effective demand for goods and services and so the demand for output and for the employment of labour.'[38] Meade extends this model by regarding the system as one in which the injections, the flows of investment + government expenditure + exports into the system = the leakages, the flows of savings + tax revenue + imports out of the system. He states, 'The left-hand side is the Keynesian dog and the right-hand side is the Keynesian tail. The inflow on the left-hand side, by a series of repercussions, raises the demand for consumption goods until incomes are earned on such a scale that there is an equal outflow on the right-hand side.'[39] If injections are increased in a full-employment economy, inflation results. If, for example, the rate of investment is increased, forced saving will be imposed on the community. Saving equals investment but there is inflation. Meade rightly states that 'It was Keynes's great contribution to start with investment wagging savings and to build modifications on to that model, rather than to start with savings wagging investment and to build modifications on to that model.'[40] I think that it is better to start with investment even in the cases of a full-employment and an over-full-employment economy because investment is a constituent of aggregate demand, the operative factor.

Associated with Keynes's theoretical revolution is his practical revolution in government employment policies. Meade justly claims that 'Keynes, if anyone, can be regarded as the architect of the system designed to maintain effective real demand at the full-employment level.'[41] He laments that Keynes is no longer with us to apply his mind to the solution of the problem of inflationary rises in money prices and wages rates associated with a full-employment economy. We may add to this our current problems of inflation and high unemployment – stagflation.

I have argued that Keynes was right to take investment as the starting point. Robertson in his *Lectures* of 1956–1957 puts the traditional view that an increase in savings may itself generate an increase in investment[42]. He stresses that in the real world a firm's capital outlay depends a good deal on the amount it is able to save. A firm's savings are its undistributed profits which will depend to a considerable extent on the amount of its total profits. Robertson welcomes what he regards as the return of high-brow opinion to the traditional fold by quoting Michal Kalecki, 'than whose no brow is higher'[43]. Kalecki was a distinguished Polish economist 'who discovered the General Theory independently'[44]. Robertson points out that Kalecki had become dissatisfied with theories of the behaviour of investment during the trade cycle in terms of the principle of acceleration etc. The quotation he gives is: 'A reasonable interpretation of the inter-relation between the level of income and investment decisions should be based, I think, on the fact that with the high level of income there is correlated a high level of savings, and that the stream of new savings stimulates investment because it makes it possible to undertake investment without increasing indebtedness.' Robertson adds 'The wheel has come full circle.'[45] We now appear to have savings governing investment rather than investment governing savings.

Kalecki had put forward this line of argument in his 1937 article, 'Principle of Increasing Risk' and gave a new version, Entrepreneurial Capital and Investment, in *Selected Essays* (1971)[46]. His analysis is in terms of the limitation of the size of the firm or joint-stock company apart from the market for its product. Another factor which Kalecki regards as decisive is the amount of entrepreneurial capital, the amount of capital owned by the firm. In the case of the joint-stock company, the entrepreneurial capital is not to be regarded as the total ordinary share capital which can be increased by share issues although such issues are 'restrained by the limited market for shares of a given company'[47]. It is rather the share capital of the big shareholders who wish to maintain their control of the company plus undistributed profits. A firm or company is enabled to expand by investing the undistributed profits which can be 'ploughed back' into the concern and also by investing the additional finance it can obtain from the capital market because of its larger amount of entrepreneurial capital. In the case of the joint-stock company this is obtained by the issue of ordinary shares, preference shares and debentures. A firm or company with a given amount of entrepreneurial capital cannot obtain as much additional external finance as it wishes at the prevailing rate of interest. Further 'many firms [and companies] will not use to the full the potentialities of the capital market because of the "increasing risk" involved in expansion'[48]. Kalecki explains that 'A firm considering expansion must face the fact that given the amount of the entrepreneurial capital, the risk increases with the amount invested. The greater the investment in relation to the entrepreneurial capital, the greater is the reduction in the entrepreneur's income in the event of an unsuccessful business venture.'[49] A joint-stock company is in a similar position. It is on these grounds that Kalecki maintains that investment depends on the level of income, the level of savings in the form of undistributed profits being partly dependent on this.

In Chapter 18, The General Theory of Employment Re-Stated[50], Keynes gives a summary of his system, stating which are the economic factors taken as given, which are the independent variables, and shows how these taken together determine his *quaesita*, the level of income and the amount of employment which are closely associated. It is a comparative static system. Keynes did not formulate it mathematically but a number of economists summarized it in a set of simultaneous equations soon after *The General Theory* appeared. Oscar Lange did this with a set of four simultaneous equations[51]. One of his equations is:

$$I = F(i,C)$$

where I is the investment per unit of time, i the rate of interest and C the expenditure on consumption per unit of time[52]. Keynes had analysed the inducement to invest in terms of the marginal efficiency of capital and the rate of interest. This equation states that the rate of investment depends on the rate of interest and the level of consumption. As Pigou pointed out, Keynes did state that the level of consumption was one of the factors on which the rate of investment depended. Keynes was thinking of the concept that the demand for capital goods is derived from the demand for consumers' goods as a factor of their production. Pigou correctly stated that 'When consumption is *in process of increasing* there is, indeed, a consequential demand for investment to provide new equipment. But in situations of short-period equilibrium consumption must be regarded as fixed.'[53] Keynes has a comparative static model, so that comparing short-period equilibrium positions, investment does not depend on consumption. Net investment depending on an increase in consumption involves the acceleration principle, a dynamic principle excluded from Keynes's static system[54].

Lange's statement that investment depends on the level of consumption could only be interpreted in terms of Kalecki's return to the traditional view that investment depends upon the amount of savings available which is related to the level of income. We may substitute the level of income for consumption in Lange's equation. Lange took a Keynesian view and certainly did not want to say investment depended on saving but the reverse. The attempt made by Lange and other economists to express Keynes's system in a set of simultaneous equations which included the rate of investment was not successful[55]. As Professor Shackle stressed in conversations with me, Keynes's model is open-ended with respect to the determination of the rate of investment. He wrote, 'A very notable example of such "open" or non-selfcontained models is Keynes's *General Theory of Employment*, where net investment, the flow whose size is treated as the actively dominant feature of the situation, is deliberately left free of any simple determining formula involving only the other 'internal' variables of the system.'[56] Again, Shackle wrote, 'In Keynes's own model there was a curious unbalance or lacuna. He had left investment itself ultimately unexplained, save as the outlet for a natural human adventurousness.'[57]

In Chapters 11, The Marginal Efficiency of Capital, and 12, The State of Long-Term Expectation[58], of *The General Theory* Keynes did make an important contribution to an analysis of the factors on which the rate of investment depends although he did not provide a complete theory[59]. Expectations play a vital role. The marginal efficiency of capital is regarded in terms of the expected, not the current, yield of capital goods[60]. The importance of uncertainty is emphasized. Keynes writes, 'The outstanding fact is the extreme precariousness of the basis of knowledge on which our estimates of prospective yield have to be made. Our knowledge of the factors which govern the yield of an investment some years hence is usually very slight and often negligible.'[61] Thus animal spirits play an important role, Keynes writes. 'Most, probably, of our decisions to do something positive, the full consequences of which will be drawn out over many days to come, can only be taken as a result of animal spirits – of a spontaneous urge to action rather than inaction, and not as the outcome of a weighted average of quantitative benefits multiplied by quantitative probabilities.'[62] Individual initiative for the undertaking of investment will only be adequate 'when reasonable calculation is supplemented and supported by animal spirits'[63]. The dependence of the marginal efficiency of capital on expectations is given as the main reason for it being so volatile and subject to serious fluctuations[64]. Thus the rate of private investment fluctuates and causes the trade cycle. Keynes points out that in his Chapter 22, Notes on the Trade Cycle, booms and slumps are analysed in terms of fluctuations of the marginal efficiency of capital relatively to the money rate of interest[65]. Although the importance of Kalecki's analysis of the effect of saving on investment must be recognized, I agree with Meade's view that Keynes was right to start with investment as one of the determinants of the level of income at which saving was equal to investment[66]. As we have seen, Keynes regarded aggregate demand as the operative factor or motivating force in the system and investment as an important constituent of aggregate demand.

Mr J. A. Kregel argues that Keynes's model is not general in the same sense as the general equilibrium model developed by Walras and his followers which shows the simultaneous determination of all prices and economic quantities at a point of time. He states that Keynes's claim to generality is based on the fact that in his model output and employment can be at any levels[67]. Keynes himself in the Preface to *The General Theory* states that the analysis relates primarily to the determinants of the levels of employment and output as a whole and writes 'We are thus led to a more general theory, which includes the classical theory with which we are familiar, as a special case.'[68] Kregel states that 'Keynes's position is indeed closer to Marshall's partial or one-at-a-time method, although his system is interdependent in a sense that Marshall's is not. This also implies that Keynes's view of the "generality" of his theory is incompatible with the "Generalized General Theory" that Hicks suggests when, for reasons of "Mathematical elegance", he turns the theory into a simultaneous equation system in three variables, income, the rate of interest, and the value of investment.'[69] The reference to Hicks is to his 1937 *Econometrica* article, 'Mr Keynes and the "Classics"'[70], to which Keynes gave his general approval[71]. Kregel refers approvingly to Mr Pasinetti's criticism of Hicks's type of generalization.

Pasinetti regards Hicks's analysis as typically un-Keynesian. He writes that 'Hicks has in fact broken up Keynes's basic chain of arguments. The relations have been turned into a system of simultaneous equations, i.e. precisely into what Keynes did *not* want them to be . . . . So Keynes's contribution on effective demand is wiped out at a stroke.'[72] This seems to me to be going too far. As I stated above, Keynes summarized his comparative static system in Chapter 18 of *The General Theory*. The system implied a set of simultaneous equations but Keynes retained causality in his analysis. The simple mathematical models in the form of sets of simultaneous equations as developed by Lange and Hicks to which I have referred, and also by Professor Modigliani[73], make the basic structure of the Keynesian system explicit. In this way they are useful, the main fundamental relationships are crystallized out, but of course they do not tell the whole story. Thomas Sowell has stated that 'Keynes's theory was one of general equilibrium, or of a simultaneous determination of the respective values of related variables, though sometimes expressed as if it were a theory of unidirectional causation.'[74] As we have seen, Keynes himself did this by making aggregate demand his starting point. I would not agree that the simultaneous equation models wiped out effective demand at a stroke. One can trace the effect of aggregate demand on the level of income as being the operative factor or motivating force while being aware of the interdependence of the economic variables[75].

At the beginning of this chapter I referred to Kahn, Harrod and Joan Robinson as Keynesians. Hutchison refers to these three well-known authorities as 'Pseudo-Keynesians whose enormous influence and prestige brought them numerous followers, allies, partners, popularisers and subsidiaries'[76]. He states that these three prime Pseudo-Keynesians, although differing on a number of issues, 'share a very great deal of common ground; *and especially, all three have been repeatedly, for decades, concerned to invoke, quite unjustifiably, the magic, charismatic name of Keynes on behalf of their own particular doctrines*'[77]. Austin Robinson justifiably objects to this labelling 'some of us Keynesians and some of us Pseudo-Keynesians'[78]. There are conflicts in the objectives of economic policy, the level of employment, the degree of price level stability, the balance of payments and so on. The relative importance to be attached to particular objectives and the targets to be aimed at at any time are difficult matters of judgement involving economic and non-economic considerations. It is obvious that Keynes's followers would not always know what policies Keynes would have recommended. Hutchison complains that 'Only belatedly, in the 'seventies, when the problems of the British economy had indeed become baffling, were Lord Kahn and Sir Roy Harrod sometimes to be found dismissing as a "nonsense question" what Keynes would be advocating today'[79]. I think that Hutchison's criticism is too harsh. Admittedly, his 'three prime Pseudo-Keynesians' did at times venture to state what policies Keynes would have recommended. However, they were often merely putting forward Keynesian policies for the demand management of the economy on the general lines of Keynes's thought. In the very difficult area of the advocacy of specific policies for particular situations they, like other economists, were of course not infallible. Kahn, Harrod and Joan Robinson are Keynesians in that they accept the fundamental importance of the model in *The General Theory* and have used it as a basis for the development of their economic thought. Kahn refers to the Keynesian argument for 'a direct curbing influence on the behaviour of money wages' when discussing the present high rate of cost inflation. He writes, 'I use the word *Keynesian* as describing the natural development of Keynes's thinking under the influence of the conditions against which economists, as well as statesmen, have been struggling.'[80]

Kahn is the Keynesian economist who provided Keynes with the multiplier. Indeed, he played a very important role in the development of Keynes's ideas which led to *The General Theory*. Harrod refers to Kahn as Keynes's most outstanding pupil of the inter-war period and points out that Keynes quickly realized his quality and 'roped him in to advise him and help him in his major tasks'[81] when he was writing *A Treatise on Money* (1930)[82]. In the Preface, Keynes acknowledged his great indebtedness to Kahn when he wrote, 'In the gradual evolution of the book into its final form and in the avoidance of errors my greatest debt is to Mr R. F. Kahn of King's College, Cambridge, whose care and acuteness have left their trace on many pages'[83]. Austin Robinson points out that it was Kahn who retailed to Keynes the results of the deliberations of the Cambridge 'circus' of economists who had weekly discussion of the *Treatise*[84]. It was at this time that Keynes began to develop his theory of changes in the levels of employment and output as a whole. An impression of the importance of Kahn to Keynes during the period when Keynes was developing his thought which led to *The General Theory* may be obtained from their correspondence between the dates of the publication of *A Treatise* and of *The General Theory*[85]. In 1934 after a long visit from Kahn, Keynes told his mother that 'as usual he was extraordinarily helpful'[86]. In the Preface to *The General Theory*, Keynes wrote, 'In this book, even more perhaps than in writing my *Treatise on Money*, I have depended on the constant advice and constructive criticism of Mr R. F. Kahn. There is a great deal in this book which would not have taken the shape it has except at his suggestion.'[87] In The British Academy's Fourth Keynes Lecture in Economics, *On Re-Reading Keynes*, Kahn in 1974 referred to *The General Theory*, as 'a world-shattering book'[88].

Kahn in his 1956 article, 'Full Employment and British Economic Policy', showed his awareness of the dangers of inflation when he wrote 'a price level which is known to be persistently and strongly rising fails to provide a secure basis for economic prosperity and progress'[89]. He was concerned as to 'whether a satisfactory behaviour of money wages is compatible with the very low ratios of unemployment which have recently been ruling'[90]. Kahn was writing when the unemployment percentage was at the exceptionally low figure of 1.1. He refers to the high unemployment percentages during the 1930s and contrasts the post-World War II period during which the percentage never exceeded 3 apart from a few weeks at the time of the 1947 fuel crisis. He points to the facts that for most of the period unemployment had been less than 2 per cent and for over two years less than 1½ per cent[91]. Kahn refers to Beveridge's aim to reduce unemployment to an average of 3 per cent and quotes here from Keynes's letter to Beveridge, 'No harm in aiming at three per cent unemployment, but I shall be surprised if we succeed.'[92] Kahn points out that in 1955 the unemployment percentage fell to 1 per cent and the United Kingdom was in international balance of payments difficulty. The Government took various restrictive measures. Kahn writes that 'since the latter part of 1955, the concern of the Government has been with the persistent rise of money wages, and the consequent effect on prices'[93]. The Government at that time relied on an appeal for wage and price restraint. Kahn quotes, apparently with approval, from a White Paper in which it is stated that we all want full employment and stable prices, and 'The experience of the past ten years has shown that the fuller employment is the more liable prices are to rise; but the Government does not believe that there is any inevitable conflict between the two objectives.'[94]

Kahn states that the Government's appeal for wage and price restraint may prove unsuccessful. Thus, it is clear that in 1956 Kahn was much concerned with the problems of reconciling policies aimed a very high level of employment and a stable general level of prices. He accepted that money wages should generally rise with increasing productivity and that there should be some flexibility in relative wages. His hopes for a solution of the problem rested on what he regarded as appropriate fiscal and growth policies. Kahn wrote, 'The fiscal system has already contributed a great deal to redistributing income and building up the social services, and it is only on that basis that trade unions can be expected to refrain from pressing home the advantages offered by a sellers' market for labour.'[95] He pointed out that the growth of productivity depended very largely on a high level of physical investment[96]. Kahn wrote, 'that is why it seems so important to find a means of reconciling high rates of investment and employment with an acceptable behaviour of the money-wage level and to avoid being driven into a policy involving really effective restraints on investment designed perhaps to bring the ratios of unemployment close to Lord Beveridge's obsolete 3 per cent'[97]. Some reference to criticisms of Kahn having advocated inflationary policies will be considered later, but it is clear from this article that he was concerned about inflation in 1956 and was putting forward rational policies which he hoped would prevent it. These hopes did not materialize and he put forward an incomes policy which we shall consider later. As we have seen, the rate of inflation was relatively moderate in the 1950s and 1960s although not to be taken lightly. From 1969 it has been a most serious problem.

In the same year, 1956, Kahn gave two radio talks on the B.B.C., Lord Keynes And Contemporary Economic Problems[98]. The first talk was entitled Inflation and he began by saying that he was not intending in these talks 'to try to guess what Keynes would be thinking or saying if he were alive today'[99]. Kahn points out that Keynes was well aware of the problem of inflation in a full-employment economy. He refers to Keynes's *Economic Journal* article of June–September 1943 in which Keynes considers the argument that a capitalist country is doomed if it attempts to maintain full employment because of a progressive increase of money wages. Kahn quotes from Keynes, 'According to this view severe slumps and recurrent periods of unemployment have been hitherto the only effective means of holding efficiency wages within a reasonably stable range. Whether this is so remains to be seen. The more conscious we are of this problem, the likelier shall we be to surmount it.'[100] Further, Kahn writes with a quotation from Keynes, 'And, again: "It is one of the chief tasks ahead of our statesmanship to find a way to prevent" money wages from forever soaring upwards.'[101] Kahn recognized that the inflation of 1956 which so much concerned the Government was due both to cost-push (trade unions pushing money wages up too fast) and to demand-pull (excessive money demand given the existing productive resources and their current prices). He points out that wage inflation has occurred even when there was thought to be too much slack in the economy, as in 1953. Kahn approved of Mr Butler's 1953 expansionist Budget in general[102]. Kahn said that if in 1953 'the regulation of the economy had been conducted with an eye to the behaviour of wages rather than to the level of activity, it would have meant not only the persistence but the aggravation of economic waste – of unemployment as a means of checking wage increases'[103].

Kahn pointed out that 'In the Keynesian system the money wage is the fulcrum on which the price structure rests. The behaviour of prices depends on that of money wages rather than the other way round.'[104] This is true in the case of a cost-push inflation but not in the case of a demand-pull inflation[105]. Kahn recognized that 'credit conditions' affected the amount of employment, given the general level of wages. He referred to Keynes's recognition of the inflationary problem in How to Pay for the War (1940)[106] and the necessity of putting a coherent plan to the trade unions. Kahn considers the crucial point to be 'the need to get the trade unions' representatives to consider the wage level as a whole and not in terms of the sectional interests of individual trade unions or workers'[107]. He points out that the difficult problem of relative wages (wage differentials) is somewhat eased if the rise in real wages made possible by increasing productivity is reflected in rising money wages rather than a fall of prices. The co-operation of trade union leaders is said to depend on an appropriate system of taxation as it affects the distribution of disposable income[108]. What is regarded as the appropriate distribution of productive resources between producing consumption goods and producing capital goods depends on the circumstances of the time. Kahn took the view that 'Today so much turns on increasing our productivity, and this calls for a high rate of investment.'[109] He thus supported relatively high taxation and low interest rates.

Kahn associates with the above argument an attack on the quantity theory of money. He refers to Keynes's ironical statement in a letter to the Editor of the Financial News of 3 January 1940, which I have already mentioned[110], that 'If you are not too old, as to which I have no information, I strongly recommend an operation. By modern methods an inflamed Quantity Theory can be removed with much less danger than formerly.'[111] However, as explained in the section on the Quantity Theory of Money in Chapter 5, the quantity equation is a useful truism and the quantity theory must be synthesized with Keynesian theory. Keynes was critical but, as pointed out, he contributed to the development of the quantity theory in important ways. Keynes's followers were actually more critical than Keynes, I think. Nevertheless one can in general agree with Kahn that Keynes's analytical framework, developed largely to solve the problem of unemployment in peace-time, proved well suited to deal with the shortage of productive resources in wartime and provides the basis '"for most of the sensible things which are said" – about the problems of inflation in peace-time'. It must be remembered, however, that Keynes produced a theoretical model, an apparatus of thought, which can be used well or badly. Good judgement is needed and expert use made of the available empirical information. Economics is an inexact science and mistakes will be made. It was in 1956, the year of Kahn's thought which we are considering, that Milton Friedman began the Counter-Revolution in monetary theory, Monetarism, with the publication of his contribution, The Quantity Theory of Money – A Restatement[112]. Many economists who would not describe themselves as monetarists would agree that this development was necessary. As I have already stated, a more complete theory is obtained by a synthesis of the quantity theory and Keynes's basic model of *The General Theory*.

Kahn's views in the 1950s are also to be found in his long Memorandum of Evidence Submitted to the Radcliffe Committee[113]. Kahn writes that 'there is no reason for belittling the importance of the monetary mechanism as a component of the whole economic system'[114], so long as the objectives are regarded as being independent of the means employed. His two important ends are the general level of economic activity and the balance between consumption and investment. Kahn holds that consumption is largely influenced by taxation while investment is mainly influenced by the monetary and credit mechanism[115]. On this basis, Kahn argues that it is of the greatest importance to what extent the general level of activity is controlled by means of monetary and budgetary policies. Kahn states that the choice between the relative amounts of consumption and investment is ultimately a political decision but is concerned about 'the bias of a democratic society towards an ill-considered short-sighted preference for immediate consumption at the expense of investment – and so at the expense of additional consumption in the future'[116]. Kahn explains how this is partly due to the tendency to use budgetary policy to stimulate the economy and monetary policy to restrain it.

Kahn considers that monetary policy has a substantial influence on investment although it is slow and unpredictable in its effects. He states that there are other means of influencing investment but 'there always must be a monetary policy'[117]. This statement should be particularly noted in view of the unjustified criticism that Keynes and almost all Keynesians neglected monetary policy. Kahn expresses it 'in terms of rates of interest on loans of various maturities and of the amount of bank advances'[118]. Kahn then proceeds to deal with the level of economic activity at which it is desirable to aim. He had expressed earlier concern about the restraint on investment since 1955 although he admitted that it was necessary to some limited extent[119]. Kahn does not analyse in detail here the problem of the level of activity but refers to the growth of productive capacity and technical knowledge and writes that 'the record of the last three years is depressing. Production has scarcely increased.'[120] Kahn advised the Committee to avoid the use of the terms 'demand inflation' and 'cost inflation'. He emphasized that the price level rose if money wages increased more than proportionately to productivity. He wrote, 'If reliance is placed on regulation of demand in order to secure a tolerable behaviour of [money wages and] prices, it must almost certainly mean maintaining unemployment at a level which would represent very serious economic waste as well as political unacceptableness.'[121] Kahn thought this was the case if complete stability of the price level was the aim and liable to be so[122] if the aim was to prevent the price level rising faster than in other countries such as West Germany and the United States. He is highly critical of the use of monetary policy for this purpose as this involves regulating demand by restricting productive investment and, certainly, the growth of productivity. This reduces the rate of increase of money wages which is possible with stable prices because of increasing productivity.

Kahn is thus led strongly to advocate a wages policy although he would not expect complete success. Kahn wrote 'The more unbridled are the procedures for negotiating wages, the less feasible is it to run the economic system under really full pressure. But in the absence of anything like what might be called a wages policy, it would, I am convinced, be economically expedient as well as politically inevitable to abandon any idea of stability of the price level. The only relevant question would be in what degree a progressive rise in prices should be tolerated for the sake of avoiding undue restriction of demand.'[123] Kahn attributes major responsibility for the rate of increase of money wages in this country, except in the case of a marked shortage of labour, to the competitive struggle between trade unions and within some trade unions – leap-frogging[124]. Kahn stresses the importance of agreement about relative wages of different labour groups. He writes, 'I believe that negotiations of some kind of national wage structure, conceived in terms of relative wages, at least for the most important sections of labour, is an essential pre-requisite to securing over any term of years a tolerable behaviour of the absolute wage level.'[125] Kahn realizes the difficulties of his proposal but believes that if the relative wage problem could be solved, an appropriate behaviour of the absolute wage level could be achieved. He recognizes that allowance would have to be made for adjustments in relative wages according to the changing conditions of the supplies of and demands for particular labour groups, but refers to the required adjustments as being slight. The problem of 'wage drift', employers bidding up wages above negotiated rates, is also discussed[126].

Kahn is critical of the traditional quantity theory of money although as I have explained in Chapter 5 it has been formulated in an acceptable way. He states that the quantity of money operates on the economy in only three ways; investment is affected by the effect of changes in the quantity of money on the rate of interest, bank advances and the effect of these two on the stock exchange. He writes, 'My contention that it is not the quantity of money in itself which determines the size of the stream of total demand requires that the velocity of circulation of money should be regarded as a purely passive factor.'[127] Kahn further states that 'The velocity of circulation, as normally conceived, is an entirely bogus concept.'[128] I agree with Kahn on the importance of an incomes policy but cannot accept his attitude to the quantity theory of money. The velocity of circulation is by no means a bogus concept. The factors on which the income-velocity of circulation or the corresponding constituent in the demand for money depends and the causes of their changing are discussed in Chapter 5. It is true that in deep depression an increase in the quantity of money may be offset by a decline

in the velocity of circulation so that there is no increase in money demand –
a special case. It is also true that in a boom a decrease in the quantity of
money may be offset by an increase in the velocity of circulation but there
are limits to such an increase so that a policy of decreasing the quantity of
money will ultimately reduce money demand.

The Radcliffe Report[129] is a very detailed examination of the United
Kingdom monetary system and, despite the criticism it has received, it
remains a valuable document. Unfortunately, the Radcliffe Committee in
its Report took a similar position to that of Kahn with regard to the
velocity of circulation. The concept is only mentioned in three
paragraphs[130]. In para. 391 it is stated that 'We have not made more use of
this concept because we cannot find any reason for supposing, or any
experience in monetary history indicating, that there is any limit to the
velocity of circulation: it is a statistical concept that tells us nothing directly
of the motivation that influences the level of total demand.' In my 1953
article I showed that the velocity of circulation cannot be infinite[131] and
discussed some of the factors on which it depends. I also showed that the
constituent of the demand for money which corresponds to the velocity of
circulation can be discussed in terms of the motives for holding money.

Kahn states that placing the emphasis on the quantity of money is
misleading. What is important in his view is that the monetary authority
achieves the appropriate structure of interest rates although he recognizes
the importance of 'the background of a monetary policy which operates on
rates in general'[132]. The Radcliffe Committee stated that they followed
Kahn 'in insisting upon the structure of interest rates rather than some
notion of the 'supply of money' as the centre-piece of monetary action; this
does not however imply an absence of special interest in the activity of the
banks'[133].

The Radcliffe Report is often considered to be the culmination of the line
of thought that 'money doesn't matter'. As we have seen, Milton Friedman
had already started the Counter-Revolution in 1956[134] and it was he and
the other monetarists who emphasized that 'money does matter'[135].
However, the Radcliffe Committee did not go quite as far as represented
by some of its critics. The Committee stated, 'Though we do not regard the
supply of money as an unimportant quantity, we view it as only a part of
the wider structure of liquidity in the economy. It is the whole liquidity
position that is relevant to spending decisions, and our interest in the
supply of money is due to its significance in the whole liquidity picture.'[136]
After considering the amount of liquidity rather than just the quantity of
money, the Committee wrote, 'We would nevertheless emphasize that the
amount of money, in the sense of the amount of notes and bank deposits, is
of considerable significance.'[137]

As far as monetary policy is concerned, the Radcliffe Committee
emphasized the control of interest rates rather than the control of money
although the two are closely associated. The longterm rate of interest was
regarded as more important than the short-term rate, but the Committee
did not attach much importance to the effect of changes in interest rates on
investment[138]. More importance was attached to the monetary authority's
control of 'the liquidity condition of financial institutions and of business
firms and people generally so that those wanting money to spend (whether

for capital development or other purposes) find it more (or less) difficult to get than it was before'[139]. It is emphasized that changes in the rate of interest are an important cause of changes in liquidity[140]. The Committee thus concentrated on the availability of funds[141]. The emphasis is on bank advances rather than bank deposits[142]. The Committee concluded that interest rate policy was not suitable as a 'major short-term stabilizer of demand'[143] but that the monetary authorities must control appropriately the longterm rate of interest. The Report states that if the view is that a fall in demand indicates 'a more lasting collapse in the demand for capital development, definite measures to bring down the whole structure of interest rates – amounting to a change of gear – would be appropriate'[144]. The Committee held that monetary measures could not 'alone be relied upon to keep in nice balance an economy subject to major strains from both without and within'[145]. Direct controls and fiscal measures are not discussed in detail in view of the Committee's terms of reference but their relevance to the use of monetary policy is indicated[146]. In the case of a severe slump, the Committee takes the traditional view that monetary policy in the form of reducing interest rates etc. can have little effect and quotes the proverb that 'you can take a horse to the water but you cannot make him drink'[147]. In the case of headlong inflation, the Committee advocates a 'combination of controls of capital issues, bank advances and consumer credit'[148] as the appropriate policy.

However, the Radcliffe Committee did go too far in playing down the role of the quantity of money. A number of examples may be noted. In dealing with headlong inflation, the Committee rejects 'any restriction of "the supply of money"'[149]. This is quite unacceptable. In summarizing their review of monetary measures, the Committee states, 'we find control of the supply of money to be no more than an important facet of [national] debt management'[150]. After emphasizing the general liquidity position, the Committee stated, 'the supply of money itself is not the critical factor' and after stressing the importance of the interest-rate structure, it stated, 'This does not mean that the supply of money is unimportant, but that its control is incidental to interest-rate policy.'[151] As we have seen, Robertson continued to maintain that the quantity of money was important and Milton Friedman and the other monetarists reasserted its importance. Today, most of the economists who would not describe themselves as monetarists do recognize the importance of the quantity of money.

Returning to Kahn's Evidence to the Radcliffe Committee, Kahn discusses the relationship between the quantity of money and the Government's 'overall' deficit, the amount by which the total Government expenditure (including capital expenditure) exceeds total tax revenue. Kahn points out that the deficit may be financed by the issue of government securities to the general public and/or by the issue of securities which are purchased by the banking system, and is associated with an increase in the quantity of money. He states that 'It is the behaviour of interest rates which matters and their influence on the level of demand, not the behaviour of the quantity of money.'[152] This is a complicated matter to which Kahn returns in later publications discussed below[153].

In the 1970s Kahn again became active in the discussion of appropriate monetary and fiscal policies for the management of the economy. With Mr Michael Posner he submitted in 1974 a Memorandum, The Effects of

Public Expenditure on Inflation and the Balance of Payments, to The Expenditure Committee[154]. It should be noted that the *Report* does not accept Kahn's views on prices and incomes policies. The Committee's view was that 'a permanent, statutory prices and incomes policy is in modern Britain politically both impracticable and objectionable'[155]. They held that 'the utmost current possibility is to secure whatever can be secured by the voluntary agreement of the many parties involved'[156]. Kahn and Posner do not accept the analysis and policy recommendations of the New Cambridge School[157], represented by Francis Cripps, Wynne Godley and Martin Fetherston. Kahn and Posner discuss the reasons put forward for not using changes in public expenditure as a method of controlling the economy, but state that it has a role to play. The local authorities and nationalized industries should be encouraged 'to store plans on ice' and have lists of 'potential delays of "starts" '[158]. They do not accept the view of Mr Godley and his associates that 'the only potentially destabilizing agents are the Government's own actions with regard to expenditure, taxation and credit on the one hand, and, on the other, foreign influences, particularly export demand and world commodity prices'[159]. On the contrary, Kahn and Posner expect that 'the private sectors, if left to themselves, will generate fluctuations in economic activity'[160]. They do not pretend that 'the objective of "fine tuning" can be achieved. On the other hand, we do believe that some ironing out of fluctuations is both desirable and possible.'[161]

Kahn and Posner, as in Kahn's earlier writings, emphasize the importance of productive investment. They lament the inflationary effect of the low rate of growth of productivity in the United Kingdom which only allows a low rate of increase of money wages without inflation and a low rate of rise in the standard of living which causes pressure for a higher rate of increase in money wages. Kahn and Posner emphasize the importance of containing 'the rates of growth both of public expenditure and of personal consumption, so as to allow a higher rate of growth of productive investment'[162].

Inflation is then discussed in terms of 'demand inflation' and 'cost inflation'[163] and their relationship. Kahn and Posner 'have no belief in the notorious Phillips Curve'[164] and so stress cost inflation *per se*, in particular rising money wages due to trade union action. It is stated that 'To cope with the problem of cost inflation, in the sense of rapidly rising money wages and prices, . . . , we regard statutory control of money wages (as well as of other incomes and prices) as absolutely vital.'[165]

On the general question of managing the level of demand, Kahn and Posner do not believe that it can contribute to the curbing of cost inflation except when unemployment is very low (say 2¼ per cent) and there are serious shortages of labour and physical bottlenecks. The behaviour of money wages is not regarded as the only criterion. At times it may be necessary to keep demand low enough to release productive resources for appropriate increases in the production of exports and productive equipment, involving a temporary loss of output and employment. However, they stress that 'it is both pointless and wasteful to release productive resources in this way unless there exist adequate incentives to industrialists to increase their production of exports and to install additional equipment'[166].

In considering the desirable level of taxation, Kahn and Posner stress the importance for the management of the economy of achieving the right public sector financial deficit. This depends on the level of public expenditure, the behaviour of the private sector of the economy and of the levels of exports and imports[167]. Closely related to the public sector deficit is the public sector borrowing requirement[168]. They argue strongly that if demand inflation is avoided (by taxation being high enough, the borrowing requirement low enough), public expenditure financed by borrowing is not inflationary. This is a truism but requires elucidation. It is pointed out that the demands on resources are the same for house-building whether it is financed by private or local authority borrowing and for the expansion of the steel industry whether it is privately or publicly owned. Kahn and Posner recognize that there may be an inflationary influence to the extent that the borrowing requirement is financed by an expansion of the quantity of money by the banking system purchasing Government securities such as Treasury Bills. This occurs if the Government does not prevent it by permitting interest rates to rise sufficiently by obtaining the necessary funds from individuals, companies and from abroad. In this case however, demand inflation has not been avoided[169].

Kahn consistently put forward in publications subsequent to the 1974 Evidence the views on the quantity of money, its velocity of circulation, the public sector borrowing requirement and the great importance of an incomes and prices policy for cost inflation which I have discussed[170].

Kahn tends to minimize the importance of changes in the quantity of money while the monetarists maximize it. He writes 'It can be readily conceded to the monetarists that an increase in the quantity of money, though not the *cause* of inflation, is a necessary condition.'[171] Unfortunately, Kahn does not develop his point and we are left in a semantic confusion regarding causation. Of course, an increase in the quantity of money which is not spent has no effect on prices or real output. Kahn quite correctly points out that the relationship between the size of the public sector borrowing requirement and the change in the quantity of money is very erratic. However, to the extent that it is financed by an increase in the quantity of money, there is a tendency for prices and/or real output to rise[172]. He correctly emphasizes the importance of considering the effect of the public sector financial deficit on effective demand but underplays the importance of the extent to which it is financed by an increase in the quantity of money and/or its velocity of circulation[173].

Kahn is critical of Mr. Eltis not having given his views on the importance of money wages and trade union policy. He points out that 'If reliance had to be placed exclusively on a reduction in the rate of increase in the quantity of money and in the public sector financial deficit, the causal process would take the form of . . . growing unemployment.'[174] In 1977 Kahn and Posner maintain that the emphasis should be on the levels of activity and employment and stress the importance of investment to increase industrial productivity while North Sea oil eases the international balance of payments problem. Their aim is to reduce the rate of inflation and they do not consider that 'the state of credit, largely dependent on the behaviour of the quantity of money, should be tailored to match an unacceptably high rate of wage inflation'[175]. Although there are occasional references to the quantity of money, it is unfortunate that Kahn did not integrate the quantity theory of money with aggregate demand theory instead of tending to denigrate it.

Harrod is the second of the three Keynesians considered. Although a student and don at Oxford, he had gone to Cambridge to learn some economics under Keynes[176]. When criticizing the proofs of *The General Theory*, Harrod tells us he wrote 'in a strain of ardent admiration and with a sense of his mighty achievement'[177]. In 1937 he wrote an appreciative summary of *The General Theory*, his only criticism being that Keynes's system was still static[178]. Harrod states that 'Keynes gave this article his blessing.'[179] In 1951 Harrod recognized the general applicability of Keynesian doctrines, that in 1935 they pointed to expansion while since the outbreak of World War II they 'pointed in the opposite way, namely, towards economy . . .'[180]. Harrod refers to Keynes's system as a reclassification of economic phenomena and writes 'It is by actual use and application, not by logic, that Keynes has been, and will, I am confident, continue to be, triumphantly vindicated.'[181] He emphasizes the importance of Keynes's new conceptual framework 'which has enabled us to transform all our thinking about the level of output as a whole'[182]. Harrod regards the central concept of Keynes's theory to be that of aggregate demand[183] and his classification provides this. Harrod had pointed out in his 1937 *Econometrica* article on the static system of Keynes's *General Theory* the importance of the development of economic dynamics and growth theory. Harrod may be regarded as the founder of modern dynamic economics and growth theory with his path-breaking article 'An Essay in Dynamic Theory' of 1939[184]. D. H. Robertson could justly claim that he was an earlier pioneer in this development of economic thought, but for personal and other reasons most modern theory in this area stems rather from Harrod's 'dynamisation' of Keynesian theory. Harrod in his Retrospect on Keynes (1963) stated that Keynes may be truly regarded as 'the father of dynamic theory' because his 'macroeconomic theory of statics was an indispensable foundation'[185]. Referring to his book, *The Trade Cycle* (1936), Harrod writes that he 'worked with great assiduity on incorporating a dynamic element in the Keynesian scheme . . . The essence of my book was a conflation of Keynes's "multiplier" theory with what has since come to be called the "acceleration principle".'[186] Harrod goes on to state that his *Trade Cycle* 'still contained no basic axiom relating to growth theory. I continued thinking furiously, and two years later excogitated such an axiom.'[187] Thus was born the famous Harrod growth equation of the 1939 article.

Harrod attempts to give the basis of a dynamic theory in the form of a 'marriage of the "acceleration principle" and the "multiplier theory"'[188]. He presents a theory of a moving equilibrium of economic growth and states that 'a new method of approach – indeed, a mental revolution – is needed'[189]. His concept, the 'warranted rate of growth' is 'that rate of growth which, if it occurs, will leave all parties satisfied that they have produced neither more nor less than the right amount'[190]. Thus, this rate of growth will be maintained. Harrod shows that this moving equilibrium of a given rate of increase of output is highly unstable, which is of interest for trade cycle analysis[191]. The 'actual rate of growth' will diverge for various reasons from the warranted rate of growth. In the real world of uncertainty, this is to be expected. Harrod also has a concept of a 'natural rate of growth' which is 'the maximum rate of growth allowed by the increase of population, accumulation of capital, technological improvement and the work/leisure preference schedule, supposing that there is always full employment in some sense'[192]. He maintains that there is no inherent tendency for the warranted and natural rates of growth to coincide[193]. We cannot assume a full-employment equilibrium will be spontaneously achieved.

After World War II, Harrod returned to his growth analysis in lectures delivered in the University of London in February 1947. Here he restated and elaborated his ideas. The lectures appeared as his important book, *Towards a Dynamic Economics* (1948). In the Foreword, Harrod stresses the Keynesian problem of stagnation although in the immediate post-war years he recognizes that the pressures on the economy are giving rise to 'full employment'. In the case of Great Britain, he envisages the possibility of a considerable period during which there is no tendency to stagnation although the problem of periodic depressions will remain. However, the United States, Harrod thinks, is likely to be faced with the problem of chronic depression. Thus, Harrod deals both with the theory and its application to policy[194].

In referring to this book, I have pointed out elsewhere that Harrod 'extended Keynesian theory in a very important way. Keynes's theory was static and short-period analysis . . . . Harrod, with a bow to the classical economists, re-emphasized the importance of dynamic theory and long-period analysis. He considered the interrelations between the expansion of man-power, output or income per head and the quantity of capital available in an expanding economy. He examined "the necessary relations between the rates of growth of the different elements in a growing economy"[195]. A complete theory of the trade cycle is not presented, but Harrod suggests that the instability of the line of advance provides a framework for such a theory.'[196]

The core of Harrod's contribution to dynamic economics is to be found in his fundamental equations which are given in the 1939 article, *Towards a Dynamic Economics* (1948) and *Economic Dynamics* (1973). In one form the equation is a truism. Harrod writes[197]:

$$GC = s$$

G is the rate of growth per unit of time, the increment of total production (income) as a fraction of total production (income), $\Delta Y/Y$ (Y standing for income) = say 2 per cent per annum or 1/50. C is the incremental capital : income or : output ratio. If K stands for capital and I for investment,

$$C = \frac{\Delta K}{\Delta Y} = \frac{I}{\Delta Y} = \text{say } 4.$$

The fraction of income saved is $s = S/Y$, S standing for the amount of saving. The $s = $ say 8 per cent or 8/100. The equation thus takes into account the accelerator, the ratio of an increase in capital to an increase in income and the multiplier which depends on the proportion of income saved. The marginal propensity to consume (save) may be assumed to be equal to the average propensities. Giving the above arithmetical values to the equation (truism) GC = s, we have

$$\frac{1.4}{50} = \frac{8}{100}$$

The second form of the equation expresses the equilibrium of a steady advance and Harrod writes[198]:

$$G_wC_r = s$$

G_w is the warranted rate of growth which Harrod defines as 'that over-all rate of advance which if executed, will leave entrepreneurs in a state of mind in which they are prepared to carry on a similar advance'[199]. This over-all rate of progress will perpetuate itself although individual entrepreneurs may adjust their outputs upwards or downwards[200]. The equation is no longer a truism because G_w is the warranted rate of growth and C_r is the required capital:output ratio[201]. Here the capital:output ratio is constant because it is assumed that inventions are neutral in Harrod's sense[202] and the rate of interest is constant[203]. G_wC_r is the amount of investment during a period as a fraction of income and this must equal s, the fraction of income saved. In *Economic Dynamics* Harrod makes the equilibrium condition clearer by writing s_d for s; s_d being the fraction of income which persons, companies and government desire to save[204].

Harrod's third concept is the natural rate of growth (G_n) which is the rate of growth obtainable from the full utilization of the increasing productive resources, the full-employment dynamic equilibrium. If the warranted rate of growth tends to be less than the natural rate of growth the economy is faced with the problem of chronic unemployment (stagnation). A tendency of the actual rate of growth to diverge from the warranted rate of growth is regarded as the trade cycle problem[205].

Harrod follows his dynamic theory with a consideration of economic policy. In his discussion of contra-cyclical policy[206] he argues that monetary (interest rate) policy can only play a minor role. Public works policies are considered important despite certain difficulties. Harrod then stresses budgetary deficit spending in the form of reducing taxation. His third weapon is a plan for government-financed buffer stocks. Employment would be provided during the depression by the government buying and holding a number and variety of goods which could be sold during the boom. Harrod strongly advocates international buffer stocks for dealing with world slumps.

In his last lecture, Is Interest Obsolete?, Harrod discusses the secular problem. He argues that 'there is a strong *a priori* presumption that saving will tend to redundancy'[207]. The possibility that a more equal distribution of income may reduce the propensity to save is considered. Harrod does not rule out the possibility that the absorption of saving by an increase in the capital:output ratio because of a falling rate of interest may be substantial but he has serious doubts. The effect of a very low rate of interest on saving is not known[208]. Harrod is concerned that budget-deficit financing should not involve growing interest payments on the National Debt and suggests that 'debt incurred for the sole purpose of sustaining purchasing power in a slump should carry no interest'[209]. Deficits by reducing taxation should provide sufficient purchasing power, money, to maintain full employment, carefully defined to avoid regimentation or inflation[210]. Harrod states that 'Inflation must be avoided.'[211] He points out that we do not know whether there will be a chronic tendency to stagnation but this is provided for by his scheme.

In his Manchester lectures Harrod stressed the importance of an economy being managed so as to achieve its growth potential. If monetary and fiscal policies are inadequate, indicative planning is needed to encourage industrial investment[212]. Insufficient demand is a major evil while excess demand is only a nuisance, thus the error of economic policy-makers should be on the side of excess demand. Harrod adds, 'I am not, however, denying that price inflation is an evil of substantial importance. The primary weapon of policy for checking this evil should be the "incomes policy".'[213] Harrod argues that 'incomes policy should be at the very centre of the picture in regard to policy making'[214]. It is the cure for the spiralling of wages and prices. International balance of payments deficits should not be allowed to impede growth and the usual policies, devaluation, etc. are discussed. He strongly recommends import controls in certain circumstances but as a lifelong free-trader this is in *faute de mieux*[215]. Harrod puts growth, subject to any desirable increase in leisure, as the top priority and this is done in terms of modern dynamic economics[216].

Economic Dynamics (1973)[217] shows clearly that Harrod was not an inflationist. He was concerned about the unprecedented rate of inflation in the UK and USA at times during 1969–1971 because of excessive wage increases, was critical of the acceptance of a moderate degree of annual inflation as 'lamentable defeatism' and gave a sociological explanation[218]. He writes that we should not 'acquiesce in the great evil', the method of dealing with it is 'incomes policy' (involuntary or statutory) and the target stable prices[219]. Harrod does not accept the Phillips curve but admits that if monetary and fiscal policies were adopted to create massive unemployment wage-cost inflation might be dampened. This is quite unacceptable and therefore an 'incomes policy' is required[220]. Harrod writes 'Unemployment and inflation are both evils; the former is the greater evil.'[221], but he stresses the importance of avoiding inflation. In dealing with some conflict cases, Harrod does say that it may be desirable to tolerate some demand-pull inflation to reduce unemployment but that an 'incomes policy' is required to prevent wage-price spiralling[222]. He believes the problem of achieving growth potential is complex and criticizes the simple monetarist view that it is solved by a suitable rate of growth of the money supply although he is a great believer in its importance[223]. At this point Harrod again refers to his belief in the importance of 'indicative planning'[224].

It may be noted here that Hicks's elegant 1950 model of the trade cycle[225] drew on Samuelson's model[226] and Harrod's work on dynamic economics. Hicks combines a modified Keynesian multiplier with the accelerator and produces a cyclical movement about a long-period upward economic trend. Hicks first of all develops a 'real' theory of the trade cycle for which the accelerator is 'ultimately responsible'[227]. The path of output is shown to rise to the 'full employment' ceiling, creep along it for a very limited time and then move in a downward direction to reach the bottom of the slump. Hicks shows that a bottom to the slump is inevitable and on his upward trend assumption recovery is certain and so the cycle continues[228]. He approaches a little nearer to the real world in the last two chapters which introduce the monetary factor. Such abstract models are useful but their limitations must be realized[229].

I take as my third Keynesian economist, Professor Joan Robinson. She was closely associated with Keynes when he was writing *The General Theory*, read the proofs and made numerous notes. In a eulogistic letter to Keynes, Joan Robinson referred to it as making 'an impression of great power and coherence'[230]. In her Introduction to the first volume of her *Collected Economic Papers*, Joan Robinson refers to the second section as consisting of 'various attempts to expound and defend the *General Theory*,' while the third section on dynamic economics and the fourth on international trade 'are also deeply influenced by Keynes'[231]. As early as 1937 she published *Introduction to the Theory of Employment*, a simplified exposition of Keynes's *General Theory*. Joan Robinson showed concern about inflation in her 1946 paper, 'Obstacles to Full Employment', in which she stated that 'A successful employment policy, just because it is successful, entails a chronic danger of inflation.'[232] The danger arises from the tendency for money-wage rates to rise with full employment. Actually, she had begun to consider the problem of inflation in relation to full employment in her 1935 essay Full Employment written before the publication of *The General Theory*[233]. Joan Robinson's early interest in dynamic economics, to which she was to make important contributions, is shown in her appreciative but critical review, Mr. Harrod's Dynamics[234].

The second volume of Joan Robinson's *Collected Economic Papers*[235] consist of contributions made in the 1950s to post-Keynesian economics. In her Introduction, 1974, she points out that following Harrod a number of economists were developing a Keynesian analysis of the long run, departing from static equilibrium analysis. The theme of her essays is the analysis of a dynamic equilibrium[236]. Her first main attempt to dynamize *The General Theory* was her essay, The Generalization of the General Theory, which concerned the rate of output of goods and services in an expanding economy[237]. She soon realized the defects of her analysis and made a second attempt in the form of her important book, *The Accumulation of Capital* (1956)[238]. Once again Joan Robinson attempts to extend Keynes's short-period analysis to the development of a theory of an expanding economy in the long run because of the accumulation of capital, technical progress and an increasing population. In her 1958 paper Full Employment and Inflation, she rejoices at the unexpectedly very low level of unemployment achieved during the post-war period but points out that 'as we feared, the high level of employment has been accompanied by a continuous fall in the value of money'[239].

The third volume[240] contains Joan Robinson's papers of the early 1960s, including groups which continue the development of the post-Keynesian tradition reinforced by the Anglo-Italian theory of the distribution of incomes[241]. The papers relate to Keynes and to Marx. Joan Robinson points out that the main lines of *The General Theory* are identical with Michal Kalecki's analysis based on Marx[242]. In her 1964 essay, Kalecki and Keynes, she points out that Kalecki independently found the same solution as Keynes. She writes that 'His book, *Essays in the Theory of Business*

Cycles, published in Polish in 1933, clearly states the principle of effective demand in mathematical form.'[243] Joan Robinson points out that 'All the same, as Michal Kalecki is the first to admit, the "Keynesian Revolution" in Western academic economics is rightly so called. For without Keynes' wide sweep, his brilliant polemic, and, above all, his position within the orthodox citadel in which he was brought up, the walls of obscurantism would have taken much longer to breach'.[244] We did not have a Kaleckian Revolution because his early work was in Polish, except a little known article in French and one very mathematical article[245], and he was a Marxist[246].

In the September 1962 *Economic Journal*, Joan Robinson made the first of her many attacks on the neoclassical synthesis, coining her famous phrases, the bastard-Keynesian model and the bastard Keynesians[247]. In her 1961 paper, Beyond Full Employment, Joan Robinson admits that 'capitalism with full employment which we have known since the war, is an impressive sight – the rapid growth in many countries, the spread of luxury and the reduction of misery; the greater freedom and self-respect of individuals, no longer cringing to keep a job or rotting without one'[248]. However, she sees two main difficulties, the international monetary problem and the continuously rising wages and prices associated with a high level of employment. She stresses the disadvantages of inflation. Once full employment is achievable, there remains the problem of what goods and services should be provided, the allocation of productive resources to various forms of investment and to various consumption goods and services. This allocation will depend on the monetary and fiscal policies adopted. The problem is normative, involving ethical and other considerations, for example, the personal distribution of incomes after taxes and subsidies. This is, of course, a general problem and not only one for those like Joan Robinson who were labelled 'left-wing Keynesians'[249]. However, she rightly stresses its importance. In this connection she discusses the advantages obtainable from economic growth[250].

For Joan Robinson's important contribution to the theory of economic growth I refer to her *Essays in the Theory of Economic Growth* (1962)[251]. The second essay, A Model of Accumulation, adopts a Keynesian approach to long-period problems and outlines a generalization of *The General Theory* which she hopes will be more perspicacious than her former attempts[252]. She builds up a causal model, starting not from equilibrium relations 'but from the rules and motives governing human behaviour'[253]. She takes a simple model of modern capitalism depicting 'a system in which production is organized by individual firms and consumption by individual households, interacting with each other without any overriding control'[254].

The determinants of equilibrium are grouped under seven headings: (1) technical conditions; (2) investment policy; (3) thriftiness conditions; (4) competitive conditions; (5) the wage bargain; (6) financial conditions; (7) the initial stock of capital goods and the state of expectations formed by past experience. Joan Robinson then considers 'the characteristics of the determinants to be postulated for a model designed to discuss, in very general terms, the growth of a pure private-enterprise economy and what are the cross-connections between them'[255]. Under technical conditions, the numbers and quality of the labour force and its growth through time are considered and the state of the industrial arts and its improvement are considered. She stresses the cross-connections, investment in education affecting the labour force, and investment in research influencing the growth of technical knowledge[256]. Under investment policy, the rate of accumulation of productive capital by firms is discussed. After referring to various complications, she assumes that a higher rate of accumulation requires a higher level of profits because of risk and because finance is more readily available[257]. Keynes had stressed the importance of uncertainty in the case of investment and that entrepreneurs' decisions to invest depended largely on the level of 'animal spirits'[258]. In Joan Robinson's model animal spirits also play an important role. With regard to thrift, the model leans towards von Neumann's assumption that all wages are spent and all profits saved[259]. Dealing with competitive conditions, Joan Robinson states that an economy with a large number of monopolistic firms 'is not necessarily less dynamic or growing more sluggishly'[260]. Regarding the wage bargain, she generally assumes constant money-wage rates[261]. Under finance, she considers the borrowing powers of firms and interest rates. Under her assumptions, monetary (interest rate) policy plays a very minor role[262].

After some rather complicated analysis, Joan Robinson proceeds 'to confront the desired rate of growth (resulting from the "animal spirits" of the firms) with the rate of growth made possible by physical conditions (resulting from the growth of population and technical knowledge)'[263]. Smooth, steady growth with full employment is nicknamed 'A Golden Age'[264]. In this case the desired rate of capital accumulation is equal to the rate made possible by the rate of growth of population and of output per head, starting with near full employment and an appropriate composition of the capital stock, the former being maintained. Disturbances to this equilibrium are negligible because conditions are and have been tranquil. Expectations are being realized. On the model's assumptions the real-wage rate rises as technical progress raises output per head while the rate of profit on capital remains constant. This equilibrium must not be described as an optimum situations as this would involve value judgements regarding the appropriate rate of capital accumulation and the personal distribution of incomes.

Joan Robinson distinguishes a number of other 'ages'. Among which we may note 'A Limping Golden Age' in which there is a steady rate of capital accumulation but less than full employment[265]. Conversely, there is 'A Restrained Golden Age' in which the desired rate of capital accumulation cannot be realized. The excess demand for labour causes rising money-wage rates, prices and demand for credit. The rate of interest then rises to check investment and the demand for labour equals the supply[266]. In dealing with 'A Galloping Platinum Age' Joan Robinson points out that 'So far, we have considered situations in which the composition of the stock of capital is already adjusted to the rate of growth that is going on, so that the ratio of plant for producing plant to plant for producing commodities is such that it can maintain itself.'[267] In 'A Galloping Platinum Age' there is a lack of basic plant to produce plant. If 'animal spirits' are high and there is mass unemployment there is a gallop to the appropriate stock of such plant unless it is interrupted by full employment being reached[268]. Another type of limit upon the rate of accumulation appears in 'A Bastard Golden Age'. This is when there is general unemployment and the real wage is the acceptable minimum so that trade unions would increase money wages to prevent any reduction in real wages by rising prices[269]. Joan Robinson's steady growth paths depend on her assumed conditions of tranquillity. She proceeds to discuss the causes of instability[270]. The economy is subject to shocks, for example, a burst of attractive innovations or a chance fall in profits. It may also be subject to unsteady control by government. The model contains inherent instability, because the behaviour of expectations is such 'that a rise in the level of profits sets up an expectation of a further rise, and a fall, of a further fall'[271]. For these reasons the model exhibits unsteady growth although an economy may have the characteristic features of one of her steady 'ages'. There follows a brief discussion of the effects of changes in money-wage rates and prices on the behaviour of the economy in real terms[272].

The fourth volume of Joan Robinson's *Collected Economic Papers* contain her papers of 1965–1972[273]. In her 1971 lecture, The Second Crisis of Economic Theory[274], she states that 'The first crisis arose from the breakdown of a theory which could not account for the *level* of employment. [Hence the Keynesian Revolution] The second crisis arises from a theory that cannot account for the *content* of employment.'[275] I have already acknowledged that the 'content' is a very important economic and social problem[276]. However, I would not regard it as the second crisis of economic theory. What I regard as the important crises and developments in Post-Keynesian economics are discussed in this book.

In *Economic Heresies* (1971)[277], Joan Robinson is again concerned with the problem of inflation. She points out that at the time of *The General Theory* (1936) 'It seemed obvious that the continuous full employment would be accompanied by a continuous fall in the value of money which might disrupt the basis of the whole system.'[278] She explains the processes of 'demand-pull' and 'cost-push' in terms of the behaviour of firms and trade unions. Joan Robinson points out that hyper-inflation has been avoided but that the consequences of continuous inflation are extremely demoralizing. She refers to the difficulties of an incomes policy and states that 'the general level of prices has become a political problem'[279].

Joan Robinson's Presidential Address to the Economics Section of the British Association Meeting, 1972, was entitled 'What has become of the Keynesian Revolution?'[280] She rightly stresses the importance of uncertainty in the revolution. She laments the neoclassical synthesis, her bastard-Keynesian model, which admittedly led to emasculated expositions of Keynesian theory in many textbooks[281], but has played an important role in the development of post-Keynesian economics. Further she ignores the reinterpretations of Keynes discussed in Chapter 12 which had already begun. She rightly stresses Keynes's analysis of the general level of prices being primarily determined by the level of money-wage rates and his view that inflation resulting from trade union wage-bargaining under 'full employment' conditions would be a difficult political problem[282].

Joan Robinson wrote an article during the present depression entitled, What has become of Employment Policy?[283]. She criticized the bastard

Keynesian doctrine of the government 'merely' having to organize investment to equal desired saving. She wrote, 'Against this background, the
slump of 1973–1974 was a considerable shock.'[284] and added, 'The bastard
Keynesian economists are quite disconcerted and the spokesmen for
capitalism have got their brief muddled up.'[285] This criticism is, I think,
unfair as the slump came as a shock to economists in a wide spectrum of
economic thought. We are now experiencing depression after the long
period of relatively steady growth since World War II[286]. Now we have
stagflation, stagnation, relatively high unemployment and inflation.

Joan Robinson discussed the situation as she saw it in 1976. She
considers the relation between inflation and trade unions and concludes
that successful co-operation between unions and government depends on
the extension of 'the influence of the unions beyond wage control'[287]. Joan
Robinson gives a brief analysis of the causes of the depression[288]. She sees
the Keynesian revolution being replaced by the pre-Keynesian orthodoxy
with consequently much higher unemployment, recurrent crises, and
considerable human misery. This is attributed to the failure of modern
economies 'to develop the political and social institutions, at either
domestic or international level, that are needed to make permanent full
employment compatible with capitalism'[289]. The non-communist world is
certainly facing the most serious economic problems since the 1930s
although they are not so acute[290]. Joan Robinson offers little that is
constructive, but there is no reason to despair when considering the
outlook for private capitalist, mixed and social democratic economies.

In recent years there has been much criticism of Keynesian policies, of
their advocacy by Keynesian economists, and a questioning as to how far
Keynes's disciples were misrepresenting the views of their master. In this
chapter I have discussed Keynes's basic model and considered the work of
three distinguished Keynesian economists, Harrod, Kahn and Joan Robinson. It has been made clear that Keynes, and the Keynesians were well
aware of the danger of inflation in a full-employment economy. Both
inflation and unemployment are great social evils and the question as to
how far a full-employment policy should be pursued is very difficult. The
'trade-off' between inflation and the level of employment is also a very
complicated matter. I argued in 1950 that the full-employment policy
should not be pressed to the point of preventing unemployment because of
rising money wages, the appropriate monetary policy should be maintained, and that 'trade unions may well re-learn this lesson'[291]. However, I
did not maintain this rigid position in the following years and like many
Keynesian economists I advocated an incomes policy to allow a high level
of employment to coexist with a reasonably stable price level. Incomes
policies are also necessary in the case of the new phenomenon of
stagflation. This difficult politico-economic problem remains to be resolved.

In view of all these difficulties I have already suggested that Hutchison in
Keynes versus the 'Keynesians' . . .? (1977) was unduly harsh in his
criticism of the Pseudo-Keynesians as he calls Harrod, Kahn, Joan
Robinson and others[292]. Mr Walter Eltis had taken a somewhat similar line
in 1976 in his article, 'The Failure of the Keynesian Conventional
Wisdom'[293]. In 1977, Worswick in a moderate defence of Keynesian
demand management asks 'where are those Keynesians who do not believe

that full employment might be threatened by inflation?'[294] An extremely critical view of Keynesian policies is put forward in *The Consequences of Mr Keynes* (1978)[295]. The summary view is that 'Intellectual error of monumental proportion has been made, and not exclusively by the politicians. Error also lies squarely with the economists. The "academic scribbler" who must bear substantial responsibility is Lord Keynes, whose thinking was uncritically accepted by establishment economists in both America and Britain. The mounting historical evidence of the ill-effects of Keynes's ideas cannot continue to be ignored. Keynesian economics has turned the politicians loose; it has destroyed the effective constraint on politicians' ordinary appetites to spend and spend without the apparent necessity to tax. Sober assessment suggests that, politically, Keynesianism represents a substantial disease that over the long run can prove fatal for the survival of democracy.'[296] We can be deeply concerned with the politico-economic problems faced by the advanced economies of democratic states and yet not accept this extreme indictment which is unjustified.

Notes

1. *See C.W.*, Vol. XIII (1973a).
2. 1st edn, 1956; 2nd edn, 1965.
3. *See* Gilbert, 'The Demand for Money: The Development of an Economic Concept (1953).
4. Robertson, *Lectures on Economic Principles* (1963a), pp. 338 *et seq*.
5. *C.W.*, Vol. VII (1936, 1973), p. xxxiv.
6. Friedrich A. Hayek, *Prices and Production* (2nd edn, 1935), p. 18. *See also* 'A Note on the Development of the Doctrine of "Forced Saving"' (November 1932), reprinted in Hayek, *Profits, Interest and Investment* (1939).
7. David Hume, *Essays Moral, Political and Literary* (1903 edn), p. 293; *David Hume, Writings on Economics*, edited and introduced by Eugene Rotwein (1955), p. 37. For comments on this passage *see* Gilbert, 'Economic Theory and Policy' (1959), pp. 16–17.
8. *See* Haberler, *Prosperity and Depression* (4th edn, 1958), p. 87, for economists who developed the acceleration principle early in this century. Part I of this book gives an excellent analysis of trade cycle theories.
9. Austin Robinson, *John Maynard Keynes Economist. Author. Statesman* (1971).
10. *Ibid*.
11. *Ibid*.
12. *Ibid*., pp. 13–14.
13. *Ibid*., p. 15.
14. *Ibid*.
15. *Ibid*. Lydia Lopokova was Keynes's wife.
16. *Ibid*.
17. *Ibid*., p. 16.
18. Cmnd 6527 (1944).
19. *Ibid*., p. 3.
20. *Ibid*., p. 18.
21. These statistics and those given below up to 1975 are taken from editors A. R. Prest and D. J. Coppock, *The U.K. Economy A Manual of Applied Economics* (6th edn, 1976), Chapter 1 by M. C. Kennedy, pp. 38, 44, 50–51. Kennedy gives the definitions and sources. Kennedy's Chapter 1, The Economy as a Whole, is an excellent survey of the United Kingdom's economy from the early 1950s to the mid-1970s.
22. Prest and Coppock (1976), pp. 35–36 and p. 35, n.4.
23. Sir Alexander Cairncross, 'Control of the Economy – What Does it Take?' (June 1970), p. 345. This article was based on a paper given at the Boston Meeting of the American Association for the Advancement of Science in December 1969.

24. *Ibid.*
25. G. D. N. Worswick, 'The End of Demand Management?' (January 1977), p. 7.
26. *Ibid.*, pp. 2 and 12.
27. *Ibid.*, p. 16.
28. Austin Robinson (1971), p. 20.
29. However, the percentage was 7.1 in 1972 compared with 9.4 in 1971.
30. December 1980.
31. *C.W.*, Vol. VII (1936, 1973), p. 24.
32. This, of course, involves a simplification of reality.
33. *C.W.*, Vol. XIV (1973b), p. 179. The statement is from a set of Keynes's rough notes.
34. *Ibid.*, p. 180. The supply conditions are assumed to be given.
35. *Ibid.*
36. Meade was a member of the 'circus' at Cambridge which discussed Keynes's *A Treatise on Money* on publication and which had an important influence on Keynes's development towards *The General Theory*. *See* Robinson in Lekachman, *Keynes' General Theory, Reports of Three Decades* (1964), p. 55. Kahn in a footnote to his classic article, 'The Relation of Home Investment to Unemployment' acknowledges his great indebtedness to Meade (Kahn (1931 in Kahn, *Selected Essays on Employment and Growth* (1972), p. 16). Soon after the publication of *The General Theory*, Meade produced a mathematical model of Keynes's basic model in the form of a set of simultaneous equations. *See* J. E. Meade, 'A Simplified Model of Mr Keynes' System', *Review of Economic Studies* (February 1937). Reprinted in Harris, *The New Economics* (1948).
37. James Meade, The Keynesian Revolution, in Milo Keynes, *Essays on John Maynard Keynes* (1975), p. 82.
38. *Ibid.*, p. 84.
39. *Ibid.*, p. 85.
40. *Ibid.*, p. 87.
41. *Ibid.*, p. 88.
42. *Lectures on Economic Principles* (1963a), p. 421.
43. *Ibid.*, p. 421.
44. Joan Robinson, *Economic Philosophy* (Penguin Books, Harmondsworth, 1964, reprinted 1966, p. 891). This book was first published in 1962.
45. Robertson (1963a), p. 422. The quotation is from Michal Kalecki, 'A New Approach to the Problem of Business Cycles' (1949/1950).
46. Michal Kalecki, *Selected Essays on the Dynamics of the Capitalist Economy 1933–1970* (1971).
47. *Ibid.*, p. 108.
48. *Ibid.*, p. 106.
49. *Ibid.*
50. *C.W.*, Vol. VII (1936, 1973), pp. 245–254.
51. Oscar Lange, 'The Rate of Interest and the Optimum Propensity to Consume' (February 1938) reprinted in American Economic Association, *Readings in Business Cycle Theory* (Philadelphia, 1944).
52. *Ibid.*, p. 171. I and C are measured in real terms, in this case in terms of Keynes's wage-units (*see* p. 82).
53. A. C. Pigou, *Keynes's 'General Theory' A Retrospective View* (1950), p. 13. Gross investment, consisting only of depreciation in the form of replacement for wear and tear is, of course, related to consumption.
54. There are a few implicit references in *The General Theory*.
55. In an econometric model based on Keynes this problem has to be overcome in one way or another.
56. G. L. S. Shackle, *A Scheme of Economic Theory* (1965), p. 98.
57. *Ibid.*, p. 132.
58. The relationship between short-term and longterm expectations is discussed on pp. 46–47.
59. Much work has been done on the theoretical and empirical aspects of investment since Keynes, but much further research is required. A useful general survey is P. N. Junankar, *Investment: Theories and Evidence* (1972). *See also* G. P. Marshall, A. A. Sampson and R. Sedgwick, 'The Rate of Investment and the Supply Schedule for New Capital Goods', *Bulletin of Economic Research* (November 1975) and earlier articles in the *Bulletin* referred to in n.1 on p. 287.

60. It would only be correct to take the current yield in the static state. *C.W.*, Vol. VII (1936, 1973), p. 145.
61. *Ibid.*, p. 149.
62. *Ibid.*, p. 161.
63. *Ibid.*, pp. 143–144.
64. *Ibid.*, pp. 149 *et seq.*
65. *Ibid.*, p. 144. *See* Chapter 22 and particularly p. 313.
66. Milo Keynes (1975), pp. 83–84. There is a complication here because $S \equiv I$, an identity, in the *General Theory*.
67. J. A. Kregel, 'Economic Methodology in the Face of Uncertainty' (June 1976), p. 217, n.2.
68. *C.W.*, Vol. VII (1936, 1973), p. xxiii.
69. Kregel (1976), p. 218, continuation of n.2 on p. 217.
70. Reprinted in John Hicks, *Critical Essays in Monetary Theory* (1967).
71. *See* p. 80.
72. Luigi L. Pasinetti, *Growth and Income Distribution* (1974), pp. 46–47.
73. Franco Modigliani, 'Liquidity Preference and the Theory of Interest and Money', *Econometrica* (January 1944), reprinted in American Economic Association, *Readings in Monetary Theory* (1952).
74. Thomas Sowell, *Say's Law* (1972), p. 204.
75. Reference has been made in the discussion to effective demand and aggregate demand. Effective demand is the short-term equilibrium aggregate demand.
76. Hutchison, *Keynes versus the 'Keynesians' . . .?* (1977), p. 61.
77. *Ibid.*
78. *Ibid.*, p. 58.
79. *Ibid.*, p. 36. The references are to Lord Kahn, *On Re-Reading Keynes* (1975), p. 33 and to Sir Roy Harrod in D. E. Moggridge, *Keynes: Aspects of the Man and His Work (The First Keynes Seminar Held at the University of Kent at Canterbury, 1972)* (1974), pp. 8–9.
80. Lord Kahn, 'Mr Eltis and the Keynesians' (April 1977), p. 10.
81. Harrod, *The Life of John Maynard Keynes* (1951), p. 432.
82. *C.W.*, Vols V and VI (1930, 1971).
83. *C.W.*, Vol. V (1930, 1971), pp. xviii–xix.
84. In Lekachman (1964), p. 55.
85. *C.W.*, Vol. XIII (1973a).
86. *Ibid.*, p. 484.
87. *C.W.*, Vol. VII (1936, 1973), p. xxiii.
88. Lord Kahn (1975), p. 11.
89. Nihon Keizai Shimbun, 1956, reprinted in Richard Kahn (1972), pp. 99–100.
90. Kahn (1972), p. 100.
91. *Ibid.*, p. 97.
92. *Ibid.*, pp. 97–98. Beveridge reported 3 per cent 'as a conservative, rather than an unduly hopeful, aim' (*Full Employment in a Free Society* (1944), p. 128).
93. *Ibid.*, p. 99. The rate of inflation was relatively low at that time as compared with the rates experienced since 1969. United Kingdom retail prices increased by 4.5 per cent in 1955 and by 2.0 per cent in 1956. *See* Prest and Coppock (1976), p. 44.
94. *The Economic Implications of Full Employment*, Cmnd 9725 (March 1956), quoted by Kahn (1972), p. 100.
95. Kahn (1972), p. 102.
96. This, of course, would be associated with technical progress.
97. Kahn (1972).
98. Printed in *The Listener*, 3 and 10 May 1956, reprinted in Kahn (1972).
99. Kahn (1972), p. 103.
100. *The Economic Journal* (June–September 1943), p. 187. Kahn (1972), p. 104.
101. Kahn (1972). The quotation is from Keynes's note, 'A Rejoinder', *The Economic Journal* (December 1944), p. 430, in answer to a note in the same issue by F. D. Graham entitled 'Keynes v Hayek on a commodity reserve currency'.
102. Kahn would have preferred a greater stimulus to investment and a smaller stimulus to consumption by tax reliefs.
103. Kahn (1972), p. 104. Kahn added that 'Denmark today provides an impressive indication of the amount of unemployment required to act as a moderating – and not so very moderating at that – influence on wage increases'.

104. *Ibid.*, p. 105.
105. These two causes of inflation may be operative at the same time, one of them being dominant. At the time of writing it is cost-push inflation with which we are concerned.
106. *C.W.*, Vol. IX (1972).
107. Kahn (1972), p. 106.
108. *Ibid.*, p. 107. Kahn at this point is taking as given the expenditure on defence, the social services and so on.
109. *Ibid.*, p. 109. Note his approval of Mr Macmillan's budgeting for a surplus, public saving. Kahn quotes Keynes's view in July 1939 that 'Clearly the effect of high taxation in discouraging outlay should be tried before recourse is had to a high rate of interest'. 'Borrowing by the State', *The Times*, 24 July 1939.
110. *See* p. 79.
111. Quoted by Kahn (1972), p. 110.
112. Milton Friedman, *Studies in the Quantity Theory of Money* (1956a).
113. Committee on the Working of the Monetary System, *Principal Memoranda of Evidence, 1959.* H.M.S.O. [written 27 May 1958], reprinted in Kahn (1972).
114. Kahn (1972), p. 124.
115. Kahn recognizes that monetary policy has some direct effect on consumption and certain forms of budgetary policy influence investment. *Ibid.*, p. 125.
116. *Ibid.*, p. 126. Kahn's interest in growth theory is shown by his article, 'Exercises in the Analysis of Growth', *O.E.P.* (June 1959), reprinted in Kahn (1972).
117. *Ibid.*, p. 128.
118. *Ibid.* Kahn explains here the ways in which changes in interest rates and the availability of bank advances affect investment.
119. *Ibid.*, p. 129.
120. *Ibid.*, p. 131. It should be noted that Great Britain's unemployment percentages were very low at that time being 1.0 in 1955 and 1956, 1.3 in 1957 and 1.9 in 1958 (*see* Prest and Coppock (1976), p. 44). Kahn states later (p. 139) that 'Stagnation of output is expressed in uneconomic use of employed labour more than in positive unemployment'.
121. *Ibid.*, p. 139.
122. Kahn added 'though in much lesser degree'. It must be remembered that he was writing this in the 1950s and not in the 1970s.
123. Kahn (1972), p. 140. Kahn adds 'And in view of the poor response of the behaviour of wages to restriction of demand, I do not believe that it would be desirable to go beyond avoiding such positive shortage of labour as could, in moderate measure, be usefully tolerated if an effective wages policy was being operated.' (pp. 140–141).
124. *Ibid.*, p. 142.
125. *Ibid.*, pp. 143–144.
126. *Ibid.*, p. 144.
127. *Ibid.*, p. 147.
128. *Ibid.* Robertson expressed his disagreement with this statement of Kahn. *See* his *Memorandum Submitted to the Canadian Royal Commission on Banking and Finance* (1936b), p. 16, n.
129. *Committee on the Working of the Monetary System Report*, Cmnd 827 (August 1959).
130. *Ibid.* paras 391, 392, 523. In para. 392, n., it is stated that 'the more efficient the financial structure, the more can the velocity of circulation be stretched without serious inconvenience being caused'. The Report emphasized the importance of the non-bank financial intermediaries in the monetary system. Professor N. J. Gibson questioned 'the extreme position taken up by the Radcliffe Committee towards non-bank financial intermediaries as a threat to traditional monetary policy'. N. J. Gibson, *Financial Intermediaries and Monetary Policy* (2nd edn, 1970), p. 18.
131. Gilbert, 'The Demand for Money: the Development of an Economic Concept' (1953), p. 150.
132. Kahn (1972), pp. 148–149. For the structure of interest rates *see* p. 249, n. 2
133. *Radcliffe Report* (1959), para. 395.
134. *See* p. 105.
135. Economists who could not be described as monetarists, such as D. H. Robertson, also held this view.
136. Radcliffe Report (1959), para. 389. The Committee emphasized the general liquidity of the economic system having in mind all financial assets and liabilities.

137. *Ibid.*, para. 392.
138. 'We have sought, without much success, for convincing evidence of its presence in recent years.' *Ibid.*, para. 386.
139. *Ibid.*, para. 385.
140. *Ibid.* For example, a fall in the rate of interest raises the capital value of fixed-interest securities.
141. *Ibid.*, paras 387 *et seq.*
142. *Ibid.*, para. 395.
143. *Ibid.*, para. 498.
144. *Ibid. See also* paras 499 and 500. Here, the Committee refers to the power of the monetary authorities as managers of the National Debt to influence interest rates. *See also* para. 514 and Chapter VII.
145. *Ibid.*, para. 514. Hire purchase controls were included in monetary measures but considered of limited usefulness.
146. *Ibid.*, paras 515–519.
147. *Ibid.*, para. 521.
148. *Ibid.*, para. 524. *See also* paras 525–529.
149. *Ibid.*, para. 524. It is true that the measures advocated did in fact involve the control of the quantity of money multiplied by its income-velocity of circulation. The Committee's analysis in terms of general liquidity etc. is important but it is unfortunate that the traditional form of analysis was abandoned.
150. *Ibid.*, para. 514.
151. *Ibid.*, para. 397.
152. Kahn (1972), p. 149. If, for example, 'the rate of interest' (simplifying) is regarded as being at the right level and an issue of Government securities to the general public would raise the rate of interest, it is appropriate to sell government securities to the banking system bearing the current rate of interest and allow the quantity of money to increase.
153. *See* p. 158.
154. *Ninth Report from the Expenditure Committee (1974) Public Expenditure, Inflation and the Balance of Payments*, HC 328 (July) London: H.M.S.O.
155. *Ibid.*, para. 44. *See also* paras 45–47.
156. *Ibid.*, para. 47. The parties involved include, of course, the trade unions. The Report continued, 'Perhaps, upon occasion, people will agree to a temporary, statutory incomes policy'.
157. For the New Cambridge School *see* Public Expenditure and the Management of the Economy, Memorandum by Francis Cripps, Wynne Godley and Martin Fetherston, University of Cambridge: Department of Applied Economics in *Ninth Report from the Expenditure Committee* (1974), For an advanced presentation *see* Francis Cripps and Wynne Godley, 'A Formal Analysis of the Cambridge Economic Policy Group Model' (November 1976), and the very useful references appended to it.
158. *Ninth Report from the Expenditure Committee* (1974), paras 11–18. This would also apply to some classes of central government expenditure.
159. *Ibid.*, Godley, para. 15, quoted by Kahn and Posner, para. 19.
160. *Ibid.*, para. 19. There are also possibilities of offsetting, to some extent, unfavourable foreign influences.
161. *Ibid.*, para. 21. Godley and his associates had proposed that the Government should decide public expenditure and fix an appropriate rate of tax. Kahn and Posner recognise the difficulties of economic forecasting but do not despair regarding demand management. *See* paras 23–25.
162. *Ibid.*, para. 31. Kahn and Posner regret the relatively high rates of consumption and public expenditure during the past twenty-five years. The international balance of payments aspect of a low rate of productive investment is considered in para. 27.
163. Kahn had previously advised the Radcliffe Committee not to use these terms.
164. *Ninth Report from the Expenditure Committee* (1974), para. 40.
165. *Ibid.*, para. 41. A footnote states 'While Mr Posner believes that a fully articulated, explicit policy for prices and incomes must be vigorously pursued, he feels that his position as an Official Adviser precludes him from endorsing every word of paragraph 41.' *See also* Appendix 4, Supplementary Memorandum by Professor Lord Kahn and Mr Michael Posner (1974), p. 163.
166. *Ibid.*, para. 43. As far as exports are concerned, the country's competitive position must be taken into account and this depends on the foreign exchange rate and other factors.

167. *Ibid.*, para. 50. They want 'just the right *level* of the public sector deficit at any point of time, and just the right amount of *change*'. They realize that this 'just rightness' cannot be judged precisely (para. 51).
168. The differences between the two concepts may be ignored here.
169. The analysis in paras 57–72 is complicated and Kahn and Posner might not agree completely with my presentation of their position. *See* especially para. 72 which deals with increases in the quantity of money. It should be noted that an increase in the quantity of money which is associated with an increase in money incomes in proportion to the increase in real output need not be inflationary. Kahn's and Posner's analysis relating to demand inflation assumes a high level of employment and money demand increasing more rapidly than real output.
170. *See* Lord Kahn (1975); Lord Kahn, *'Thoughts on the Behaviour of Wages and Monetarism'*, *Lloyds Bank Review* (January 1976); Lord Kahn, 'Mr Eltis and the Keynesians', *Lloyds Bank Review* (April 1977a); Richard Kahn and Michael Posner, 'Inflation, Unemployment, and Growth', *National Westminster Bank Quarterly Review* (November 1977b); *see also* Richard Kahn, Unemployment as seen by the Keynesians, in editor G. D. N. Worswick, *The Concept and Measurement of Involuntary Unemployment* (London 1976).
171. Kahn (1976b), p. 6.
172. This may also occur with a constant quantity of money if factors associated with the borrowing requirement cause an increase in the velocity of circulation. If there is general unemployment the main effect will tend to be on output. There is also an international balance of payments problem.
173. Kahn (1976b), pp. 9–10.
174. Kahn (1977), p. 9. This is a criticism of Walter Eltis, 'The Failure of the Keynesian Conventional Wisdom' (October 1976).
175. Kahn and Posner (1977), p. 36. Unlike the monetarists, they see the great danger of wage inflation as 'an issue of high politics, to be resolved only by political imagination and action. It is hard to see from where this might come' (p. 37).
176. Harrod (1951), p. vi. Harrod died in 1978. For bibliographical information *see* Robert Blake, A Personal Memoir, in editors W. A. Ellis, M. F. G. Scott, J. N. Wolfe, *Induction, Growth and Trade* (1970), Harrods's autobiographical references in R. F. Harrod, *The Prof.: Personal Memoir of Lord Cherwell* (1959) and Brown, Henry Phelps 'Sir Roy Harrod: a biographical memoir' (March 1980) and 'Sir Roy Harrod: A Note' (March 1981).
177. Harrod (1951), p. 452.
178. R. F. Harrod, 'Mr Keynes and Traditional Theory', *Econometrica* (January 1937), reprinted in Harris (1948) and Lekachman (1964).
179. Harrod (1951), p. 453, n.1.
180. *Ibid.*, p. 462.
181. *Ibid.*, p. 463.
182. *Ibid.*, p. 464.
183. Sir Roy Harrod, Keynes's Theory and its Application, in D. E. Moggridge (1974), p. 4. *See also* Roy Harrod, *Economic Dynamics* (1973), p. 8.
184. *Economic Journal* (1939), reprinted in R. F. Harrod, *Economic Essays* (1st edn, 1952) to which references are made. Harrod had some years earlier begun to think along these lines. *See* R. F. Harrod, 'The Expansion of Credit in an Advancing Community' (August 1934). Evsey D. Domar in the United States developed independently a similar theory to that of Harrod in his articles, 'Capital Expansion, Rate of Growth, and Employment' (1946) and 'Expansion and Employment' (1947).
185. Harrod in Lekachman *Keynes' General Theory Reports of Three Decades* (1964), p. 140.
186. Harrod, *Economic Essays* (2nd edn, 1972), p. ix. Another important model of the trade cycle, based on the two relationships (the multiplier and the accelerator) was developed by P. A. Samuelson in his article 'Interactions between the Acceleration Principle and the Multiplier' (May 1939). *See* Gilbert, 'Economic Theory and Policy' (1959), p. 4.
187. *Ibid.*
188. Harrod *Economic Essays* (1st edn, 1952), p. 254.
189. *Ibid.*, p. 256.
190. *Ibid.*
191. *Ibid.*, pp. 264–265.
192. *Ibid.*, p. 273.

193. *Ibid.*
194. Harrod (1948), pp. v and vi. The fact that the post-World War II period has not experienced stagnation (the present serious depression is not related to this concept) does not affect the importance of Harrod's work. Harrod's model, like Keynes's, is of general importance and does not depend on the stagnation thesis.
195. J. C. Gilbert, 'Economic Theory in Great Britain Today' (May 1957), p. 19.
196. *Ibid.*, p. 29.
197. Harrod (1948), p. 77.
198. *Ibid.*, p. 81.
199. *Ibid.*, p. 82.
200. Harrod is not envisaging a dynamic equilibrium with perfect adjustment which is thus similar to his static equilibrium in this respect (*ibid.*, p. 81). This allows for a degree of uncertainty.
201. It is important to note that for the fully developed theory C_r is a marginal concept but here we may assume that the average and marginal capital:output ratios are the same.
202. *See* Harrod (1948), pp. 83 and 22 *et seq*. Neutral inventions are distinguished from those which increase or decrease the capital:output ratio. According to Hicks's classification, a neutral invention leaves unchanged the ratio of the marginal product of capital to that of labour, assuming these two factors of production. A capital-saving invention decreases this ratio and a labour-saving invention increases this ratio. *See* J. R. Hicks, *The Theory of Wages* (1st edn, 1932), pp. 121 *et seq*. Inventions play an important role in economic growth theory as, for example, in the various growth models of Lord Kaldor where he developed a technical progress function. *See* the articles by Kaldor cited by F. H. Hahn and R. C. O. Mathews in the American Economic Association and Royal Economic Society, *Surveys of Economic Theory*, Vol. II (London, 1967), p. 118, including N. Kaldor and J. A. Mirrlees, 'A New Model of Economic Growth' (June 1962).
203. A fall in the rate of interest tends to increase the capital:output ratio, and a rise to decrease it.
204. Harrod (1973), p. 17.
205. Harrod (1948), p. 91.
206. *Ibid.*, pp. 115–128.
207. *Ibid.*, p. 130.
208. *Ibid.*, pp. 132–134.
209. *Ibid.*, p. 136.
210. Harrod's proposed mechanism actually involves a balanced budget and payments into the Exchequer by an independent expert Authority which would normally be used to reduce taxation. *Ibid.*, pp. 138–139.
211. *Ibid.*, p. 140.
212. Sir Roy Harrod, *Towards a New Economic Policy* (1967), Lectures Given in the University of Manchester, p. 49. Harrod has in mind here the indicative planning by France and the British 'National Plan' of 1965 which was soon suspended.
213. *Ibid.*, p. 53.
214. *Ibid.*, p. 54.
215. *Ibid.*, pp. 56 *et seq*. Harrod emphasizes the importance of providing an adequate international monetary system.
216. *Ibid.*, p. 70. However, the maximum growth of the gross national product must not be regarded as a 'sacred cow'. *See* p. 7. *See also* Harrod (1973), pp. 168–170.
217. This is a complete rewriting of *Towards a Dynamic Economics*. Harrod remains one of my three Keynesians despite the statement on the dust jacket that Harrod views Keynes 'as a transitional figure, mainly of historic interest now, since he did not embark into *dynamic* theory'.
218. Harrod (1973), pp. 82, 83 and 91–92. The rate of inflation greatly accelerated later.
219. *Ibid.*, pp. 92–93.
220. *Ibid.*, p. 97. Again he writes, 'Inflation is an evil'. The argument regarding the Phillips curve is repeated on p. 117.
221. *Ibid.*, p. 98.
222. *Ibid.*, p. 117.
223. *Ibid.*, p. 119. On p. 179 Harrod writes, 'I have retained the opinion over a very long period that monetary policy has effects of crucial significance'. A reference to monetary policy in the short period is made on p. 177. For a discussion of monetarism, *see* Chapter 10.

224. *Ibid.*, pp. 119–121.
225. J. R. Hicks, *A Contribution to the Theory of the Trade Cycle* (1950).
226. *See* Samuelson (1939).
227. Hicks (1950), pp. 136–137.
228. This very brief account is taken from Chapter VIII, The Cycle in Outline. Hicks emphasizes the cycle constrained by the ceiling and not the free cycle in which the ceiling is not reached.
229. For Hicks's own reassessment of his model, *see* the extract from 'Real and Monetary Factors in Economic Fluctuations', *S.J.P.E.* (November 1974), reprinted in *Economic Perspectives* (1977), pp. 177–181. *See also* G. L. S. Shackle, *A Scheme of Economic Theory* (1965), pp. 131 *et seq.* and 191–192.
230. *C.W.*, Vol. XIII (1973a), p. 638. Letter from Joan Robinson, 16 June 1935.
231. Joan Robinson, *Collected Economic Papers*, Vol. I (1966), p. ix. The first printing was 1951.
232. Robinson (1951, 1966), p. 114. The paper had been published in *Nationalokonomisk Tidsskrift* (1946).
233. *Collected Economic Papers*, Vol. IV (1973a), p. 174. This essay was originally published in Joan Robinson, *Essays in the Theory of Employment* (London, 1st edn, 1937; Oxford, 2nd edn, 1947) and reprinted in Joan Robinson (1973a).
234. *Collected Economic Papers*, Vol. IV, pp. 155–174. This is a reprint of a review of R. F. Harrod, *Towards a Dynamic Economics*, in *Economic Journal* (March 1949).
235. Joan Robinson, *Collected Economic Papers*, Vol. II (1st edn, 1960; 2nd edn, 1975).
236. *Ibid.*, p. iii.
237. Joan Robinson, *The Rate of Interest and Other Essays* (1952), p. 71.
238. Joan Robinson (1960, 1975), p. vi. The reference is to Joan Robinson, *The Accumulation of Capital* (1st edn, 1956; 3rd edn, 1969).
239. Joan Robinson (1960, 1975), p. 272. She is referring to the rise of consumer-goods prices at an average rate of 4 per cent a year since 1946, a relatively low rate compared to that of the 1970s.
240. Joan Robinson, *Collected Economic Papers*, Vol. III (Oxford, 1st edn, 1965; 2nd edn, 1975).
241. *Ibid.*, p. xiii.
242. Joan Robinson's statement that 'Kalecki's version of the General Theory, rather than Keynes', has been incorporated in the post-Keynesian tradition.' (p. xiv) should only refer, I think, to one particular stream of thought.
243. *Ibid.*, p. 94. Joan Robinson states that Kalecki published a version of his theory in prose in *Polska Gospodarcza*, No. 43 (1935). She describes Kalecki's special contributions, *ibid.*, pp. 94–99.
244. *Ibid.*, p. 98.
245. M. Kalecki, 'A Macrodynamic Theory of Business Cycles' (1935), a paper presented at the meeting of the Econometric Society, Leyden, October 1933. For further information on Kalecki, *see* Joan Robinson, Michal Kalecki, a review of his *Selected Essays on the Dynamics of the Capitalist Economy 1933–1970* (1971) in *Cambridge Review* (October 1971), reprinted in Joan Robinson (1973a); G. C. Harcourt's review of George R. Feiwel, *The Intellectual Capital of Michal Kalecki: A Study in Economic Theory and Policy* (1975) in *Economica* (February 1977).
246. We also do not talk of a Swedish Revolution in economics in the 1930s in spite of the developments in employment theory and policy there. *See* Donald Winch, 'The Keynesian Revolution in Sweden' (April 1966).
247. Joan Robinson (1965, 1975), pp. 100–102. This is part of a review of Harry G. Johnson, *Money, Trade and Economic Growth* (1962).
248. *Ibid.*, p. 105. The paper is a reprint of an article in *Annals of Collective Economy* (Liège, April–June 1961).
249. *Ibid.*, p. 109. Joan Robinson quotes from Keynes's *The General Theory* (p. 379), 'I see no reason to suppose that the existing system seriously misemploys the factors of production which are in use . . . It is in determining the volume, not the direction, of actual employment that the existing system has broken down.' (*Ibid.*, p. 110). Keynes certainly defended private capitalism, the mass unemployment problem having been solved. However, it is misleading to suggest that Keynes was not concerned with the direction of employment in spite of this statement. This is clear from the reading of the whole of Chapter 24 of *The General Theory* where he refers to the 'arbitrary and

inequitable distribution of wealth and incomes' (p. 372), the scale on which consumption might be restricted in the interests of capital accumulation (p. 377), and that 'the modern classical theory has itself called attention to various conditions in which the free play of economic forces may need to be curbed or guided.' (pp. 379–380). The general philosophy of the 1942 Beveridge report, *Social Insurance and Allied Services* (Cmnd 6404) accorded with Keynes's views (Harrod (1951), p. 535). *See also* Joan Robinson, *Economic Philosophy* (1964), reprinted 1966, pp. 91–93 and 121–130 for a detailed discussion of the 'content' of full employment.

250. *Ibid.*, pp. 110–112.
251. London. Her book, *The Accumulation of Capital* (1956, 1969), is difficult. Lord Kaldor's views are akin to Joan Robinson's and he has produced a number of 'Keynesian' economic growth models. *See* his latest model in N. Kaldor and J. A. Mirrlees, 'A New Model of Economic Growth' (1962) and the first footnote which refers to earlier models.
252. Joan Robinson (1962), p. v.
253. *Ibid.*, p. 34.
254. *Ibid.*, p. 35.
255. *Ibid.*, p. 36.
256. *Ibid.* To simplify her model, Joan Robinson assumes no scarcity of natural resources at this stage.
257. *Ibid.*, pp. 37–38. The general characteristics of the economy are given. Presumably, the rate of interest is given.
258. *C.W.*, Vol. VII (1936, 1973), pp. 161–162.
259. Joan Robinson (1962), p. 38. This is, of course, a simplification and Joan Robinson does allow for some element of the alternative assumption that saving depends on the individual preferences of the recipients of income.
260. *Ibid.*, p. 41. Joan Robinson discusses briefly the behaviour of prices, profits, output and real wages under monopolistic conditions (pp. 41–42).
261. However, money-wage rates rise if there is excess demand for labour or the real wage is depressed below what workers are willing to accept (*ibid.*, p. 42).
262. *Ibid.*, pp. 43–44. The importance of monetary policy is reduced to a minimum except 'as a stopper to inflation'.
263. *Ibid.*, p. 52. Joan Robinson points to the relationship between Harrod's and her models but states that there are some important differences.
264. *Ibid.*, indicating its mythical nature.
265. *Ibid.*, pp. 53–54.
266. *Ibid.*, p. 54. Other types of restraint are also concerned (pp. 55–56).
267. *Ibid.*, p. 56.
268. *Ibid.*, pp. 56–57. An alternative interruption is 'striking the minimum acceptable real-wage rate'.
269. *Ibid.*, p. 58. 'In such a situation, the rate of accumulation is limited by the "inflation barrier"' (p. 59).
270. *Ibid.*, pp. 63–69.
271. *Ibid.*, p. 67. Uncertainty is, of course, involved here and the upward and downward oscillations of the economy are analysed (pp. 67–69).
272. *Ibid.*, pp. 70–74. The third essay, A Model of Technical Progress is important for the analysis of progress in the form of neutral, capital-saving and capital-using inventions and other matters.
273. Joan Robinson, *Collected Economic Papers*, Vol. IV (1973a). This volume contains some papers from Essays in the Theory of Employment (1st edn, 1937) and the essays in *On Re-reading Marx* (1953).
274. Richard T. Ely Lecture, delivered to the American Economic Association, December 1971.
275. Joan Robinson (1973a), pp. 99–100. The 'content' problem is discussed on pp. 100–105. *See also* Economics Today, a lecture delivered at the University of Basel, December 1969, p. 128.
276. The problem also has important political aspects, for example the amount of expenditure on armaments to which Joan Robinson refers. *See* the preceding footnote references. This involves a political decision taking into account all the relevant circumstances.
277. Joan Robinson (1971), reprinted 1972.

278. *Ibid.*, p. 91.
279. Page 94.
280. Published in Joan Robinson, *After Keynes* (1973b) to which reference is made. *See also* Milo Keynes (1975).
281. Joan Robinson (1973b), pp. 5–6.
282. *Ibid.*, p. 8. Joan Robinson adds that we can have wage-inflation during a recession. In the version in Milo Keynes (1975), p. 129, she states that wage-inflation under new full employment conditions is neither the fault of trade unions nor of businessmen but that 'It is the fault of an economic system inappropriate to the state of development of the economy.'
283. *Cambridge Journal of Economics* (1971), reprinted in Joan Robinson, *Contributions to Modern Economics* (1978). It was written in collaboration with Frank Wilkinson (p. xvi).
284. *Ibid.*, p. 257. Joan Robinson states that 'By 1976, Samuelson's faith in macroeconomic policies . . . had been badly shaken.' (p. 256, n.4, continued on p. 257). This is based on the comparison of the passage in Paul A. Samuelson, *Economics* (10th edn, 1976), p. 373 with the corresponding passage in 8th edn (1970), p. 348.
285. *Ibid.*, p. 257.
286. There were recessions during this period but in most industrial countries they involved merely a slowing down of the rate of growth of output. In the depression of the 1970s there have been actual reductions in countries' gross domestic product as was the case in trade-cyclical depressions before World War II.
287. *Ibid.*, p. 261. This conclusion raises, of course, important political issues.
288. *Ibid.*, pp. 261–265.
289. *Ibid.*, p. 265.
290. Inflation, a serious problem today, did not exist in the 1930s.
291. That is, that inappropriate increases in money wages, given an appropriate monetary policy, will cause unemployment. *See* J. C. Gilbert, 'Exchange Rate Adjustments' (January 1950), pp. 8–10.
292. Hutchison (1977), p. 61.
293. *Lloyds Bank Review* (October 1976). *See also* Walter Eltis, 'The Keynesian Conventional Wisdom', *Lloyds Bank Review* (July 1977) which is a reply to Lord Kahn, 'Mr Eltis and the Keynesians', *Lloyds Bank Review* (April 1977).
294. Worswick, The End of Demand Management? (1977), p. 14. In a postscript Worswick criticizes Eltis's October 1976 article. For an advanced treatment of four schools of thought on demand management, *see* Michael Posner, *Demand Management* (National Institute of Economic and Social Research Economic Policy Papers 1, London, 1978).
295. J. M. Buchanan, John Burton, R. E. Wagner, *The Consequences of Mr Keynes* (1978).
296. *Ibid.*, p. 27.

Chapter 10

The neoclassical synthesists

The 'Neoclassical Synthesis' stems from Hicks's famous 1937 *Econometrica*[1] article which has in some respects its culmination in Patinkin's monumental *Money, Interest and Prices* (1956 and 1965). Hicks was greatly influenced at the time by the general-equilibrium analysis of Walras and the neoclassical synthesis is sometimes referred to as Neo-Walrasian Equilibrium Analysis. Its critics refer to it as the Neoclassical-Bastard Keynesian theory[2]. Hicks had produced a 'potted version' of *The General Theory* which in 1967 he thought was 'not a bad representation of Keynes'[3] and in a 1972 paper concluded that Keynes accepted it as a fair statement of the nucleus of his position[4]. Walras had produced a general-equilibrium system in which all the economic factors were interdependent, everything depending on everything else. Hicks summarized Keynes's basic model in the form of three simultaneous equations in the Walrasian framework. Keynes's short-period equilibrium level of income (and hence employment) and rate of interest are simultaneously determined at the point on the ISLM diagram where the demand for money is equal to the supply in real terms and the rate of investment is equal to the rate of saving[5]. As perfect certainty is not assumed, this equilibrium may be regarded as a result of Walras's tâtonnement, groping process, but cannot be assumed to persist.

A number of economists developed this line of thought. Patinkin[6] in Part One, Microeconomics, of his book introduces money explicitly into general-equilibrium analysis in order to achieve an integration of monetary theory and value theory (the theory of relative prices of goods and services)[7]. The real-balance effect which takes into account the real value of money balances held (their purchasing power) plays a vital role in the integration. In Part Two, Macroeconomics, Patinkin develops Keynesian theory within this general framework. He simplifies by dealing with four aggregates – labour services, commodities, bonds and money and their corresponding markets. Both the static and dynamic cases of full employment are discussed in terms of general-equilibrium analysis. Patinkin then enters the Keynesian world of unemployment by developing his theory of involuntary unemployment which he defines as the excess supply of labour existing at the prevailing real-wage rate[8]. I have stressed that Keynes's basic model is one of comparative statics although a number of economists

are now interpreting Keynes in terms of dynamic disequilibrium economics. Patinkin despite his Walrasian approach writes, 'Thus Keynesian
economics is the economics of unemployment *dis*equilibrium.'[9]

Harry Johnson recognized Patinkin's achievement while discussing the
criticisms which were made against the first edition of *Money, Interest and
Prices* (1956)[10]. Johnson, writing after the second edition (1965), gives a
further assessment of Patinkin's work[11]. Samuelson, a member of this
school of thought, refers to Patinkin having arrived 'at a synthesis
consistent with what I believe was the best of neoclassical theory' and
'going beyond anything previously appearing in the literature'[12].

In the neoclassical synthesis Keynes's theory becomes a special case of
the more general neoclassical system. The classical and neoclassical
economists would have agreed with Keynes that inflexibility of money
wages and prices could cause unemployment. Keynes was making a
realistic assumption when he assumed that money wages were inflexible
downwards but he also analysed the effects of falling money wages and
prices. What happens to Keynes's less than full-employment equilibrium in
this case? The fall in prices increases the real value of the quantity of
money and lowers the rate of interest. The rate of investment may,
however, show little response to the fall in the rate of interest so that even
at a zero rate of interest the rate of investment may not be high enough for
full employment. Further, even if the rate of investment is very responsive
(interest elastic), the rate of interest cannot fall below a certain minimum
because of Keynes's speculative motive or the cost of bringing borrowers
and lenders together[13]. These conditions are not sufficient for Keynes's
under-employment equilibrium because under the flexible wage and
competitive assumptions, money wages and prices would continue to fall,
which would be inconsistent with equilibrium. As is shown in Chapter 4 the
Pigou effect gives a full-employment equilibrium by increasing consumption using comparative static analysis.

To show that Keynes's basic static model is a special case in the
neoclassical synthesis is not as derogatory as is often stated. The neoclassical synthesists are well aware of the extent of the abstractions from the
real world which they have made. They recognize that even a competitive
economy cannot be regarded as a self-regulating mechanism which provides full employment[14]. They appreciate the way in which Keynes
formulated his basic model which emphasized effective demand and
support Keynesian full-employment policies. Referring in 1963 to the
writings of such American economists as Solow, Tobin and himself,
Samuelson states that 'attention was focused on a managed economy which
through skilful use of fiscal and monetary policy channeled the Keynesian
forces of effective demand into behaving like a neoclassical model'[15]. In
1976 Samuelson wrote 'By means of appropriately reinforcing monetary
and fiscal policies, a mixed economy can avoid the worst excesses of boom
and slump. This being understood, the paradoxes that robbed the older
classical principles dealing with small-scale "microeconomics" of their
relevance and validity now lose much of their sting. The broad cleavage
between microeconomics and macroeconomics is closed by active public
use of fiscal and monetary policy (save for the unsolved dilemma of
stagflation in the mixed economy!).'[16] One is reminded of Keynes's

statement that 'if our central controls succeed in establishing an aggregate volume of output corresponding to full employment as nearly as practicable, the classical theory comes into its own again from this point onwards'[17]. Admittedly, the neoclassical synthesis was often formulated on the assumption of perfect certainty, or minimal uncertainty, which was, of course, an emasculation of Keynes's theory. However, the policy recommendations took account of the uncertain real world[18].

Professor James Tobin's work may be taken for more detailed consideration as an example of the work of the neoclassical synthesists. Tobin, like Friedman and Patinkin, has had a powerful influence on the development of monetary economics since the 1950s. Tobin and his associates are referred to as the Yale School. Referring to the New Economists, the Kennedy–Johnson economists of the 1960s, Tobin stated that 'We adhered to the "neoclassical synthesis", which emphasized that monetary and fiscal ingredients could be mixed in varying proportions to achieve desired macroeconomic results.'[19] Tobin also wrote 'I do not know what to call those of us who take an eclectic nonmonetarist view. "Neo-Keynesian" will do, I guess, but so would "neoclassical". The synthesis of the last twenty-five years certainly contains many elements not in the *General Theory* (Keynes 1936). Perhaps it should be called Hicksian . . . One thing the nonmonetarists should *not* be called is "fiscalists." . . . Whereas neo-Keynesians believe that *both* monetary and fiscal policies affect nominal income, monetarists believe that only monetary policies do so.'[20]

Tobin started from Keynes's liquidity preference theory of the demand for money and developed the portfolio approach to the demand for money as did some of his contemporaries such as Friedman. Tobin's work in this area is of outstanding importance. In his article of 1947 and 1948, Liquidity Preference and Monetary Policy, Tobin contended that 'the demand for cash balances is unlikely to be perfectly inelastic with respect to the rate of interest, and that policy conclusions which depend on the assumption that the demand for cash balances is interest-inelastic are therefore likely to be incorrect'[21]. It is not required that the elasticity is greater than 1 but that there is considerable elasticity.

Tobin used United States data for 1922 to 1945 to obtain a statistical relationship between 'idle' bank deposits and the short-term interest rate. The procedure for estimating 'idle' deposits (money as a store of value) taken to be total deposits minus deposits held for the transactions-motive was not satisfactory but his result remained important. Tobin found the inverse relationship between the interest rate and the demand for money postulated by Keynes's liquidity preference theory[22]. In reply to criticism by Dr Warburton, Tobin computed 'idle' balances in a different way, related them to the longterm interest rate and did not obtain a markedly different result[23].

Tobin's 1956 article, The Interest Elasticity of Transactions Demand for Cash, shows that the demand for money for the transactions-motive depends inversely on the interest rate because of 'the cost of transactions between cash and interest-bearing assets'[24]. For Keynes the transactions demand for money depended on income given certain institutional arrangements and he almost ignored the interest rate[25]. Tobin refers to Baumol's emphasis on the importance of these transactions costs in his classic article[26]. In my 1953 article, The Demand for Money, I emphasized the importance of costs of investment when dealing with my first fundamental reason for holding money, time[27]. Receipts and expenditures are not perfectly synchronized. Tobin asks 'Why not hold transactions balances in assets with higher yields than cash [money], shifting into cash only at the time an outlay must be made?'[28] The advantage is yield, the disadvantage is the cost, pecuniary and non-pecuniary, of frequent small investments and disinvestments. The higher the short-term rate of interest the greater the advantage of temporary investments of money balances and vice versa. Thus the demand for money held for the transactions-motive is related inversely to the rate of interest. Tobin's paper contains a detailed analysis of the maximization of the individual's interest earnings, net of transactions costs, on a number of assumptions. Interest rates must be high enough in relation to transactions costs to justify such investments[29].

Tobin made a fundamental contribution to the analysis of the demand for money as a store of value in his 1958 article, Liquidity Preference as Behaviour towards Risk[30]. However, I do not think that his interpretation of Keynes's speculative-motive is acceptable. In my (1953) article, The demand for money, my 'second fundamental reason for holding money is uncertainty as to the future capital value of a fixed-interest bearing asset [called a bond]'[31]. I point out that 'Keynes's speculative motive introduced the uncertainty factor as an independent factor, our second fundamental reason for holding money . . . no money would be held for this motive if the future capital value of bonds was certain, that is, the future rate of interest was certain and there was no default risk.'[32]

Tobin states that the explanation for holding money as a store of value 'to which Keynes gave the greatest emphasis is the notion of a "normal" longterm rate, to which investors expect the rate of interest to return. When he refers to uncertainty in the market, he appears to mean disagreement among investors concerning the future of the rate of interest rather than subjective doubt in the mind of an individual investor.'[33] It is true that Keynes emphasized the importance of a difference of opinions and Tobin quotes from The General Theory, 'It is interesting that the stability of the system and its sensitiveness to changes in the quantity of money should be so dependent on the existence of a variety of opinion about what is uncertain . . .'[34]

Tobin assumes there are only two monetary assets, cash [money] and consols. He writes that '"cash" should not necessarily be identified with means of payment, i.e. currency and bank [demand] deposits. In most advanced economies these are dominated for investment balances by equally safe and lossproof assets which bear interest, notably time and saving deposits. This article really refers to the choice and interest differential between those assets and market instruments on which capital losses [and gains] may occur as a result of interest rate movements.'[35] Tobin assumes, however, that the yield of cash is zero and the current yield of the other monetary asset, 'consols', is r per 'year'. A fixed money income per 'year' in perpetuity of $r is obtained if $1 is invested in consols. The investor decides the proportions of his total investment balance to be held in cash, A_1, and consols, A_2, for his investment period[36]. Certain interest expectations are assumed, the expected rate is r_e. Investors either expect a rise or fall in the rate of interest, a capital loss or capital gain g. The investor will hold the whole of his investment balance in cash or consols according to whether r (the current rate) +g is less or greater than zero. There is thus a critical level of the current rate of interest r_c dependent on the expected rate so that if the current rate r is less than this the total balance is held in cash while if it is greater the total balance is held in consols.

Tobin now assumes that the expected rate of interest and the critical rate are functions of the current rate. Once again there is a critical rate r_c such that the investor holds no cash or no consols according to whether r is greater or less than this[37]. Tobin shows how for the economy as a whole the Keynesian liquidity preference curve showing extensions and contractions in the demand for cash in response to falling and rising interest rates can be derived on the assumption that individual investors differ in their critical rates[38]. Each investor has a certain interest expectation and a critical rate. At the market rate of interest he holds either only cash or only consols.

This interpretation of Keynes is not acceptable in view of the fact that one of the main characteristics of *The General Theory* is the emphasis on uncertainty. In his discussion of the demand for money Keynes does refer to calculations of probability[39]. When dealing with the uncertainty of the future rate of interest and the precautionary-motive, he takes the case of a need for cash conceivably arising and the risk of a loss if a longterm bond is purchased and has to be sold instead of cash being held. Keynes writes, 'The actuarial profit or mathematical expectation of gain calculated in accordance with the existing probabilities – if it can be so calculated, which is doubtful – must be sufficient to compensate for the risk of disappointment.'[40] Thus Keynes not only emphasizes uncertainty but is doubtful whether calculations in terms of probabilities can be made. Further in his important *Quarterly Journal of Economics* article of 1937, The General Theory of Employment , Keynes states, 'partly on reasonable and partly on instinctive grounds, our desire to hold money as a store of wealth is a barometer of the degree of our distrust of our own calculations and conventions concerning the future'[41].

Tobin also maintains that 'Keynesian theory implies that each investor will hold only one asset [cash or bonds]'[42]. This follows from Tobin's interpretation of Keynes that investors have differences of opinion but have certain interest expectations. If we interpret Keynes as assuming uncertain interest expectations this need not be the case. Keynes had stated that a necessary condition for holding wealth in the form of money 'is the existence of *uncertainty* as to the future of the rate of interest . . .'[43]. An investor who expects the rate of interest to fall has an incentive to hold bonds but he is not certain and may hold some money as a store of value 'to be on the safe side'. An investor who expects the rate of interest to rise sufficiently has an incentive to hold money but as he is uncertain he may hold some bonds for which he receives a certain yield. Keynes does not analyse this problem of diversification and at one point refers to the possibility of the 'bull' holding no cash when he writes 'whilst the individual who differs from the market in the other direction [expects the rate of interest to fall] will have a motive for borrowing money for short periods in order to purchase debts of longer term'[44]. However, in view of what I have stated above I do not think that Keynes's uncertain investors should be assumed to have only undiversified portfolios.

Despite this criticism of Tobin's interpretation of Keynes's liquidity preference schedule, Tobin's own theory of liquidity preference in terms of uncertainty and risk aversion is a very valuable contribution. This remains true although the applicability of probability theory making use of subjective probabilities is debatable, as is the assumption that the individual investor and perhaps the institutional investor will be able or will attempt to make all the detailed calculations required. Further, institutional investors may not conform to Tobin's assumptions of individual financial behaviour 'for example, they may be almost entirely concerned with the interest income of assets, intending to hold them until maturity, or very nearly so'[45].

Tobin's analysis of liquidity preference assuming uncertainty and risk aversion is a very important development of Keynes's theory. He continues with two assets, cash and consols, but the investor is not certain of the future rate of interest on consols and runs the risk of a capital gain or loss. The investor is faced with a situation in which 'The higher the proportion of his investment balance [cash + consols] that he holds in consols, the more risk the investor assumes. At the same time, increasing the proportion in consols also increases his expected return . . . the investor can expect more return if he assumes more risk.'[46] The investor is uncertain about his capital gain or loss g but bases his actions on his estimate of its probability distribution, the expected value of which is zero and which is independent of the current rate of interest. The return R on a portfolio which consists of a proportion A_1 of cash and A_2 of consols, proportions independent of its size, is:

$$R = A_2(r + g) \tag{1}$$

Tobin states that since g is a random variable with expected value zero, the expected return on the portfolio is:

$$E(R) = \mu_R = A_2 r \tag{2}$$

Tobin states that 'The Risk attached to a portfolio is to be measured by the standard deviation of R, σ_R. The standard deviation is a measure of the dispersion of possible return around the mean value μ_R. A high standard deviation means, speaking roughly, high probability of large deviations from μ_R, both positive and negative. A low standard deviation means low probability of large deviations from μ_R; in the extreme case, a zero standard deviation would indicate certainty of receiving the return μ_R.'[47] Thus an investor with a high standard deviation portfolio has the chance of large capital gains and the equivalent chance of large capital losses. If he has a low standard deviation portfolio the investor will have little prospect of capital gain or loss. Tobin writes, 'The standard deviation of R depends on the standard deviation of g, σg, and on the amount invested in consols . . . . Thus the proportion the investor holds in consols A_2 determines both his expected return μ_R and his risk σ_R.'[48] The investor can obtain greater expected return by assuming more risk.

Tobin classifies investors into risk lovers (gamblers) and risk averters who will only accept more risk for greater expected return. The risk

averters are either diversifiers or plungers[49]. Professor Dwayne Wrightsman takes the typical investor and explains that Tobin 'assumes that the
"risk averter" is subject to diminishing marginal utility of income and
increasing marginal disutility of risk. Starting from a position of no
securities and only money . . . the proportion of securities in the portfolio
is increased by one increment which, correspondingly, increases income
and risk by one increment . . . And so the process [continues] . . . until it is
no longer possible at the margin to add more utility from income than
disutility from risk.'[50]

Tobin proceeds to analyse the effects of changes in the rate of interest,
assuming no change in the investor's estimate of the risk of capital gain and
loss. A rise in the interest rate has a substitution effect, an incentive to
switch from money to consols. It also has an income effect; the investor can
obtain more security and more yield by making some switch from consols
to money. For the normal investor it may be assumed that the substitution
effect is predominant, in which case we have the investor's demand for
money inversely related to the rate of interest, Keynes's liquidity preference schedule.

Tobin adopted the assumption that investors expect on balance no
change in the rate of interest while clearly they do form such expectations
in which they differ. However, he states that his formal apparatus 'will
serve just as well for a non-zero expected capital gain or loss as for a zero
expected value of g'[51].

In his 1958 article Tobin began to tackle the more complex problem of
choices of a number of assets other than cash but he confined the analysis
to monetary assets all of which share the risk of changes in the purchasing
power of money[52]. Professor Gardner Ackley accepts the didactic advantages of the simplifying assumption of two assets, money and bonds, while
emphasizing the importance of having a macroeconomic model which
includes many types of financial assets[53]. Referring to Keynes's speculative-motive and Tobin's risk aversion, he writes 'Once we admit the
existence of a second interest-yielding asset with fixed (or even with
nearly-fixed) market values, Keynes's story collapses – and so does
Tobin's.'[54] Ackley recognizes their importance for the term structure of
interest rates but considers that only the Baumol–Tobin interest-elasticity
of transactions demand is important for the explanation of the demand for
money. Further work is required in this area but the substantive contributions of Keynes and Tobin must be emphasized.

Tobin developed his liquidity analysis into the portfolio approach to the
theory of money. The individual's and institution's portfolios consist of
money and a number of other assets according to the complexity of the
model set up. Such assets include short-term and longterm government
securities, deposits with non-bank financial intermediaries, for example,
building societies, equities (ordinary shares) and physical capital goods.
Money includes currency and demand deposits (current accounts).
Whether time deposits (deposit accounts) are included or treated as a
near-money is a question of convenience. I have followed Keynes and
included deposit accounts in money. On the one hand there are the
portfolio preferences, the asset demand functions, of individuals and
institutions which 'are based on expectations, estimates of risk, attitudes

towards risk, and a host of other factors'[55]. On the other hand there are the relative supplies of the various kinds of asset. The analysis of portfolio balance and the process of adjustment when portfolio imbalance occurs involves a theory of choice based on the advances made 'in the theory of decision-making under uncertainty and in inventory theory'[56]. Tobin's own contributions to risk aversion and inventory theories have already been considered[57].

The portfolio approach when fully developed provides 'a general multi-equation equilibrium of the entire spectrum of assets and debts: all financial markets, and all financial institutions replace the narrower traditional concentration on the quantity of money and the commercial banking system. No one equation – not even equality of demand and supply of money – is regarded as the determining equation for macroeconomics.'[58] This general equilibrium includes the holdings of the wide variety of physical capital goods. Keynes's liquidity preference theory has the simplifying assumption of two financial assets, money and longterm government bonds, the rate of interest on which is 'the rate of interest', although he frequently refers to the complex of rates of interest. For example, Keynes refers to the complex of rates of interest for debts of different maturities and of varying degrees of risk[59]. In Tobin's important 1961 paper, Money, Capital, and Other Stores of Value, it is shown that the concept of the entire spectrum involves a whole structure of rates of return. Tobin writes, 'The structure of rates may be pictured as strung between two poles, anchored at one end by the zero own-rate conventionally borne by currency . . . and at the other end by the marginal productivity of the capital stock.'[60] The structure of rates will depend upon the relative supplies of assets which are not perfect substitutes. He states, 'In general, an increase in the supply of an asset – e.g., longterm government bonds – will cause its rate to rise relative to other rates, but less in relation to assets for which it is directly or indirectly a close substitute . . . than in relation to other assets.'[61]

Tobin's portfolio approach provides a monetary macroeconomic model in which the 'rate of interest' plays an important role in the determination of the level of income and employment. He writes in his 1965 review article of Friedman's and Schwartz's magnum opus, 'Personally I think that interest rates rank high among the gauges that measure the impact of monetary policies and conditions on economic activity'[62]. Keynes's analysis of the inducement to invest was mainly in terms of the marginal efficiency of capital and the rate of interest but he also used the alternative of the relationship between stock exchange valuations and the costs of capital goods. He wrote that the daily revaluations of the Stock Exchange 'inevitably exert a decisive influence on the rate of current investment. For there is no sense in building up a new enterprise at a cost greater than that at which a similar enterprise can be purchased.'[63] Section V of Chapter 12 is a brilliant piece of writing on the precariousness of stock exchange market valuations. Keynes gives an example of irrationality: 'It is said, for example, that the shares of American companies which manufacture ice tend to sell at a higher price in summer when their profits are seasonally high than in winter when no one wants ice.'[64]

Tobin uses two methods of analysis similar to those of Keynes but greater emphasis is placed on the stock market valuation process for which his model is famous. Brainard and Tobin in their 1968 paper, Pitfalls in Financial Model Building, write, 'One of the basic theoretical propositions motivating the model is that the market valuation of equities, relative to the replacement costs of the physical assets they represent, is the major determinant of new investment. Investment is stimulated when capital is valued more highly in the market than it costs to produce it, and discouraged when its valuation is less than its replacement cost.'[65] Alternatively, it can be stated that investment is stimulated when the market yield on equity is below the expected real return to physical investment. This equity yield is also referred to as the supply price of capital, 'the rate of return that the community of wealth-owners require in order to absorb the existing capital stock (valued at current prices) . . . into their portfolios'[66]. Tobin rejects Keynes's use of the longterm bond rate and insists that equity yield is the strategic variable[67]. However, it may be argued that a decrease in either rate may stimulate investment.

An increase in the market valuation of equities may be caused by an increase in the marginal efficiency of capital, the expected profitability of investment because of inventions and other non-financial changes affecting expectations. The market valuation of equities may also increase because of financial changes which reduce the market yield on equity. Tobin writes, 'Indeed, this is the sole linkage in the model through which financial events, including monetary policies, affect the real economy.'[68] Monetary policy may be used to increase the market valuation of equities, the valuation of investment goods, relatively to their costs of production and therefore increase the rate of investment[69]. Tobin's model which takes the relationship between the market valuation of equities and the costs of production of new capital goods as the determinant of the rate of investment is of course a simplification. He recognizes that, 'There are many kinds of physical capital and many markets where existing stocks are valued – not just markets for equities, but other markets for operating businesses and for houses, other kinds of real estate, cars and other durable goods, etc.'[70] In reply to Friedman's claim to greater catholicity in the list of assets, Tobin states that his 'own conception of "capital" has always included consumer durables'[71].

In his 1963 paper, An Essay on the Principles of Debt Management, prepared for the Commission on Money and Credit, Tobin undertakes a detailed analysis of the monetary effect of government debt on aggregate demand. This is shown to depend on the size or composition of the debt. Changes in the size of the debt result from budget deficits and surpluses. The monetary and debt management authorities can change its composition. The Federal Reserve System, the central bank, can for example increase the supply of money (demand debt) and decrease the supply of interest-bearing debt by purchases of open market securities. The monetary and debt management authorities can for example change the relative amounts of short-term and longterm debt. The monetary effect is measured by the supply price of capital or the market valuation of equities. Events and policies which decrease the supply price of capital are expansionary and vice versa. Tobin states that 'increase in federal debt – whether as demand debt [money] or as interest-bearing debt of short or long maturity – are expansionary. Likewise, substitution of demand debt for short or long debt, and substitution of shorter debt for longer debt, are expansionary. Altering the composition of the debt in one of these ways, or in reverse if contraction of aggregate demand is desired, is the principal tool of monetary control.'[72]

If there is an increase in the supply of money by purchase of open market securities there is portfolio imbalance and rates of return throughout the spectrum of assets must fall. Equity yield falls, the market valuation of equities rises relative to the cost of production of capital and the rate of investment increases[73].

Tobin states that a substitution of short-term for longterm government debt is also expansionary[74]. This is because the longterm rate of interest will fall and also the supply price of capital (equity yield) which increases the rate of investment. He warns that in analysing the monetary effect of changes in the size and composition of the government debt, changes in the supply of money (demand debt) is not the only financial asset to be considered. Money is not regarded as a unique asset. Attention should be directed to the strategic variable, the supply price of capital. However, money is unique as a generally acceptable means of payment and aggregate money demand cannot be increased without an increase in the quantity of money and/or its velocity of circulation. If the quantity of money is constant, any change which is expansionary must involve an increase in velocity.

If Tobin's model is to be operational, empirical research should show that an increase in the supply of money causes a rise in equity prices and that a rise in equity prices relative to the cost of production of capital goods increases the rate of investment. David Gowland writes, 'Belief in a relationship between the money supply and share prices seems to be surprisingly widespread in academic and city circles. It is surprising that it survived the year commencing May 1973, in which M_3 rose by 23 per cent and the stock market fell by 39 per cent measured by the FT-Actuaries 500 Share Index. It is less surprising that it survived the author's attempt to disprove the relationship.'[75] Of course, share prices fluctuate for all sorts of reasons. Tobin is aware that 'Market valuations fluctuate violently and erratically'[76] in the short run but the question is whether there is some relationship between increases in the supply of money and equity prices.

In his *Current Economic Problems* paper Gowland reviews recent American literature in which it is argued that there is an indirect and a direct influence between changes in money supply and share prices. He concludes that both theoretical and empirical work in the United States seem to show that 'there may be a connection between money and share prices . . . . However, it is not clear what form it takes.'[77] Gowland also reviews previous United Kingdom work which he finds unsatisfactory[78]. His own empirical work is on United Kingdom data for 1954–1972 and 1963–1972. Gowland concludes that in general 'empirical work in both the time and frequency domains seems to prove that there is no relationship in the UK between money and share prices'[79]. The discussants, Professors Marcus H. Miller and C. W. J. Granger were critical and the whole matter remains very much in the air[80].

Not much empirical support has been given to a rise in equity prices relatively to the cost of production of capital goods increasing investment. Victoria Chick writes, 'Empirically the relationship between equity values, the desire to invest, actual investment and subsequent growth of the firm, is tenuous to say the least.'[81] Ackley referring to the statistical testing of investment theories states 'the results remain rather unimpressive'[82]. He discusses four (including Tobin's model) of the five models which Charles Bischoff subjects to statistical testing[83]. Bischoff used United States data from 1953 to 1968 and also 1969 to 1970. Ackley's general conclusion is that economists 'still do not have any fully satisfactory or widely accepted theory of investment'[84]. However, in referring to Tobin's theory, he points to the changes of the ratio of market value of non-financial corporations to replacement cost of net assets from 1960 to 1976 for the United States and asserts that 'this ratio is at least roughly correlated with the ratio of real business investment to real GNP in those particular years'[85]. It is interesting to note that the Central Statistical Office includes as one of its five longer leading indicators of the business cycle in United Kingdom economic activity the Financial Times-Actuaries 500 share index. It is stated that 'the Financial Times-Actuaries 500 share index has an average lead time of 8 months, but this has varied between 3 and 20 months with the lead in more recent periods becoming longer'[86]. This is based on monthly data from May 1962. Tobin has provided a formal model and like any other it must be used with skill and judgement.

For Tobin 'money matters' but also 'fiscal policy matters'. Pure fiscal policy involves for example an increase in government expenditure financed by the sale of government securities without any increase in the supply of money. If the income-velocity of money is approximately constant the increased government expenditure can only cause a diversion of total expenditure and no increase in money income, nor increases in real output (employment) and the price level. However, the rate of interest rises and Tobin rightly believes that income-velocity will increase in response to this rise. Some allowance may have to be made for a decline in private investment but the fiscal policy does have an expansionary effect. The elasticity of demand for money in response to a rise in the rate of interest is less than 1 but considerable (*see* pages 118–119). Thus income-velocity increases considerably. Much the same analysis would apply to fiscal policy involving a decrease in taxation[87].

Notes

1. 'Mr Keynes and the "Classics"' (1937), reprinted in J. R. Hicks, *Critical Essays in Monetary Theory* (1967). *See also* Hicks, *Value and Capital* (1st edn, 1939; 2nd edn, 1946) particularly Part II.
2. *See* p. 164.
3. Hicks (1967), p. vii.
4. Hicks, 'Recollections and Documents' (February 1973), reprinted in Hicks, *Economic Perspectives* (1977), *see* p. 146.
5. *See* Hicks (1967), particularly pp. 134 and 138.
6. Patinkin (1956, 1965), *see also* for example Oscar Lange, *Price Flexibility and Employment* (1944) and Franco Modigliani, 'Liquidity Preference and the Theory of Interest and Money', *Econometrica* (1944), reprinted in The American Economic Association; *Readings in Monetary Theory* (1952).

7. The role of money in Walras has been much discussed. *See* my discussion of Professor Arthur W. Marget's work in J. C. Gilbert, The Demand for Money: the Development of an Economic Concept, *Journal of Political Economy* (1953), pp. 151–152, Michio Morishima, *Walras' Economics, a Pure Theory of Capital and Money* (1977) and Professor William Jaffe's eulogistic but critical review of this book in *Economic Journal (September 1978)*.
8. *Patinkin (1956, 1965), p. 315.*
9. *Ibid.*, pp. 337–338. This line of thought is discussed in Chapter 10.
10. Harry G. Johnson, 'Monetary Theory and Policy' (June 1962), reprinted in his *Essays in Monetary Economics* (2nd edn, 1969b), pp. 17–25.
11. 'Recent Developments in Monetary Theory – A Commentary', in David R. Croome and Harry G. Johnson, *Money in Britain 1959–1969* (1970), reprinted in Harry G. Johnson, *Further Essays in Monetary Economics* (1972), pp. 32–37). One criticism of the neoclassical synthesis is discussed in this chapter.
12. P. A. Samuelson, 'What classical and neoclassical monetary theory really was', *Canadian Journal of Economics*, 1 (1968), pp. 1–15, reprinted in R. W. Clower, *Monetary Theory Selected Readings* (1969), p. 187.
13. *See* p. 221.
14. Neoclassical economists such as Pigou and Robertson also recognized this.
15. Paul A. Samuelson (1963b). A brief survey of post-Keynesian developments. In Robert Lekachman, *Keynes' General Theory: Reports of Three Decades* (1964), p. 341. Samuelson refers to J. Tobin, A Dynamic Aggregative Model, *Journal of Political Economy* (April 1955), R. M. Solow, 'A Contribution to the Theory of Economic Growth' (February 1956) and T. W. Swan, 'Economic Growth and Capital Accumulation' (November 1956).
16. Paul A. Samuelson, *Economics* (10th edn, 1976), p. 373.
17. Keynes, *C.W.*, Vol. VII (1936, 1973), p. 378. Keynes understandably did not pay sufficient attention to the normative problem of the direction of employment although he was aware of it. Quotations from Chapter 24 can be misleading in this respect and the whole of the chapter should be read.
18. The importance of uncertainty in Keynes's theory has been emphasized in recent years. A number of economists such as Shackle and Joan Robinson have done this all along.
19. James Tobin, *The New Economics One Decade Older* (1974), p. 12.
20. Tobin in Gordon, *Milton Friedman's Monetary Framework* (1974), p. 77, n.1. Tobin adds 'Friedman agrees that this gives "the right flavour of our conclusions"'. Regarding the derivation from Hicks, Tobin refers to Hicks's classic articles of 1935 and 1937 reprinted in Hicks (1967).
21. James Tobin, 'Liquidity Preference and Monetary Policy', *Review of Economics and Statistics*, 29 (May 1947 and November 1948). In Tobin, *Essays in Economics Volume I: Macroeconomics* (1971), p. 27.
22. Tobin (1971), p. 37.
23. *Ibid.*, p. 41.
24. James Tobin, 'The Interest Elasticity of Transactions Demand for Cash', *Review of Economics and Statistics*, 38 (August 1956). In Tobin (1971), p. 229.
25. Keynes, *C.W.*, Vol. VII (1936, 1973), pp. 171, 172, 196–197, 201.
26. W. J. Baumol. 'The Transactions Demand for Cash: An Inventory Theoretic Approach' (November 1952).
27. J. C. Gilbert, 'The Demand for Money: The Development of an Economic Concept' (April 1953).
28. Tobin (1971), p. 230.
29. *Ibid.*, p. 236.
30. *Ibid.*
31. Gilbert (1953), p. 155.
32. *Ibid.*, p. 157.
33. Tobin (1971), p. 248.
34. Keynes, *C.W.*, Vol. VII (1936, 1973), p. 172, Tobin (1971), p. 270, n.9.
35. Tobin (1971), p. 270, n.6.
36. *Ibid.*, pp. 244 and 270, n.7.
37. *Ibid.*, p. 246.
38. *Ibid.*, pp. 245–247.
39. Keynes, *C.W.*, Vol. VII (1936, 1973), pp. 169, 201, 202

40. *Ibid.*, p. 169.
41. Keynes, *C.W.*, Vol. XIV (1973b), p. 116.
42. Tobin (1971), p. 266.
43. Keynes, *C.W.*, Vol. VII (1936, 1973), p. 168.
44. *Ibid.*, p. 170.
45. David G. Pierce and David M. Shaw, *Monetary Economics: Theories, Evidence and Policy* (1974), p. 119.
46. Tobin (1971), p. 249.
47. *Ibid.*, pp. 249–250.
48. *Ibid.*, p. 251.
49. *Ibid.*
50. Dwayne Wrightsman, *An Introduction to Monetary Theory and Policy* (1971), pp. 139–140.
51. Tobin (1971), p. 267.
52. *Ibid.*, pp. 261–265.
53. Gardner Ackley, *Macroeconomics: Theory and Policy* (1978), p. 729.
54. *Ibid.*, p. 727.
55. Tobin (1971), p. 338.
56. *Ibid.*, p. xiii.
57. *See also* H. Markowitz, *Portfolio Selection* (1959).
58. Tobin (1971), p. xiii.
59. *C.W.*, Vol. VII (1936, 1973), p. 205.
60. Tobin, 'Money, Capital, and Other Stores of Value', *American Economic Review (Papers and Proceedings)*, 51 (May 1961). In Tobin (1971), p. 225.
61. Tobin (1971), p. 226.
62. Tobin, 'The Monetary Interpretation of History', *American Economic Review*, 55 (June 1965). In Tobin (1971), p. 474. This is a review of Milton Friedman and Anne Jacobson Schwartz, *A Monetary History of the United States, 1867–1960* (1963).
63. Keynes, *C.W.*, Vol. VII (1936, 1973), p. 151.
64. *Ibid.*, p. 154.
65. William C. Brainard and James Tobin, 'Pitfalls in Financial Model Building', *American Economic Association (Papers and Proceedings)*, 58 (May 1968). In Tobin (1971), p. 357.
66. Tobin (1971), p. 226.
67. *Ibid.*, pp. 226, 385–386. Tobin believes that the longterm government bond rate should not be used 'as an unerring gauge of the tightness of monetary control of the economy. The differential between a long-term bond interest rate and the rate of return investors require of equity is surely as variable as any differential in the whole gamut of the structure of interest rates.'
68. *Ibid.*, p. 357.
69. The analysis of economic growth in terms of a positive rate of investment and capital accumulation in a monetary macroeconomic model was undertaken by Tobin in three important articles, A Dynamic Aggregative Model (1955), Money and Economic Growth (1965) and Notes on Optimal Monetary Growth (1968). In Tobin (1971).
70. Tobin (1971), p. 358.
71. Tobin in Gordon (1974), p. 89.
72. Tobin (1971), p. 447. This view is in line with the views of the Radcliffe Report, Committee on the Working of the Monetary System, Cmnd 827 (1959) and John G. Gurley and Edward S. Shaw, *Money in a Theory of Finance* (1960).
73. Tobin writes, 'Neo-Keynesian econometric models, notably the Federal Reserve MIT-Penn model, link monetary policies via financial markets and intermediaries to the markets for producing capital, houses, and durable goods'. In Gordon (1974), p. 89.
74. Tobin (1971), p. 403.
75. David Gowland, *Monetary Policy and Credit Control* (1978), p. 78. M_3 is defined on p. 198. He is referring here to his paper, The Money Supply and Stock Market Prices, in Michael Parkin and A. R. Nobay, *Current Economic Problems* (1975).
76. Tobin (1971), p. 401.
77. Parkin and Nobay (1975), p. 220.
78. *Ibid.*, pp. 321–234.
79. *Ibid.*, pp. 226–227.
80. *Ibid.*, pp. 234–240.

81. Victoria Chick, *The Theory of Monetary Policy* (1973), p. 100, n.2. She refers to the following works: A. C. Rayner and I. M. D. Little, *Higgledy-Piggledy Growth Again* (1966); A. J. Merrett *et al.*, *Equity Issues and the London Capital Market* (1967); A. Singh and G. Whittington, *Growth, Profitability and Valuation* (1968).
82. Ackley (1978), p. 655.
83. Charles Bischoff, 'Business Investment in the 1970s: A Comparison of Models' (1971).
84. Ackley (1978), p. 659.
85. *Ibid.*, p. 655. The diagram is on p. 57, reproduced from the *Annual Report of the Council of Economic Advisers* (1977), contained in the *Economic Report of the President* (1977), U.S. Government Printing Office.
86. Central Statistical Office Press Notice, Cyclical Indicators for the U.K. Economy Recent Movements of the Indicators (17 September 1980), p. 4.
87. For Tobin's views on fiscal policy *see*, for example, Tobin (1971), p. 491 and Gordon (1974), p. 78. He makes it explicit that his position does not depend on absolute liquidity preference (the trap). *See* Gordon (1974), p. 78, n.3.

Chapter 11

The fundamentalists

Professor Allan Coddington refers to Professor Shackle's work as 'Perhaps the most uncompromising, and certainly the most eloquent, exposition of fundamentalist Keynesianism'[1]. The fundamentalists are thus represented by one of the most distinguished economists of the post-World War II period. Coddington states, 'In posing a threat to the "Classical" system – or at least to a recognizable caricature of it – Keynes also called into question the method of analysis by which this system was constructed.'[2] Coddington refers to the classical (or neoclassical) system as 'reductionism', the reduction of market phenomena to stylized individual choices on which were based the theories of markets and general equilibrium. Fundamentalist Keynesians see the revolutionary importance of Keynes's work in his frontal assault on this reductionist method[3].

Whether Keynes's assault on classical and neoclassical economics had to be so vehement in order to make the required impact on contemporary economic thought is debatable. I agree with Professor B. Corry that in the process 'Keynes's treatment of Pigou in *The General Theory* was grossly unfair.'[4] Keynes's model of classical or neoclassical economics is based on Pigou's *The Theory of Unemployment*[5] of 1933. Corry argues that Keynes should have taken into account Pigou's other work and states that Pigou himself emphasized that his 1933 book should be taken in conjunction with his *Industrial Fluctuations*[6].

To the fundamentalist the essence of Keynes's contribution is his emphasis on choice, decision-taking, in the face of uncertainty. This is to be found particularly in Chapter 12 of *The General Theory*, The State of Long-Term Expectation, and in his classic 1937 *Quarterly Journal of Economics* article, The General Theory of Employment'[7]. In answering his critics Keynes was able to state his position more clearly than he had done in *The General Theory*. Coddington points out that the fundamentalists attach great importance to this article and writes, 'it is, first and foremost, an attack on the kind of choice theory that is required for the reductionist program. As against the clearly specified and stable objections and constraints required by reductionist theorizing, Keynes emphasizes that the basis of choice lies in vague, uncertain and shifting expectations of future events and circumstances: expectations that have no firm foundation in circumstances, but take their cues from the beliefs of others, and that will be sustained by hopes, undermined by fears and continually buffeted by "the news".[8] Further, Coddington writes that for the fundamentalist, 'Keynes's ideas require the rethinking and reconstruction of the whole body of reductionist theory: its choice-theoretic basis and the equilibrium theory of markets that rests on it.'[9]

The fundamentalist regards Keynes's own ideas as only a first step in a complete revision of economic theory. Keynes himself retained the concept of equilibrium, making use of the method of comparative statics. The concept of equilibrium has been attacked by fundamentalist Keynesians but I would say that it has also been accepted with recognition of its limitations.

Shackle is classed as a fundamentalist Keynesian because of his emphasis on uncertainty in his interpretation of Keynes's theory. His original work on uncertain expectations and time in economics is of undoubted importance. Shackle has pursued these related themes from the time of his first book of 1938, *Expectation, Investment and Income*[10] to his most recent book of 1979, *Imagination and the Nature of Choice*[11]. In the Introduction to *Uncertainty and Expectations in Economics Essays in Honour of G. L. S. Shackle*, Sir Charles Carter and Professor Ford, referring to the 1938 book, state that its title 'reminds us already of Shackle's special interest in *expectations*, in which he was building on an essential part of Keynes's ideas, but at the same time searching for a better theoretical expression than even the *Treatise on Probability* had provided'[12]. They refer to Shackle's greatest and most original work as being *Expectation in Economics*[13] of 1949. Shackle, making use of his concepts of 'potential surprise' and 'focus-outcomes', attempts to deal with choice under uncertainty. The main point is that such decisions are unique and crucial; there are no *a priori* or statistical frequency-ratios, so that the theory of probability is not applicable. This book was not completely successful and Shackle attempted to clarify and develop his thought in the essays included in Part I of his 1955 book *Uncertainty in Economics*[14]. There followed many further books and articles listed in the Bibliographical Data in the Shackle *Festschrift*, but important problems remain outstanding.

Shackle's main interest is in a decision which is unique in the sense that it is not one of a whole series of similar decisions where a frequency-ratio is relevant, and is crucial in the sense that the decision may change significantly the situation of the decision-taker. It follows that 'A crucial or even contingently crucial experiment [decision] must be treated by the decision-maker as in effect unique and never-to-be-repeated'[15]. Carter writes that Shackle's 'criticism of the use of the concept of probability in such circumstances is conclusive. Actuarial or statistical probability has no application to an experiment which is non-divisible and non-seriable; and it makes no sense to apply the arithmetical processes which belong to actuarial probability to a purely subjective estimate of probability.'[16] Carter has been interested in Shackle's approach over many years but he is critical of Shackle's theory of choice under uncertainty. Indeed, in his *Festschrift* paper he offers an alternative theory but it begins with Shackle's work. One can agree with Carter and Ford that Shackle 'is an initiator of original ideas, whose full effect on the corpus of economic theory is still to come. Generations of scholars will find in his writings a stimulus to fresh thought.'[17]

One has only to think of Keynes's emphasis on uncertainty, for example, in his analysis of the factors determining the rate of investment, to realize that Shackle, the developer of a theory of choice under uncertainty, is rightly classed as a fundamentalist Keynesian. The theme of his 1972 book *Epistemics and Economics* is 'what we substitute for knowledge in that vital and limitless area where we are eternally denied it, "tomorrow"'[18]. Keynes's *The General Theory*, Shackle states, 'was an immensely more destructive subversion of received theory . . . than even his admirers have acknowledged . . . . The method has the look of an appeal to equilibrium. Yet the *meaning* is that rational, fully-informed equilibrium is excluded by the denial to us of anything but fragmentary suggestion of what will be the sequel of today's efforts and plans.'[19] Shackle defines epistemics as the theory of thoughts and states that economics is about thoughts, the thoughts of economic agents regarding the intended uses of their productive resources and their conjectures about each other's thoughts in this field[20]. Shackle writes, 'It is not even the lack of exactness in its measurements (the more fundamental and inherent imprecisions are those of meaning) but the extent to which their subject-matter consists of *thoughts* and not of *objects*, which makes the assimilation of economic analysis to mechanical science dangerous.'[21] Further, Shackle writes, 'Economics has veritably turned imprecision into a science: economics, the science of the quantification of the unquantifiable and the aggregation of the incompatible. It has followed this road at so violent a gallop, that much which is of significance and influence has been trampled on, much territory has been claimed which cannot be held.'[22] This is harsh criticism from a major economist of our time but one which is hardly applicable to many economists who are well aware of the nature of their subject-matter. Despite all the difficulties of quantification, economists have to live with index-numbers. However, economists will do well to heed what Shackle writes as a warning of the dangerous rocks on which their ships will founder unless they navigate with careful judgement as well as technical expertise. The same view can be taken of his strong statement that economics 'has tried for a precision, certainty and reach of prediction whose basis is not there'[23]. Indeed, Shackle himself admits that the imprecision must be accepted and that governmental economic policies can only be formulated in broad terms making use of such aggregates as 'consumption', 'investment', 'capital' etc.[24]. As far as aggregation is concerned the problem is the appropriate degree of disaggregation, given the available data and the policy objectives. Shackle rightly asserted much earlier that economists 'should regard uncertainty as the very nerve and essence of their subject or great parts of it'[25].

To Keynes and the fundamentalist Keynesians Professor Frank H. Knight's distinction between risk and uncertainty in his path-breaking book of 1921, *Risk, Uncertainty and Profit*, is of the greatest importance. Knight distinguished two categorically different things included in 'risk' as used loosely in everyday speech and in economics. He confines risk to quantities susceptible to measurement and uncertainty to phenomena which are unmeasurable, cases of the non-quantitative type[26]. It is surprising that Keynes did not refer to Knight's distinction in *A Treatise on Money* and in *The General Theory*. It is uncertainty that plays such a vital role in the theories of Keynes and the fundamentalist Keynesians. Shackle in *Imagination and the Nature of Choice* distinguishes the two forms of risk very clearly. Firstly, there is risk in the terms of the actuary and the theorist of probability. This risk is calculable. In the actuary's sense it 'is an aspect of a practical means, in one particular type of context, of eliminating unknowledge and its effects to some degree . . . . When the actuary speaks of *risk* he is concerned with knowledge of a kind, not perfect but of high practical value . . . . In life at large the 'systems' which yield frequency-tables consist of the policy-holders of insurance companies, and the repeated trials made with these systems arise from their members' exposure to accidents, misfortunes or mortality.'[27] The individual can insure against his loss by regular payments of premiums. The insurance company's actuary relates the premium payments of its policy-holders to their claims as a whole. Secondly, there is the risk corresponding to Knight's uncertainty which is described by Shackle as 'The risk which cannot be insured against, the risk arising from irremediable unknowledge, is not calculable in the sense in which risks handled by insurance companies are . . . . It is plain that if the action whose sequel is in question is of a kind which *by its nature cannot* be repeated, there can be neither derivation of frequency-ratios nor use of them by projection on to stretches of time-to-come.'[28]

Professor Paul Davidson, a fundamentalist Keynesian, stresses the importance of uncertainty in the Knight–Keynes sense in his *Money and the Real World*[29]. Professor Herschel I. Grossman in a review of this book writes, 'In established theory, the concepts of risk aversion and subjective probability have superceded Knight's distinction between measurable risk and unmeasurable uncertainty. However, according to Davidson, uncertainty, in contrast to risk, "is significant in its effects on all economic activity" (p. 12), and "probability statements based on frequency distributions have nothing to say about uncertainties" (p. 15) . . . . Davidson simply rejects subjective probability as useless out-of-hand (pp. 15, 206–209).'[30]

Davidson's book is no doubt open to many criticisms, but I do not see any justification for this particular criticism. Knight's distinction is between risk which is confined to objective probabilities and uncertainty which includes subjective probabilities, but is unmeasurable. Knight's concept of uncertainty is justifiably used by Davidson in his exposition of Keynesian theory. There remains the question of the use to be made of subjective probabilities. Shackle points out that objective probability gives us knowledge in the form of a set of frequency-ratios[31], but subjective probability is a different matter. If the list of rival hypotheses is complete, the decision-maker can give his various conjectures a consistent relation. He states, 'For then each of the subjectively-adjusted weights or probabilities will be assigned to its particular member of the list some fraction out of a total which stands for certainty that the eventual answer will belong to the list. We have still to ask precisely what role this kind of consistency performs; whether the air it gives to the whole proceeding, of sharing in the authority which belongs to a statistically derived set of probabilities, is dangerously misleading; and above all, in what circumstances the omnicompetence of the system of classification of answers, the list of outcomes, can be logically guaranteed; and if not, what is to be done?'[32] My own position is eclectic. I accept the great importance of Knight's unmeasurable uncertainty while acknowledging that the use of subjective probabilities for some problems is appropriate. Shackle is naturally appreciative of Davidson's book. In a review he refers to Davidson having brought together strands of thought from many economists but mainly from Keynes whose work he interprets. Shackle writes, 'From these strands he has made an ingenious and intricate composition, through which there runs a single theme like a tide carrying everything along, the effects of uncertainty in making life, business or human history what they are.'[33]

In Keynes's discussion of the inducement to invest, the interest elasticity of the marginal efficiency of capital curve and its instability are important. Keynes believed that in certain circumstances the rate of investment would increase significantly in response to a fall in the rate of interest while in others it would not. One of the aims of Shackle's 1946 *Economic Journal* article, 'Interest-rates and the Pace of Investment', was to give a theoretical explanation of why businessmen's replies to the Oxford Economists' Research Group's questions were on the whole that changes in rates of interest did not affect their investment decisions[34]. Various reasons have been given including the unsatisfactory methods of the enquiry. Shackle's emphasis is on uncertainty in this connection, a line taken by many economists. An allowance must be made for uncertainty, for doubt, in addition to the pure rate of interest. If the entrepreneur takes 10 to 15 per cent as a minimum return on capital value, Shackle states that the 'value of an investment will be insensitive to even very large proportionate changes in the pure rate of interest; for if, . . . the revenue-earning life of the instrument is assured to be long, allowance for doubt will render negligible the net returns of all but a few years immediately ahead; while if it is assumed to be short, the influence of the pure rate of interest is weak even without any allowance for doubt.'[35] Shackle gives figures to show that the effect of changes in the rate of interest may well be unimportant once an allowance for doubt has been taken into account. He asks whether the entrepreneur will 'even trouble himself to revise his estimates at all on account of such changes as have ordinarily occurred in recent decades in the long-term rate of pure interest?'[36] Shackle does agree that the influence of changes in the rate of interest on the rate of investment will be strong in the case of investments in instruments 'which men believe can be depended on to continue earning net returns for many decades after they are constructed'[37].

There has been a long debate and much empirical research undertaken on the elasticity of the rate of investment with respect to the rate of interest. William H. White gives a critical discussion of a number of pre-war and post-war surveys of businessmen's attitudes in his paper, Interest Inelasticity of Investment Demand – the Case from Business Attitude Surveys Re-examined. His conclusion is 'In view of all their defects, no definite conclusion can be drawn from the surveys of business attitudes toward capital costs. The surveys do indicate that investment is to *some* degree less interest-elastic than thought by proponents of interest-rate policy. But they do not establish that the interest elasticity falls *seriously* below what its proponents claimed. Further investigations . . . must be carried out before any reliable conclusions can be reached.'[38] Pierce and Shaw refer to 'the results of econometric tests in the early 1960s which indicated that long-term fixed investment was significantly interest-elastic'[39]. They refer to V. Argy's summary of the major factors determining the investment interest elasticity. However, they also refer to C. G. F. Simkin's review of the arguments for and empirical evidence on the interest insensitivity of aggregate demand[40]. Friedman's and Tobin's views on the effect of changes in the rate of interest on investment have been discussed widely to include durable consumers' goods. (*See* pp.128, 186). However, Shackle's 1946 article remains a significant contribution.

A change in the rate of investment with a given interest rate, the instability of a shifting marginal efficiency of capital curve, is shown by Keynes to be a cause of economic instability and here uncertainty plays a vital role. He attached, of course, great importance to the instability of the marginal efficiency of capital (investment-demand) schedule. Shackle points out that 'Uncertainty is the very bedrock of Keynes's theory of employment'[41]. He expresses surprise that Keynes did not give much formal analysis of uncertainty when discussing the marginal efficiency of capital, a concept in which expectations are so important. In *The General Theory* the only scheme Shackle finds mooted 'for formally including uncertainty in the analysis of businessmen's decisions, is the third footnote to p. 24: "An entrepreneur, who has to reach a practical decision as to his scale of production, does not, of course, entertain a single undoubting expectation of what the sale-proceeds of a given output will be, but several hypothetical expectations held with varying degrees of probability and definiteness. By the expectation of proceeds I mean, therefore, that expectation of proceeds which, if it were held with certainty, would lead to the same behaviour as does the bundle of vague and more various possibilities which actually make up his state of expectation when he reaches his decision." '[42] In *A Scheme of Economic Theory* Shackle states that in his book of 1938, *Expectation, Investment and Income* he gave to this Keynesian concept 'the name of *certainty equivalent*, which has become established in the literature. Keynes here applies it to decisions on how much to produce, but it would equally well apply to decisions on how much to invest.'[43] Thus Shackle states, 'we may perhaps understand the series of annuities, which the marginal efficiency of capital discounts to equality in total present value with the construction cost of the plant, as *certainty equivalents* wherein the "objective" estimate of unsureness and the attitude towards it are both subsumed.'[44] It is of the utmost importance always to bear in mind that this does not mean uncertainty is eradicated. It remains the case that decisions are taken under uncertainty.

In *The General Theory* Keynes emphasized 'the extreme precariousness of the basis of knowledge on which our estimates of prospective yield have to be made. Our knowledge of the factors which will govern the yield of an investment some years hence is usually very slight and often negligible. If we speak frankly, we have to admit that our basis of knowledge for estimating the yield ten years hence of a railway, a copper mine, a textile factory, the goodwill of a patent medicine, an Atlantic liner, a building in the City of London, amounts to little and sometimes to nothing; or even five years hence.'[45] Keynes's famous reference to animal spirits is relevant here. He wrote, 'Most, probably, of our decisions to do something positive, the full consequences of which will be drawn out over many days to come, can only be taken as a result of animal spirits – of a spontaneous urge to action rather than inaction, and not as the outcome of a weighted average of quantitative benefits multiplied by quantitative probabilities.'[46] This uncertain basis on which investment decisions are taken is the reason for the shifting about of the marginal efficiency of capital (investment-demand) curve so that at a given rate of interest the rate of investment may vary widely upwards and downwards. Chapter 12 is devoted to this theme with which many economists including, of course, the fundamentalist Keynesians, would agree, but not the monetarists, who tend to believe in the inherent stability of a private enterprise economy. At the end of Chapter 11, The Marginal Efficiency of Capital, Keynes had already emphasized the importance of future expectations to this concept.

Professor Brian J. Loasby in his *Choice, complexity and ignorance* of 1976 is highly appreciative of Shackle's work. He himself points out that 'Keynes makes quite clear that it is not a modification of accepted economic rationality but its destruction by ignorance which he is writing about.'[47] Loasby stresses Keynes's repeated insistence on the instability of the marginal efficiency of capital. He gives a number of examples from *The General Theory*: '"Long-term expectations . . . are liable to sudden revision" (p. 51); the marginal efficiency of capital is "subject to . . . somewhat violent fluctuations" (p. 144); it is "fickle and highly unstable" (p. 204); "liable to change without much warning, and sometimes substantially" (p. 249); being "determined . . . by the uncontrollable and disobedient psychology of the business world" (p. 317).' Further, he points out that 'None of these quotations are taken from Chapter 12, which is devoted entirely to the proposition that the marginal efficiency of capital cannot helpfully be specified as a dependent variable in any equation system.'[48] Loasby is emphasizing here, as Shackle, the break which Keynes made from classical and neoclassical general-equilibrium theory by the introduction of uncertainty which he used to explain the instability and disorder of the economy. He is also agreeing with Shackle that Keynes's model is open-ended or non-self-contained where 'net investment, the flow whose size is treated as the actively dominant feature of the situation, is deliberately left free of any simple determining formula involving only the 'internal' variables of the system'[49]. Self-contained models have been produced since Keynes and they undoubtedly have their uses, but Keynes with his grasp of the real world was right to create an open model in which investment decisions are taken in the face of uncertainty and are not in a straightjacket, tied, for example, to changes in the level of income. Loasby in the context of his own work is a fundamentalist Keynesian similar to Shackle. He writes, 'It is the impossibility of foreknowledge that is at the root of Shackle's argument – and, in our view, of Keynes's.'[50]

The fundamentalist Keynesians support their interpretation of Keynes not only on the basis of *The General Theory* but also on that of his 1937 *Quarterly Journal of Economics* article, 'The General Theory of Employment', described by Shackle as apocalyptic. They quote from a classic passage of this article in which Keynes explains what he means by uncertain knowledge with particular reference to investment. He writes, 'The sense in which I am using the term is that in which the prospect of a European war is uncertain, or the price of copper and the rate of interest twenty years hence, or the obsolescence of a new invention, or the position of private wealth owners in the social system in 1970. About these matters there is no scientific basis on which to form any calculable probability whatever. We simply do not know.'[51] Action, however, has to be taken in the face of uncertainty and Keynes refers to three techniques used: (1) an undue reliance on the present as a guide to the future; (2) an assumption that 'the *existing* state of opinion as expressed in prices and the character of existing output is based on a *correct* summing up of future prospects, so that we can accept it as such unless and until something new and relevant comes into the picture'; (3) an 'endeavour to conform with the behaviour of the majority or the average'[52]. Keynes emphasizes that views of the future based on such a flimsy foundation are liable to sudden and violent changes. Further, Keynes writes, 'I accuse the classical economic theory of being itself one of these pretty, polite techniques which tries to deal with the present by abstracting from the fact that we know very little about the future.'[53]

Shackle thinks that Keynes discovered in this article 'the soul of his own work'[54]. He writes in his book of 1974, *Keynesian Kaleidics*, that Keynes's treatment of action under uncertainty here pronounces 'the dissolution of the view of business conduct as rational, as the application to men's affairs of *fully-informed* reason'[55]. Shackle states that Keynes 'ascribes the possibility of involuntary general unemployment to the existence of a liquid asset in a world of uncertainty . . . . It is in the *General Theory*, and above all in the QJE [1937 article], that we find the appeal to uncertainty, to unknowledge of the outcomes of available courses of action, as the origin of the difficulty of maintaining the flow of investment at a level which can engender full employment in face of a considerable propensity to save.'[56]

Shackle has contributed in an important way to the theory of choice under uncertainty. He shows that Keynes did not do this[57]. Hutchison also points out that Keynes did not, as Patinkin states, 'develop a theory of economic behaviour under uncertainty'[58]. He refers to Professor Herbert A. Simon's emphasis on the importance of shifting to the study of decision-making under uncertainty from equilibrium theories based on certainty or adequate knowledge[59]. These criticisms should be regarded as criticisms of Keynes's model and not of Keynes, as he had enough on hand. Further, the vitally important emphasis of the fundamentalist Keynesians and other economists on uncertainty should be made without ignoring the degree of economic stability often to be found, the equilibrating forces operative, and the possible stabilizing economic policies of governments.

Shackle provides two very useful classifications of types of economic theory according to their time and uncertainty assumptions and in doing so throws much light on the nature of Keynes's model[60]. He distinguishes between: A. Economics of Perfect Adjustment. 'Time has no significant place, and uncertainty no place, in the analysis.' (Typically: Walras.); B. Calculable Dynamics. 'Time enters the analysis significantly in the form of

lagged reactions or of steady growth. Uncertainty has no significant role.'
(Typically: Hicks, *Trade Cycle*.); C. Aggregative Comparative Statics.
'Uncertainty enters in the form of liquidity preference and as an element in
the schedule of the marginal efficiency of capital. Expectational time but
not dynamic time is present.' (Typically: Keynes, *The General Theory*.);
D. Economics of Uncertain Expectation. 'Uncertainty has an essential
significance and its effects are traced in dynamic time. Both expectational
and dynamic time are present.'[61] Keynes's basic model is that of comparative statics as he uses the equilibrium method. Uncertainty plays an
important role but at a point of time given expectations and other factors
are assumed. At another point of time the given expectations and other
factors will be different and a different equilibrium will exist[62].

In addition to the mechanical time of Calculable Dynamics and expectational time, Shackle distinguishes evolutionary time which is found in
Marshall's theory of economic evolution[63]. Shackle orders eight types of
theory by assigning to each three numbers (0 to 7) locating it with respect
to mechanical time, evolutionary time and expectational time. Thus
general timeless equilibrium is (0, 0, 0) and Hicks's model of the trade
cycle is (7, 0, 0). Keynes's Aggregative Comparative Statics referred to as
Keynesian kaleido-statics is (2, 0, 6). This recognizes the central role of
expectations in Keynes's theory. Shackle gives 2 to mechanical time
because there are passages such as Chapter 22 on the trade cycle in which
Keynes uses time-lagged reactions. Shackle's own theory is one in which
expectational time is completely dominant and is referred to as non-
distributive expectation (0, 0, 7). Shackle takes an eclectic view, thinking
that all the theories described are necessary and should be used as
appropriate[64].

Keynes's basic model in *The General Theory* is that of comparative
statics. He had used the dynamic method in *A Treatise on Money*. In the
mid-1970s Shackle in conversation expressed strongly the view that it was
very unfortunate that Keynes changed his method from the dynamics of
1930 to the statics of 1936. While recognizing the importance of economic
dynamics and the limitations of economic statics, I think the method of
comparative statics was appropriate for his purpose. Keynes was writing
during a period of mass unemployment. He was not much concerned with
changes in the aggregate supply function, but with increases in expected
aggregate demand which would give higher levels of employment.

Keynes's equilibrium at a point of time depends on various circumstances including expectations. These change and a new equilibrium is
established. Shackle uses the kaleidoscope as an analogue. He writes 'A
twist of the hand, a piece of "news", can shatter one picture and replace it
with a different one . . . [this] suggests a name for Keynes's method:
kaleido-statics.'[65] In the Tilton papers volume of Keynes's *Collected
Writings* there is a letter from Keynes to Sir Hubert Henderson in which he
writes 'I should, I think, be prepared to argue that in a world ruled by
uncertainty with an uncertain future linked to an actual present, a final
position of equilibrium, such as one deals with in static economics, does
not properly exist.'[66] Keynes's equilibrium is a static equilibrium, but
certainly entails that the given expectations included in the data cannot be
correct and that the equilibrium cannot persist.

Notes

1. Coddington, Alan (1976). Keynesian Economics: the Search for First Principles', *Journal of Economic Literature*, 14, p. 1260.
2. *Ibid.*, p. 1258.
3. Professor Joan Robinson is another fundamentalist Keynesian discussed by Coddington. I have discussed her work in Chapter 9.
4. B. Corry, Keynes in the History of Economic Thought: Some Reflections (1978). In A. P. Thirlwall, *Keynes and Laissez-Faire* (1978), p. 11.
5. A. C. Pigou, *The Theory of Unemployment* (1933).
6. A. C. Pigou, *Industrial Fluctuations* (1st edn, 1927; 2nd edn, 1929).
7. J. M. Keynes, 'The General Theory of Employment' (1937b). In *The General Theory and After: Part II Defence and Development. C.W.*, Vol. XIV (1973b).
8. Coddington (1976), p. 1260.
9. *Ibid.*, p. 1261.
10. G. L. S. Shackle, *Expectation, Investment and Income* (1st edn, 1938; 2nd edn, 1968).
11. G. L. S. Shackle, *Imagination and the Nature of Choice* (1979).
12. C. F. Carter and J. L. Ford, *Uncertainty and Expectations in Economic Essays in Honour of G. L. S. Shackle* (1972), p. viii.
13. G. L. S. Shackle, *Expectation in Economics* (1st edn, 1949; 2nd edn, 1952).
14. G. L. S. Shackle, *Uncertainty in Economics and Other Reflections* (1955).
15. Shackle (1955), p. 7.
16. C. F. Carter, On Degrees Shackle: or, The Making of Business Decisions. In Carter and Ford (1972), p. 30.
17. Carter and Ford (1972), p. vii.
18. G. L. S. Shackle, *Epistemics and Economics* (1972), Preface.
19. *Ibid.*
20. *Ibid.*
21. *Ibid.*, p. 66.
22. *Ibid.*, p. 360.
23. *Ibid.*, p. 362.
24. *Ibid.*, p. 363.
25. Shackle (1955), p. 255.
26. Frank H. Knight, *Risk, Uncertainty and Profit* (1921, 1948), pp. 19–20. *See also* Chapter VII.
27. Shackle (1979), p. 134.
28. *Ibid.*, p. 135.
29. Paul Davidson, *Money and the Real World* (1st edn, 1972; 2nd edn, 1978).
30. Herschel I. Grossman, Review of *Money and the Real World*, by Paul Davidson. *Journal of Money, Credit and Banking* 7 (August 1975), pp. 405–406.
31. Shackle (1972), p. 18.
32. *Ibid.*, pp. 20–21.
33. Shackle, Review of *Money and the Real World*, by Paul Davidson. (June 1973), p. 533.
34. Shackle in T. Wilson and P. W. S. Andrews, *Oxford Studies in the Price Mechanism* (1951).
35. Shackle (1955), pp. 140–141.
36. *Ibid.*, p. 144. The high interest rates of recent years are mainly due to inflationary expectations.
37. *Ibid.*
38. William H. White, Interest Inelasticity of Investment Demand – the Case from Business Attitude Surveys Re-examined. In M. G. Mueller, *Readings in Macroeconomics* (1967), p. 113.
39. David G. Pierce and David M. Shaw, *Monetary Economics: Theories, Evidence and Policy* (1974), Preface.
40. Pierce and Shaw (1974). The references are to V. Argy, 'The Impact of Monetary Policy on Expenditure with Particular Reference to the U.K.', *I.M.F. Staff Papers* (June 1969), p. 65 and to C. G. F. Simkin, *Economics at Large* (1968), p. 195.
41. Shackle, *The Years of High Theory* (1967), p. 112.
42. *Ibid.*
43. Shackle, *A Scheme of Economic Theory* (1965), p. 81.

44. Shackle (1967), pp. 112–113.
45. Keynes, *C.W.*, Vol. VII (1936, 1973), pp. 149–150.
46. *Ibid.*, p. 161.
47. Brian J. Loasby (1976). *Choice, Complexity and Ignorance* (1976), p. 159.
48. *Ibid.*, p. 168.
49. Shackle (1965), p. 98.
50. Loasby (1976), p. 170.
51. Keynes, *C.W.*, Vol. XIV (1973b), pp. 113–114.
52. *Ibid.*, p. 114.
53. *Ibid.*, p. 115.
54. Shackle (1965), p. 45.
55. Shackle, *Keynesian Kaleidics* (1974), p. 39.
56. *Ibid.*, p. 28.
57. *Ibid.*, p. 37.
58. T. W. Hutchison, *On Revolutions and Progress in Economic Knowledge* (1978), p. 206. He is quoting from D. Patinkin, 'Keynes's Monetary Thought: A Study of its Development' (1976b), p. 142. Hutchison also refers (p. 212) to Dr Kregel's critical description of Keynes's choice of assumptions about expectations. *See* J. A. Kregel, 'Economic Methodology in the Face of Uncertainty' (1976), pp. 209 *et seq*.
59. Hutchison (1978), pp. 211–212. The reference is to Herbert A. Simon (1976). From Substantive to Procedural Rationality. In Spiro J. Latsis, *Method and Appraisal in Economics* (1976), pp. 129 *et seq*.
60. *See* his 1953 article, A Chart of Economic Theory, reprinted in Shackle (1955) and Chapter VII, A Scheme of Economic Theory, in Shackle (1965).
61. Shackle (1955), p. 218 and chart facing p. 218.
62. Shackle states that *The General Theory* also belongs to the Economics of Uncertain Expectations. *See* Shackle (1955), p. 222.
63. Shackle (1965), pp. 187–188.
64. *Ibid.*, pp. 191–195.
65. *Ibid.*, p. 48.
66. Keynes, *C.W.*, Vol. XXIX (1979), p. 222. The letter is dated 28 May 1936. Shackle (1965), p. 44, refers to *The General Theory* being 'founded on the idea of expectations and their precarious and trembling balance even in what is formally equilibrium'. Further, Shackle (1974), p. 77, refers to 'a *haunted* equilibrium' in *The General Theory*.

Chapter 12

Some reinterpretations of Keynes's theory

Professor Robert Clower's 1965 paper, The Keynesian Counter-Revolution: a theoretical appraisal, initiated a very important development in post-Keynesian economics. The counter-revolution to which he refers is the one 'launched by Hicks in 1937 and now being carried forward with such vigour by Patinkin and other general equilibrium theorists'[1]. The reference to Hicks relates to his famous article, Mr Keynes and the Classics, which Keynes himself found acceptable (*see* page 30) and to his great work *Value and Capital*. Patinkin's work in this area led to his *magnum opus*, *Money, Interest, and Prices* of 1956 and the definitive edition of 1965[2]. Clower states that the '"counter-revolution" to which I refer is clearly not a conscious revolt against Keynesian economics, for all the writers involved are, in a practical sense, strong supporters of what they conceive to be the Keynesian Revolution'[3]. The paper deals with the question whether these economists are Keynesians in terms of Keynes's theory. The counter-revolution which Clower is appraising and in fact attacking is the neoclassical synthesis, the objective of which is to incorporate Keynesian theory within Walrasian general equilibrium analysis. Léon Walras's *Eléments d'économie politique pure*[4] was one of the great intellectual achievements of the marginal revolution in economics in the 1870s. Clower states that he is attempting 'to show that the same highly special theoretical presuppositions which led to Keynes's original attack on orthodox economics continue to pervade contemporary price theory and that the Keynesian Counter-Revolution would collapse without them'[5]. I regard the importance of Clower's work to be the interpretation of Keynes's theory in terms of one of its main aspects and elaborating this aspect. *The General Theory* is a seminal work and there are a number of other important aspects such as the one stressed by the fundamentalist Keynesians.

Clower writes, 'Like us, Keynes does not in any way deny the generality of orthodox equilibrium analysis; he only denies that orthodox economics provides an adequate account of disequilibrium phenomena.'[6] This view is important. Clower states further that '*either Walras's Law is incompatible with Keynesian economics, or Keynes had nothing fundamentally new to add to orthodox economic theory*. This may seem an unnecessarily brutal way to confront one sacred cow with another. But what other conclusion is possible?'[7] My own view is that all the work done on the neoclassical synthesis has by no means been a waste of time. Certain aspects of Keynesian theory have been illuminated by placing it within the Walrasian framework but some important parts could not be included. To do so requires fundamental modifications of the Walrasian or neo-Walrasian general equilibrium theory. Thus for the time being, it is necessary to be eclectic and have a number of interpretations of Keynes. The development of a synthetic microeconomic and macroeconomic model of a monetary economy which takes account of the great achievements of Walras, Keynes and other economists is not possible at present and must be regarded as a distant objective. Such a model will include static and dynamic equilibrium, disequilibrium, an analysis of their nature and the processes which occur in such states.

In orthodox equilibrium analysis no distinction is made between planned and realized magnitudes relating to the behaviour of households and firms. By means of Walras's tâtonnement process or auctioneer, or Edgeworth's system of recontracting, all purchases and sales are made at an equilibrium set of prices. However, in states of disequilibrium, Clower emphasizes, it is vital to distinguish between transactor-planned or notional magnitudes and transactor-realized or actual magnitudes. Clower develops his analysis of individual decision processes on what he calls *Say's Principle*, that 'no transactor consciously *plans* to purchase units of any commodity without at the same time *planning* to finance the purchase either from profit receipts or from the sale of units of some other commodity'[8]. Clower further points out that when households are part of a connected market system, 'What is then presupposed about planned sales and purchases cannot possibly be true of realized sales and purchases unless the system as a whole is always in a state of equilibrium; that is to say, not every household can buy and sell just what it pleases if supply exceeds demand somewhere in the economy.'[9]

The key element in Clower's work is the dual decision hypothesis. He assumes involuntary unemployment in Keynes's sense which is '*Men are involuntarily unemployed if, in the event of a small rise in the price of wage-goods relatively to the money-wage, both the aggregate supply of labour willing to work for the current money-wage and the aggregate demand for it at that wage would be greater than the existing volume of employment.*'[10] Wage-goods are the goods on which money-wages are spent. If realized current money receipts are considered to impose a restraint on current consumption plans it follows that 'planned consumption as expressed in effective market offers to buy will necessarily be less than desired consumption as given by the demand functions of orthodox analysis'[11]. These demand functions are those of a full-employment equilibrium. The other side of involuntary unemployment is thus involuntary under-consumption. Clower asks 'whether Keynes can reasonably be considered to have had a dual decision theory of household behaviour at the back of his mind when he wrote *The General Theory*'[12]. He thinks this is the case on the basis of indirect evidence although he can find no direct evidence.

Clower shows that 'Walras's Law, although valid as usual with reference to *notional* market excess demands, is in general irrelevant to any but full-employment situations.'[13] In a state of involuntary unemployment *notional* demand, full-employment equilibrium demand, is greater than *effective* demand which depends mainly on current money receipts. It is this effective demand which determines employment and the level of output. There is an excess supply of labour. Clower regards his contribution as clarifying the theoretical basis of the Keynesian Revolution. He writes 'In a line, Keynesian economics brings current transactions into price theory whereas traditional analysis explicitly leaves them out.'[14] Clower recognizes the usefulness of present general-equilibrium analysis for thinking about economic problems in abstract terms but warns of the danger of thinking about practical problems without taking into account complications of crucial relevance which are necessarily omitted from such analysis. He concludes that 'we would do well to think twice before accepting as "useful" or "general", doctrines which are incapable of accommodating Keynesian economics'[15]. It is only fair to add that neoclassical synthesists do show awareness of the limitations of their abstract model.

Clower developed his interpretation of Keynesian theory in his important 1967 article, A reconsideration of the microfoundations of monetary theory[16]. This constitutes further criticism of the neoclassical synthesis as developed by Hicks, Lange and Patinkin to whom he adds Samuelson[17]. He states that they have produced a model 'suspiciously reminiscent of the classical theory of a barter economy . . . [and] that the conception of a money economy implicit in these constructions is empirically and analytically vacuous'[18]. He proposes an alternative micro-foundation for the theory of a monetary economy.

In reformulating accepted theory Clower analyses the restrictions on transactor behaviour in an economy in which money plays a distinctive role in contrast to a barter economy. He rightly points out that the important distinction between money and non-money commodities is that money acts as a means of payment, a generally acceptable medium of exchange. Money also serves as a unit of account, a standard of deferred payments and a store of value, but other commodities may or do perform these functions. Exchange relations in a money economy are complicated and Clower confines his analysis to that of '*pure money economies* in which one and only one commodity can be traded directly for any other commodity'[19]. This is stated in his famous aphorism: '*Money buys goods and goods buy money; but goods do not buy goods.*'[20] This restriction is regarded as basic for the theory of a monetary economy. Clower emphasizes that 'choice alternatives in a money economy must be so defined as to satisfy the requirement that money be offered or demanded as one of the commodities entering into every trade. Analytically, what this entails is a clear separation between goods demanded for purchase (offers to sell money) and goods offered for sale (offers to buy money).'[21] Clower returns to the traditional point that effective demand in a money economy involves both desire and an ability to pay: As a result of his preliminary analysis of the micro-foundations regarded as suitable for the theory of a money economy, he states that he has provided 'a model where, in sharp contrast with established theory, money commodities play a peculiar and central role . . .'[22].

Clower in his paper, Theoretical foundations of monetary policy, given to the 1970 Sheffield Money Seminar argues, as I state in the Introduction to the volume of Proceedings, 'strongly for much more analysis of a monetary economy in micro-economic rather than in macro-economic terms'[23]. I point out that Clower 'does not regard monetary policy as a sensitive or reliable instrument of control at present and urges that research should be undertaken into the dynamics of observable processes of monetary adjustment and the related possibilities of economic control'[24]. There was a division of opinion on this important matter at the Seminar. Professor F. P. R. Brechling supported Clower's approach in his Laidler Discussion Paper while Harry Johnson in his Clower Discussion Paper argued against it, taking a monetarist point of view. Milton Friedman in the general discussion criticized Clower's interest in the technology of monetary exchanges while Clower restated his position that monetary theory must be based on actual monetary trading processes.

Clower stresses the importance of the means of payment function of money in a theory of a monetary economy. He defines money theoretically 'in terms of explicitly postulated restrictions on trading alternatives that assign a special role to certain commodities as payment media in organized markets'[25]. For Clower, currency, demand deposits (current accounts) and trade credit constitute money in the United States and United Kingdom. He states, 'The essential issue here is whether the tender of any given financial instrument permits a buyer to take delivery of a commodity from a seller. On this criterion, trade credit qualifies as money – trade credit being interpreted to include credit card and overdraft facilities, department store credit and travellers' checks, as well as commercial paper and book credits.'[26] Shackle in his Discussion Paper argues 'that time deposits (deposit accounts) and unused overdraft permission should be included, while trade credits should be excluded, if we accept the definition that money is a means of payment'. Shackle points out that the process of increasing trade credit is the putting off of the making of payments and that it is in the influencing of the velocity of circulation that trade credit plays its part[27]. My own conclusion was that theoretical and empirical definitions of money 'are a matter of convenience, and "assets" which could possibly be included on the supply side and are not must be taken into account on the demand side'[28].

Clower in his 1977 article, 'The anatomy of monetary theory', contributes to the development of the modern theory of monetary exchange. He explores the roles of transactions costs and any other possible conditions which are necessary for the existence of monetary exchange in an economic system which otherwise conforms to an abstract general-equilibrium model of the Arrow–Debreu type. Four requirements are stated as mandatory for any theory of a monetary economy: '(1) The theory should imply that trade is an ongoing process in time rather than a once-for-all affair that ends in the permanent elimination of incentives for further trade. (2) The theory should imply that, on average over any finite time interval, each individual holds positive stocks of all goods that are regularly traded. (3) The theory should imply that the bulk of all trades occur not through essentially random pairing of individuals, who happen to share a double coincidence of wants, but rather through systematic pairing of specialist with non-specialist traders in a relatively small number of organized, continuously operating markets. (4) The theory should imply that at least one and at most a few distinctive "money" commodities are transferred (or promised for future delivery) by one party to another in virtually all exchange transactions.'[29]

The first requirement that trade is an ongoing process is satisfied if either or both the assumptions are correct – that individuals view future endowment flows of goods and labour services as probable rather than certain and that they 'can negotiate trades only by engaging in extensive search and bargaining activities'[30]. As far as the second requirement that stocks are held is concerned, it is clear that stocks will be held because trading costs imply that individuals will trade at points of time and not continuously. However, Clower shows that the influence of storage costs must be taken into acount when considering the holding of positive average stocks. The third requirement is that most trade takes place in organized markets. This follows if search and bargaining costs are significant and provides great social benefits. Clower points out that since Aristotle writers have tended to identify 'money' and 'organized markets'. He emphasizes that they are logically distinct although historically they have generally co-existed. The fourth requirement is that 'money' is used in virtually all exchange transactions. Clower refers to recent work which shows that an individual who receives a flow of units of good X 'will – except in very special cases – minimize total trade-related costs by purchasing many or even most consumption goods at dates that differ significantly from those at which he sells units of X'[31]. At this point storage costs are again introduced into the analysis. Clower states, 'If there exists some commodity that is already a common object of exchange and which has distinctly lower storage costs than all or most other commodities, a rational individual will choose to acquire or dispose of units of this good in virtually all exchange transactions.'[32] If such a good also possesses the other well-known qualifications, such as portability, it will be the means of payment, money.

Clower has established the *necessary* conditions for the existence of money in an economic system which otherwise conforms to an Arrow –Debreu economy. He also indicates some factors on which the *sufficient* conditions depend. He does not claim final results but emphasizes that much further theoretical work is required.

Professor Axel Leijonhufvud was a research student of Clower's who took over his ideas on Keynesian theory and developed them. His book, *On Keynesian Economics and the Economics of Keynes*[33], published in 1968 caused considerable excitement among academic economists. It was an attack on the prevailing view that 'the Income-Expenditure model' which goes back to Hicks's 1937 article, 'Mr Keynes and the "Classics"'[34], was an appropriate conceptual framework for the presentation of *The General Theory*. Leijonhufvud's main thesis '*is that Keynes's theory is quite distinct from the "Keynesian" income-expenditure theory*'[35]. His "Economics of Keynes" is an alternative model with a very different structure which he strongly maintains is '*more consistent with the textual evidence of Keynes's two major works – [A Treatise on Money and The General Theory] – and with pre-Keynesian, "Classical" theories.*'[36] Leijonhufvud's book had some very favourable reviews. Harry Johnson in a 1969 paper referred to the book as a 'monumentally scholarly work of exegesis and interpretation of the *General Theory*'[37]. Professor A. G. Hines in his 1971 book, *On the Reappraisal of Keynesian Economics*, takes a very favourable view of the work of Clower and Leijonhufvud. He thinks that they are correct in their assessment of Keynes's theoretical contribution[38] but he does not agree with Leijonhufvud's abandoning the income-expenditure model. The uneasy response to the book is partly attributed to Leijonhufvud's insistent attack on this model as a framework for the expression and development of Keynes's main ideas. Hines suspects that the work-a-day economist when faced with the real world will use the income-expenditure model to handle short-run stabilization problems. He points out that Leijonhufvud 'is asking the economist to throw away a substantial part of his analytical equipment and, since in his book he offers no alternative formal apparatus to take its place, this is asking rather a lot'[39]. Further, Hines writes 'Fortunately, I think it is possible to show that Keynes's major theoretical insights can be conveyed within the context of the income-expenditure model.'[40]

Richard Jackman in his 1973 Money Study Group paper, 'Keynes and Leijonhufvud', is very critical of Leijonhufvud's treatment of the income-expenditure model. He is also critical of Leijonhufvud's interpretation of Keynes on a number of major issues[41]. Professor C. J. Bliss in his 1974 paper to the Association of University Teachers of Economics, The reappraisal of Keynes's economics: an appraisal, makes a number of very important criticisms but before mounting them he writes, 'I have shared, and continue to share, some of the infectious enthusiasm to which the book gives rise. It is a valuable contribution which gives a far more accurate picture of what Keynes was on about than does many a textbook on macroeconomics. Furthermore some of its important claims are correct.'[42] Professor Mark Blaug in his Discussion Paper welcomes Bliss's paper as he agrees that Leijonhufvud's interpretation of Keynes is open to serious criticism. He writes, 'If we were considering Leijonhufvud's book as a contribution to disequilibrium economics, our verdict might be favourable. But as a reassessment of Keynes it suffers from gross exaggeration.'[43]

The problem of interpeting Keynes is difficult and there are important differences of opinion as to the appropriate interpretation of elements of his theory and his theory as a whole. Sometimes it is a question of the interpretation of a functional relationship and sometimes a question of the emphasis to be placed on an aspect of his theory. There is not always *the* interpretation to be found as it may depend on the context. *The General Theory* is basically equilibrium analysis in terms of comparative statics but it contains forays into dynamic equilibrium analysis and disequilibrium analysis. Leijonhufvud states that he is critical of the usual interpretation of Keynes and therefore has to consider in detail 'what Keynes really said'. This doctrine-historical objective is however strictly secondary. The primary objective is to 'provide a fresh perspective from which the income-expenditure theory may be reconsidered.'[44] For this purpose, 'it is Keynes's *Gestalt*-conception [vision] of how a modern capitalist economy works, and not "what he really said", that we ultimately want to grasp'[45]. To complicate matters further, Leijonhufvud goes somewhat beyond Keynes on some issues[46]. His disequilibrium analysis *per se* is important.

Leijonhufvud does not accept that *The General Theory* is basically equilibrium analysis in terms of comparative statics. He regards the question of whether it is static or dynamic as one of form versus substance. He admits that Keynes's formal method of analysis was in many respects static but writes that 'The theoretical problems with which he was concerned were problems of the "short run", i.e. of disequilibrium. His model was static, but his theory was dynamic.'[47] Further, Leijonhufvud states that 'what is being analyzed is not an equilibrium state but an equilibrating process, i.e. a succession of disequilibrium states'[48]. He also refers to the importance of the lag-structure assumed. There is, of course, no lag-structure in Keynes's basic comparative static theory; he only has lags when he occasionally departs from it as in Chapter 22, Notes on the Trade Cycle. Again, Leijonhufvud writes, 'Keynes dealt with dynamic processes by means of a "comparative statics" period-analysis [and] the subject of his work is not "unemployment equilibrium" but the nature of the macroeconomic process of *adjustment* to a disequilibrating disturbance.'[49] However, it is in *A Treatise on Money* that Keynes's disequilibrium analysis is to be found.

It is interesting that Patinkin who developed the neoclassical synthesis to a high point in his *Money, Interest, and Prices*, the school subject to so much attack from Leijonhufvud, says in his *Keynes's Monetary Thought* of 1976 that he has 'interpreted the *General Theory*, not as a static theory of unemployment equilibrium, but as a dynamic theory of unemployment *dis*equilibrium'[50]. Patinkin in *Money, Interest, and Prices* wrote that 'Keynesian economics is the economics of unemployment *dis*equilibrium.'[51]

Bliss views Keynes's equilibrium economics as the economics of temporary equilibrium and points to such equilibrium conditions in Keynesian theory as the equality between the wage rate and the marginal product of labour and that between the rate of interest and the marginal efficiency of capital. Thus Leijonhufvud's disequilibrium analysis is not the 'Economics of Keynes'; he is going beyond Keynes[52].

It was realized straightaway that Keynes had changed his methodology when he moved from *A Treatise on Money* to *The General Theory*. He abondoned dynamic period analysis in which disequilibrium analysis was possible and adopted comparative statics. Harrod wrote in 1937 that Keynes's theory was not dynamic 'For it is still a static equilibrium which the anticipations along with other circumstances serve to determine'[53]. Kahn's multiplier is a period multiplier[54] but Keynes's multiplier is a static multiplier[55].

It is quite clear from *The Collected Writings* of Keynes that he made the change to statics after long consideration and for good reasons at the time. Keynes wrote to Professor Ohlin regarding the *ex post* and *ex ante* method, 'This is in fact almost precisely on the lines that I was thinking and lecturing somewhere about 1931 and 1932, and subsequently abandoned. My reason for giving it up was owing to my failure to establish any definite unit of time and I found that that made very artificial any attempt to state the theory precisely. So, after writing out many chapters along what was evidently Swedish lines, I scrapped the lot and felt that my new treatment was much safer and sounder from the logical point of view . . . I used to speak of the period between expectation and result as "funnels of process", but the fact that the funnels are all of different lengths and overlap one another meant that at any given time there was no aggregate realized result capable of being compared with some aggregate expectation at some earlier date.'[56]

The basic equilibrium condition in *The General Theory* is that the aggregate supply price of the output from a given level of employment of labour is equal to the aggregate demand price for this output[57]. The aggregate demand price is the proceeds which entrepreneurs expect to receive during a small unit of time under uncertainty. This temporary equilibrium cannot persist because the given expectations will not be correct, even assuming no change in other circumstances. In terms of comparative statics, different hypothetical rates of new investment and different marginal propensities to consume (multipliers) can be assumed, giving different temporary equilibrium states, different levels of employment. These temporary equilibria are snapshot photographs. As Shackle puts it so well, 'At each curtain rise the *General Theory* shows us, not the dramatic moment of inevitable action but a tableau of posed figures. It is only after the curtain has descended again that we hear the clatter of violent sceneshifting.'[58]

To Leijonhufvud Keynesian Economics as distinct from the Economics of Keynes is the familiar Hicks–Hansen[59] IS–LM model of the textbooks and indeed the class of sophisticated models developed by the neoclassical or neo-Walrasian synthesists which go back to Hicks. Leijonhufvud refers to this model as the income-expenditure model. He states that verbal expositions of this model generally refer to five aggregates: consumer goods, capital goods, labour services, money, government debt ('bonds') but the standard income-expenditure model 'contains only *three* variables which can be interpreted as price relations, i.e. the money price level, the money wage rate, and the interest rate'[60]. The number of goods (aggregates) must therefore be reduced to four. The most common formulation is to combine consumer goods and capital goods to create a one-commodity model. This is a serious limitation as Keynes's theory involves changes in the relative prices and quantities of consumer goods and capital goods.

Leijonhufvud states that *The General Theory* also contains the five goods but only three relative values. He regards this model as a two-commodity model, consumer goods and capital goods being separate. According to Leijonhufvud, 'Keynes's basic model treats capital goods and "bonds" as one aggregate.'[61] which he refers to as 'non-money assets' and which are titles to prospective income-streams. He writes that 'Keynes's "representative" non-money asset is a long-term asset. Thus the representative bond has a long term to maturity, the representative capital good is very durable.'[62] Keynes's model is thus said to have the four goods, consumer goods, non-money assets, labour services and money. Leijonhufvud admits that Keynes often has a larger number of goods and that the income-expenditure model may have more than four goods.

It is very undesirable to aggregate capital goods and bonds in a model of Keynes's theory. Leijonhufvud's justification is that 'Bond-streams and equity-streams are treated as perfect substitutes, a simplification which Keynes achieved through some quite mechanical manipulations of risk and liquidity premia.'[63] A distinction between the rate of interest and the marginal efficiency of capital is required and their equality is an equilibrium condition. From the marginal efficiency of capital must be deducted the cost of bringing borrowers and lenders together and an allowance to cover the leader's risk and uncertainty[64]. Such a distinction goes back at least to Knut Wicksell's *Interest and Prices* of 1898 in which he distinguished between the money and natural rates of interest[65]. Goodhart states that in his view the analysis of the determination of investment expenditures 'requires explicit recognition of the significant distinctions between real assets and bonds'[66]. If we are to have straitjackets, the five goods/four relative values model is the minimum level of aggregation, I think. The five goods are consumer goods, capital goods, labour services, money and bonds.

Leijonhufvud was unduly critical of the income-expenditure model. As already stated, Hines finds the model appropriate for the expression of Keynes's major theoretical insights. Jackman quotes Keynes's summary of the factors determining income and employment on pages 246–247 of *The General Theory* which seems to him 'to cast some doubt on the view that Keynes's theory of income determination is "quite distinct from" the IS–LM model, for the factors mentioned are the behavioural functions underlying the IS and LM curves, together with an exogenously determined money wage'[67]. Money certainly plays an important role in *The General Theory* but Jackman regards Leijonhufvud's argument that the IS–LM model has led to 'strange new doctrines of the "unimportance of money" and the "ineffectiveness of monetary policy"'[68] as curious. He points out that 'the ineffectiveness of monetary policy cannot in any case be deduced from the IS–LM model as such, but only from particular assumptions about the shape of the underlying behavioural functions'[69]. Competent income-expenditure theorists base their views on what are the appropriate monetary and fiscal policies on a number of considerations.

The problem of the interest elasticities of investment, consumption and the demand for money involves theoretical and empirical difficulties. Leijonhufvud argues that according to his interpretation of Keynesian theory in which bonds and real capital are close substitutes and the representative capital good is long-lived, the interest elasticity of investment is high on *a priori* theoretical grounds. Keynes's *General Theory* has been interpreted both as showing high and low elasticities. Jackman does not accept Leijonhufvud's arguments and states, 'The magnitude of the interest-rate elasticity of investment (in the "Keynesian" short run) must clearly be an empirical, rather than a theoretical, matter.'[70] In the early years following *The General Theory*, Keynesian economists tended to accept that investment was interest-inelastic. Later, a survey of empirical work by William H. White of 1956 (*see* page 196) suggested that the interest-elasticity is sufficient to justify the proponents of interest-rate policy. Hines points out that recent empirical studies by Catephores and himself and Weber 'in which the relevant hypotheses and the underlying lag structures are carefully specified suggest that . . . expenditure functions *are* interest-elastic.'[71] Friedman (*see* page 128) and Tobin (*see* page 186) attach importance to the influence of the rate of interest on the rate of investment, widely defined.

Keynes dismissed as insignificant the intertemporal effect of a change in the rate of interest on consumption out of current income but he emphasized the importance of its effect on consumption by causing changes in capital values. Leijonhufvud quotes from *The General Theory*, adding italics: 'Windfall changes in capital-values . . . should be classified amongst *the major factors* capable of causing *short-period* changes in the propensity to consume.'[72] Such 'windfall effects' (distinct from the Pigou effect) can be caused by a shift in the marginal efficiency of capital schedule or a change in the rate of interest. Leijonhufvud considers the former to be irrelevant for Keynes's short-period analysis although it can be assumed in comparative statics. He concentrates on the latter, a change in the rate of interest. Leijonhufvud points out that 'It is asserted that a rise in asset values due entirely to a fall in interest rates – the "country is no richer" – will raise the propensity to consume out of current income.'[73] In this case the increase in the value of net worth is an increase in perceived wealth. Leijonhufvud points out that Keynes did not provide a choice-theoretical explanation and he attempts to do so. The problem is compli-cated but it should be noted that Leijonhufvud's rationalization seemed unconvincing to Jackman[74]. Mr J. S. Fleming states that 'the wealth effect of interest changes on consumption, developed by Leijonhufvud as an interpretation of Keynes, is not securely founded'[75]. Goodhart refers to a 1969 study in the United States which showed 'A large proportion of the total effect, particularly in the short run, of monetary forces comes about through wealth effects upon personal consumption, mainly a result of monetary changes causing fluctuations in stock-market prices.'[76] He adds that in the United Kingdom there is less firm evidence of this relationship. However, there is no doubt that Keynes attached importance to it.

The third relationship is the elasticity of the demand for money. The speculative motive plays a vital role in Keynes's analysis of liquidity-preference. Keynes emphasized that the speculative demand for money tended to stabilize the longterm rate of interest, preventing required interest rate adjustments. He considers the two assets money and longterm government bonds in order to simplify the analysis. Keynes assumed that bond-holders had inelastic interest-rate expectations. If the rate of interest was regarded as being at about the normal level, an increase in the real quantity of money would have little effect in lowering it. As the rate of interest fell, speculators would expect it to rise again and would therefore hold larger money balances and the bonds would be held bearing a not much lower yield, the rate of interest. There is no doubt that Keynes attached great importance to low longterm interest rates and as Leijonhuf-vud writes, he feared that 'conventional monetary policies would not suffice to bring about a large enough and rapid enough change in the long rate of interest'[77]. Keynes advocated fiscal policy, increasing government expenditure relatively to government revenue in certain circumstances such as deep depression. If entrepreneurs' confidence had been under-mined, pump-priming was required. However, Keynes believed in the efficiency of both fiscal and monetary policies. Leijonhufvud rightly points out that 'He did argue that new instruments needed to be added to the traditional armory of Central Banks, i.e. open market operations in long-term and "risky" securities.'[78] Keynes undoubtedly regarded monet-ary policy as important. Leijonhufvud states that the Liquidity Trap notion was explicitly repudiated by Keynes[79]. Economists have taken different views on Keynes's concept of 'absolute liquidity-preference' (liquidity trap); that is, the interest elasticity of demand for money is infinite. There is a minimum rate of interest which cannot be reduced by increasing the real money stock. The views taken have been based on numerous quotations from *The General Theory* which show the difficulty of interpreting Keynes. My own view is that Keynes did not consider the liquidity trap to be a contemporary problem but did consider that it could be important. Further, he believed the interest elasticity was high. The relevant empirical work has already been discussed (*see* pages 118–119). It should also be noted that Keynes attached importance to shifts in both the liquidity preference and marginal efficiency of capital curves.

Loasby points out that a decision-maker may be faced with partial ignorance because of a failure of communication or because the future is unknowable. In Leijonhufvud's interpretation of Keynes the emphasis is placed on the former (because of the cost of communication); in Shackle's interpretation, on the latter. Loasby takes Shackle's view[80]. Taking this view does not prevent an appreciation of the aspect of Keynesian theory developed by Clower and Leijonhufvud. Clower's important distinction between notional and effective demands is emphasized by Leijonhufvud. He points out that effective demand which determines production and employment may be less than notional demand, the demand which would manifest itself in a Walrasian general equilibrium with full employment of productive resources. In this case there is an excess supply of labour, an unemployment disequilibrium in his terms.

An individual is assumed to fail to realize some of his notional sales, say the sale of his labour services. His notional demand quantities are unknown so that 'notional demands do *not* "provide the relevant market signals". The information which traders acquire is based primarily on the actually realized exchanges.'[81] The initial contraction is accentuated through the income-constrained or multiplier process. Transactors will have unemployed resources and will reduce their expenditures in other markets. Effective demands are thus reduced in these markets. 'Unemployed resources emerge in these markets also and *the search instituted by unemployed workers and producers with excess capacity will yield information on "effective" demands, not on "notional" demands.*'[82] The distinction between a money and barter economy is vital here. The unemployed when seeking work ask for money, not commodities. This means that 'Their notional demand for commodities is *not communicated* to producers; not being able to perceive this potential demand for their products, producers will not be willing to absorb the excess supply of labour at a wage corresponding to the real wage that would "solve" the Walrasian problem.'[83] It should be noted that the payment of unemployment insurance and other social benefits reduce the importance of this process, providing 'automatic stabilizers'. Leijonhufvud himself points out that the magnitude of the multiplier is reduced to the extent that 'unemployed households still have a "cushion" of liquid assets, such as savings deposits'[84].

Leijonhufvud regards the revolutionary element in *The General Theory* as being Keynes's reversal of the Marshallian ranking of price – and quantity – adjustment speeds. 'In the shortest period flow quantities are freely variable, but one or more prices are given.'[85] In the case of the labour market Leijonhufvud is justified. All that is required is downward stickiness of money-wage rates, not rigidity. Professor E. Roy Weintraub states that Leijonhufvud abandoned his 1968 inversion of adjustment speeds analysis in a University of California, Los Angeles, Discussion Paper of 1974[86]. However, its application to the labour market seems useful.

Keynes discussed a number of reasons for this inflexibility of money wages[87]. Leijonhufvud who was influenced by Professor A. A. Alchian's unpublished work[88] analyses the unemployment disequilibrium in terms of wage stickiness and lack of information in the labour market. He writes, 'Alchian has shown that the emergence of unemployed resources is a predictable consequence of a decline in demand when traders do not have perfect information on what the new market-clearing price would be.'[89] A more realistic assumption is made than that of perfect certainty in Walrasian equilibrium theory. The individual transactor is faced with information costs. Leijonhufvud writes that the unemployed worker 'may start with a reservation price close or equal to his old wage . . . Search – acquisition of information – is costly, both in direct expense and in foregone earnings. At some point, therefore, employment at the best wage then known will be accepted.'[90]

In his 1976 paper Leijonhufvud continued to emphasize the co-ordination problem and stated that it 'will ultimately require the development of methods of "dynamic", "disequilibrium" process analysis'[91]. Despite the criticisms to which it has been subject, Leijonhufvud's book remains important.

Notes

1. Robert Clower (1965). The Keynesian Counterrevolution: A Theoretical Appraisal. In F. H. Hahn and F. P. R. Brechling, *The Theory of Interest Rates* (1965), p. 103.
2. Patinkin also refers to Oscar Lange, *Price Flexibility and Employment* (1944) and Franco Modigliani, Liquidity Preference and the Theory of Interest and Money (1944). In American Economic Association, *Readings in Monetary Theory* (1952).
3. Hahn and Brechling (1965), p. 103, n.1.
4. Walras, Léon, *Elements of Pure Economics* (1954), translated and edited by W. Jaffé from the definitive edition (1926) of the *Eléments d'économie politique pure*.
5. Hahn and Brechling (1965), p. 104.
6. *Ibid.*, p. 109.
7. *Ibid.*, pp. 110–111.
8. *Ibid.*, p. 116.
9. *Ibid.*, p. 117.
10. Keynes, *C.W.*, Vol. VII (1936, 1973), p. 15.
11. Hahn and Brechling (1965), p. 118.
12. *Ibid.*, p. 120.
13. *Ibid.*, p. 122.
14. *Ibid.*, p. 124.
15. *Ibid.*, p. 125.
16. R. W. Clower, A Reconsideration of the Microfoundations of Monetary Theory (1967). In Clower, *Monetary Theory Selected Readings* (1969).
17. P. A. Samuelson, *Foundations of Economic Analysis* (1947).
18. Clower (1969), p. 202.
19. *Ibid.*, p. 207.

20. *Ibid.*, pp. 207–208.
21. *Ibid.*, p. 208.
22. *Ibid.*, p. 211.
23. Clower in G. Clayton, J. C. Gilbert, R. Sedgwick, *Monetary Theory and Monetary Policy in the 1970s (1971), p. 2.*
24. *Ibid.*, p. 2.
25. *Ibid.*, pp. 2, 17.
26. *Ibid.*, p. 18. n.9.
27. *Ibid.*, p. 3.
28. *Ibid.*
29. Robert W. Clower, The Anatomy of Monetary Theory, *American Economic Review*. American Economic Association, *Papers and Proceedings*, 67 (February 1977), pp. 206–207.
30. *Ibid.*, pp. 207–208.
31. *Ibid.*, p. 210.
32. *Ibid.*, p. 211.
33. Axel Leijonhufvud, *On Keynesian Economics and the Economics of Keynes* (1968).
34. J. R. Hicks, 'Mr Keynes and the "Classics"' (1937). In Hicks, *Critical Essays in Monetary Theory* (1967).
35. Leijonhufvud (1968), p. 8.
36. *Ibid.*
37. Harry G. Johnson (1970). Recent Developments in Monetary Theory – A Commentary. In Harry G. Johnson, *Further Essays in Monetary Economics* (1972), p. 29.
38. A. G. Hines, *On the Reappraisal of Keynesian Economics* (1971), p. 9.
39. Hines (1971), p. 25.
40. *Ibid.*, p. 25.
41. Published in *Oxford Economic Papers*, 26, (July 1974).
42. In Michael Parkin and A. R. Nobay, *Current Economic Problems* (1975), p. 203.
43. In Parkin and Nobay (1975), p. 215.
44. Leijonhufvud (1968), p. 10.
45. *Ibid.*, p. 10.
46. *Ibid.*, p. 11.
47. *Ibid.*, p. 36.
48. *Ibid.*, p. 36.
49. *Ibid.*, p. 50.
50. Don Patinkin, *Keynes' Monetary Thought* (1976a).
51. Don Patinkin, *Money, Interest, and Prices* (1st edn, 1956; 2nd edn, 1965), pp. 337–338. Note that as early as 1948 Patinkin had written that 'the real significance of the Keynesian contribution can be realized only within the framework of *dynamic* economics', in his article, Price Flexibility and Full Employment. In American Economic Association (1952), pp. 279–280.
52. Bliss in Parkin and Nobay (1975), p. 204.
53. R. F. Harrod (1937). Mr. Keynes and Traditional Theory. In Harrod, *Economic Essays* (1952), p. 252.
54. R. F. Kahn (1931). The Relation of Home Investment to Unemployment. In Kahn, *Selected Essays on Employment Growth* (1952).
55. Keynes, *C.W.*, Vol. VII (1936, 1973), p. 115.
56. Keynes, *C.W.*, Vol. XIV (1973b), pp. 184–185. *See also* the statement in his 1937 lectures (rough notes survive) regarding his method in his 1931–1932 lectures, *ibid.*, p. 180.
57. Keynes, *C.W.*, Vol. VII (1936, 1973), p. 25.
58. G. L. S. Shackle, *The Years of High Theory* (1967), p. 182.
59. Professor Hansen was an important advocate of Keynesian theory in the United States and made use of Hick's IS–LM model in such textbooks as Alvin H. Hansen, *Monetary Theory and Fiscal Policy* (1949) and Alvin H. Hansen, *A Guide to Keynes* (1953).
60. Leijonhufvud (1968), p. 131.
61. *Ibid.*, p. 135.
62. *Ibid.*, p. 135.
63. *Ibid.*, p. 41.
64. Keynes, *C.W.*, Vol. VII (1936, 1973), p. 309.
65. Knut Wicksell, *Interest and Prices* (1898, 1936). Keynes's abandonment of Wicksell's natural rate of interest is not relevant here. *C.W.*, Vol. VII (1936, 1973), pp. 242–244.

66. C. A. E. Goodhart, *Money, Information and Uncertainty* (1975), p. 177.
67. Jackman (1974), pp. 259–260.
68. *Ibid.*, p. 260. Jackman is quoting Leijonhufvud (1968), p. 25.
69. *Ibid.*, p. 260.
70. *Ibid.*, p. 262.
71. Hines (1971), p. 36. The references are to A. G. Hines and G. Catephores (1970). Investment in U.K. Manufacturing Industry, 1956–1967. In K. Hilton and D. F. Heathfield, *Econometric Study of the United Kingdom* (1970) and W. E. Weber (1970). 'Effect of Interest Rates on Aggregate Consumption' (September 1970).
72. Leijonhufvud (1968), p. 191. The quotation is from Keynes, *C.W.*, Vol. VII (1936, 1973), pp. 92–93.
73. Leijonhufvud (1968), p. 193.
74. Jackman (1974), pp. 263–264.
75. J. S. Fleming (1974). Wealth Effects in Keynesian Models (1974), p. 257.
76. Goodhart (1975), pp. 180–181.
77. Leijonhufvud (1968), p. 158.
78. *Ibid.*, p. 404. Leijonhufvud refers to Keynes, *A Treatise on Money*, *C.W.*, Vols V, VI (1930, 1971), Chapter 37 and *C.W.*, Vol. VII (1936, 1973), pp. 197, 202–208.
79. *Ibid.*, p. 158.
80. Brian J. Loasby, *Choice, Complexity and Ignorance* (1976), pp. 169–170.
81. Leijonhufvud (1968), p. 84. The quotation is from Clower (1965).
82. *Ibid.*, pp. 84–85.
83. *Ibid.*, p. 90.
84. A. Leijonhufvud, *Keynes and the Classics* (1969), p. 44.
85. Leijonhufvud (1968), p. 52.
86. Published in E. Roy Weintraub, *Microfoundations: The Compatibility of Microeconomics and Macroeconomics* (1979), p. 82.
87. *See* Jackman's discussion in Jackman (1974), pp. 268–269.
88. *See* now A. A. Alchian, 'Information Costs, Pricing and Resource Unemployment', *Western Economic Journal* (June 1969) and Edmund S. Phelps *et al.*, *Microeconomic Foundations of Employment and Inflation Theory* (1974). For work in the same area *see* Robert J. Barro and Herschel I. Grossman, *Money, Employment and Inflation* (1976).
89. Leijonhufvud (1968), p. 38.
90. *Ibid.*, p. 78.
91. A. Leijonhufvud (1976). Schools, 'Revolutions' and Research Programmes in Economic Theory. In Spiro J. Latsis, *Method and Appraisal in Economics* (1976), p. 94.

Part IV

The policy implications

Chapter 13

The stagnation thesis

The stagnation thesis, which Keynes puts forward in various places in *The General Theory*, is that there is a tendency to chronic depression, low levels of employment and output, because of a deficiency of aggregate money demand in advanced economies. Some economists have maintained that this is the essence of *The General Theory*; others that Keynes was only giving hints of possibilities; while others have maintained that Keynes regarded stagnation as a serious problem although it was not the essence of his contribution. I take this middle-of-the-road position. In this chapter I assume money-wage rates are fixed so that unemployment does not cause them to fall. In the following chapter money-wage rates are assumed to be flexible downwards and some effects of falling money wages are examined.

According to Keynes, stagnation may arise because saving at a full-employment[1] level of income would be greater than investment and a deflationary pressure is exerted on the economy, giving a lower level of income and employment at which the lower rate of saving is equal to the rate of investment[2]. At a high level of income the rate of saving will be high, while a wealthy community which has accumulated a large stock of capital (factories, machines etc.) will have exhausted many of the profitable investment opportunities and the rate of investment will be low. Without state intervention, this rate of investment in combination with the multiplier will determine a less than full-employment level of income which may involve a high level of unemployment.

It is necessary to give a number of quotations from Keynes relating to the stagnation problem as there has been so much misunderstanding. He refers to the problem early in his book, *The General Theory*, when explaining the paradox of poverty in the midst of plenty. He writes, 'a poor community will be prone to consume by far the greater part of its output, so that a very modest measure of investment will be sufficient to provide full employment; whereas a wealthy community will have to discover much ampler opportunities for investment if the saving propensities of its wealthier members are to be compatible with the employment of its poorer members. . . . But worse still. Not only is the marginal propensity to consume weaker in a wealthy community, but, owing to its accumulation of capital being already larger, the opportunities for further investment are less attractive unless the rate of interest falls at a sufficiently rapid rate.'[3] Thus Keynes envisages that 'an insufficiency of effective demand may, and often will, bring the increase of employment to a standstill *before* a level of full employment has been reached'[4]. Here and elsewhere Keynes has in mind, I think, a theoretical concept of an unemployment equilibrium although some economists consider that this is a misinterpretation of Keynes.

The stagnation thesis is based on the possibility that there is a secular tendency for the marginal efficiency of capital, the expected rate of return on an additional unit of investment in capital goods, to be lower than the minimum rate of interest possible, if the rate of investment is sufficient to equal the rate of saving out of a full-employment level of income. In this case there will be chronic unemployment as it will be unprofitable to undertake the rate of investment required for full employment. Keynes states that the rate of interest 'may fluctuate for decades about a level which is chronically too high for full employment'[5]. Keynes put forward the concept of a minimum rate of interest because of what he called the speculative motive[6]. If the rate of interest falls to a level at which people expect that it will rise rather than fall, they will hold more money[7] if the monetary authority increases the quantity of money, and not bid up the prices of bonds, fixed-interest government securities. The monetary authority cannot in these circumstances reduce the rate of interest any further. This is the so-called liquidity trap. Keynes writes, 'Unless reasons are believed to exist why future experience will be very different from past experience, a long-term rate of interest of (say) 2 per cent leaves more to fear than to hope, and offers, at the same time, a running yield which is only sufficient to offset a very small measure of fear.'[8] A rise in the rate of interest causes a fall in the price of bonds and capital losses for the holders, while a fall in the rate of interest gives them capital profits. Keynes refers again to this liquidity-trap[9] situation later and writes, 'But while this limiting case might become practically important in future, I know of no example of it hitherto.'[10] There has been much controversy over the liquidity trap and this sentence is often quoted. Keynes's following sentence is, however, generally omitted. He writes, 'Indeed, owing to the unwillingness of most monetary authorities to deal boldly in debts of long term there has not been much opportunity for a test.'[11] There has been a great deal of econometric research done on the liquidity trap and it is doubtful if any case has been discovered[12]. However, the theoretical concept remains valid and it is a practical possibility. As Keynes points out, the minimum rate of interest because of the speculative motive can only appear if the monetary authority pushes its easy monetary policy far enough. Patinkin shows that the monetary authorities in the United Kingdom and in the United States could have reduced interest rates in the 1930s to even lower levels by greater increases in the quantity of money[13]. Dr Dalton as Chancellor of the Exchequer pursued an ultra-cheap money policy from 1945 to 1947 when it broke down. This was because he had forced the longterm rate of interest on Consols and his similar Treasury stock to 2½ per cent, which was much below the rate of interest which would have reflected the degree of capital scarcity in the high-employment economy at that time. It would be interesting to have a detailed econometric study of this period in relation to the concept of the liquidity trap[14].

Apart from the speculative motive, there are other reasons for a minimum rate of interest. Keynes points out that in a society with a monetary system the rate of interest cannot be negative, as people can save by holding money which 'will "keep" and involves negligible costs of storage and safe custody'[15]. We assume here a stable general level of prices. If the price level is rising, the real value of a money balance held falls and there is a negative rate of interest. The costs of bringing borrowers and lenders together sets a lower limit to the rate of interest[16]. In the case of loans to business and industry in the private sector of the economy, an allowance for lender's risk must be added to this rate of interest. This risk is related to voluntary and/or involuntary default by the borrower[17]. The default may, of course, be partial. Keynes refers to a further source of risk, the possibility of a rise in the general price level. He maintains that institutional and psychological factors determine a minimum rate of interest much above zero. He writes, 'In particular the costs of bringing borrowers and lenders together and uncertainty as to the future of the rate of interest . . . set a lower limit, which in present circumstances may perhaps be as high as 2 or 2½ per cent on long term.'[18]

Keynes argues that, if his estimate of the minimum rate of interest should prove correct, this situation 'may soon be realized in actual experience'[19]. He points out that 'The post-war experiences of Great Britain and the United States are, indeed, actual examples of how an accumulation of wealth, so large that its marginal efficiency has fallen more rapidly than the rate of interest can fall in the face of the prevailing institutional and psychological factors, can interfere, in conditions mainly of *laissez-faire*, with a reasonable level of employment and with the standard of life which the technical conditions of production are capable of furnishing.'[20] Here, Keynes is considering stagnation as actually existing, not just a possibility in the future. The rate of saving at a full-employment level of income would be too high to be compatible with stability and this level of income is not sustainable because of insufficient investment opportunities. He somewhat dramatically refers to the possibility that this evil day may be postponed if the wealthy build mighty mansions, pyramids and cathedrals. Keynes rightly states that where there is a tendency to stagnation, employment and output will be increased by the digging of holes in the ground, the work being paid for out of the savings of the higher level of income[21]. However, in many places, Keynes shows that a high level of income and employment may be maintained by the appropriate control of fruitful investment and consumption by means of fiscal and monetary policies.

Keynes took a very optimistic view of the possibility of eliminating the scarcity of capital, making capital goods so abundant that the marginal efficiency of capital, the expected rate of return on investment, was zero. On certain assumptions, he guesses that an advanced economy, the population of which was not increasing rapidly, could reach a quasi-stationary equilibrium with the marginal efficiency of capital approximately equal to zero within a single generation. It would be quasi-stationary because progress and change would continue because of changes in technique, tastes etc.[22]. Keynes states that he feels 'sure that the demand for capital is strictly limited in the sense that it would not be difficult to increase the stock of capital up to a point where its marginal efficiency had fallen to a very low figure'[23]. The return from the use of capital goods would then only have to cover the costs of replacement because of depreciation (wastage and obsolescence) and some payment for risk-bearing and the skill of the entrepreneur[24]. Keynes is thus able to look forward to the euthanasia of the rentier which would occur gradually and, he thinks, would be of social advantage[25]. The 'pure' rate of interest, the yield on longterm government bonds, would be above zero by only the cost of bringing borrower and lender together if it was generally believed that capital scarcity had finally been eliminated and there would be no rise in the rate of interest. Again, Keynes shows his optimism by referring to 'our aim of depriving capital of its scarcity-value within one or two generations'[26].

In Chapter 22, Notes on the Trade Cycle, Keynes states that the remedy for the trade cycle is not to abolish booms but to abolish slumps and keep the economy in a state of quasi-boom. Linked with his theory of stagnation was his theory of the weak boom. He writes,'Except during the war, I doubt if we have any experience of a boom so strong that it led to full employment.'[27] He also considers it very possible that the maintenance of approximately full employment in countries as wealthy as Great Britain or the United States would be associated with a rate of investment, given the existing propensity to consume, which would eventually lead to the elimination of capital scarcity in the sense that aggregate gross yield from capital investment would only cover about its replacement cost. Keynes's optimism is again shown by his thinking that this situation might be reached within twenty-five years or less[28]. In Chapter 18, The General Theory of Employment Re-Stated, Keynes puts the same view of stagnation and weak booms. He writes that our economic system 'seems capable of remaining in a chronic condition of sub-normal activity for a considerable period . . . . Moreover, the evidence indicates that full, or even approximately full, employment is of rare and short-lived occurrence.'[29] The upward fluctuations of output and employment are considered to be relatively weak.

Keynes did not regard stagnation as a problem in the nineteenth century and early in this century. He writes, 'During the nineteenth century, the growth of population and of invention, the opening-up of new lands, the state of confidence and the frequency of war . . . seem to have been sufficient, taken in conjunction with the propensity to consume, to establish a schedule of the marginal efficiency of capital which allowed a reasonably satisfactory average level of employment to be compatible with a rate of interest high enough to be psychologically acceptable to wealth-owners.'[30] Keynes refers to evidence for a period of almost one hundred and fifty years showing that rates of interest were low enough, given the investment opportunities, 'to encourage a rate of investment consistent with an average employment which was not intolerably low'[31]. Professor Alan Sweezy states that there is not a hint of the stagnation thesis in Keynes's *The Economic Consequences of the Peace* (1919)[32]. Rather, the danger is that we shall have too little saving[33]. In 'Economic Possibilities for our Grandchildren', Keynes sees mankind solving its economic problem by the increase of capital equipment and technical progress and that in about a hundred years the accumulation of wealth will no longer be of high social importance[34]. The optimism is here, but not the pessimism because of stagnation resulting from the economy not adapting appropriately to capital abundance. Sweezy points out that in Keynes's *A Treatise on Money* (1930) one gets a few glimpses of declining investment opportunity in relation to the rate of saving[35]. However, Sweezy quotes a letter by Keynes to *The New York Times*, June 1934, in which he considered the current economic situation in the United States and Roosevelt's New Deal programme. Here there is no suggestion of a problem of chronic stagnation[36]. It is in *The General Theory* that Keynes becomes seriously concerned with the problem.

Thus, Keynes writes in *The General Theory* that 'To-day and presumably for the future the schedule of the marginal efficiency of capital is, for a variety of reasons, much lower than it was in the nineteenth century. The acuteness and the peculiarity of our contemporary problem arises, therefore, out of the possibility that the average rate of interest which will allow a reasonable average level of employment is one so unacceptable to wealth-owners that it cannot be readily established merely by manipulating the quantity of money.'[37] Keynes is taking the tendency to chronic stagnation seriously and is a strong advocate for state intervention to raise the level of aggregate money demand to provide full employment. He proposes public investment as his practical judgement is that there are great social advantages to be obtained from eliminating the scarcity of capital. However, Keynes is ready to concede that the wisest course is to advance on both fronts, to have a socially controlled rate of interest to bring about a progressive decline in the marginal efficiency of capital and to pursue policies for increasing consumption out of a given level of income[38]. Later, Keynes makes clear that his case is for the socialization of investment while preserving a free-enterprise economy[39]. In his Galton Lecture, 'Some Economic Consequences of a Declining Population', given to the Eugenics Society in 1937, Keynes is much concerned with the problem of economic stagnation. Hitherto, Keynes maintains that the demand for new capital has come about equally from the demands of a growing population and the demands of inventions which increase output per head[40]. With a stationary population (and even more so with a declining population), Keynes argues that the maintenance of a high level of employment depends on policies which increase consumption (reduce the rate of saving) by a more equal distribution of incomes and force down the rate of interest to increase capital intensity, the ratio of capital to output[41]. If these conditions are not satisfied, Keynes forecasts a chronic tendency towards the under-employment of resources and the destruction of capitalist society. The concept of an optimum population has logical difficulties, but what has been said above is consistent with the fact that an economy's standard of living may be affected unfavourably by overpopulation or by its population increasing faster than its stock of capital. This point is particularly relevant for developing (underdeveloped) countries.

Keynes's views on stagnation are now considered from his *How to Pay for the War* (February 1940) until his death. In that book he developed his novel idea of compulsory saving in the form of pay deferred to contribute to the combating of inflation. A great advantage of the scheme was that it would allow for the release of the savings at the time of the first post-war slump[42]. There is no reference to chronic stagnation but the possibility of a slump was uppermost in his mind. However, Keynes emphasized the stagnation problem in writing of conditions in the United States in an article in the *New Republic* in July 1940. Dealing with its war potential, he wrote, 'At all recent times, investment expenditure has been on a scale which was hopelessly inadequate to the problem of maintaining full employment; and it is not unlikely that this would have remained true, except temporarily, even if the attendant political considerations had stimulated private-enterprise investment instead of retarding it.'[43] Professor Moggridge and Miss Susan Howson refer to the National Debt Enquiry Committee which met during the first half of 1945. Its early stages, dealing with monetary policy and debt management, were dominated by Keynes. One of his underlying assumptions for the post-war period was that 'After the transition, which might be lengthy, deflation rather than inflation would prove to be the more likely danger.'[44] Moggridge and Howson state that 'In general, Keynes was more optimistic than his colleagues as to when the problem of deflation would prove serious. In 1943 he suggested that the problem might not arise for 10 to 15 years after the war ("the long-term problem of full employment", 25 May 1943).' They point to the increase in his optimism since his concern in 1940 over the post-war slump to which I have referred. They also point to Keynes's optimism in 1946 about international economic conditions on which Great Britain's prosperity largely depended[45]. However, Moggridge and Howson also refer to Keynes's view that there was a general tendency towards deficient demand[46], which I have already discussed.

The modern stagnation thesis we owe to Keynes, but his basic model in *The General Theory* did not necessarily lead to this. The stagnation thesis was not a theory but a speculation of possibilities, of what the magnitudes of certain economic relationships might be. Keynes at times attached more or less importance to chronic stagnation. He clearly considered it a serious possibility. No doubt, if he had lived into the post-World War II period, he would have given it less importance and put it into a better perspective. It is still a question of debate whether Keynes's tendency to chronic stagnation existed during the inter-war period.

Robertson's attitude to Keynes's stagnation thesis varied over time. Writing to Keynes, 3 February 1935, commenting on a draft of *The General Theory*, Robertson referred to Keynes's change in the objective of his analysis from fluctuations around a norm to a chronic failure to reach a norm. He writes, 'I don't see much in pre-war history to persuade me of its then truth . . . . But I'm certainly not able to reject it *a priori* as an interpretation of the present and the probable future. I'm impressed by the evidence of slumpiness in the American boom, and by the difficulties created by certain modern changes not directly connected with the rate of interest, – the slackening of population growth, the ending of the era of geographical exploration, the tendency (cf. McKenna's speech) for big combines not to come to the banks for working capital. Coupled with the unwillingness of the banks to provide fixed capital.'[47] In a later letter to

Keynes, dated 10 February 1935, Robertson writes, 'I don't think I'm unsympathetic to what I feel to be the newest and practically the most important thing which you are saying, – viz. that in the post-war world there have been certain long-term depressive influences at work of a kind which most critics hitherto have regarded as purely slump-phenomena, explicable in terms of the events of a preceding boom. I don't think there is much reason for supposing this to have been true pre-war: and I think it is early to judge whether it is going to be true in the future, i.e. how far it is a strictly-post-war phase and how far a rich-20th-century phase. But I'm far from certain it isn't the latter.'[48] Thus, Robertson sounds a note of caution. In his paper of September 1936, 'The Snake and the Worm', Robertson refers to the conflicting views that trade-cyclical fluctuation is the most serious problem of private capitalism and that a chronic and endemic tendency towards stagnation is the great problem. The former he refers to as the snake and the latter as the worm. Robertson asks, 'Is he a real worm, or is he the figment of generous imaginations tortured by the tragedies of the worst and deepest slump of history?'[49] He goes on to say that he dare not swear that he is an unreal worm, but he offers one or two reasons 'why he might be thought to exist even if he does not'[50]. Again, Robertson sounds a note of caution.

Writing in 1947, Robertson points out that many able economists have been converted to the stagnation thesis as a result of reflecting on the events of the 1920s, the great depression of the early 1930s and the incomplete recovery which followed in the latter years of the decade[51]. The doctrine is stated in its usual form, that in the wealthy countries of the Western World the desire to save is chronically outrunning the opportunities for investment and secular depression, with occasional partial recoveries, is to be expected. Robertson draws our attention to the fact that such prophecies have been made before and not been fulfilled, 'Dame Nature or Dame History having always in the end turned out to be keeping another card up her sleeve, though she has sometimes been rather long in shaking it down'[52]. However, he tries to assess what the probabilities are of the wolf of stagnation appearing in the future. Robertson recognizes that it may not be possible to give a clear-cut answer, but suggests that England will not be faced with stagnation, at any rate for a good while ahead. On the other hand, he tells his North American readers that 'if there is a wolf, or as I have called him elsewhere a worm, on the look-out for a victim, you have a good many qualifications for the part'[53]. Robertson is now writing after the death of Keynes and during the period of full employment which followed World War II. Keynes might well have not differed from Robertson's view as stated here. However, referring to *The General Theory* in 1948, Robertson states that Keynes's 'embrace, on the strength of one bad depression, of 100 per cent "stagnationism" [was] at least premature'[54].

In both Parts II and III of his *Lectures* of 1956–1957, Robertson returns to the problem of chronic stagnation. In Chapter IV of Part II, Interest on Capital: Demand, Robertson repeats some of the causes already mentioned for a possible large decrease in the intensity and elasticity of demand for fixed capital and adds the growing demands for personal services involving little demand for equipment and the non-appearance during the 1930s of a real successor to the petrol engine as an invention requiring much capital[55]. Later, Robertson sketches the changes in the degree of capital scarcity from 1750 to 1930[56]. Chapter IV of Part III is devoted to The Stagnation Thesis. Robertson considers the case of the forces of productivity and thrift having created a situation in which the rate of interest has fallen to zero or to a level a little above zero. If in this situation the desire to save continued, Robertson agrees that there would be a progressive fall in money income which the monetary authority would find it very difficult to prevent. He considers later whether this situation would necessarily involve massive unemployment, but admits that it would be difficult. Robertson argues that the situation may not arise because of a strong inducement to decumulate capital which would occur and writes, 'I am inclined to say which did in the 1940s show strong signs of coming into force – at very low levels of interest, and which would inhibit any further fall'[57].

Robertson concludes this chapter by discussing how much there is in the stagnation thesis. He refers to the long post-war boom since 1945, but reminds us of some of the reasons given for long-run pessimism already mentioned, to which he adds the unresponsiveness of some kinds of investment to a decrease in the rate of interest. He also reminds us of three considerations on the other side. Firstly, it is not clear that populations with increasing incomes per head do tend to consume a diminishing proportion of their income. People in general adjust their spending habits to their higher incomes. Robertson quotes Professor Williams with regard to the United States: 'what the estimates seem to indicate is a constant long-run relation between income, investment and consumption since as far back as 1880'[58]. As income increases, however, the absolute amount of saving increases, which requires a higher absolute amount of investment, other things being equal, if stagnation is to be avoided. Secondly, Robertson points out that many kinds of capital outlay – docks, nuclear reactors and the like – are not closely geared to the demand for consumption goods, unlike machines, but depend on general estimates of the economic progress of whole regions. He states that these types of investment are admittedly sensitive to changes in the rate of interest. A fall in the rate of interest will cause capital deepening, an increase in the ratio of capital to output. Robertson's third consideration is that 'Nobody has ever yet succeeded in predicting just what is round the corner in the way of invention and technical change.'[59] He writes that the future course of 'the tussle between Invention and Fecundity on the one hand and Affluence and Thrift on the other is wrapped in mystery!'[60] Later, he refers again to the point that the proportion of income saved by a community does not appear to increase as income per head increases and suggests that this 'seems to remove one of the linch-pins from the stagnation thesis'[61]. Admittedly, Keynes did refer to a decline in the marginal propensity to consume, a decline in the proportion of income spent, in these circumstances[62]. However, the linch-pin is not removed because, as pointed out above, the absolute amount of saving increases. Keynes, the great exponent of stagnationism in this country, was not relying on a declining marginal propensity to consume as income per head increased. He wrote to Professor A. C. Pigou, 10 December 1938, 'You are quite right . . . . My assumption is that when incomes increase there is a larger absolute amount of saving. As regards larger proportions, I make no assumption and simply say that in certain conditions, the proportion may as a matter of fact be larger. You will find the most relevant passage on pages 96 and 97 (of *The General Theory*).'[63]

Finally, in his *Lectures*, Robertson, when referring to the problem of maintaining a high level of employment after an expansion, states that 'it may well be that Kalecki and other devotees of the "stagnation thesis" overestimate the need for artificial stimuli to the "propensity to consume" '[64]. Robertson's reasoning is that as far as expansion has involved repressing the propensity to consume through 'forced levies', "letting the propensity to consume have its head" might do much to stimulate employment in the consumption goods industries[65]. The concept of 'forced levies' or 'forced saving' plays an important role in Robertson's writings on the upswing of the trade cycle. It should be noted that Robertson was lecturing during the long period of post-war boom and at that time was concerned with the problem of 'over-employment' and inflationary pressure[66]. He did make many important proposals for dealing with trade-cyclical depression from 1915 onwards.

Wilson in his 1953 article says that part of the essential content of Keynes's thought is to be found in the theory of weak booms rather than in the theory of secular stagnation[67]. He does not accept the verdict of the American Professor, John H. Williams, published in 1948, that the theory of stagnation is 'the essential content' of Keynes's theory[68]. Wilson points out that Robertson wrote, 'I know of no shrewder appraisal of the "new economics"', when referring to Williams's article[69]. On the other hand, Wilson points out that 'The prophecy that mature, wealthy economies would suffer from stagnation has now been subjected to a great deal of criticism, and even Professor Hansen is no longer so robust a defender of the faith. This was Keynes at his most donnish and least scientific.'[70] It is the weak boom which Wilson emphasizes, referring to the weak booms of the inter-war period after 1920. Thus, he criticizes Robertson's view that by moderating the boom, 'the worst evils of trade depression could thereby be averted'.[71] However, this raises the complicated problem of the conflicting claims of progress and stability which occupied Robertson so much. He refers to Keynes's mild reproof in *The General Theory* (p. 327) for his having set his sights too low regarding a sustainable level of employment[72]. Keynes himself, however, was advocating in articles in *The Times* in January 1937 the reduction of postponable investment to restrain the 'boom' of 1937 when unemployment was 11 to 12 per cent, only a partial recovery having taken place from the deep depression of 1930 –1932. He argued against an increase in the longterm rate of interest because this would make it difficult to reduce the rate sufficiently to the level which would be required later. Keynes believed that we were approaching, or had reached, the point where there was not much advantage in stimulating aggregate demand. His reason was that a rightly distributed demand was now more needed. The problem was structural, for example the depressed areas, and not a deficiency of aggregate money demand. Keynes made the same proposals to the Committee on Economic Information and they were adopted in their Report of February 1937. Robertson objected to the Keynes proposals on monetary policy as he believed that interest rates should be increased to avoid inflation[73]. The main point I wish to make is that whether a boom is weak or strong, its nature must be carefully examined before the appropriate policies can be proposed.

The economic conditions in the United States in the 1930s provided a suitable climate for the development of the stagnation thesis. From 1922 to 1929 the country had been very prosperous. The Great Depression which began in 1929 was by far the worst in history. It began before the great crash on Wall Street when stock exchange prices collapsed in October 1929. During the early 1930s the depression deepened, national income declining drastically and unemployment rising to a very high level. Recovery did not begin until 1933 and before it was complete the United States experienced the depression of 1937–1938.

Professor Alvin H. Hansen of Harvard University became Keynes's leading disciple and interpreter in the United States and the great exponent of the stagnation thesis. His review of Keynes's *The General Theory* in October 1936 had not been enthusiastic[74], but he became one of the 'converts' and did much to popularize Keynesian views in the United States. In particular, he elaborated the stagnation thesis. In December 1938, Hansen gave his Presidential Address to The American Economic Association, entitled 'Economic Progress and Declining Population Growth'[75]. He described stagnation in his address: 'Not until the problem of full employment of our productive resources from the long-run, secular standpoint was upon us, were we compelled to give serious consideration to those factors and forces in our economy which tend to make business recoveries weak and anaemic and which tend to prolong and deepen the course of depressions. This is the essence of secular stagnation – sick recoveries which die in their infancy and depressions which feed on themselves and leave a hard and seemingly immovable core of unemployment.'[76]

Hansen makes use of Sir Ralph Hawtrey's distinction between capital deepening, an increase in the ratio of capital to output, and capital widening, an increase of capital in the same proportion as the increase in output[77]. Capital deepening occurs as a result of certain changes in technique, in the character of output as a whole and a reduction in the rate of interest, which is not regarded as being of much significance. Capital widening occurs when the capital-output ratio is maintained constant, capital increasing in the same proportion as the increase in population (the labour force) and/or the increase in productivity per head because of causes other than an increase in the capital-output ratio[78]. Hansen argues that the demand for capital is decreasing because of the declining rate of population growth and that the capital-output ratio tends to be constant as shown by his rough estimates[79]. He also points to the fact that the opening of new territory is almost complete. The increasing populations and the opening up of new territories in the developing countries are not regarded as providing an important outlet for investment because of the difficulties in the way of foreign investment[80]. Hansen concludes, 'Thus the outlets for new investment are rapidly narrowing down to those created by the progress of technology.'[81] He expresses some concern about 'the apparently growing importance of capital-saving inventions'[82], but concludes that an acceleration in the progress of science and technology is required. Hansen states that bold action must be taken to prevent the growing power of trade unions, the development of monopolistic competition, and so on, from restricting technological innovation. Nevertheless, he does not think sufficient investment outlets will be provided to ensure full employment[83]. The remainder of Hansen's address is devoted to the problem of dealing with the secular stagnation envisaged[84].

Winch points out that the stagnationists believed that continuous budgetary deficits would be needed and quotes Hansen's words, 'owing to deep-seated causes inherent in the essential character of a non-expanding economy, secular stagnation stalks across the stage, or at least shows its face'[85]. Winch states that Hansen's stagnation thesis was not only Keynesian but contained elements of non-Keynesian origin[86]. Winch's view is that it is doubtful if the limited evidence of the 1930s 'was sufficient to conclude that the incentives for private investment were permanently weakened [in the United States]'[87]. He refers to the work of the leading opponent of stagnationism, G. Terborgh, whose *The Bogey of Economic Maturity* was published in 1945[88]. Alan Sweezy examines the case for and against stagnationism in his 1947 contribution to *The New Economics* and concludes that the United States is likely to be confronted with the problem of secular lower rate of private investment. He takes a more optimistic view than Hansen in his American Economic Association address as to the ease with which the deficiency in private investment can be compensated. He points to the possibilities of reductions in the high level of taxation and large increases in socially valuable expenditure by the government[89]. Hansen did, however, raise serious problems for consideration[90]. The United States was prosperous during the post-war years although suffering from a number of recessions. The succeeding recoveries, however, were weaker so that the longterm trend of unemployment was rising. Winch points out that a number of basic questions were raised as to the state of the economy when another dip occurred in 1960 following the recovery from the 1957–1959 recession which was hardly complete[91]. In 1960 a large number of distinguished economists came to Washington to serve the new Kennedy Administration. A group under Samuelson was appointed to examine the current recession and propose remedies. Their report distinguished between 'the immediate recession and the more fundamental problem of underlying sluggishness in the economy'[92]. The report was Keynesian and we see here a return to the emphasis on stagnation. The Kennedy–Johnson economic recovery of 1961–1965 was a great success. As Winch mentions, twenty years after his death, Keynes's picture was on the cover of *Time* magazine and a few weeks later *Business Week* stated that the prestige of economists had been raised 'to an all-time high' by the economic expansion[93]. Since that time for various reasons economists have not been so acclaimed.

Robertson referred in his 1960 Marshall Lectures to Professor William Fellner's real horror of the destructive effect on our institutional system if the decline in the rate of profit on capital should go at all fast or far. He thinks we may want to consider 'whether Harry Johnson, in reviewing his book, was not justified is suspecting that "Fellner may have been led from a spurious problem to a spurious conclusion"'[94]. On the other hand,

Samuelson took a critical view of Johnson in 1963, referring to a remark he made in his Invited Lecture before the American Economic Association at the St. Louis convention in December 1960. Samuelson writes, 'His oral statement that nobody takes seriously any more the problem of stagnation or underconsumption was received with some lifting of eyebrows . . . (because) many economists shared with the public a concern over the apparent sluggishness of the American economy since the mid-fifties; and, of course, events in the last two years have accentuated the concern over sluggish labor markets and lagging growth.'[95] Samuelson refers to the decade 'when our problems of unemployment have seemingly become chronic'[96].

Harry Johnson in his 1961 article, 'The General Theory after Twenty-Five Years', raises the question whether mass unemployment is the typical situation of an advanced capitalist economy, which he regards as the theme and prevailing tone of *The General Theory*, and which was held to be the case by the stagnationists following Keynes. Johnson admits that a conclusive argument on this question is impossible because of a number of factors which contributed to a high level of employment in the post-war period. However, he believes 'that Keynes drastically overgeneralized a particularly bad depression which was made worse by errors of economic policy'[97]. Johnson tells us that stagnationists still exist, but they are concerned either with the underdeveloped countries or with the relatively slow rate of growth of capitalist economies. My references to Samuelson above show that this is not correct. Some economists do take seriously the stagnation thesis as described in this chapter. Again, in his 1970 article, Johnson refers critically to the general belief that deep depression would follow the end of the war, this belief being based on 'Keynesian analysis – elaborated by American Keynesians, and especially Alvin Hansen of Harvard, into a general theory of the tendency of capitalism to wallow in secular stagnation'[98]. It is true that the widely held belief proved to be unjustified, but Keynes himself, although much concerned with the longterm problem of stagnation, did not expect the problem of deflation to arise until after a lengthy post-war period.

Stagflation, a situation in which money incomes and prices rise while there is considerable unemployment, is a problem which has become serious in advanced capitalist or 'mixed' economies[99] in recent years. Indeed, it appeared in the United States in the late 1950s. Stagflation does not necessarily involve secular stagnation. It may refer to inflation continuing during a recession or depression in an economy without a tendency to such stagnation. The causes of the depression which began in 1973 in the advanced capitalist economies are being analysed by economists and different explanations are being put forward. The explanations are in the main compatible with the view that there is not at present a tendency to secular stagnation.

Whether advanced capitalist economies have experienced secular stagnation in the past and what is the likelihood that they will be faced with the problem in the future are questions that remain unanswered. We cannot say of the economist, with Omar, 'He knows about it all; he knows, he knows.'

Notes

1. Here full employment does not mean 100 per cent employment as there will be fractional unemployment in the form of seasonal and structural unemployment etc.
2. In Keynes's basic model S ≡ I, an identity. I have departed from this concept here.
3. Keynes, *C.W.*, Vol. VII (1936, 1973), p. 31.
4. *Ibid.*, pp. 30–31. Effective demand is the proceeds which entrepreneurs expect to receive from the sale of output at a given level of employment. *See ibid.*, pp. 25 and 55.
5. *Ibid.*, p. 204.
6. The point is made as simply as possible here. I give a more detailed discussion in my *Journal of Political Economy* article, J. C. Gilbert, 'The demand for money: the development of an economic concept' (1953), pp. 155 *et seq*.
7. Money throughout this discussion is measured in real terms; an increase in the nominal quantity of money with a constant price level is an increase in the real quantity of money.
8. Keynes, *C.W.*, Vol. VII (1936, 1973), p. 202.
9. Keynes did not himself use this term.
10. Keynes, *C.W.*, Vol. VII (1936, 1973), p. 207.
11. *Ibid.*, p. 207.
12. *See* Don Patinkin, *Money, Interest, and Prices* (2nd edn, 1965), p. 349, n.24 and A. A. Walters, *Money and Banking Selected Readings* (1973), Editorial, Introduction, p. 15.
13. Patinkin (1965), p. 354, n.29.
14. For an analysis of monetary policy during the period, *see* R. S. Sayers, *Modern Banking* (7th edn, 1967) Appendix 2, The Ultra-Cheap Money Operations of 1945–7, especially pp. 317–318.
15. Keynes, *C.W.*, Vol. VII (1936, 1973), p. 217.
16. *Ibid.*, p. 219.
17. *Ibid.*, p. 144.
18. *Ibid.*, pp. 218–219. A considerable margin would have to be added for lender's risk in the case of loans made in the private sector.
19. *Ibid.*, p. 219.
20. *Ibid.*, p. 219.
21. *Ibid.*, p. 220.
22. *Ibid.*, pp. 220–221.
23. *Ibid.*, p. 375.
24. *Ibid.*, p. 375. *See also* p. 221 where Keynes points out that there will be 'a positive yield to skilled investment in individual assets' but that a positive or negative yield on the aggregate of capital goods depends on the unwillingness or eagerness of entrepreneurs to undertake risks to obtain possible profits.
25. *Ibid.*, p. 376.
26. *Ibid.*, p. 377.
27. *Ibid.*, p. 322.
28. *Ibid.*, pp. 323–324.
29. *Ibid.*, pp. 249–250.
30. *Ibid.*, p. 307. The schedule of the marginal efficiency of capital gives the rates of investment per unit period of time at different rates of interest.
31. *Ibid.*, p. 308.
32. Keynes, *C.W.*, Vol. II (1919, 1971).
33. Alan Sweezy, Declining investment opportunity, in Seymour E. Harris, *The New Economics* (1948), p. 427.
34. Keynes, *C.W.*, Vol. IX, *Essays in Persuasion* (1972a), p. 329.
35. Keynes, *C.W.*, Vol. VI, p. 168, for example. Sweezy in Harris (1948), p. 428.
36. Sweezy in Harris (1948), pp. 428–429.
37. Keynes, *C.W.*, Vol. VII (1936, 1973), pp. 308–309.
38. *Ibid.*, p. 325.
39. *Ibid.*, p. 378.
40. Keynes, 'Some Economic Consequences of a Declining Population', *Eugenics Review* (April 1937), reprinted in *C.W.*, Vol. XIV (1973b), p. 130. Keynes had some rough estimates of the relevant statistics for 1860 and 1913 between which dates the British population increased by about 50 per cent. *See* p. 128.

41. *Ibid.*, p. 132. Keynes was not always so optimistic about the responsiveness of the rate of investment to a reduction in the rate of interest.

42. Keynes, *C.W.*, Vol. IX (1972a), especially pp. 391–408. Keynes's scheme appeared in the form of post-war credits, but the amounts raised were much less than Keynes had proposed.

43. J. M. Keynes, 'The United States and the Keynes Plan' (29 July 1940), quoted by Sweezy in Harris (1948), p. 430.

44. D. E. Moggridge and Susan Howson, 'Keynes on Monetary Policy, 1910–1946' (July 1974), p. 243.

45. *Ibid.*, p. 243, footnote 3. The reference is to Keynes's article, 'The Balance of Payments of the United States' (June 1946).

46. *Ibid.*, p. 245 and footnote 2.

47. Keynes, *C.W.*, Vol. XIII (1973a), p. 500. The reference to McKenna's speech is to his speech as chairman of the Midland Bank to shareholders, 24 January 1935.

48. *Ibid.*, p. 506.

49. Sir Dennis Robertson, *Essays in Money and Interest* (1966).

50. *Ibid.*, p. 92.

51. Robertson, *Money* (4th edn, 1947), p. 214.

52. *Ibid.*, p. 215.

53. *Ibid.*, p. 216.

54. In New Introduction to D. H. Robertson, *A Study of Industrial Fluctuation* (1948), p. xvi.

55. Sir Dennis Robertson, *Lectures on Economic Principles* (1963a), p. 222. *See also* pp. 229–230 for Robertson's analysis of the decrease in the demand for capital resulting from the process of capital accumulation which he explains, assuming no changes in population, and technical knowledge.

56. *Ibid.*, p. 249.

57. *Ibid.*, pp. 390–391. There would be positive and negative saving by individuals. The question is under what conditions net saving of an economy falls to zero – a very complicated one.

58. *Ibid.*, p. 391. Robertson refers to populations which are 'increasing in wealth per head' but the context justifies my substitution of 'increasing incomes per head'. The pioneering empirical work for the United States was done by Simon Kuznets who found a secular tendency for the proportion of income consumed to be constant. *See* Simon Kuznets, *National Product Since 1869* (1946).

59. *Ibid.*, p. 392.

60. *Ibid.*, p. 392.

61. *Ibid.*, p. 425. Robertson refers to the community growing rich but the context justifies my wording. Keynes, *C.W.*, Vol. VII (1936, 1973).

62. *See* p. 219 where the relevant quotation is given, *C.W.*, Vol. VII (1936, 1973), p. 31. Keynes is contrasting a poor and a wealthy community but is clearly thinking of income per head.

63. Keynes, *C.W.*, Vol. XIV (1973b), p. 272.

64. Robertson (1963a), p. 437. The reference is to M. Kalecki's contribution, Three Ways to Full Employment, to The Oxford University Institute of Statistics, *The Economics of Full Employment* (1945). Lord Beveridge was another stagnationist. *See* his *Full Employment in a Free Society* (1944).

65. Robertson (1963a), p. 437.

66. Page 438.

67. T. Wilson, 'Professor Robertson on Effective Demand and the Trade Cycle' (1953), p. 568.

68. *Ibid.*, p. 567. The reference is to J. H. Williams, 'An Appraisal of Keynesian Economics' (May 1948).

69. *Ibid.*, p. 567. The reference is to D. H. Robertson's 1951 'Some Notes on the Theory of Interest'. This is now reprinted in Robertson, *Essays in Money and Interest* (1966), p. 202.

70. *Ibid.*, pp. 467–468.

71. *Ibid.*, p. 468. The quotation is from Robertson, *Money* (4th edn, 1947), p. 214.

72. Robertson (1963a), pp. 437–439. Reference is also made to the associated problem of inflation.

73. This is a simple account of a complicated problem about which there has been controversy. *See* D. E. Moggridge and Susan Howson (1974), pp. 240–241; Professor

Hutchison's *Keynes versus the 'Keynesians' . . .?* (1977), pp. 10–14, A Comment by Professor Lord Kahn, pp. 48 *et seq.*, A Comment by Professor Sir Austin Robinson, pp. 58–60, Rejoinder by T. W. Hutchison, pp. 61–64, Appendix A, J. M. Keynes, 'How to Avoid a Slump' (articles in *The Times*, 12, 13, 14 January 1937), Appendix B, J. M. Keynes, 'Borrowing for Defence: Is it Inflation?' (article in *The Times*, 11 March 1937).

74. A. H. Hansen, 'Mr Keynes on Underemployment Equilibrium' (October 1936). For references to this review, *see* Harris (1948), pp. 35–36 and Donald Winch, *Economics and Policy* (1972), p. 389, n.73.

75. Printed in *American Economic Review* (March 1939); reprinted in The American Economic Association, *Readings in Business Cycle Theory* (1944).

76. American Economic Association (1944), p. 370.

77. *Ibid.*, p. 372. There are difficulties in measuring changes in capital and output. It should be noted that capital deepening is also used in the sense of increasing the ratio of capital to labour as productive resources.

78. *Ibid.*, p. 374. *See also* p. 372 regarding the rate of interest.

79. *Ibid.*, pp. 375–376.

80. *Ibid.*, pp. 377–378.

81. *Ibid.*, p. 378.

82. *Ibid.*, p. 378.

83. *Ibid.*, pp. 380–381.

84. Hansen developed and strongly supported the stagnation thesis in his books, *Full Recovery or Stagnation?* (1938), *Fiscal Policy and Business Cycles* (1941) and *Economic Policy and Full Employment* (1947).

85. Winch (1972), p. 260. The whole quotation given is from Hansen (1938), pp. 301–302.

86. *Ibid.*, pp. 260–261.

87. *Ibid.*, p. 262.

88. Beveridge, *Full Employment in a Free Society* (1944), p. 104, n.1 refers to earlier criticism of the stagnation thesis by Mr Richard Bissell in Seymour E. Harris, *Post-War Economic Problems* (1943) and Mr Harold G. Moulton in his *The New Philosophy of Public Debt* (1943).

89. In Harris (1948), pp. 434–435.

90. Hansen in American Economic Association (1944), pp. 381–384.

91. Winch (1972), pp. 312–313.

92. *Ibid.*, p. 315. Note 46 on p. 395 states that the report, entitled 'Economic Frontiers', was published in M. B. Schnapper, *New Frontiers of the Kennedy Administration* (1961).

93. *Ibid.*, p. 319. *See* note 53 on p. 395 for the dates; *Time*, 31 December 1965 and *Business Week*, 5 February 1966. *See also* James Tobin, *The New Economics One Decade Older* (1974).

94. Robertson, *Growth, Wages, Money* (1961). The reference is to William Fellner, *Trends and Cycles in Economic Activity* (1965). The quotation from Harry Johnson's review of this book is from *American Economic Review* (March 1957), p. 166.

95. Samuelson (1946) in Lekachman, *Keynes' General Theory Reports of Three Decades* (1964), p. 342.

96. *Ibid.*, p. 343.

97. Harry G. Johnson, *Money, Trade and Economic Growth* (2nd edn, 1964), p. 143. The article was first published in *American Economic Review* (May 1961) and reprinted here.

98. Harry G. Johnson, *Further Essays in Monetary Economies* (1972), p. 80. The article, 'Monetary theory and Monetary Policy', reprinted here was first published in *Euromoney* (December 1970).

99. The advanced capitalist economies now have relatively large public sectors.

Chapter 14

Monetary and fiscal policy

The problem of the relative importance of monetary and fiscal policies for the control of inflationary booms and depressions has long been debated. Monetary policy is pursued by changes in interest rates and changes in the availability of bank credit, the degree of credit rationing at a given rate of interest. Here I refer to the short-term interest rate, say the rate of interest charged for a bank loan, and the longterm interest rate, the yield on irredeemable government bonds such as Consols, to which interest rates for longterm borrowing for fixed capital investment are related by additions for risk and uncertainty. Hitherto I have referred to *the* rate of interest and the present distinction between the short-term and the longterm rates of interest is still a simplification. If we take rates of interest on British Government securities, there is a whole family of interest rates from the short-term Treasury Bill rate to the longterm rate on Consols, the rates varying according to the maturity dates. Short-term rates are normally below longterm rates[1]. In addition, there are interest rates on loans to business and industry which vary according to maturity dates and allowances for risk and uncertainty, partly related to the former. Thus, there is the very difficult problem of the factors which determine relative rates of interest, the structure of interest rates. Many theories have been formulated and the problem has not yet been completely resolved[2]. Fiscal policy is pursued by the government changing the amounts of taxation and/or expenditure for a given period which, as far as central government is concerned, involves changes in its budgetary surplus or deficit. I discuss Keynes's changing views on monetary and fiscal policy in some detail because there has been much misunderstanding and divergence of opinion among economists on this matter.

Moggridge and Susan Howson trace the evolution of Keynes's views on monetary policy and show that he attached importance to interest rate policy until the end of his life although, like Robertson and many other economists, he realized that it was ineffective in deep depression. It is misleading to think that Keynes discarded interest rate policy from say 1936, the year of *The General Theory*, and replaced it completely by fiscal policy. It is also incorrect to think of Keynes as not being concerned with inflation when it was a serious problem.

In February 1920, at the time of the post-World War I inflationary boom, Keynes had advised the Chancellor of the Exchequer to adopt dear money[3]. Moggridge and Howson quote from a letter by Keynes to Kahn, 12 January 1942, regarding Treasury discussions in 1920. 'Blackett, Hawtrey, Pigou and myself – all said practically the same thing, namely a very sharp and rapid shock of ultra-dear money in order to break the boom . . . . I doubt if I should have advised differently in my present state of mind in the same situation.'[4] What characterized this situation in particular was that all controls had been abandoned and that it was not possible to reintroduce them and to introduce additional controls which were required. He continues in his letter to Kahn that there are important lessons for the next time, the main one being 'that all controls – rationing, raw material control, new issue control, bank credit control and high taxation – must be retained in principle for at least two years and only gradually relaxed as and when consumption goods become available in greater quantities'[5]. In an article in *The Sunday Times*, 4 September 1921, 'Europe's economic outlook III – the depression in trade', Keynes explained his view that monetary policy should be directed at the cost of short-term credit. In times of inflationary boom, short-term interest rates should be raised which would damp down businessmen's price and profit expectations and traders would thus reduce their holdings of stocks of goods. In times of depression, short-term interest rates should be lowered which would encourage traders to increase their stocks and thus stimulate economic recovery[6].

Moggridge and Howson point out that 'This theory of monetary policy was of course the same as that which Hawtrey consistently held.'[7] In *Currency and Credit*, Sir Ralph Hawtrey gives a detailed analysis of the cause of trade-cyclical fluctuations in terms of fluctuations in short-term interest rates and changes in dealers' stocks associated with changes in orders to manufacturers, which led to producers increasing or decreasing output and employment. *Currency and Credit* was one of the main books on monetary theory which I had to read at The London School of Economics in the 1920s. Hicks tells us that Sir Austin Robinson assured him that it was the standard work on monetary theory used in the Cambridge Tripos during the twenties[8]. According to Hawtrey 'the trade cycle is a *purely* monetary phenomenon'[9]. However, I was not brought up to accept this extreme monetary point of view and I doubt whether Keynes ever held it. In Keynes's *A Tract on Monetary Reform* (1923)[10], the emphasis was on the use of monetary policy to stabilize the price level and so maintain a high level of output and employment. The instrument of monetary policy was Bank Rate[11] with which other short-term interest rates were closely associated. By changes in Bank Rate, businessmen's behaviour could be moulded 'by altering expectations of future price levels and the cost of financing production with a given level of price expectations'[12]. Moggridge and Howson point out that traders' stocks now played a much less important role than in his 1921 article and in Hawtrey's theory.

In *A Treatise on Money* (1930)[13] an important change was made. Here Keynes made changes in the longterm rate of interest, the main instrument of monetary policy, rather than changes in the short-term rate. His position now was that the demand for working capital was insensitive to changes in short-term interest rates but that the demand for fixed capital was responsive to changes in the longterm rate of interest. The monetary authorities could only control directly the short-term rate, but Keynes convinced himself that changes in short-term rates had a significant influence on the longterm rate[14]. Keynes criticized Hawtrey's view that dealers were sensitive to changes in Bank Rate when deciding the amount of stocks to hold. He argues that whether a dealer is paying 5 or 6 per cent for a bank loan has little influence 'compared with the current and prospective rate of off-take for the goods he deals in and his expectations as to their prospective price movements'[15]. In his third lecture, The Road to Recovery, of his 1931 series of three Harris Foundation lectures, An Economic Analysis of Unemployment, Keynes emphasized the importance of the longterm rate of interest. He admitted that when confidence is very low the rate of interest may play a comparatively small part and that it may be the case that the rate of interest is never the dominating factor influencing investment in manufacturing plants. However, he writes, 'But, after all, the main volume of investment always takes the forms of housing, of public utilities and of transportation. Within these spheres the rate of interest plays, I am convinced, a predominant part.'[16] Keynes refers to the extreme difficulty of reducing interest rates sufficiently and the time it will take. Nevertheless, he states that 'a sufficient change in the rate of interest must surely bring within the horizon all kinds of projects which are out of the question at the present rate of interest'[17]. He regards the achievement of an appropriately low rate of interest as 'the prime object of financial statemanship'[18]. Although the banking system only controls directly the short-term rate, Keynes sees no insuperable difficulty because of the normal relation between the short-term and longterm rates of interest. He suggests a number of devices for hastening the effect of a change in the short-term rate on the longterm rate[19]. Keynes had already advocated in A Treatise on Money, that in deep depression the central bank, say the Bank of England, should not only pursue its traditional open-market policy by buying short-term securities, increasing the cash reserves of the commercial banks and increasing the total quantity of money which would tend to lower longterm rates of interest as well as short-term rates, but should also buy longterm securities. He stated that 'It should not be beyond the power of a central bank (international complications apart) to bring down the longterm market rate of interest to any figure at which it is itself prepared to buy longterm securities.'[20] In the post-World War II period the Treasury has used the large resources of the 'Public Departments' to influence relative interest rates. These 'Departments' include the Post Office Savings Bank, the trustee savings banks and the social insurance funds. The National Debt Commissioners, who include the Chancellor of the Exchequer and the Governor of the Bank of England, can, for example, substitute holdings of longterm government securities for Treasury Bills, thus reducing the amount of the former held by the public. This will tend to lower the longterm rate of interest[21]. The government by funding or unfunding the National Debt, changing the relative amounts of longterm and short-term securities which constitute it, can influence relative interest rates. Keynes criticized the government in the 1930s for funding part of the

National Debt when he was advocating lower interest rates[22]. There is a minimum longterm rate of interest given existing institutional arrangements[23].

From late 1932 Keynes's emphasis on the role of monetary policy changed from that in *A Treatise on Money*. In *The Means to Prosperity* (1933)[24], monetary policy had a supporting role but loan-financed public works were required to start and to continue the recovery from a slump. A fall in short-term interest rates must be followed by a fall in longterm rates, but it is emphasized that private investment will not increase until after profits have risen and that a very large proportion of our normal loan-expenditure is undertaken by public and semi-public bodies[25].

There has been much discussion as to the relative importance attached by Keynes to monetary and fiscal policies in *The General Theory*. In the basic theoretical model, the rate of interest plays an important role. The inducement to invest depends upon the rate of interest and the marginal efficiency of capital. The rate of interest is much more important in his liquidity preface theory, his theory of the demand for money, than it had been hitherto. However, the emphasis to be placed on monetary and on fiscal policies depends on the forms of the functional relationships of his theoretical model. They include the elasticity of the rate of private investment with respect to changes in the rate of interest, the shifts which occur in the marginal efficiency of capital schedule[26], and the elasticity of the demand for money with respect to the rate of interest. In *The General Theory* full-employment equilibrium is a special case but it is admitted. In this case the private enterprise economy provides a rate of investment which is equal to the rate of saving at a full-employment level of income without inflation imposing saving on the community. In this special case, all that is required is an appropriate monetary (interest rate) policy. State intervention in the form of fiscal policies contributing to an increase or decrease in aggregate money demand is not required. An economy may be in a similar position as a result of the government's fiscal policy pursued for reasons other than the implementation of full-employment, such as redistribution of personal incomes through the budget and public investment on social grounds. A situation is then created in which a practicable interest rate is associated with a rate of private investment which is consistent with full-employment equilibrium. No fiscal policies are required as instruments of employment policy.

In *The General Theory*, Keynes emphasized that full employment was a special case and he analysed the factors which determined the levels of income and employment, showing that levels of under-employment equilibrium were included in his general theory. Indeed, the emphasis was on the fact that a private-enterprise economy could not be relied on to provide full employment without state interventions. The marginal efficiency of capital schedule could be too low, the demand for capital inelastic with respect to a fall in the rate of interest, and there was the possibility of a minimum rate of interest being reached. The mass unemployment could be due to cyclical depression or to a chronic deficiency of aggregate money demand. The latter case is the stagnation thesis examined in Chapter 13.

The General Theory of Employment Interest and Money is a theory of a monetary economy. Mistaken attempts have been made to 'demonetize'

Keynes's theory, but money and the money rate of interest are integral parts of his theory. In certain circumstances, monetary policy is ineffective but it was not Keynes who thought 'money doesn't matter'. Keynes has been accused of an inflationary bias, but as is shown, he was quick to apply his apparatus of thought to inflationary situations in the late 1930s and during World War II. In *The General Theory* (1936) itself, he was mainly concerned with depression and mass unemployment but he did refer to inflation in a number of passages. Keynes writes 'When full employment is reached, any attempt to increase investment still further will set up a tendency in money-prices to rise without limit, irrespective of the marginal propensity to consume, i.e. we shall have reached a state of true inflation.'[27] Again, he writes, 'When a further increase in the quantity of effective demand produces no further increase in output and entirely spends itself on an increase in the cost-unit fully proportionate to the increase in effective demand, we have reached a condition which might be appropriately designated as one of true inflation.'[28]

Keynes also states that during an economic recovery, the increase in output and employment will be associated with a rise in the general level of prices. Keynes's analysis is for the short-period during which capital equipment is given, and on this basis he shows that the supply of total output is not perfectly elastic. Increasing output will be associated with diminishing returns and rising prices even with constant money wages. He writes 'It is probable that the general level of prices will not rise very much as output increases, so long as there are available efficient unemployed resources of every type. But as soon as output has increased sufficiently to begin to reach the "bottle-necks", there is likely to be a sharp rise in the price of certain commodities.'[29] Given that recovery is occurring at constant money-wage rates, Keynes regards the rise of prices as 'merely a by-product of the increased output'. He adds, 'No one has a legitimate vested interest in being able to buy at prices which are only low because output is low.'[30] In addition, Keynes points out that prices will also tend to rise because money-wage rates tend to rise before full employment is reached. He refers to the upward pressure on money-wages exerted by groups of workers in these circumstances and to the importance of the psychology of the workers and the policies of employers and trade unions. Admittedly, Keynes refers to such increases in money-wages as semi-inflation[31]. It is difficult to understand why, for example, Fellner wrote in 1952 that Keynes 'showed no awareness of the fact that a consistent Full-Employment program of his variety would result in substantial inflationary pressure . . .'[32], and also why Dennison wrote in 1968 that 'the implications for policy of Keynes's system were unambiguously inflationary'[33]. Recovery involving a rising price-level would have been accepted by most economists at the time.

Admittedly, Keynes in *The General Theory* placed the emphasis on a high level of output and employment rather than a stable general level of prices, but he was writing during a period of depression. He certainly attached importance to a reasonably stable level of prices. I do not think that the charge against Keynes, that he had developed a system with an inflationary bias, is justified. The psychological and social distress of unemployment, in spite of the improved social security system during the post-World War II period, is so great that a very high priority is given to full employment on normative grounds quite apart from the lost output because of unemployment. The disagreements among economists relate to how far a full-employment policy should be pursued and by what policies, taking into account the inflationary pressure on the economic system, the extent to which economic progress (increasing real output per head and reduction in weekly hours worked) requires some slack in the system, and international balance of payments problems which have led to 'stop–go' policies. The 'stop' policies led to lower levels of employment and economic growth. There has been criticism that at times the United Kingdom has experienced over-full employment which was partly due to policies advocated by overzealous Keynesians. From what I have said above it is clear, I think, that Keynes was not an inflationist. If he had lived, he would no doubt have turned his trenchant mind to our post-war problems of the level of employment, the rate of inflation and the international balance of payments. The serious depression, which started in 1973 in the major advanced economies, led in the United Kingdom to much higher rates of unemployment than had previously occurred during the post-war period and also to exceptionally high rates of inflation. There has been disagreement among economists over the appropriate policies for dealing with the unemployment and inflation of this depression period.

The General Theory, like *The Means to Prosperity* (1933), included the longterm rate of interest as an influence on private investment and Keynes emphasized that its manipulation could not be relied on to stabilize the economy at full employment. However, he did attach importance to the level of the longterm rate of interest. Keynes writes that the longterm rate of interest exercised 'at any rate in normal circumstances, a great though not a decisive, influence on the rate of investment. Only experience, however, can show how far management of the rate of interest is capable of continuously stimulating the appropriate volume of investment.'[34] Keynes adds that he is now somewhat sceptical of the success of a merely monetary (rate of interest) policy and that he expects the State will take 'an ever greater responsibility for directly organising investment'. This is because it seems likely that fluctuations in the marginal efficiency of capital will be 'too great to be offset by any practicable changes in the rate of interest'[35]. However, Keynes is clearly attaching importance to interest rates when he writes, 'Perhaps a complex offer by the central bank to buy and sell at stated prices gilt-edged bonds of all maturities, in place of the single bank rate for short-term bills, is the most important practical improvement which can be made in the technique of monetary management.'[36] Keynes in Chapter 22, Notes on the Trade Cycle, states that the depression which follows the boom is the result of a collapse in the marginal efficiency of capital, the expected rate of return on investment in capital goods. This collapse in the marginal efficiency of capital may be so great that for the moment no practicable reduction in the rate of interest will bring about recovery by itself. Keynes adds, however, that later on the 'decline in the rate of interest will be a great aid to recovery and, probably, a necessary condition of it'[37]. He analyses the causes of the lapse of time before recovery begins and concludes that 'the current volume of investment cannot safely be left in private hands'[38]. Thus, although interest-rate policy is considered to be important it does not suffice. Government fiscal policy is required in the form of public investment expenditure which must be increased during depression to offset the fall in private investment. This is the case for loan-financed public works. In Chapter 24, Concluding Notes, Keynes refers to the scale of investment being promoted by a low rate of interest but advises that we should 'not attempt to stimulate it in this way beyond the point which corresponds to full employment'[39]. Here, he is not thinking of the stagnation thesis which is discussed in Chapter 13.

In January 1937 Keynes was concerned with the boom in the United Kingdom although unemployment was still high. The second of his three articles in *The Times* under the general heading of 'How to Avoid a Slump' was entitled '"Dear" Money'. He maintained that we must avoid dear money 'as we would hell-fire'[40]. He recognized that aggregate investment might rise too much and that it would have to be restrained by going slow with postponable investment, but he argued that this must not be achieved by a higher rate of interest. His argument was that if we allowed the rate of interest to rise we could not easily reverse the movement. Thus, he writes, 'The long-term rate of interest must be kept *continuously* as near as possible to what we believe to be the long-term optimum. It is not suitable to be used as a short-period weapon.'[41] Keynes thought that the phase of the recovery might be at hand when aggregate demand should be damped down. The methods which he considered were increased taxation, the postponement of new capital expenditure by local authorities where possible and the encouragement of imports by a temporary rebate on tariffs'[42].

Further evidence of Keynes's view on the longterm rate of interest is given in a letter he wrote, 6 June 1941, to an American economist, M. Ezekiel. Keynes wrote, 'I am far from fully convinced by the recent thesis that interest rates play a small part in determining the volume of investment. It may be that other influences, such as an increase in demand, often dominate in starting a movement. But I am quite unconvinced that low interest rates cannot play an enormous part in *sustaining* investment at a given figure, and, when there is a movement from a higher rate to a lower rate, in allowing a greater scale of investment to proceed over a very much longer period than would otherwise be possible.'[43] He added that he would like to do further work on the problem. He no doubt had at least partly in mind the investigations of the Oxford Economists' Research Group in the late 1930s which took the form of a questionnaire to a sample of businessmen. It appeared to show that neither changes in short-term nor longterm interest rates had much effect on their investment decisions. The results of the investigations were presented in 1938 with care and the limitations of the inquiry explained[44]. Certain criticisms have been made of this particular research and much econometric work has been done since.

A National Debt Enquiry Committee, of which Keynes was a member, met during the first half of 1945. He warned that after the war the Treasury should not fund the debt which would raise longterm interest rates. If, however, after a post-war transitional period, 'the prevailing long-term rate became *chronically* too low in the sense that it encouraged new capital formation on an inflationary scale, Keynes advocated a rise in long-term rates'[45]. It is interesting to note that Keynes recognized that the monetary authorities could use changes in short-term rates of interest and in the volume of accommodation in support of short-term management during the transition[46]. Wilson writing in 1953 does not think that Keynes would have approved of the easy money policy over the past few years of strong inflationary pressure and quotes Professor John H. Williams, 'Keynes changed his mind, and almost the last time I saw him was complaining that the easy money policy had been greatly overdone and interest rates were too low both in England and here.'[47]

As we have seen, Keynes continued to attach importance to monetary (interest rate) policy throughout his life, but it is his advocacy of fiscal policy that has received the greater attention. Winch states that in *A Treatise on Money* (1930) Keynes 'even went as far as to claim that investment could be influenced "to any required extent" by the appropriate monetary policy'[48]. However, Keynes, with the case of the United Kingdom very much in mind, refers to a country on an international gold standard which cannot lower the rate of interest without stimulating foreign lending, which causes a strain on the foreign exchange rates and a loss of gold which it cannot afford. In these circumstances, the Government must subsidize certain types of domestic investment or itself undertake domestic schemes of public investment[49]. Moggridge and Howson refer to this as the *Treatise*'s special case because of the international constraint on lowering the rate of interest. They point out that it was the basis for Keynes's British policy advice in 1930 and in 1931 until the United Kingdom left the gold standard in the September[50]. Keynes had put forward the same view before 1930. He was associated with the Liberal Yellow Book, *Britain's Industrial Future* (1928), in which public investment to combat unemployment was proposed, and had written, with Hubert Henderson, the famous pamphlet, *Can Lloyd George Do It?* (1929)[51]. This was in support of Lloyd George's general election pledge to reduce unemployment by public spending, particularly on roads and railways. The 'Treasury view', referred to in Chapter 3, the argument that public works will merely divert employment from other uses, is wrong in a situation of general unemployment. Keynes examines the sources of the savings to finance the additional public investment and it is shown that savings will not be diverted from financing other capital equipment[52]. It is pointed out that the problem has been debated by economists in recent years and the result shows 'the conclusion of this chapter [IX] as sound and orthodox and the Treasury's dogma as fallacious'[53].

Moggridge and Howson point out that from late 1932 Keynes no longer relied on the special case of *A Treatise on Money* for the advocacy of loan-financed public works to increase employment and output in a depression[54]. In the initial stages of recovery monetary policy only played a supporting role. Actually, before we left the gold standard in September 1931, Keynes had stated in a Harris Foundation lecture in Chicago in June 1931, that he had been a strong advocate of measures of public investment in Great Britain and 'I believe that they can play an extremely valuable part in breaking the vicious circle everywhere.'[55] Keynes developed this view of the great importance of countercyclical public works in *The Means to Prosperity* (1933)[56] and in *The General Theory* (1936). In the latter book, public investment was also an important remedy for stagnation if it occurred[57].

Although the limitations on the effectiveness of monetary policy of changes in the longterm rate of interest are recognized in *The General Theory*, they play an important role, but not so dominant a role as in *A Treatise on Money*. There has been an important move towards the necessity for fiscal policies. This appears mainly in the context of Keynes's speculation as to the possibilities of economic stagnation. There is not a great deal about fiscal policies as remedies for cyclical depression, presumably because his treatment of the trade cycle was limited to one chapter, the emphasis being on the comparative static analysis of the determination of the level of employment and output. It is in his policy writings that we find his advocacy of countercyclical fiscal policies. However, there are a number of important passages in *The General Theory*. Keynes stresses that the increase in loan-financed public investment, say public works, will not be the net increment of investment if monetary policy does not prevent a rise in the rate of interest which will cause a reduction in private investment[58]. The fashionable phrase in recent years is that 'crowding out' will occur. Thus, in association with the public works policy the central bank must increase the quantity of money to prevent a rise in the rate of interest. In a deep depression, the central bank may not need to take much action as the velocity of circulation of money may be abnormally low and it will rise with the increase in public works and general level of economic activity. The effect on total income and employment will depend on the investment and employment multipliers. The issue of government securities which increases the budgetary deficit or, more generally, the public sector borrowing requirement[59], may be associated with an increase in the velocity of circulation of money and/or an increase in the quantity of money. Further, fiscal policy can be used to increase consumption if it is used to bring about a more equal distribution of incomes. Keynes also points out that we must take account of the effect on consumption of government sinking funds for the repayment of the national debt out of taxation. These funds represent government saving and reduce consumption. Keynes writes that 'It is for this reason that a change-over from a policy of government borrowing to the opposite policy of providing sinking-funds (or vice versa) is capable of causing a severe contraction (or marked expansion) of effective demand.'[60] Reducing taxation at the expense of the sinking fund is a very limited form of stimulating expenditure by reducing taxes[61]. During the post-World War II period, demand management by means of fiscal policy has mainly been in the form of changes in taxation and not in public expenditure which would have caused great difficulties.

In *The General Theory* Keynes states that he expects the State will take 'an ever greater responsibility for directly organising investment; since it seems likely that the fluctuations in the market estimation of the marginal efficiency of different types of capital . . . will be too great to be offset by any practicable changes in the rate of interest'[62]. Keynes believed that the trade cycle was characterized by fluctuations in the marginal efficiency of capital and this is a clear statement of the necessity for a countercyclical public investment programme. In Chapter 22, Notes on the Trade Cycle,

Keynes states that the essence of the change from boom to slump is 'the collapse in the marginal efficiency of capital, particularly in the case of those types of capital which have contributed most to the previous phase of heavy new investment'[63]. This is the temporary-exhaustion-of-investment-opportunities explanation of the cyclical downturn. In view of the wide fluctuation in the marginal efficiency of capital, depression unemployment cannot be combated by interest-rate policy and Keynes concludes that 'the duty of ordering the current volume of investment cannot safely be left in private hands'[64].

Keynes in his policy writings after 1936 continued to be a strong advocate of fiscal policies. I have already referred to his three articles in *The Times* in January 1937 when he considered it might be necessary to damp down aggregate demand. The policies proposed were increased taxation, the postponement of new capital expenditure by local authorities, and the encouragement of imports. At the same time, Keynes proposes the reversal of these policies with the onset of depression. He points out that the Government should incur debt during the slump, decrease taxes, urge local authorities to increase capital expenditure (having their plans ready) and check imports. Indeed, in his third article, Keynes states that 'our main preoccupation should be concerned not so much with avoiding the perils of a somewhat hypothetical boom as with advance precautions against that sagging away of activity which, if it is allowed to cumulate after the usual fashion, will once again develop into a slump'[65].

Keynes put the same views on fiscal and monetary policy to the Committee on Economic Information (of which he was a member) which adopted them in its report of February 1937. The Treasury accepted the report[66]. At long last, Keynes had won over the Treasury to appropriate fiscal countercyclical policies including public works. Keynes continued to be concerned during 1937 with the necessary preparations for avoiding a slump. In a letter to *The Times* of 28 December 1937 he advocated the preparation of public works schemes to be held in readiness[67]. Hutchison also quotes from a letter of 3 January 1938 in which Keynes stated, 'The weight of authority and of public opinion in favour of meeting a recession in employment by organised loan expenditure is now so great that this policy is practically certain to be adopted when the time comes.'[68] However, rearmament expenditure continued and then war came.

In general, Keynes and Robertson were in agreement on monetary and fiscal policies although there were certain differences in view and in judgement. Robertson thought that Keynesian theory was inflationary. In his 1948 New Introduction to *A Study of Industrial Fluctuation*, Robertson refers with disapproval to the general public's belief that in the mid-1930s a revolutionary discovery was made about 'effective demand'. Further he writes, 'And the highly inflationary twist then given to that schematic statement of the whole problem which has won the widest measure of attention from the world seems to me to have had an unfortunate effect on policy in England and the United States, since the end of the war.'[69] Earlier, in 1937, Robertson had objected to the paragraphs in the February report of the Committee on Economic Information because 'he believed that avoiding dear money would add fuel to the inflation and that Keynes's whole argument . . . [was] unduly influenced by peculiarities in the situation of 1929–32'[70]. Actually, the inflationary boom did not develop and we do not know how successful the fiscal restraints alone would have proved. Hicks in his 1966 Memoir writes, 'That the Keynesian system did have some restraints (its own canons of budgetary policy, for instance, . . .) he [Robertson] was reluctant to acknowledge. It would lead (as indeed it has led) to inflation – to "Boost and Bolster" – to deliberate departure from his own ideal of ordered progress and monetary stability.'[71] The following points should be noted. Firstly Keynes did not dispense with interest-rate policy altogether. In 1945 he envisaged the possibility that the longterm rate of interest might have to be increased some time after the war to prevent inflation. Secondly, as discussed in this chapter, Keynes was well aware of the dangers of inflation and paid some attention to the problem in *The General Theory* written during depression, although this has not always been recognized. We may add his statement in the House of Lords in May 1944 that 'We intend to prevent inflation at home.'[72] Thirdly, during the post-war years of inflationary pressure about which Robertson showed continuous concern some 'Keynesian' economists and others may have been too enthusiastic in advocating full-employment policies *à l'outrance*. However, Keynes, in developing his basic model in the way he did and in his advocacy of policies to maintain a high level of employment, cannot be held responsible for this.

Robertson supported public works as a remedy for depression in 1915 and refers in 1948 to thinking that he then may have made 'the first formal attack on what long afterwards came to be known as the "Treasury view" of the inefficiency of policies of "public works"'[73]. Over a long period Robertson and Keynes were strong advocates of this policy. Wilson shows how advanced Robertson was in 1915 with regard to other aspects of the responsibility of government for the control of investment[74]. The attack on the Treasury view was in a sense a combined attack by Robertson and Keynes[75]. In 1953 Wilson, writing in retrospect, states that 'In the end it was his [Keynes's] rhetoric and his new mystique which carried the day, although Professor Robertson's earlier attacks contributed in no small measure to his success.'[76] Keynes's emphasis on the point that there will be an increase in saving to match the increase in investment, starting from general unemployment, was of vital importance. In his last publication, written in 1962, Robertson again puts the case for fiscal policy as a remedy for depression. He does not think that we can rely solely on the 'built-in stabilizers' of modern fiscal systems such as the payment of unemployment relief and the effect of a progressive income tax. Positive government action may well be needed and Robertson puts the emphasis on public works rather than reduced taxation. Like Professor John Kenneth Galbraith, he believes that the United States is short of social capital[77]. The same applies to the United Kingdom.

Robertson is his book, *Money*, argues that a trade-cyclical boom may require restraint which involves central bank action to reduce the cash reserves of the commercial banks which determine the level of their deposits and to raise Bank rate. The commercial banks will reduce or restrain the growth of loans and deposits by raising interest rates, qualitative control, and rationing[78]. In the case of depression, the monetary weapons are less efficient. There is no counterpart to the method of bank-loan rationing apart from its reduction and the reduction in interest rates may have little stimulating effect on investment and economic activity. Under existing institutional arrangements, the banks cannot lend at zero or negative money rates of interest[79]. The case for government intervention with a policy of public investment, public works, clearly follows[80]. Robertson took up the same general position regarding monetary and fiscal policies in 1962[81]. Thus there was very little difference between Keynes and Robertson on monetary and fiscal policies[82].

During the post-World War II period, Robertson thought that the reaction against monetary policy as a means of combating inflation had gone too far[83]. He no doubt thought he was dealing with Keynes's 'inflationary twist' but Keynes might well have taken the same line as Robertson. His criticism was really directed toward certain 'Keynesian' economists and others who were concerned to maintain the very high levels of employment in spite of the continuing inflation. As Samuel Brittan has pointed out, 'During the period there was a strong relationship between unemployment and political popularity.'[84] Robertson was writing during a period of inflationary pressure and what he regarded as over-full employment[85]. What appropriate level of employment is to be taken as the objective involves difficult economic problems and value judgements.

In a lecture given in December 1948, Robertson said that he had 'a hunch that the reaction among the neo-Keynesians against the importance of the causal influence of the rate of interest on capital outlay has been carried too far'[86]. At the same time, in the immediate post-war years we had a very low interest-rate policy of which Robertson disapproved[87]. He gives reasons for this, including the danger of wage inflation. He pointed out that if the monetary authorities are prepared to create 'whatever *flow of money* is needed to discharge whatever wage-bill is needed to reconcile full employment with whatever *wage-rate* is demanded by the Trade Unions, they have in effect abdicated from exercising that sovereignty over the standard of value which we thought we had committed to their charge'[88]. Robertson said that some of the enthusiasts for hyper-employment had looked for a substitute for the old policeman and found Police-Constable Public Finance. He had recognized his importance in 1915 and had no doubt that the scope for his employment was far greater now. However, Robertson thinks he needs saving from those who 'belittle the importance of an indefinite growth in the public debt'[89] and that we must not put too much on his broad shoulders. Firstly, it is difficult to replace budgetary deficits with budgetary surpluses when necessary[90]. Secondly there are lags in both the introduction and working of fiscal measures. Thirdly, if fiscal policy is made administratively more flexible, it remains to be seen how well the tax system survives frequent and swift changes 'which might be needed to make fiscal policy function successfully as the sole regulator of economic activity'[91]. Fourthly, Robertson argues that it is much better to control the increase of money than retrieve it by increased direct taxes which affect incentives and indirect taxes which will give another twist to the vicious spiral of rising money incomes. It is interesting to note that Keynes also believed that high taxation could be an indirect cause of inflation[92].

Returning to Robertson's concern over the growth of the national debt as a result of budget deficit financing as a remedy for cyclical depression or stagnation[93], it should be pointed out that it is the taxation required to pay the interest on it which is regarded as the problem. The payments on internal national debt are transfer payments and the taxation must be considered in terms of its effects on the incentives to effort, enterprise and risk-bearing. Under Keynes's influence it was often assumed that the debt would be financed at very low rates of interest, but this may not be the case. It has been pointed out that the burden of the transfer will depend on the size and growth of the debt in relation to the size and growth of the national income[94]. It must be remembered that the real national income will be higher as a result of the adoption of successful budgetary deficit employment policies. There are circumstances in which one could share Robertson's concern. Nevertheless, it may not be possible to use budgetary surpluses at times to reduce the national debt for a reason other than the one he gives in his reference to Cripps. The aim of employment policies includes the avoidance of a tendency to inflation requiring offsetting budgetary surpluses.

In his *Lectures* of 1956–1957, Robertson puts forward views of monetary and fiscal policies in the case of depression similar to those we have already considered[95]. When advocating public works, he refers to the difficulties of timing and making the public demand for labour an adequate substitute for the decrease in private demand – the problem of the mobility of labour[96]. Robertson is now more hopeful of government borrowing to finance consumption by means of tax reductions, gifts and subsidies[97]. While he regards public finance as perhaps the main instrument of anti-cyclical policy, he thinks monetary policy must play a role. Robertson agrees with the Douglas Sub-Committee that the shortcomings of fiscal policy 'make "an appropriate, vigorous and flexible *monetary* policy" a most desirable adjunct'[98]. In 1957, his immediate concern was not with depression but the tendency to *over*-employment. He recognizes that politically and psychologically this is a very difficult problem. Economically, it is essentially the same old problem – 'how much slack does a modern economy require in order to avoid ossification of its industrial structure and a progressive undermining of its standard of value?'[99]

Robertson in his 1960 Marshall Lectures wishes to see an active monetary policy and expresses disagreement with the Radcliffe Committee Report which gave it only a subordinate role[100]. He approves of the rise in short- and longterm interest rates since 1957, emphasizes the importance of exorcising the spectre of inflation and the appropriate control of the money supply[101]. Robertson criticizes the Report for going too far in reaching its unfavourable verdict regarding 'the short-term efficiency or otherwise of the direct influence *on borrowers* of the traditional instruments of monetary policy'[102].

In his *Memorandum*, written in 1962, Robertson states that he is 'still persuaded that "credit squeezes" can be made to bite over a sufficient range to be very effective, though they may take rather longer to operate and may require to be furnished with more varied teeth than used to be supposed, and though they may have differential effects which are not wholly welcome'[103]. He recognizes that a Monetary Authority may be faced as a result of trade union and other pressures with cost–push inflation, which may be spontaneous, derived from demand–pull, or mixed. In this case there is a conflict between the fullest possible immediate employment and the smallest possible divergence from monetary stability[104]. In these circumstances, Robertson who confesses never to have been an enthusiast for a national incomes policy, states that he does not regard it as fundamentally unsound provided the policy is a supplement and not a substitute for monetary and fiscal policies. He now goes so far as to write, 'during the past year I have felt it to be the duty of responsible persons in Britain to hope and work for its success'[105].

Finally, reductions in money and/or real wages must be considered as an alternative or addition to monetary and fiscal policies for increasing the level of employment. The cutting of money wages is not a practical policy for trade-cyclical depression. Most economists in Great Britain, including Robertson and Pigou, did not advocate this policy in the 1930s. The assumption of general money-wage cuts or perfect flexibility of money-wage rates was made in the 1920s and 1930s in highly abstract analysis by Pigou and others, quite legitimately[106]. Since Keynes's *General Theory* of 1936, there has been a good deal of analysis of the effects of general money-wage reductions on employment in a fluctuating economy on various assumptions. It would be very useful to have a comprehensive survey of the problem taking comparative static and dynamic models and making various assumptions including those of certainty and uncertainty. In the latter case, different assumptions relating to expectations would be considered.

In *The General Theory* Keynes criticized the 'classical' school for slipping in an illicit assumption when it was assumed that the money-wage bargain determined the real wage. He writes, 'There may exist no expedient by which labour as a whole can reduce its *real* wage to a given figure by making revised *money* bargains with the entrepreneurs. This will be our contention.'[107] It is substantiated by an analysis which shows, on certain assumptions, that the prices of wage-goods[108] fall proportionately with the fall in money wages leaving real wages unchanged. Keynes is making here the important point that money wages are not only a cost of production but also a constituent of aggregate money demand, money income. In Chapter 19, Keynes considers other possibilities and admits that 'A reduction in money-wages is quite capable in certain circumstances of affording a stimulus to output, as the classical theory supposes.'[109] However, Keynes rejects the 'classical' analysis of a direct effect, increasing employment, because it assumes that aggregate demand is not reduced in full proportion to the reduction in money-wages[110]. In Keynes's model, money-wage reductions can only increase employment by their effects on the community's propensity to consume, the marginal efficiency of capital, and the rate of interest. Keynes shows that employment could increase because of an increase in exports, an increase in investment and consumption if money-wages are expected to rise in the future, an increase in investment owing to the fall in the rate of interest (which depends on the real supply of and demand for money – the former being increased by the fall in prices), and an increase in entrepreneurs' optimism. Two other possible repercussions are the effect on consumption of the redistribution of income (people whose money incomes are fixed have increased real incomes with the fall in prices) and the depressing effect on entrepreneurs of the increased real value of their debt (possibly increasing bankruptcies) to which must be added the increased real burden of the national debt and, hence, of taxation. The former is regarded as likely to be unfavourable while the latter is of course unfavourable.

Assuming a closed system[111], Keynes is left with only two possible causes of an increase in employment: an increased marginal efficiency of capital and a fall in the rate of interest. He finds little hope in the former, while the latter is obtained more easily by increasing the nominal quantity of money with money-wages constant and the lower rate of interest may give little stimulus. Keynes concludes that the general level of money-wages should be maintained stable in the short-period[112].

Robertson in his *Lectures* of 1956–1957 continued to maintain that money-wage reductions could directly increase employment. Taking a dynamic view, he approves of Professor Viner's lag point and the restoration of profit margins[113]. Robertson writes, 'The lag, so Viner argues, between the wage reduction and any consequent decline in sales will suffice to give entrepreneurs the *inducement* to set in hand all sorts of postponable expenditure on equipment, etc., which they have perforce been postponing during depression, and will also increase their *power* of acting in this way by improving their credit status.'[114] Robertson admits that once plans and expectations are introduced, anything may happen. He distinguishes between a fairly large cut in money wages and a series of expected cuts, the latter being unfavourable to investment. He refers to Haberler's proposal that wage reductions could be combined with an expansionary policy such as public works[115]. Robertson also points to Pigou's historical evidence which contrasts the average unemployment in the sixty years before 1914 with the much greater unemployment and the greater rigidity of wages in the inter-war period[116]. He concludes that it is one thing to say that money-wage reductions in depression are politically impossible but 'it is quite another thing to claim that by this change the economic system has gained in stability or recuperative power'[117]. Much analytical skill has been devoted by economists to this problem[118]. Robertson's discussion is useful but not exhaustive.

Keynes stated in *The General Theory* that 'with a given organisation, equipment and technique, real wages and the volume of output (and hence of employment) are uniquely correlated, so that, in general, an increase in employment can only occur to the accompaniment of a decline in the rate of real wages'[119]. Keynes acknowledges his agreement with the 'classical' economists on this point. It is clear that Keynes's analysis relates to the short period and it should be noted that he obtains his fall in real wages by a rise in the price level of wage-goods while money-wage rates remain constant or rise less than proportionately. Professor Viner in his 1936 review stated that this conclusion resulted from too unqualified an application of the law of diminishing returns and needed to be modified for cyclical unemployment and other possibilities. He showed that during the recovery both employment and real wages could increase[120]. Keynes had made his point in different terms when he stated that 'When money-wages are rising . . . it will be found that real wages are falling'[121]. In 1939 in an article, 'Relative Movements of Real Wages and Output'[122], Keynes discusses J. G. Dunlop's investigation into the British statistics which appear to show that money and real wages have usually risen together and L. Tarshis's similar results for recent years in the United States[123]. Keynes concludes his article by stating that further statistical enquiry is necessary and urging us not to be too hasty in revising our short-period theory[124]. Whatever the final outcome of this debate, it is important to remember that if in the private sector the real-wage rates of labour groups are fixed by trade unions above the economic value of the labour employed or seeking employment, unemployment will result[125].

Notes

1. *The Bank of England Quarterly Bulletin* gives yield curves for British Government securities which relate yields (rates of interest) to maturity dates of the securities at given dates.
2. *See* J. C. Dodds and J. L. Ford, *Expectations, Uncertainty and the Term Structure of Interest Rates* (1974), for a survey of existing theories and of the empirical work which has been done, including their own at Sheffield University. *See also* Harry G. Johnson, *Macroeconomics and Monetary Theory* (1971), Chapter 1.
3. D. E. Moggridge and Susan Howson, *Keynes on Monetary Policy, 1910–1946* (1974), p. 230.
4. *Ibid.*, p. 231.
5. *Ibid.*, p. 231.
6. *Ibid.*, p. 232.
7. *Ibid.*, p. 232. They refer to the main books in which he expounded his theory: R. G. Hawtrey, *Good and Bad Trade* (1913), *Currency and Credit* (1919, 1st edn, and later editions) and *A Century of Bank Rate* (1938 and later editions).
8. John Hicks, *Economic Perspectives* (1977), p. 118 and n.3.
9. R. G. Hawtrey, 'The Genoa Resolutions on Currency' (September 1922), p. 298.
10. Keynes, *C.W.*, Vol. IV (1923, 1971).
11. Bank Rate was the rate of interest at which the Bank of England would discount (buy) Treasury Bills. It was replaced by the Bank of England's Minimum Lending Rate in October 1972. The Minimum Lending Rate was abolished on 20 August 1981, except in certain circumstances. The Bank of England, however, continues to pursue an interest rate policy by using an undisclosed band of interest rates.
12. Moggridge and Howson (1974), p. 232.
13. Keynes, *C.W.*, Vols V and VI (1930, 1971).
14. Keynes, *C.W.*, Vol. VI (1930, 1971), pp. 315–324.
15. Keynes, *C.W.*, Vol. V (1930, 1971), p. 174.
16. Keynes, *C.W.*, Vol. XIII (1973a), pp. 364–365.
17. *Ibid.*, p. 365.
18. *Ibid.*, p. 365.
19. *Ibid.*, p. 366.
20. Keynes, *C.W.*, Vol. VI (1930, 1971), p. 332. Such a policy will involve the central bank in capital losses if it has to reverse its action and sell bonds at lower prices, but this is regarded as being in the public interest (pp. 334–335). The international complications are discussed on pp. 335–338. If the country is a member of an international monetary system with fixed exchange rates, a fall in rates of interest relatively to those ruling in other countries will tend to cause an increase in foreign lending and a strain on the foreign-exchange rates.
21. R. S. Sayers, *Modern Banking* (7th edn, 1967), pp. 309–310. The ultra-cheap money policy of 1945–1947 failed (*see* p. 318). Professor Sayers points out that 'in the nineteen-fifties it was primarily by varying securities held in the Issue Department (of the Bank of England) that the authorities operated on the gilt-edged market' (p. 309).
22. Moggridge and Howson (1974), p. 240 and notes.

23. *See* p. 222.
24. Keynes, *C.W.*, Vol. IX (1972).
25. *Ibid.*, pp. 353–355.
26. The schedule or curve which relates rates of investment at different rates of interest. A shift of the curve to the left reflects a lower rate of investment at a given rate of interest.
27. Keynes, *C.W.*, Vol. VII (1936, 1973), pp. 118–119.
28. *Ibid.*, p. 303. *See* p. 82 for the concept of the cost-unit.
29. *Ibid.*, p. 300.
30. *Ibid.*, p. 328.
31. *Ibid.*, p. 301. It should be noted that a period of recovery and prosperity is possible without a rising price level as was the case in the United States during the 1920s. Keynes always assumed that prices would rise more than money-wages and that real wages would be reduced. This assumption has been criticized. *See* A. A. Sampson and R. Sedgwick, 'Wages, Prices, and Employment in General Disequilibrium' (July 1977), p. 216, and their references to J. T. Dunlop and L. Tarshis). *See also* J. M. Keynes, 'Relative Movements of Real Wages and Output', *Economic Journal* (March 1939), reprinted as Appendix 3 in *C.W.*, Vol. VII (1936, 1973).
32. William Fellner, 'The Robertsonian Evolution' (1952), p. 277.
33. S. R. Dennison, *Robertson, Dennis Holme (1890–1963)* (1968), p. 531.
34. Keynes, *C.W.*, Vol. VII (1936, 1973), p. 164.
35. *Ibid.*, p. 164. *See also* p. 204.
36. *Ibid.*, p. 206. Keynes discusses the limitations to which the monetary authority is subject on pp. 207–208.
37. *Ibid.*, p. 316.
38. *Ibid.*, p. 320.
39. *Ibid.*, p. 375.
40. T. W. Hutchison, *Keynes versus the 'Keynesians'* . . .? (1977), Appendix A, p. 68.
41. *Ibid.*, Appendix A, p. 68. The longterm rate Keynes had in mind was 2½ per cent. *See* Moggridge and Howson (1974), p. 241.
42. *Ibid.*, pp. 69–70.
43. This valuable quotation is given by Moggridge and Howson (1974), p. 242.
44. *See* T. Wilson and P. W. S. Andrews, *Oxford Studies in the Price Mechanism* (1951) for reprints from *Oxford Economic Papers* (October 1938) of H. D. Henderson, 'The Significance of the Rate of Interest' (particularly p. 24) and J. E. Meade and P. W. S. Andrews, 'Summary of Replies to Questions on Effects of Interest Rates'. It was this first inquiry which received a great deal of attention. *See also* R. S. Sayers, 'The Rate of Interest as a Weapon of Economic Policy', written at the beginning of 1949 and included in the volume. Professor Sayers refers to the second inquiry of 1939, the relevant articles, and mentions that this inquiry confirmed the earlier results (p. 6). In this article, Sayers inclines to the view that 'changes in the interest rate may have considerable effect on business activity through their effects on both capital outlay and consumption outlay' (p. 15), but he emphasizes that the efficiency of the interest rate changes over time for various reasons (pp. 15–16).
45. Moggridge and Howson (1974), p. 244, n.3.
46. Moggridge and Howson (1974), p. 244.
47. T. Wilson, 'Professor Robertson on Effective Demand and the Trade Cycle', (1953), p. 572. The quotation is from J. H. Williams, 'An Economist's Confessions' (March 1952), p. 14.
48. Donald Winch, *Economies and Policy* (2nd edn, 1972), p. 172.
49. Keynes, *C.W.*, Vol. VI (1930, 1971), pp. 337–338.
50. Moggridge and Howson (1974), p. 236. This included his own 'evidence' to the Macmillan Committee on Finance and Industry which reported in 1931. Keynes did advocate public investment before the return to the gold standard, but on a different basis. *See* Winch (1972), pp. 165–166, for Keynes's proposals made in 1923 and 1924.
51. Keynes, *C.W.*, Vol. IX (1972).
52. *Ibid.*, pp. 116–120.
53. *Ibid.*, p. 121. Hutchison states that in 1929 'A majority of economists in Britain supported the case for public works (e.g. Keynes, Henderson, Pigou, Robertson, Clay, etc.).' He adds that public works policies were opposed by Hawtrey of the Treasury and later by the supporters of the Austrian monetary over-investment theory of the trade cycle. *See* T. W. Hutchison, *Economics and Economic Policy in Britain, 1946–1966*

(1968), p. 277. Blaug points out that 'The rigorous case for countercyclical public works was stated for the first time in the *Minority Report of the Poor Law Commission* (1909). This was largely the work of the Webbs and A. L. Bowley. *See* Mark Blaug, *Economic Theory in Retrospect* (2nd edn, 1968), p. 654.
54. Moggridge and Howson (1974), pp. 238–239.
55. Keynes, *C.W.*, Vol. XIII (1973a), p. 364.
56. Keynes, *C.W.*, Vol. IX (1972).
57. *See* Chapter 13.
58. Keynes, *C.W.*, Vol. VII (1936, 1973), p. 119.
59. This phrase was not used in Keynes's day.
60. Keynes, *C.W.*, Vol. VII (1936, 1973), p. 95. *See* R. F. Harrod, *The Life of John Maynard Keynes* (1951), pp. 441–442, for a discussion of Keynes's treatment of this matter in *The Means to Prosperity*.
61. In *The Means to Prosperity*, Keynes added to the relief of taxation by suspending the Sinking Fund that obtained 'by returning to the practice of financing by loans those services which can properly be so financed, such as the cost of new roads charged on the Road Fund and that part of the dole which can be averaged out against the better days for which we must hope' (*C.W.*, Vol. IX (1972), p. 348). He also refers to the advantages of increased spending by the taxpayer as compared with government-loan expenditure. Winch refers to Keynes's attempts at this time to reassure people about the balancing of the Budget and that increasing the national income would lead to reduced dole payments and increased tax yields (Winch (1972), pp. 175–176). He writes that 'Keynes's motive for holding back from deliberate advocacy of unbalanced budgets was probably that he did not wish to give the public too much to swallow at one gulp' (Winch (1972), p. 378, n.66).
62. Keynes, *C.W.*, Vol. VII (1936, 1973), p. 164.
63. *Ibid.*, p. 316.
64. *Ibid.*, p. 320.
65. Hutchison (1977), p. 71. Keynes stresses the importance of early intervention, the reduction of taxation to increase the consumption of the lower income-groups, and the setting up of a board of public investment to prepare sound projects in detail. He also stresses the importance of an appropriately low longterm rate of interest (pp. 71–73).
66. Moggridge and Howson state that this acceptance was mainly due to Sir Frederick Phillips of the Treasury who came round to Keynes's view in December 1936. Moggridge and Howson (1974), p. 241, n.1. *See also* Hutchison (1977), p. 15, n.1, where he quotes from S. Howson and D. Winch, *The Economic Advisory Council 1930–1939* (1977), with reference to the Committee's first recommendation. This relates to advising the government to postpone investment projects which are not urgent, in view of the economic situation at the time.
67. Hutchison (1977), p. 13.
68. *Ibid.*, p. 14.
69. D. H. Robertson, *A Study of Industrial Fluctuation* (1948 edn), p. XVII.
70. Moggridge and Howson (1974), p. 241, n.1.
71. D. H. Robertson, *Essays in Money and Interest* (1966), p. 17.
72. Hutchison (1977), p. 15.
73. Robertson (1948), p. XV. With regard to Hawtrey's attack on the public works proposal, Robertson states that it 'scarcely deserves formal refutation' (p. 253, n.1).
74. Wilson (1953), p. 569.
75. Other economists were also involved.
76. Wilson (1953), p. 570.
77. Robertson writes, 'Perhaps I am out of date, but I hope that she will not go through another major depression without doubling the number (viz. one) of public lavatories which in 1943 I was able to discover in her capital city.' Sir Dennis Robertson, *A Memorandum Submitted to the Canadian Royal Commission on Banking and Finance* (1963b), p. 18, note. He opts for public works rather than the reduction of taxes paid by wealthy persons and corporations because the taxes remitted may not be quickly spent. We have seen, however, that tax reductions are an important weapon of fiscal policy.
78. D. H. Robertson, *Money*, pp. 155–174. The definitive edition is 1948, but this reference and the reference below are to Chapter VIII which is the same as in the 1928 edition.
79. *Ibid.*, pp. 176–178. Reference is also made to the possibility of banks making loans for the purchase of consumers' durable goods as a useful expedient.

80. *Ibid.*, p. 178.
81. Robertson (1963b), pp. 16–18.
82. Robertson was earlier than Keynes in putting forward the view that low interest rates were ineffective in acute depression. As we have seen, he did so in *Money* (1928). He had made the point earlier in *Banking Policy and the Price Level* (1926) (1st edn, 1926; 2nd edn, 1949), p. 81. Referring to Robertson's evidence in May 1930 to the Macmillan Committee on Finance and Industry, Winch writes, 'Unlike Keynes of the *Treatise*, he was pessimistic about the remedial effects on investment of lower rates.' *Economics and Policy* (1972), p. 169.
83. Mr R. A. (now Lord) Butler became Chancellor of the Exchequer in October 1951 and Bank rate was increased (from 2 to 2½ per cent) for the first time since the war, in November 1951. This was the beginning of the 'new monetary policy' which was pursued at a time of international balance of payments crisis, part of the 'Stop–Go' pattern of economic activity. Robertson would not have thought that the Government had the right mix of fiscal and monetary policies.
84. Samuel Brittan, *Steering the Economy* (1971 edn), p. 455).
85. In the immediate post-war years the unemployment percentage was well below Beveridge's average of 3 per cent, regarded by Keynes as over-ambitious, and there was open and suppressed (by controls) inflation. From 1953 to 1969 the average of the annual percentage increases in United Kingdom retail prices was 3.3, while the average of the unemployment percentaes was 1.6. During the relevant period for Robertson, up to 1961, the retail prices percentage increases ranged from 0.6 (1959) to 4.5 (1955) and the unemployment rates from 1.0 per cent (1955 and 1956) to 2.0 per cent (1959). The unemployment percentages refer to wholly unemployed in Great Britain. *See* M. C. Kennedy in A. R. Prest and D. J. Coppock, *The U.K. Economy, A Manual of Applied Economics* (6th edn, 1976), pp. 38 and 44.
86. What has Happened to the Rate of Interest?, reprinted in Robertson (1966), p. 192.
87. *Ibid.*, pp. 193–197.
88. *Ibid.*, pp. 196–197.
89. *Ibid.*, p. 198. *See also* Robertson, *Lectures on Economic Principles* (1963a), p. 434.
90. As Robertson puts it, Sir Stafford Crippses 'do not grow on gooseberry bushes', *ibid.*, p. 198. Cripps was Chancellor of the Exchequer from November 1947 until October 1950. The policies of Dr Dalton, the previous Chancellor of the Exchequer, were open to much criticism but he did obtain a disinflationary budget surplus in 1947. *See* Winch (1972), p. 294.
91. Robertson (1966), p. 198.
92. Colin Clark quotes a letter he received from Keynes, dated 1 May 1944, on submission of his article 'Public Finance and Changes in the Value of Money' which appeared in the *Economic Journal* (December 1945). Clark had maintained that where taxation exceeded 25 per cent of net national income at factor cost, inflation would follow. Keynes wrote 'In Great Britain after the war I should guess that your figure of 25 per cent as the maximum tolerable proportion of taxation may be exceedingly near to the truth. I should not be at all surprised if we did not find a further confirmation in our post-war experience of your empirical law.' Colin Clark, *Taxmanship* (1970), p. 21. In Chapter IV Clark confirms the relationship in a review of post-war experience in many countries. Empirical laws, however, must be treated with great care.
93. *See* Chapter 13.
94. United Nations, *National and International Measures for Full Employment* (1949), p. 43.
95. Robertson (1963), pp. 430–435.
96. *Ibid.*, p. 432.
97. *Ibid.*, pp. 433–434.
98. *Ibid.*, p. 435. This was the United States Congressional Sub-Committee under the chairmanship of an economist, Senator Paul Douglas, which was set up in 1949 (*see* p. 404).
99. *Ibid.*, p. 456. Robertson had wrestled throughout his life with the problem of stability and progress beginning with his first work on the trade cycle of 1915, *A Study of Industrial Fluctuations*. *See also* his 1956 address, Stability and Progress: The Richer Countries' Problem, reprinted as Annex I to *Lectures on Economic Principles* (1936a).
100. Robertson, *Growth, Wages, Money*, p. 44. The reference is to the *Committee on the Working of the Monetary System Report*, Cmnd 827 (1959).

101. *Ibid.*, pp. 52–56. In his *Lectures on Economic Principles* (1963a), p. 449, Robertson had insisted that in the last resort it was the duty of Governments and not Trade Unions to stop inflation and this involved a firm control of the supply of money.
102. *Ibid.*, p. 62. *See also* p. 63. By implication, Robertson clearly attaches importance to the direct incentive effect of restrictive monetary policy (p. 64).
103. Robertson (1963b), p. 20.
104. *Ibid.*, p. 23. Robertson adds that 'the long-run prospects of growth and employment may be gravely damaged by any serious lapse from monetary stability'.
105. *Ibid.*, p. 24. Robertson refers to formidable difficulties (pp. 24–25). He also discussed the problem in *Growth, op. cit.*, pp. 36–43.
106. Hutchison (1968), pp. 22–24, 283–284, 290–291, 293–294, 300.
107. Keynes, *C.W.*, Vol. VII (1936, 1973), p. 13.
108. Wage-goods are the goods on which wages are spent.
109. Keynes, *C.W.*, Vol. VII (1936, 1973), p. 257.
110. *Ibid.*, pp. 259–260.
111. No international trade.
112. Keynes, *C.W.*, Vol. VII (1936, 1973), pp. 262–271. Keynes deals with seven reactions of money-wage reductions which he regards as the most important. I refer to six of them.
113. Jacob Viner, 'Mr Keynes on the Causes of Unemployment', *Quarterly Journal of Economics* (November 1936), reprinted in Robert Lekachman, *Keynes' General Theory Reports of Three Decades* (1964), pp. 248–249.
114. Robertson (1963a), p. 445. *See also* his statement of 1948, *Essays in Money and Interest* (1966), pp. 192–193.
115. Gottfried Haberler, *Prosperity and Depression* (reprint of 1943 edn, New York, 1946), p. 503.
116. Robertson (1963a), p. 446. There were of course, other factors involved.
117. *Ibid.*, p. 446. This amounts to a criticism of Keynes.
118. *See*, for example, Haberler, *Prosperity and Depression* (1943, 1946), pp. 239–244, 395–405, 491–503; James Tobin, Money Wage Rates and Employment, Chapter XL of Seymour E. Harris, *The New Economics* (1948).
119. Keynes, *C.W.*, Vol. VII (1936, 1973), p. 17.
120. Viner in Lekachman (1964), pp. 237–238.
121. Keynes, *C.W.*, Vol. VII (1936, 1973), p. 10. As money wages rise during the recovery, it follows that the increase in employment is associated with a fall in real wages.
122. *Economic Journal* (March 1939), reprinted as Appendix 3, *C.W.*, Vol. VII (1936, 1973).
123. J. G. Dunlop, 'The Movement of Real and Money Wage Rates' (September 1938); L. Tarshis, 'Changes in Real and Money Wages' (March 1939) and his 'Real Wages in the United States and Great Britain' (August 1939).
124. Keynes, *C.W.*, Vol. VII (1936, 1973), p. 412. *See* now A. A. Sampson and R. Sedgwick, 'Wages, Prices and Employment in General Equilibrium' (July 1977).
125. This statement relates to the theory that real wages measure the marginal productivity of labour.

References

ACKLEY, GARDNER (1961; 3rd reprinting, 1973), *Macroeconomic Theory*, New York: Collier Macmillan.

ACKLEY, GARDNER (1978), *Macroeconomics: Theory and Policy*, London: Collier Macmillan.

AFTALION, A. (1913), *Les Crises Périodiques De Surproduction*, Paris: Rivière.

ALCHIAN, A. A. (1969), Information costs, pricing and resource unemployment. *Western Economic Journal* (June).

AMERICAN ECONOMIC ASSOCIATION (1944), *Readings in Business Cycle Theory*, Philadelphia: Blakiston.

AMERICAN ECONOMIC ASSOCIATION (1952), *Readings in Monetary Theory*, London: Allen & Unwin.

AMERICAN ECONOMIC ASSOCIATION AND ROYAL ECONOMIC SOCIETY (1967), *Surveys of Economic Theory*, Vol. II, London: Macmillan.

ANDERSON, L. C. AND JORDAN, J. L. (1968), Monetary and fiscal actions: a test of their relative importance in economic stabilization. *Federal Reserve Bank of St Louis Monthly Review*, 50 (November).

ANNUAL REPORT ON THE COUNCIL OF ECONOMIC ADVISERS (1977), In *Economic Report of the President*, 1977: U.S. Government Printing Office.

ANDO, A. and MODIGLIANI, F. (1965a), Rejoinder. *American Economic Review*, 55 (September).

ANDO, A. and MODIGLIANI, F. (1965b), The relative stability of monetary velocity and the investment multiplier. *American Economic Review*, 55 (September).

ARGY, V. (1969), The impact of monetary policy on expenditure with particular reference to the U.K. *I.M.F. Staff Papers*, 16 (June).

ARTIS, M. J. and NOBAY, A. R. (1969), Two aspects of the monetary debate: the attempt to reinstate money. *National Institute Economic Review*, No. 49 (August).

BALOGH, LORD (1978), In Thirlwall, ed. (1976).

BARRETT, C. R. and WALTERS, A. A. (1966), The stability of Keynesian and monetary multipliers in the United Kingdom. *Review of Economics and Statistics*, 48 (November).

BARRO, ROBERT J. and GROSSMAN, HERSCHEL I. (1976), *Money, employment and inflation*, London: Cambridge University Press.

BAUMOL, W. J. (1952), The transactions demand for cash: an inventory theoretic approach. *Quarterly Journal of Economics*, 56 (November).

BELL, QUENTIN (1974), *Bloomsbury*, London: Futura.

BEVERIDGE, W. H. (1909), *Unemployment, A Problem of Industry*, London, New York: Longmans Green.

BEVERIDGE, W. H. (1936), *Employment theory and the facts of unemployment*, London: The London School of Economics.

BEVERIDGE, W. H. (1942), *Report on Social Insurance and Allied Services*, Cmnd 6404, H.M.S.O.

BEVERIDGE, W. H. (1944), *Full Employment in a Free Society*, London: Allen & Unwin.

255

BISCHOFF, CHARLES (1971), Business investment in the 1970s: a comparison of models. *Brookings Papers on Economic Activity*.

BLAKE, ROBERT (1970), A personal memoir. In Ellis, Scott and Wolfe, eds (1970).

BLAKE, C. AND LYTHE, S. G. E., eds (1981), *A Maverick Institution Dundee School of Economics Fiftieth Anniversary Commemorative Essays*, London: Gee.

BLAUG, MARK (2nd edn, 1968), *Economic Theory in Retrospect*, London: Heinemann.

BLAUG, M. (1975), Discussion, in Parkin and Nobay, eds (1975).

BLISS, C. J. (1974), The reappraisal of Keynes' economics: an appraisal. In Parkin and Nobay, eds (1975).

BORDO, MICHAEL D. and SCHWARTZ, ANNA J. (1978), Clark Warburton: pioneer monetarist. In *Carleton Economic Papers*, Ottawa: Carleton University.

BRAINARD, WILLIAM C. and TOBIN, JAMES (1968), Pitfalls in financial model building. In Tobin (1971).

BRAITHWAITE, R. B. (1975), Keynes as a philosopher. In Milo Keynes, ed. (1975).

BRITTAN, SAMUEL (1971). *Steering the Economy*, Harmondsworth: Penguin.

BROWN, E. H. PHELPS (1951), Evan Durbin 1906–1948. *Economica*, 18 (February).

BROWN, HENRY PHELPS (1980), Sir Roy Harrod: a biographical memoir. *Economic Journal*, 90 (March).

BROWN, HENRY PHELPS (1981), Sir Roy Harrod: a note. *Economic Journal*, 91 (March).

BUCHANAN, J. M., BURTON, JOHN, WAGNER, R. E. (1978), *The Consequences of Mr Keynes*, London: Institute of Economic Affairs.

CAGAN, PHILLIP (1956). The monetary dynamics of hyperinflation. In Friedman, ed. (1956a).

CAGAN, PHILLIP C. (1965), *Determinants and Effects of Changes in the Stock of Money, 1867–1960*, New York: Columbia University Press.

CAGAN, PHILLIP and SCHWARTZ, ANNA JACOBSON (1975), How feasible is a flexible monetary policy? In Richard T. Selden, ed. (1975).

CAIRNCROSS, SIR ALEC (1970), Control of the economy – what does it take? *The Advancement of Science*, 26 (June).

CARTER, C. F. (1972). On degrees Shackle: or, the making of business decisions. In Carter and Ford, eds (1972).

CARTER, C. F. and FORD, J. L., eds (1972), *Uncertainty and Expectations in Economic Essays in Honour of G. L. S. Shackle*, Oxford: Blackwell.

CENTRAL STATISTICAL OFFICE (1980), Press Notice, Cyclical Indicators for the U.K. Economy Recent Movements of the Indicators. London: Central Statistical Office.

CHAMBERS, S. P. (1934–1935), Fluctuations in capital and demand for money. *Review of Economic Studies*, 2.

CHAMPERNOWNE, D. G. (1963), Expectations and the links between the economic future and the present. In Lekachman (1964).

CHICK, VICTORIA (1973), *The Theory of Monetary Policy*, London: Gray-Mills Publishing Limited.

CLARK, COLIN (1945), Public finance and changes in the value of money. *Economic Journal*, 55 (December).

CLARK, COLIN (1970), *Taxmanship*, 2nd edn. London: Institute of Economic Affairs.

CLAYTON, G. (1962), British financial intermediaries in theory and practice. *Economic Journal*, 72 (December).

CLAYTON, G., GILBERT, J. C., SEDGWICK, R., eds (1971), *Monetary Theory and Monetary Policy in the 1970s*, London: Oxford University Press.

CLOWER, ROBERT (1965), The Keynesian counter-revolution: a theoretical appraisal. In Hahn and Brechling, eds (1965).

CLOWER, R. W. (1967), A reconsideration of the microfoundations of monetary theory. In Clower, ed. (1969).

CLOWER, R. W., ed. (1969), *Monetary Theory Selected Readings*, Harmondsworth: Penguin.

CLOWER, R. W. (1971), Theoretical foundations of monetary policy. In Clayton, Gilbert, Sedgwick, eds (1971).

CLOWER, ROBERT W. (1977), The anatomy of monetary theory. *American Economic Review*. American Economic Association, *Papers and Proceedings*, 67 (February).

CODDINGTON, ALAN (1976), Keynesian economics: the search for First Principles. *Journal of Economic Literature*, 14 (December).

CODDINGTON, ALAN (1979), Hicks' contribution to Keynesian economics. *Journal of Economic Literature*, 17 (September).

COMMITTEE ON THE WORKING OF THE MONETARY SYSTEM REPORT (August 1959). The Radcliffe Report, Cmnd 827, London: H.M.S.O.

CORRY, B. (1978), Keynes in the history of economic thought: some reflections. In Thirlwall, ed. (1978).

COUNCIL OF KING'S COLLEGE CAMBRIDGE (1949), *John Maynard Keynes 1883–1946*. A Memoir. Cambridge: Cambridge University Press.

COUNCIL ON PRICES, PRODUCTIVITY AND INCOMES (1958). London: H.M.S.O.

CRIPPS, FRANCIS and GODLEY, WYNNE (1976), A formal analysis of the Cambridge economic policy group model. *Economica*, 43 (November).

CRIPPS, FRANCIS, GODLEY, WYNNE and FETHERSTON, MARTIN (1974), Public expenditure and the management of the economy. Memorandum, University of Cambridge, Department of Applied Economics. In Ninth Report from the Expenditure Committee (1974).

CROOME, DAVID R. and JOHNSON, HARRY G. (1970), *Money in Britain 1959–1969*, London: Oxford University Press.

DANES, MICHAEL (1979), An outline of Dennis Robertson's approach to the foundations of aggregative theory. Department of Economics, Queen Mary College, University of London, Paper 56 (July).

DAVIDSON, PAUL (1st edn, 1972; 2nd edn, 1978), *Money and the Real World*, London: Macmillan.

DAVIDSON, P. and WEINTRAUB, S. (1973), Money as cause and effect. *Economic Journal*, 83 (December).

DAVIS, J. R. and CASEY, F. J., Jr. (1977), Keynes's misquotation of Mill. *Economic Journal*, 87 (June).

DAVIS, R. G. (1969), How much does money matter? A look at some recent evidence. *Federal Reserve Bank of New York Monthly Review*, 51 (June).

DE LEEUW, F. and KALCHBRENNER, J. (1969), Monetary and fiscal actions: a test of their relative importance in economic stabilization: a comment. *Federal Reserve Bank of St Louis Monthly Review*, 51 (April).

DENNISON, S. R. (1968), *Robertson, Dennis Holme (1890–1963)*. International Encyclopaedia of the Social Sciences, New York: Macmillan & Free Press.

DE PRANO, M. and MAYER, T. (1965), Tests of the relative importance of autonomous expenditure and money. *American Economic Review*, 55 (September).

DE PRANO, M. and MAYER, T. (1965), Rejoinder. *American Economic Review*, 55 (September).

DERNBURG, THOMAS F. and McDOUGALL, DUNCAN M. (4th edn, 1972), *Macroeconomics*, New York: McGraw-Hill.

DODDS, J. C. and FORD, J. L. (1974), *Expectations, Uncertainty and the Term Structure of Interest Rates*, London: Robertson.

DOMAR, EVSEY, D. (1946), Capital expansion, rate of growth and employment. *Econometrica*, 14.

DOMAR, EVSEY D. (1947), Expansion and employment. *American Economic Review*, 37.

DUESENBERRY, J. S. (1949), *Income, Saving and the Theory of Consumer Behaviour*, Cambridge, Massachusetts: Harvard University Press.

DUNLOP, J. G. (1938), The movement of real and money wage rates. *Economic Journal*, 48 (September).

EASTHAM, J. K., ed. (1955), *Dundee Economic Essays*, Dundee: School of Economics, Dundee.

ELLIS, HOWARD S., ed. (1948), *A Survey of Contemporary Economics*, Philadelphia: Blakiston.

ELLIS, W. A., SCOTT, M. F. G. and WOLFE, J. N., eds (1970), *Induction, Growth and Trade*, Oxford: Clarendon Press.

ELTIS, WALTER (1976), The failure of the Keynesian conventional wisdom. *Lloyds Bank Review* (October).

ELTIS, WALTER (1977), The Keynesian conventional wisdom. *Lloyds Bank Review* (July).

EXPENDITURE COMMITTEE, NINTH REPORT (1974), *Public Expenditure, Inflation and The Balance of Payments*, HC 328 (July), London: H.M.S.O.

FEARON, PETER (1979), *The Origins and Nature of the Great Slump 1929–1932*, London: Macmillan.

FEIWEL, GEORGE R. (1975), *The Intellectual Capital of Michal Kalecki*, Knoxville, U.S.A.: University of Tennessee Press.

FELLNER, WILLIAM (1952), The Robertsonian evolution. *American Economic Review*, 42.

FELLNER, WILLIAM (1956), *Trends and Cycles in Economic Activity*, New York: Holt.

FELLNER, WILLIAM (1960), *Modern Economic Analysis*, New York: McGraw-Hill.

FISHER, G. R. and SHEPPARD, D. K. (1974), Interrelationships between real and monetary variables: some evidence from recent U.S. empirical studies. In Johnson and Nobay, eds (1974).

FISHER, IRVING (1st edn, 1911), *The Purchasing Power of Money*, New York: Macmillan.

FISHER, IRVING (1930), *The Theory of Interest*, New York: Macmillan.

FISHER, MALCOLM R. (1976), Professor Hicks and the Keynesians. *Economica*, 43 (August).

FLEMING, J. S. (1974), Wealth effects in Keynesian models. *Oxford Economic Papers*, 26 (July).

FOOT, M. D. K. W., GOODHART, C. A. E. and HOTSON, A. C. (1979), Monetary base control. *Bank of England Quarterly Bulletin*, 19 (June).

FRIEDMAN, MILTON (1952), Price, income and monetary changes in three wartime periods. In Friedman (1969).

FRIEDMAN, MILTON, ed. (1956a), *Studies in the Quantity Theory of Money*, Chicago: Harper & Row.

FRIEDMAN, MILTON (1956b), The quantity theory of money: a restatement. In Friedman (1969).

FRIEDMAN, MILTON (1957), *A Theory of the Consumption Function*, Princeton: Princeton University Press.

FRIEDMAN, MILTON (1959), The demand for money: some theoretical and empirical results. In Friedman (1969).

FRIEDMAN, MILTON (1960), *A Program for Monetary Stability*, New York: Fordham University Press.

FRIEDMAN, MILTON (1961a), The demand for money. In Friedman (1968a).

FRIEDMAN, MILTON (1961b), The lag in effect of monetary policy. In Friedman (1969).

FRIEDMAN, MILTON (1962), Should there be an independent monetary authority? In Yeager (1962). Reprinted in Friedman (1968a).

FRIEDMAN, MILTON and SCHWARTZ, ANNA JACOBSON (1963a), *A Monetary History of the United States, 1867–1960*. Princeton, N.J.: Princeton University Press.

FRIEDMAN, MILTON and SCHWARTZ, ANNA JACOBSON (1963b), Money and business cycles. In Friedman (1969).

FRIEDMAN, MILTON and MEISELMAN, DAVID I. (1963), The relative stability of monetary velocity and the investment multiplier in the United States, 1897–1958. In the Commission on Money and Credit, *Stabilization Policies*, Englewood Cliffs, N.J.: Commission on Money and Credit.

FRIEDMAN, M. (1964a), The monetary studies of the national bureau. In Friedman (1969).

FRIEDMAN, M. (1964b), Post-war trends in monetary theory and policy. In Friedman (1969).

FRIEDMAN, M. and MEISELMAN, D. (1964), Reply to Donald Hester. *Review of Economics and Statistics*, 46 (November).

FRIEDMAN, M. and MEISELMAN, D. (1965), Reply to Ando and Modigliani and to De Prano and Mayer. *American Economic Review*, 55 (September).

FRIEDMAN, M. and MEISELMAN, D. (1966), Interest rates and the demand for money. In Friedman (1969).

FRIEDMAN, M. and MEISELMAN, D. (1967), The monetary theory and policy of Henry Simons. In Friedman (1969).

FRIEDMAN, MILTON (1968a), *Dollars and Deficits*, Englewood Cliffs, N.J.: Prentice-Hall.

FRIEDMAN, MILTON (1968b), Monetary policy. In Friedman (1968).

FRIEDMAN, MILTON (1968c), Money: quantity theory. In Walters (1973).

FRIEDMAN, MILTON (1968d), The role of monetary policy. In Friedman (1969).

FRIEDMAN, M. (1969), *The Optimum Quantity of Money and Other Essays*, London: Macmillan.

FRIEDMAN, MILTON (1970a), *The Counter-Revolution in Monetary Theory*, London: Institute of Economic Affairs.

FRIEDMAN, MILTON (1970b), A theoretical framework for monetary analysis. In Gordon (1974).

FRIEDMAN, MILTON (1970c), The new monetarism: comment. In Walters (1973).

FRIEDMAN, MILTON (1971), A monetary theory of national income. In Clayton, Gilbert and Sedgwick (1971) and in Gordon (1974).

FRIEDMAN, MILTON (1972), Comments on the critics. In Gordon (1974).

FRIEDMAN, MILTON (1975), *Unemployment versus Inflation? An Evaluation of the Phillips Curve*, London: The Institute of Economic Affairs.

FRIEDMAN, MILTON (1976), Comments on Tobin and Buiter. In J. L. Stein (1976).

FRIEDMAN, MILTON (1977), *Inflation and Unemployment: The New Dimension of Politics*, London: Institute of Economic Affairs.

GANDOLFI, ARTHUR E. and LOTHIAN, JAMES R. (1977), Did monetary forces cause the great depression? A review essay. *Journal of Money, Credit and Banking*, 9 (November).

GIBSON, N. J. (2nd edn, 1970), *Financial Intermediaries and Monetary Policy*, London: Institute of Economic Affairs.

GILBERT, J. C. (1950), Exchange rate adjustments. *Yorkshire Bulletin*, 2 (January).

GILBERT, J. C. (1953), The demand for money: the development of an economic concept. *Journal of Political Economy*, 61 (April).

GILBERT, J. C. (1955), Professor Hayek's contribution to trade cycle theory. In Eastham (1955).

GILBERT, J. C. (1957), Economic theory in Great Britain today. *Yorkshire Bulletin*, 9 (May).

GILBERT, J. C. (1956/57), The compatibility of any behaviour of the price level with equilibrium. *Review of Economic Studies*, 24.

GILBERT, J. C. (1959), Economic theory and policy. *Yorkshire Bulletin of Economic and Social Research*, 11 (July).

GILBERT, J. C. (1981), The nature of economics and problems of appraisal with special reference to developments since 1931. In Blake and Lythe (1981).

GOODHART, C. A. E. and CROCKETT, A. D. (1970), The importance of money. *Bank of England Quarterly Bulletin*, 10 (June).

GOODHART, C. A. E. (1975), *Money, Information and Uncertainty*, London: Macmillan.

GORDON, R. A. (2nd edn, 1961), *Business Fluctuations*, New York: Harper.

GORDON, ROBERT J., ed. (1974), *Milton Friedman's Monetary Framework*, Chicago: The University of Chicago Press.

GOWLAND, DAVID (1975), The money supply and stock market prices. In Parkin and Nobay (1975).

GOWLAND, DAVID (1978), *Monetary Policy and Credit Control*, London: Croom Helm.

GRAHAM, F. D. (1944), Keynes v Hayek on a commodity reserve currency. *Economic Journal*, 54 (December).

GROSSMAN, HERSCHEL I. (1975), Review of *Money and the Real World*, by Paul Davidson. *Journal of Money, Credit and Banking*, 7 (August).

GURLEY, J. G. and SHAW, E. S. (1955), Financial aspects of economic development. *American Economic Review*, 45 (September).

GURLEY, J. G. and SHAW, E. S. (1956), Financial intermediaries and the saving-investment process. *Journal of Finance*, 11 (May).

GURLEY, JOHN G. and SHAW, EDWARD S. (1960), *Money in a Theory of Finance*, Washington, D.C.: The Brookings Institution.

HABERLER, GOTTFRIED (1946), *The General Theory* after ten years. In Lekachman (1964).

HABERLER, GOTTFRIED VON (1952), The Pigou effect once more. In Haberler (1958).

HABERLER, GOTTFRIED (4th edn, 1958), *Prosperity and Depression*, London: Allen & Unwin.

HABERLER, GOTTFRIED (1962), Sixteen years later. In Lekachman (1964).

HAHN, F. H. and BRECHLING, F. P. R., eds (1965), *The Theory of Interest Rates*, London: Macmillan

HAHN, F. H. (1971), Professor Friedman's views on money. *Economica*, 38 (February).

HAHN, F. H. (1980), Monetarism and economic theory. *Economica*, 47 (February).

HAHN, F. H. and MATTHEWS, R. C. O. (1967), The theory of economic growth: a survey. In American Economic Association and Royal Economic Society (1967).

HANSEN, A. H. (1936), Mr Keynes on underemployment equilibrium. *Journal of Political Economy*, 43 (October).

HANSEN, A. H. (1938), *Full Recovery or Stagnation?*, New York: Norton.
HANSEN, A. H. (1939), Economic progress and declining population growth. *American Economic Review*, 28 (March). Reprinted in American Economic Association (1944).
HANSEN, ALVIN H. (1941), *Fiscal Policy and Business Cycles*, New York: Norton.
HANSEN, A. H. (1947), *Economic Policy and Full Employment*, New York: McGraw-Hill.
HANSEN, A. H. (1949), *Monetary Theory and Fiscal Policy*, New York: McGraw-Hill.
HANSEN, ALVIN H. (1953), *A Guide to Keynes*, New York: McGraw-Hill.
HARCOURT, G. C. (1977), Review of George R. Feiwel, *The Intellectual Capital of Michal Kalecki: A Study in Economic Theory and Policy*. *Economica*, 44 (February).
HARRIS, SEYMOUR E., ed. (1943), *Post-War Economic Problems*, New York: McGraw-Hill.
HARRIS, SEYMOUR E., ed. (1948), *The New Economics*. London: Dennis Dobson (U.S. Copyright 1947).
HARROD, R. F. (1934), The expansion of credit in an advancing community. *Economica*, 1 (August).
HARROD, R. F. (1936), *The Trade Cycle*, London: Clarendon Press.
HARROD, R. F. (1937), Keynes and traditional theory. In Harrod (1952).
HARROD, R. F. (1939), An essay in dynamic theory. In Harrod (1952).
HARROD, R. F. (1948), *Towards a Dynamic Economics*, London: Macmillan.
HARROD, R. F. (1951), *The Life of John Maynard Keynes*, London: Macmillan.
HARROD, R. F. (1952; 2nd edn, 1972), *Economic Essays*, London: Macmillan.
HARROD, R. F. (1959), *The Prof: Personal Memoir of Lord Cherwell*, London: Macmillan.
HARROD, SIR ROY (1967), *Towards a New Economic Policy*, Manchester: Manchester University Press.
HARROD, SIR ROY (1974), Keynes's theory and its application. In Moggridge, ed. (1974).
HARROD, ROY (1973), *Economic Dynamics*, London: Macmillan.
HAWTREY, R. G. (1913), *Good and Bad Trade*, London: Constable.
HAWTREY, R. G. (1st edn, 1919), *Currency and Credit*, London: Longmans.
HAWTREY, R. G. (1922), The Genoa resolutions on currency. *Economic Journal*, 32 (September).
HAWTREY, R. G. (1938), *A Century of Bank Rate*, London: Longmans.
HAYEK, F. A. (1929), *Geldtheorie und Konjunkturtheorie*, Vienna.
HAYEK, F. A. (1st edn, 1931; 2nd edn, 1935), *Prices and Production*, London: Routledge.
HAYEK, F. A. (1932), A note on the development of the doctrine of 'forced saving'. *Quarterly Journal of Economics*, 47 (November).
HAYEK, F. A. (1931, 1932), Reflections on *The Pure Theory of Money* of Mr J. M. Keynes. *Economica*.
HAYEK, F. A. (1933), *Monetary Theory and the Trade Cycle*, London: Jonathan Cape.
HAYEK, FRIEDRICH A. (1939), *Profits, Interest and Investment*, London: Routledge.
HAYEK, F. A. (1941), *The Pure Theory of Capital*, London: Routledge & Kegan Paul.
HAYEK, F. A. (1942), The Ricardo effect. *Economica*, 9.
HAYEK, F. A. (1966), Personal recollections of Keynes and the 'Keynesian Revolution'. Reprinted in Hayek (1972).
HAYEK, F. A. (1st edn, 1972; 2nd edn, 1978), *A Tiger by the Tail* (compiled and introduced by Sudha R. Shenoy). London: Institute of Economic Affairs.
HAYEK, F. A. (1974a), Inflation: the path to unemployment. In Robbins *et al.* (1974).
HAYEK, F. A. (1974b), The pretence of knowledge. Reprinted in Hayek (1975).
HAYEK, F. A. (1975), *Full Employment at Any Price?*, London: Institute of Economic Affairs.
HAYEK, F. A. (1976), *Choice in Currency*, London: Institute of Economic Affairs.
HENDERSON, H. D. (1938), The significance of the rate of interest. In Wilson and Andrew, eds (1951).
HESTER, D. D. (1964), Keynes and the quantity theory: a comment on the Friedman –Meiselman CMC paper. *Review of Economics and Statistics*, 46 (November).
HICKS, J. R. (1932), *The Theory of Wages*, London: Macmillan.
HICKS, J. R. (1933), Gleichgewicht und Konjunktur. *Zeitschrift Für Nationalökonomie*, 4.
HICKS, J. R. (1935), A suggestion for simplifying the theory of money. In Hicks (1967).
HICKS, JOHN (1937), Mr Keynes and the 'classics'. *Econometrica*. In Hicks (1967).
HICKS, J. R. (1st edn, 1939; 2nd edn, 1946), *Value and Capital*, Oxford: Clarendon Press.
HICKS, J. R. (1950), *A Contribution to the Theory of Trade Cycle*, Oxford: Clarendon Press.
HICKS, JOHN (1965), *Capital and Growth*, Oxford: Clarendon Press.

HICKS, JOHN (1967), *Critical Essays in Monetary Theory*, Oxford: Clarendon Press.

HICKS, JOHN (1973), Recollections and documents, *Economica*, February. In Hicks (1977).

HICKS, J. R. (1974), Real and monetary factors in economic fluctuations. In Hicks (1977), pages 177–181.

HICKS, JOHN (1974), *The Crisis in Keynesian Economics*, Oxford: Blackwell.

HICKS, JOHN (1977), *Economic Perspectives*, Oxford: Clarendon Press.

HICKS, JOHN (1979), On Coddington's interpretation: a reply. *Journal of Economic Literature*, 17 (September).

HILTON, K. and HEATHFIELD, D. F., eds (1970), *Econometric Study of the United Kingdom*, London: Macmillan.

HINES, A. G. (1971), *On the reappraisal of Keynesian Economics*, London: Martin Robertson.

HINES, A. G. and CATEPHORES, G. (1970), Investment in U.K. manufacturing industry, 1956–1967. In Hilton and Heathfield, eds (1970).

HOLROYD, MICHAEL (1971b), *Lytton Strachey: a Biography*, Harmondsworth: Penguin (first published 1967).

HOLROYD, MICHAEL (1971a), *Lytton Strachey and the Bloomsbury Group: His Work and Their Influence*, Harmondsworth: Penguin (first published 1967).

HOWSON, SUSAN (1975), *Domestic Monetary Management in Britain 1919–38*, London: Cambridge University Press.

HOWSON, S. and WINCH, D. (1977), *The Economic Advisory Council 1930–1939*, London: Cambridge University Press.

HUME, DAVID (1903), *Essays Moral, Political and Literary*, London: The World's Classics, Grant Richards.

HUTCHISON, T. W. (1968), *Economics and Economic Policy in Britain 1946–1966*, London: Allen & Unwin.

HUTCHISON, T. W. (1976), The failure of the Keynesian conventional wisdom. *Lloyds Bank Review* (October).

HUTCHISON, T. W. (1977), *Keynes versus the 'Keynesians' . . .?*, London: Institute of Economic Affairs.

HUTCHISON, T. W. (1978), *On Revolutions and Progress in Economic Knowledge*, London: Cambridge University Press.

HUTT, W. H. (1936), *Economists and the Public*, London: Jonathan Cape.

HUTT, W. H. (1974), *A Rehabilitation of Say's Law*, Athens, U.S.A.: Ohio University Press.

JACKMAN, RICHARD (1974), Keynes and Leijonhufvud. *Oxford Economic Papers*, 26 (July).

JAFFÉ, WILLIAM (1978), Review of Morishima (1977). *Economic Journal* (September).

JENKINS, ROY (1974), *Nine Men of Power*, London: Hamish Hamilton.

JOHNSON, ELIZABETH (1973), John Maynard Keynes: scientist or politician. In Joan Robinson, ed. (1973).

JOHNSON, ELIZABETH S. and JOHNSON, HARRY G. (1978), *The Shadow of Keynes*, Oxford: Blackwell.

JOHNSON, HARRY G. (1957), Review of William Fellner, *Trends and Cycles in Economic Activity*. *American Economic Review*, 47 (March).

JOHNSON, HARRY G. (1961), The General Theory after twenty-five years. In Johnson (2nd edn, 1964).

JOHNSON, HARRY G. (1962), Monetary theory and policy. In Johnson (1969).

JOHNSON, HARRY G. (1963), Recent developments in monetary theory. In Johnson (1969b).

JOHNSON, HARRY G. (1st edn, 1962; 2nd edn, 1964), *Money, Trade and Economic Growth*, London: Allen & Unwin.

JOHNSON, HARRY G. (1969a), Inside money, outside money, income, wealth and welfare in monetary theory. In Johnson (1972).

JOHNSON, HARRY G. (1969b), *Essays in Monetary Economics*, London: Allen & Unwin.

JOHNSON, HARRY G. (1970a), Monetary theory and monetary policy. In Johnson (1972).

JOHNSON, HARRY G. (1970b), Recent developments in monetary theory – a commentary. In Johnson (1972).

JOHNSON, HARRY G. (1970c), Keynes and the Keynesians. In Johnson (1972).

JOHNSON, HARRY G. (1971a), *Macroeconomics and Monetary Theory*, London: Gray-Mills.

JOHNSON, HARRY G. (1971b), Richard T. Ely Lecture, The Keynesian revolution and the monetarist counter-revolution. In Johnson (1972).

JOHNSON, HARRY G. (1972), *Further Essays in Monetary Economics*, London: Allen & Unwin.
JOHNSON, HARRY G. (1974), Cambridge in the 1950s. In Johnson (1975).
JOHNSON, H. G. and NOBAY, A. R., eds (1974), *Issues in Monetary Economics*, Oxford: Oxford University Press.
JOHNSON, HARRY G. (1975a), *On Economics and Society*, Chicago: University of Chicago Press.
JOHNSON, HARRY G. (1975b), Keynes and British economics. In Milo Keynes, ed. (1975).
JOHNSON, HARRY G. (1976), Keynes's *General Theory*: revolution or war of independence? *The Canadian Journal of Economics*, 9 (November).
JUNANKAR, P. N. (1972), *Investment: Theories and Evidence*, London: Macmillan.
KAHN, RICHARD (1931), The relation of home investment to unemployment. In Kahn (1972).
KAHN, R. F. (1956a), Full employment and British economic policy. In Kahn (1972).
KAHN, R. F. (1956b), Lord Keynes and contemporary economic problems. In Kahn (1972).
KAHN, RICHARD (1958), Memorandum of evidence submitted to the Radcliffe committee. In Kahn (1972).
KAHN, R. F. (1959), Exercises in the analysis of growth. In Kahn (1972).
KAHN, RICHARD (1972), *Selected Essays on Employment and Growth*, London: Cambridge University Press.
KAHN, RICHARD (1975), *On Re-reading Keynes*, London: Oxford University Press.
KAHN, RICHARD (1976a), Unemployment as seen by the Keynesians. In G. D. N. Worswick, ed. (1976).
KAHN, RICHARD (1976b), Thoughts on the behaviour of wages and monetarism. *Lloyds Bank Review* (January).
KAHN, RICHARD (1977), Mr Eltis and the Keynesians. *Lloyds Bank Review* (April).
KAHN, LORD and POSNER, MICHAEL, The effects of public expenditure on inflation and the balance of payments. (Expenditure Committee, Ninth Report (1974).)
KAHN, RICHARD and POSNER, MICHAEL (1977), Inflation, unemployment and growth. *National Westminster Bank Quarterly Review* (November).
KALDOR, NICHOLAS (1941), Pigou on employment and equilibrium, *Economic Journal*, December; reprinted in Kaldor (1960).
KALDOR, NICHOLAS (1960), *Essays on Economic Stability and Growth*, London: Duckworth.
KALDOR, NICHOLAS (1970), The new monetarism. In Walters (1973).
KALDOR, N. and MIRRLEES, J. A. (1962), A new model of economic growth. *Review of Economic Studies*, 29(3).
KALECKI, M. (1935), A macrodynamic theory of business cycles. *Econometrica*, 3.
KALECKI, M. (1937), Principle of increasing risk. *Economica*, 4.
KALECKI, M. (1944), Professor Pigou on the classical stationary state – a comment. *Economic Journal*, 54 (April).
KALECKI, M. (1945), Three ways to full employment. In *The Economics of Full Employment*. (Oxford University Institute of Statistics) Oxford: Blackwell.
KALECKI, MICHAL (1949/1950), A new approach to the problem of business cycles. *Review of Economic Studies*, 17.
KALECKI, MICHAL (1967), *Studies in the Theory of Business Cycles, 1933–1939*, Oxford: Blackwell.
KALECKI, MICHAL (1971), *Selected Essays on the Dynamics of the Capitalist Economy 1933–1970*, London: Cambridge University Press.
KANTOR, BRIAN (1979), Rational expectations and economic thought. *Journal of Economic Literature*, 17 (December).
KENNEDY, M. C. (1976), The economy as a whole. In Prest and Coppock (1976).
KEYNES, J. M. (1913, 1971), *Indian Currency and Finance. The Collected Writings of John Maynard Keynes*, I. London: Macmillan.
KEYNES, J. M. (1919, 1971), *The Economic Consequences of the Peace. The Collected Writings of John Maynard Keynes*, II. London: Macmillan.
KEYNES, J. M. (1921), Europe's economic outlook III – the depression in trade. *The Sunday Times* (4 September).
KEYNES, J. M. (1921, 1973), *A Treatise on Probability. The Collected Writings of John Maynard Keynes*, VIII. London: Macmillan.

KEYNES, J. M. (1923, 1971), *A Tract on Monetary Reform. The Collected Writings of John Maynard Keynes*, IV. London: Macmillan.

KEYNES, J. M. (1926), *The End of Laissez-Faire*. In Keynes (1972) IX.

KEYNES, J. M. (1929), *Can Lloyd George Do It?*. In Keynes (1972) IX.

KEYNES, J. M. (1930, 1971), *A Treatise on Money. The Collected Writings of John Maynard Keynes*, V and VI. London: Macmillan.

KEYNES, J. M. (1931), An economic analysis of unemployment: Harris Foundation Lecture III. In Keynes (1973) XIII.

KEYNES, J. M. (1933a), *The Means to Prosperity*. In Keynes (1972) IX.

KEYNES, J. M. (1933b), *Essays in Biography*. In Keynes (1972b) X. London: Macmillan.

KEYNES, J. M. (1936, 1973), *The General Theory of Employment Interest and Money. The Collected Writings of John Maynard Keynes*, VII. London: Macmillan.

KEYNES, J. M. (1937a), Some economic consequences of a declining population. In Keynes (1973b) XIV.

KEYNES, J. M. (1937b), The general theory of employment. In Keynes (1973b) XIV.

KEYNES, J. M. (1937c), How to Avoid a Slump. *The Times*, 12, 13, 14 January.

KEYNES, J. M. (1939a), Professor Tinbergen's method. In Keynes (1973) XIV.

KEYNES, J. M. (1939b), Relative movements of real wages and output. In Keynes (1973) VII.

KEYNES, J. M. (1939c), Borrowing by the state. *The Times* (24 July, 1939).

KEYNES, J. M. (1940b), Comment [with reference to Tinbergen]. In Keynes (1973) XIV.

KEYNES, J. M. (1940a), *How to Pay for the War*. In Keynes (1972) IX.

KEYNES, J. M. (1940c), The United States and the Keynes Plan. *New Republic* (July).

KEYNES, LORD (1943), The objective of international price stability. *Economic Journal*, 53 (June–September).

KEYNES, LORD (1944), A rejoinder. *Economic Journal*, 54 (December).

KEYNES, J. M. (1946), The balance of payments of the United States. *Economic Journal*, 56 (June).

KEYNES, J. M. (1972a), *Essays in Persuasion. The Collected Writings of John Maynard Keynes*, IX. London: Macmillan.

KEYNES, J. M. (1972b), *Essays in Biography. The Collected Writings of John Maynard Keynes*, X. London: Macmillan.

KEYNES, J. M. (1973a), *The General Theory and After: Part I, Preparation. The Collected Writings of John Maynard Keynes*, XIII. London: Macmillan.

KEYNES, J. M. (1973b), *The General Theory and After: Part II, Defence and Development. The Collected Writings of John Maynard Keynes*, XIV. London: Macmillan.

KEYNES, J. M. (1973c), The general theory of employment. In *The Collected Writings of John Maynard Keynes*, XIV. London: Macmillan.

KEYNES, J. M. (1974), Comments on the critics. In Gordon (1974).

KEYNES, J. M. (1979), *The General Theory and After: A Supplement*. In *The Collected Writings of John Maynard Keynes*, XXIX. London: Macmillan.

KEYNES, J. M. (1980), *Activities 1941–6: Shaping the Post-War World: Bretton Woods and Reparations*. In *The Collected Writings of John Maynard Keynes*, XXVI. London: Macmillan.

KEYNES, MILO, ed. (1975), *Essays on John Maynard Keynes*, London: Cambridge University Press.

KEYNES, JOHN NEVILLE (1884), *Studies and Exercises in Formal Logic*, London: Macmillan.

KEYNES, JOHN NEVILLE (1891), *The Scope and Method of Political Economy*, London: Macmillan.

KING'S COLLEGE (1949), *Keynes: a Memoir*, Cambridge: Cambridge University Press.

KLEIN, LAWRENCE, R. (1st edn, 1946; 2nd edn, 1968), *The Keynesian Revolution*, London: Macmillan.

KNIGHT, FRANK H. (1921, 1948), *Risk, Uncertainty and Profit*, London: The London School of Economics and Political Science.

KREGEL, J. A. (1976), Economic methodology in the face of uncertainty. *Economic Journal*, 86 (June).

KUZNETS, SIMON (1946), *National Product Since 1869*, New York: National Bureau of Economic Research.

LACHMAN, L. M. (1973), *Macroeconomic Thinking and the Market Economy*, London: Institute of Economic Affairs.

LAIDLER, D. (1966), The rate of interest and the demand for money – some empirical evidence. *Journal of Political Economy*, 74 (December).

LAIDLER, DAVID (1969), The definition of money: theoretical and empirical problems. *Journal of Money, Credit and Banking*, 1 (August).

LAIDLER, DAVID E. W. (1st edn, 1969; 2nd edn, 1977), *The Demand for Money Theories and Evidence*, 1st edn: Scranton: International Textbook Company. 2nd edn: New York: Harper & Row.

LAIDLER, D. (1971), The influence of money on economic activity – a survey of some current problems. In Clayton, Gilbert and Sedgwick (1971).

LAIDLER, D. and PURDY, D., eds (1974), *Inflation and labour markets*, Manchester: Manchester University Press.

LAIDLER, D. E. W. (1975), *Essays on money and inflation*, Manchester: Manchester University Press.

LAIDLER, D. (1981), Monetarism: an interpretation and an assessment. *Economic Journal*, 91 (March).

LANGE, OSCAR (1938), The rate of interest and the optimum propensity to consume. *Economica*, 5 (February).

LANGE, OSCAR (1944), *Price Flexibility and Employment*, Bloomington, U.S.A.: Principia Press.

LATANÉ, H. A. (1954), Cash balances and the interest rate – a pragmatic approach. *Review of Economics and Statistics*, 36 (November).

LATANÉ, H. A. (1960), Income velocity and interest rates: a pragmatic approach. *Review of Economics and Statistics*, 42 (November).

LATSIS, SPIRO J., ed. (1976), *Method and Appraisal in Economics*, London: Cambridge University Press.

LEKACHMAN, ROBERT, ed. (1964), *Keynes' General Theory Reports of Three Decades*, London: Macmillan.

LEKACHMAN, ROBERT (1967), *The Age of Keynes*, London: Allen Lane.

LERNER, ABBA P. (1961), The General Theory after twenty-five years: discussion. *American Economic Review*, 51 (May).

LERNER, ABBA P. (1963), Keynesian economics in the sixties. In Lekachman, ed. (1964).

LEIJONHUFVUD, AXEL (1968), *On Keynesian Economics and the Economics of Keynes*. London: Oxford University Press.

LEIJONHUFVUD, AXEL (1969), *Keynes and the Classics*, London: Institute of Economic Affairs.

LEIJONHUFVUD, AXEL (1976), Schools, 'revolutions', and research programmes in economic theory. In Latsis, ed. (1976).

LILLEY, PETER (1977), Two critics of Keynes: Friedman and Hayek. In Skidelsky, R., ed. (1977).

LOASBY, BRIAN J. (1976), *Choice, complexity and ignorance*, London: Cambridge University Press.

MARKOWITZ, H. (1959), *Portfolio Selection*, New York: Wiley.

MARSHALL, A. (1890), *Principles of Economics*, London: Macmillan.

MARSHALL, G. P., SAMPSON, A. A. and SEDGWICK, R. (1975), The rate of investment and the supply schedule for new capital goods. *Bulletin of Economic Research*, 27 (November).

MARTY, A. L. (1961), Gurley and Shaw on money in a theory of finance. *Journal of Political Economy*, 69 (February).

MAYER, THOMAS *et al.* (1978), *The Structure of Monetarism*, New York: Norton.

MEADE, J. E. (1937), A simplified model of Mr Keynes' system. In Harris, ed. (1948).

MEADE, J. E. and ANDREWS, P. W. S., Summary of replies to questions on effects of interest rates. In Wilson and Andrews (1951).

MEADE, J. E. (1971), *Wages and Prices in a Mixed Economy*, London: Institute of Economic Affairs.

MEADE, JAMES (1975), The Keynesian revolution. In Milo Keynes, ed. (1975).

MEADE, JAMES E. (1980), Employment without inflation, London: *The Times* (23 June).

MELTZER, A. H. (1963), The demand for money: the evidence from the time series. *Journal of Political Economy*, 71 (June).

MERRETT, A. J. *et al.* (1967), *Equity Issues and the London Capital Market*, London: Longmans.

METZLER, LLOYD A. (1951), Wealth, saving, and the rate of interest. *Journal of Political Economy*, April (1951). In *Collected Papers* (1973). Cambridge, Massachusetts: Harvard University Press.

MILLS, T. C. (1980), Money, income and causality in the U.K. – a look at the recent evidence. *Bulletin of Economic Research*, 32 (May).

MINSKY, HYMAN P. (1976), *John Maynard Keynes*, London: Macmillan.

MISES, LUDWIG VON (1934), *The Theory of Money and Credit*, English translation of 1912 Austrian edition. London: Cape.

MODIGLIANI, FRANCO (1944), Liquidity preference and the theory of interest and money. In *American Economic Association* (1952).

MOGGRIDGE, D. E. (1973), From the *Treatise* to *The General Theory*: an exercise in Chronology. *History of Political Economy*, 5, No. 1 (Spring).

MOGGRIDGE, D. E., ed. (1974), *Keynes: Aspects of the Man and His Work*, London: Macmillan.

MOGGRIDGE, D. E. and HOWSON, SUSAN (1974), Keynes on monetary policy, 1910–1946. *Oxford Economic Papers*, 26 (July).

MOGGRIDGE, D. E. (1976), *Keynes*, Glasgow: Fontana.

MONETARY CONTROL (March 1980), Green Paper. (Cmnd 7858), London: H.M.S.O.

MOORE, G. E. (1903), *Principia Ethica*, Cambridge: Cambridge University Press.

MORISHIMA, MICHIO (1977), *Walras' Economics, A Pure Theory of Capital and Money*, London: Cambridge University Press.

MOULTON, HAROLD G. (1943), *The New Philosophy of Public Debt*, Washintgon: Brookings Institution.

MUELLER, M. G., ed. (1967), *Readings in Macroeconomics*, New York: Holt, Rinehart and Winston.

NEWLYN, W. T. and BOOTLE, R. P. (3rd edn, 1978), *Theory of Money*, Oxford: Clarendon Press.

NINTH REPORT FROM THE EXPENDITURE COMMITTEE (1974), Public Expenditure, Inflation, and the Balance of Payments. HC 328 July. London: H.M.S.O.

NOBAY, A. R. (1974). A model of the United Kingdom monetary authorities' behaviour 1959–1969. In Johnson and Nobay, eds (1974).

OHLIN, BERTIL (1937), Some notes on the Stockholm theory of savings and investment. *Economic JOurnal*, 47 (March and June). Reprinted in The American Economic Association's *Readings in Business Cycle Theory*, Philadelphia, 1944.

PARKIN, MICHAEL and SUMNER, MICHAEL T., eds (1974), *Incomes policy and inflation*, Manchester: Manchester University Press.

PARKIN, MICHAEL and NOBAY, A. R., eds (1975), *Current Economic Problems*, The Proceedings of the Association of University Teachers of Economics, Manchester, 1974. London: Cambridge University Press.

PARKIN, MICHAEL and ZIS, GEORGE, eds (1976a), *Inflation in the world economy*, Manchester: Manchester University Press.

PARKIN, MICHAEL and ZIS, GEORGE, eds (1976b), *Inflation in open economies*, Manchester: Manchester University Press.

PARKIN, MICHAEL and SUMNER, MICHAEL T., eds (1978), *Inflation in the United Kingdom*, Manchester: Manchester University Press.

PARKIN, MICHAEL (1978), Alternative explanations of United Kingdom inflation: a survey. In Parkin and Sumner, eds (1978).

PASINETTI, LUIGI L. (1974), *Growth and Income Distribution*, London: Cambridge University Press.

PATINKIN, DON (1948), Price flexibility and full employment. In American Economic Association (1952).

PATINKIN, DON (1st edn, 1956; 2nd edn, 1965), *Money, Interest and Prices*, New York: Harper & Row.

PATINKIN, DON (1969a), The Chicago tradition, the quantity theory, and Friedman. In Patinkin (1972a).

PATINKIN, DON (1969b), Money and wealth: a review article. *Journal of Economic Literature* (December).

PATINKIN, DON (1972a), *Studies in Monetary Economics*, New York: Harper & Row.

PATINKIN, DON (1972b), On the short-run non-neutrality of money in the quantity theory. *Banca Nazionale Lavoro Quarterly Review*, 25 (March).

PATINKIN, DON (1974), Friedman on the Quantity Theory and Keynesian economy. In Gordon (1974).

PATINKIN, DON (1975), The Collected Writings of John Maynard Keynes: from the *Tract* to *The General Theory*. *Economic Journal*, 85 (June).

PATINKIN, DON (1976a), *Keynes' Monetary Thought*, Durham, North Carolina: Duke University Press.

PATINKIN, DON (1976b), Keynes' monetary thought: a study of its development. *History of Political Economy*, 8.

PATINKIN, DON and LEITH, J. CLARK, eds (1977), *Keynes, Cambridge and the General Theory*, London: Macmillan.

PESEK, BORIS P. and SAVING, THOMAS R. (1967), *Money, Wealth, and Economic Theory*, London: Collier-Macmillan.

PHELPS, EDMUND S. *et al.* (1974), *Microeconomic Foundations of Employment and Inflation Theory*, London: Macmillan.

PHILLIPS, A. W. (1958), The relation between unemployment and the rate of change of money-wage rates in the United Kingdom 1861–1957. *Economica*, 25 (November).

PIERCE, DAVID G. and SHAW, DAVID M. (1974), *Monetary Economics: Theories, Evidence and Policy*, London: Butterworth.

PIGOU, A. C. (1912), *Wealth and Welfare*, London: Macmillan.

PIGOU, A. C., ed. (1925), *Memorials of Alfred Marshall*, London: Macmillan.

PIGOU, A. C. (1st edn, 1927; 2nd edn, 1929), *Industrial Fluctuations*, London: Macmillan.

PIGOU, A. C. (1933), *The Theory of Unemployment*, London: Macmillan.

PIGOU, A. C. (1936), Mr J. M. Keynes' *General Theory of Employment, Interest and Money*, *Economica*, 3 (May).

PIGOU, A. C. (1st edn, 1937; 2nd edn, 1954), *Socialism versus Capitalism*, London: Macmillan.

PIGOU, A. C. (1st edn, 1941; 2nd edn, 1949), *Employment and Equilibrium*, London: Macmillan.

PIGOU, A. C. (1943), The classical stationary state. *Economic Journal*, 53 (December).

PIGOU, A. C. (1945), *Lapses from Full Employment*, London: Macmillan.

PIGOU, A. C. (1947), Economic progress in a stable environment. Reprinted in American Economic Association (1952).

PIGOU, A. C. (1950), *Keynes's 'General Theory' A Retrospective View*, London: Macmillan.

PIGOU, A. C. (4th edn, 1960), *The Economics of Welfare*, London: Macmillan.

POOLE, W. and KOMBLITH, E. (1973), The Friedman–Meiselman CMC paper: new evidence on an old controversy. *American Economic Review*, 63 (December).

POSNER, MICHAEL, ed. (1978), *Demand Management*, London: Heinemann Educational Books.

PRESLEY, JOHN R. (1979), *Robertsonian Economics*, London: Macmillan.

PREST, A. R. and COPPOCK, D. J., eds (6th edn, 1976), *The U.K. Economy A Manual of Applied Economics*, London: Weidenfeld and Nicolson.

RADCLIFFE REPORT (1959), *See* Committee on the Working of the Monetary System Report (1959).

RAYNER, A. C. and LITTLE, I. M. D. (1966), *Higgledy-Piggledy Growth Again*, Oxford: Blackwell.

ROBBINS, LORD (1971), *Autobiography of an Economist*, London: Macmillan.

ROBBINS, LORD *et al.* (1974), *Inflation: Causes, Consequences, Cures*, London: Institute of Economic Affairs.

ROBERTSON, DENNIS HOLME (1915/1948), *A Study of Industrial Fluctuation*, London: London School of Economics.

ROBERTSON, D. H. (1st edn, 1922; 1948), *Money*, Cambridge: Cambridge University Press.

ROBERTSON, D. H. (1926), *Banking Policy and the Price Level*, London: P. S. King.

ROBERTSON, D. H. (1928), Theories of banking policy. *Economica*. Reprinted in Robertson (1966).

ROBERTSON, D. H. (1933), Saving and hoarding. *Economic Journal*. Reprinted in Robertson (1966).

ROBERTSON, D. H. (1934), Industrial fluctuations and the natural state of interest. *Economic Journal* (December). Reprinted in Robertson (1966).

ROBERTSON, D. H. (1936), Some notes on Mr Keynes's *General Theory of Employment*. *Quarterly Journal of Economics* (November).

ROBERTSON, D. H. (1938), A survey of modern monetary controversy. In Robertson (1966).

ROBERTSON, D. H. (1940), *Essays in Monetary Theory*, London: Staples.

ROBERTSON, D. H. (1948), What has happened to the rate of interest? In Robertson (1966).

ROBERTSON, D. H. (2nd edn, 1949), *Banking Policy and the Price Level*, New York: Kelly.

ROBERTSON, D. H. (1951), Some notes on the theory of interest. In Robertson (1966).

ROBERTSON, SIR DENNIS (1961), *Growth, Wages, Money*, London: Cambridge University Press.

ROBERTSON, SIR DENNIS (1963a), *Lectures on Economic Principles*, Glasgow: Collins.

ROBERTSON, SIR DENNIS (1966), *Essays in Money and Interest* (Selected with a Memoir by Sir John Hicks), Glasgow: Collins.

ROBINSON, E. A. G. (1946), John Maynard Keynes 1883–1946. In Lekachman, ed. (1964).

ROBINSON, E. A. G. (1963), Could there have been a 'General Theory' without Keynes? In Lekachman, ed. (1964).

ROBINSON, AUSTIN (1968), Pigou, Arthur Cecil. *International Encyclopedia of the Social Sciences*, New York: Macmillan & Free Press.

ROBINSON, AUSTIN (1971), *John Maynard Keynes Economist, Author, Statesman*, London: Oxford University Press.

ROBINSON, AUSTIN (1975), A personal view. In Milo Keynes, ed. (1975).

ROBINSON, JOAN (1933/1934), The theory of money and analysis of output. *Review of Economic Studies*.

ROBINSON, JOAN (1st edn, 1937; 2nd edn, 1969), *Introduction to the Theory of Employment*, London: Macmillan.

ROBINSON, JOAN (1937), Full employment. In Joan Robinson (1937, 1947) and reprinted in Joan Robinson (1973a).

ROBINSON, JOAN (1st edn, 1937; 2nd edn, 1947), *Essays in the Theory of Employment*, Oxford: Blackwell.

ROBINSON, JOAN (1949), Mr Harrod's Dynamics. *Economic Journal* (March). In Joan Robinson (1973a).

ROBINSON, JOAN (1951, 1966), *Collected Economic Papers*, Vol. I, Oxford: Blackwell.

ROBINSON, JOAN (1952), The generalization of The General Theory. In *The Rate of Interest and Other Essays*, London: Macmillan.

ROBINSON, JOAN (1952), *The Rate of Interest and Other Essays*, London: Macmillan.

ROBINSON, JOAN (1953), *On Re-reading Marx*, Cambridge: Students' Bookshop.

ROBINSON, JOAN (1st edn, 1956; 3rd edn, 1969), *The Accumulation of Capital*, London: Macmillan.

ROBINSON, JOAN (1958), Full employment and inflation. In Joan Robinson (1975).

ROBINSON, JOAN (1961), Beyond full employment. In Joan Robinson (1975), Vol. III, Oxford: Blackwell.

ROBINSON, JOAN, A model of technical progress. In Joan Robinson (1962).

ROBINSON, JOAN (1962), *Essays in the Theory of Economic Growth*, London: Macmillan.

ROBINSON, JOAN (1964a), *Economic Philosophy*, Harmondsworth: Penguin.

ROBINSON, JOAN (1964b), Kalecki and Keynes. In Joan Robinson (1965, 1975).

ROBINSON, JOAN (1969), Economics Today. In Joan Robinson (1973a).

ROBINSON, JOAN (1971a), *Economic Heresies*, London: Macmillan.

ROBINSON, JOAN (1971b), The second crisis of economic theory. In Joan Robinson (1973).

ROBINSON, JOAN (1971c), Michal Kalecki. *Cambridge Review* (October).

ROBINSON, JOAN (1972), What has become of the Keynesian Revolution? In Joan Robinson (1973).

ROBINSON, JOAN (1973a), *Collected Economic Papers*, Vol. IV. Oxford: Blackwell.

ROBINSON, JOAN, ed. (1973b), *After Keynes*, Oxford: Blackwell.

ROBINSON, JOAN (1st edn, 1960; 2nd edn, 1975), *Collected Economic Papers*, Vol. II, Oxford: Blackwell.

ROBINSON, JOAN (1st edn, 1965; 2nd edn, 1975), *Collected Economic Papers*, Vol. III, Oxford: Blackwell.

ROBINSON, JOAN (1977), What has become of employment policy? In Joan Robinson (1978).

ROBINSON, JOAN (1978), *Contributions to Modern Economics*, Oxford: Blackwell.

ROTWEIN, EUGENE, ed. (1955), *David Hume, Writings on Economics*, London: Nelson.

SAMPSON, A. A. and SEDGWICK, R. (1977), Wages, prices and employment in general equilibrium. *Oxford Economic Papers*, 29 (July).

SAMUELSON, P. A. (1939), Interactions between the acceleration principle and the multiplier. *Review of Economic Statistics*, 21 (May).

SAMUELSON, PAUL A. (1946), The General Theory. In Lekachman (1964, p. 318).

SAMUELSON, P. A. (1947), *Foundations of Economic Analysis*, Cambridge, Mass.: Harvard University Press.

SAMUELSON, PAUL A. (1963a), D. H. Robertson (1890–1963). *Quarterly Journal of Economics* (November). In Stiglitz (1966).

SAMUELSON, PAUL A. (1963b), A brief survey of post-Keynesian developments. In Lekachman (1964).

SAMUELSON, P. A. (1968), What classical and neo-classical monetary theory really was. In Clower, ed. (1969).

SAMUELSON, P. A. (10th edn, 1976), *Economics*, Tokyo: McGraw-Hill Kogakusha.

SAYERS, R. S. (1949), The rate of interest as a weapon of economic policy. In Wilson and Andrews (1951).

SAYERS, R. S. (7th edn, 1967), *Modern Banking*, Oxford: Clarendon Press.

SCHNAPPER, M. B., ed. (1961), *New Frontiers of the Kennedy Administration*, Washington: Public Affairs Press.

SCHUMPETER, J. A. (1911, 1934), *The Theory of Economic Development*, Cambridge, Massachusetts: Harvard University Press.

SCHUMPETER, JOSEPH A. (1946), Keynes, the economist. In Harris, ed. (1948). First published as 'John Maynard Keynes, 1883–1946', *American Economic Review* (September 1946).

SCHUMPETER, JOSEPH A. (1954), *History of Economic Analysis*, New York: Allen & Unwin (edited from manuscript by Elizabeth Boody Schumpeter).

SCITOVSKY, TIBOR (1940/41), Capital accumulation, employment and price rigidity. *Review of Economic Studies*, 8.

SELDEN, RICHARD T. ed. (1956), Monetary Velocity in the United States. In Friedman (1956a).

SELDEN, RICHARD T. ed. (1975), *Capitalism and Freedom*, Charlottesville: University Press of Virginia.

SHACKLE, G. L. S. (1st edn, 1938; 2nd edn, 1968), *Expectation, Investment and Income*, Oxford: Oxford University Press.

SHACKLE, G. L. S. (1946), Interest rates and the pace of investment. *Economic Journal*, 56 (March). In Wilson and Andrews (1951).

SHACKLE, G. L. S. (1st edn, 1949; 2nd edn, 1952), *Expectation in Economics*, Cambridge: Cambridge University Press.

SHACKLE, G. L. S. (1953), A chart of economic theory. Reprinted in Shackle (1955).

SHACKLE, G. L. S. (1955), *Uncertainty in Economics and Other Reflections*, Cambridge: Cambridge University Press.

SHACKLE, G. L. S. (1965), *A Scheme of Economic Theory*, London: Cambridge University Press.

SHACKLE, G. L. S. (1967), *The Years of High Theory*, London: Cambridge University Press.

SHACKLE, G. L. S. (1972), *Epistemics and Economics*, London: Cambridge University Press.

SHACKLE, G. L. S. (1973), Review of *Money and the Real World*, by Paul Davidson. *Economic Journal*, 83 (June).

SHACKLE, G. L. S. (1974), *Keynesian Kaleidics*, Edinburgh: Edinburgh University Press.

SHACKLE, G. L. S. (1979), *Imagination and the Nature of Choice*, Edinburgh: Edinburgh University Press.

SIMKIN, C. G. F. (1968), *Economics at Large*, London: Weidenfeld & Nicolson.

SIMON, HERBERT A. (1976), From substantive to procedural rationality. In Latsis, ed. (1976).

SIMONS, HENRY C. (1948), *Economic Policy for a Free Society*, Chicago: University of Chicago Press.

SINGH, A. and WHITTINGTON, G. (1968), *Growth, Profitability and Valuation*, London: Cambridge University Press.

SKIDELSKY, ROBERT, ed. (1977), *The end of the Keynesian Era, Essays on the disintegration of the Keynesian political economy*, London: Macmillan.

SOLOW, R. M. (1956), A contribution to the theory of economic growth. *Quarterly Journal of Economics*, 70 (February).

SOWELL, THOMAS (1972), *Say's Law*, Princeton: Princeton University Press.

STEIN, L. J., ed. (1976), *Monetarism*, Amsterdam: North-Holland Publishing Company.

STIGLITZ, JOSEPH E., ed. (1966), *The Collected Scientific Papers of Paul A. Samuelson*, Vol. II., Cambridge, Massachusetts: M.I.T. Press.

STREISSLER, ERICH, ed. (1969), *Roads to Freedom, Essays in Honour of Frederick A. von Hayek*, London: Routledge.

SUMNER, MICHAEL T. (1978), Wage determination. In Parkin and Sumner (1978).

SURREY, M. J. C. and ORMEROD, P. A. (1978), Demand Management in Britain 1964–1981. In Posner, ed. (1978).

SWAN, T. W. (1956), Economic growth and capital accumulation. *Economic Record*, 32 (November).

SWEEZY, ALAN, Declining investment opportunity. In Harris, ed. (1948).

TARSHIS, L. (1939), Changes in real and money wages. *Economic Journal*, 49 (March).

TARSHIS, L. (1939), Real wages in the United States and Great Britain. *Canadian Journal of Economics*, 5 (August).

TEMIN, PETER (1976), *Did Monetary Forces Cause the Great Depression?*, New York: Norton.

TERBORGH, G. (1945), *The Bogey of Economic Maturity*, Chicago: Machinery & Allied Products Institute.

THE TIMES (10th June 1977), The McCracken Committee's Report to the Organization for Economic Co-operation and Development (June 1977).

THIRLWALL, A. P., ed. (1976), *Keynes and International Monetary Relations*, London: Macmillan.

THIRLWALL, A. P., ed. (1978), *Keynes and Laissez-Faire*, London: Macmillan.

TINBERGEN, J. (1939), *A Method and its Application to Investment Activity. Statistical Testing of Business-Cycle Theories, I*, Geneva: League of Nations.

TOBIN, JAMES (1947/48), Liquidity preference and monetary policy. In Tobin (1971).

TOBIN, J. (1955), A dynamic aggregative model. In Tobin (1971).

TOBIN, JAMES (1956), The interest elasticity of transactions demand for cash. In Tobin (1971).

TOBIN, JAMES (1958), Liquidity preference as behaviour towards risk. In Tobin (1971).

TOBIN, JAMES (1961), Money, capital, and other stores of value. In Tobin (1971).

TOBIN, JAMES (1963), An essay on the principles of debt management. In Tobin (1971).

TOBIN, JAMES (1965), Money and economic growth. In Tobin (1971).

TOBIN, JAMES (1965), The monetary interpretation of history. In Tobin (1971).

TOBIN, JAMES (1968), Notes on optimal monetary growth. In Tobin (1971).

TOBIN, JAMES (1971), *Essays in Economics, Volume 1: Macroeconomics*, Amsterdam: North-Holland.

TOBIN, JAMES (1974), *The New Economics One Decade Older*, Princeton, N.J.: Princeton University Press.

TOBIN, JAMES, Money wage rates and employment. In Harris, ed. (1948).

UNITED NATIONS (1949), *National and International Measures for Full Employment*, Lake Success, New York: United Nations.

VAIZEY, JOHN (1977), Keynes and Cambridge. In Skidelsky, ed. (1977).

VILLARD, HENRY H. (1948), Monetary theory. In Ellis (1948).

VINER, JACOB (1936), Mr Keynes on the causes of unemployment. In Lekachman, ed. (1964).

WALRAS, LEON (1954), *Elements of Pure Economics*, translated and edited by W. Jaffé from the definitive edition (1926) of the *Eléments d'économie politique pure*, Paris, Lausanne. London: Allen & Unwin.

WALTERS, A. A., ed. (1973), *Money and Banking. Selected Readings*, Harmondsworth: Penguin.

WEBER, W. E. (1970), Effect of interest rates on aggregate consumption. *American Economic Review*, 60 (September).

WEINTRAUB, E. ROY (1979), *Microfoundations The Compatibility of Microeconomics and Macroeconomics*, London: Cambridge University Press.

WHITEHEAD, A. N. and RUSSELL, B. A. W. (1903), *Principia Mathematica*, Cambridge: Cambridge University Press.

WHITE PAPER (1944, Cmnd 6527), *Employment Policy*, London: H.M.S.O.

WHITE PAPER (1956, Cmnd 9725), *The Economic Implications of Full Employment*, H.M.S.O.

WHITE, WILLIAM H. (1956), Interest inelasticity of investment demand – the case from business attitude surveys re-examined. In Mueller, ed. (1967).

WHITE, WILLIAM H. (1967), Interest inelasticity of investment demand – the case from business attitude surveys re-examined. In Mueller (1967).

WICKSELL, KNUT (1936), *Interest and Prices* (Geldzins und Güterpreise, 1898). Translated from the German by R. F. Kahn. London: Macmillan.

WILLIAMS, J. H. (1948), An appraisal of Keynesian economics. *American Economic Review*, American Economic Association, *Papers and Proceedings*, 38 (May).

WILLIAMS, J. H. (1952), An economist's confessions. *American Economic Review*, 42 (March).

WILSON, T. (1953), Professor Robertson on effective demand and the trade cycle. *Economic Journal*, 63 (September), p. 570.

WILSON, T. (1980), Robertson, money and monetarism. *Journal of Economic Literature*, 18 (December).

WILSON, T. and ANDREWS, P. W. S., eds (1951), *Oxford Studies in the Price Mechanism*, Oxford: Clarendon Press.

WINCH, DONALD (1966), The Keynesian revolution in Sweden. *Journal of Political Economy*, 74 (April).

WINCH, DONALD (2nd edn, 1972), *Economics and Policy*, Glasgow: Collins.

WORSWICK, G. D. N., ed. (1976), *The Concept and Measurement of Involuntary Unemployment*, London: Allen & Unwin.

WORSWICK, G. D. N. (1977), The end of demand management? *Lloyds Bank Review* (January).

WRIGHT, A. L. (1956), The genesis of the multiplier theory. *Oxford Economic Papers*, 8 (June).

WRIGHTSMAN, DWAYNE (1971), *An Introduction to Monetary Theory and Policy*, London: Collier-Macmillan.

YEAGER, LELAND B., ed. (1962), *In Search of a Monetary Constitution*, Cambridge, Mass.: Harvard University Press.

Index

271